T5-AXH-595

CHILDREN'S RIGHTS

Multidisciplinary Approaches to Participation and Protection

Edited by Tom O'Neill and Dawn Zinga

This volume explores the implications and implementation of the United Nations Convention on the Rights of the Child (CRC) in international and Canadian contexts. The Convention, adopted in 1989 and subsequently ratified by nearly all member nations, outlines the basic rights of all persons under the age of 18, provides tools for the improvement of the condition of the world's children, and sets out a global legal framework for the enactment of appropriate legislation and policy within individual countries.

The purpose of this collection of essays is to provoke critical debate in the social sciences about children's rights that goes beyond that found in the many prescriptive and programmatic works published to date. The principal argument is that children's rights, as defined by the CRC, provide an interdisciplinary framework from which the predicaments of children can be understood and acted upon. A recurrent theme is that children's participation rights, which are an important element of the Convention, remain unrecognized in practice yet are essential as a foundation for health, identity, and citizenship.

Organized in three parts, the volume begins with essays that address the status of children's rights as a framework for understanding children's predicaments around the world. The second part explores how the CRC is applied in efforts to protect children. The book concludes with discussion of how persisting barriers to the inclusion of disabled, bullied, and marginalized children can be understood as violations of their rights, and makes a strong case for children's participation as specified in article 12 of the Convention.

Featuring thirteen essays by distinguished and emerging scholars, *Children's Rights* provides an in-depth, multidisciplinary exploration of the major issues in the area of children's rights and will be an invaluable resource to scholars and practitioners working with children and youth in institutional and educational settings.

TOM O'NEILL and DAWN ZINGA are associate professors in the Department of Child and Youth Studies at Brock University.

Children's Rights

Multidisciplinary Approaches to Participation and Protection

Edited by Tom O'Neill and Dawn Zinga

UNIVERSITY OF TORONTO PRESS
Toronto Buffalo London

© University of Toronto Press Incorporated 2008
Toronto Buffalo London
www.utppublishing.com
Printed in Canada

ISBN 978-0-8020-9785-9 (cloth)
ISBN 978-0-8020-9540-4 (paper)

Printed on acid-free paper

Library and Archives Canada Cataloguing in Publication

Children's rights : multidisciplinary approaches to participation and
protection / edited by Tom O'Neill and Dawn Zinga

ISBN 978-0-8020-9785-9 (bound) ISBN 978-0-8020-9540-4 (pbk.)

1. Children's rights.   2. Social participation.   I. O'Neill, Tom, 1957–
II. Zinga, Dawn, 1971–.

HQ789.C465 2008   323.3'52   C2008-901258-5

University of Toronto Press acknowledges the financial assistance to its
publishing program of the Canada Council for the Arts and the Ontario
Arts Council.

University of Toronto Press acknowledges the financial support for its
publishing activities of the Government of Canada through the
Book Publishing Industry Development Program (BPIDP).

Contents

Foreword

THE HONOURABLE SENATOR LANDON PEARSON[1]
AND JUDY FINLAY[2]

This collection of papers assists in advancing the dialogue on children's rights. It reinforces the interconnectedness between human rights and respect for children. Respecting children goes beyond merely listening to what they have to say. It means hearing their words with your eyes, your ears, your heart, and your undivided attention. It advocates using the voice of children to inform action. We applaud this publication as a welcome addition to the children's rights movement. It endorses children's participation as citizens.

Canada was an active player in drafting the United Nations Convention on the Rights of the Child (CRC). There were no long-standing objections from the provinces and territories that have the major responsibility for children's policy, programs, and services. The CRC was ratified by Canada in 1991 with 191 other nations internationally. In Canada, once ratified, it was not self-executing. It does not become the law of the land until it is accompanied by implementing legislation. The principles, however, have become imbedded in our laws and jurisprudence through inclusion by reference in the law such as the Youth Criminal Justice Act or in judgments that establish precedence such as the Baker case.[3] Nonetheless, there is no mechanism to enforce compliance to the principles or instruments of the Convention. There are Child and Youth Advocates appointed in nine provinces throughout Canada. These Offices serve as an essential safeguard to ensure

---

1 Retired – Landon Pearson Resource Centre, Study of Childhood and Children's Rights, Carleton University.
2 Chief Advocate, Office of Child and Family Service Advocacy, Province of Ontario; President, Canadian Council of Provincial Child and Youth Advocates.
3 *Baker v. Canada* (1999).

provision of the rights and entitlements of children as defined by provincial legislation. Indeed, the CRC serves as the foundation from which these Offices function. There is no federally appointed equivalent to the Child Advocate or Children's Commissioner in Canada. In the absence of enabling legislation or a mandated mechanism of compliance, the commitment to the positive development and the promotion of the best interests of children as rights bearers is diminished.

It is too often the belief that children should not have rights. Among the many arguments against children's rights are: children do not have the capacity to handle freedom, responsibility, or participation; children are incapable of independent judgment; children do not have a moral capacity; parents have primacy in determining the best interests of their children; children are inherent vulnerable and need protection. Child protection is often erroneously equated with children's rights. Anne McGillivray states that 'child protection is about incapacity ... weakness, powerlessness, lack of status, whereas rights are about capacity, will, power and high status.'[4] Indeed, she suggests that 'it is the status of children and not their vulnerability which promotes their exploitation.'[5] Mr Paulo Pinheiro, the independent expert for the United Nations Secretary-General's Study on Violence against Children, reinforces the importance of rights and the ensuing status that rights provide for the protection of children. He states, 'Children are not mini human beings with mini human rights. As long as adults continue to regard children as mini human beings, violence against children will persist. Every boy and girl, as any human being, must have their rights completely respected to develop with dignity.'[6] The notions of childhood as an incomplete state persist. We need to engage children as fully participatory members of society, not as adults 'in becoming.'

We promote the established rhetoric of children as our future, but at times this is at the expense of accepting children as citizens of today.[7]

---

4 Transcript of testimony of Professor Anne McGillivray before Standing Senate Committee on Human Rights, 26 September 2005, p. 2.
5 McGillivray, A. 'Why Children Do Have Rights: In Reply to Laura Purdy,' *International Journal of Children's Rights* 2 (1994), 243–58.
6 Paulo Pinheiro, Statement by the Independent Expert to the North American Regional Consultation for the United Nations Secretary-General's Study on Violence against Children, Toronto, 3 June 2005, p. 6 (www.violencestudy.org).
7 Professor Al Aynsley-Green, Children's Commissioner for England, testimony before the Standing Committee on Human Rights, 10 October 2005, as cited in Interim Report *Who's in Charge Here?* November 2005, p. 10.

Children ask that we move past the principles and practice of simple youth engagement and accept them as fully participating citizens. There are four dimensions of citizenship[8] that need to be achieved for this to happen:

- Rights and responsibilities
- Access to these rights and responsibilities
- Voice and meaningful participation
- The feeling of belonging to one's community and the identity that flows from that sense of belonging

Children understand relationships of power and authority and can articulate (albeit differently) how power is negotiated. They understand for example who makes decisions in the context of their family, their school, and their peer group. Children communicate differently and have a different social perspective, but can contribute from a unique and valuable perspective to any public debate about them. Children need to be offered the opportunity, when they have the capacity, to influence decisions that will directly or indirectly affect them, such as: choices in their day-to-day living; life-space choices; policy, programs, or practice that may affect those choices; and laws that frame those policies and practice.

We have made substantive steps in the rights revolution for children but have a considerable way to go to create either a Canada or a world fit for children, a world in which 'children are loved, respected and cherished, their rights are protected and promoted without discrimination of any kind, where their safety and well-being are paramount and where they can develop in health, peace and dignity.'[9] In our interconnected world we have to be more than just observers of children's suffering, we have to be partners with them in their struggles, talking with them and listening to them.[10] They are the experts of their lived experience. Adults are simply the observers. Together, however, we can act to effect change.

This text moves us a step closer to such change.

---

8 Judy Finlay, unpublished paper presented to the Centre for Children and Families in the Justice System, 16 June 2005, p. 7.

9 UNICEF, *A World Fit for Children* (New York: 2002), para. 9.

10 Senator Landon Pearson, 'Rights of the Child in the New Millennium,' Whittier Law School Symposium, 12 April 1999, at http://www.landonpearson.ca.

Acknowledgments

This publication has been supported by funding from Brock University, Canadian International Development Agency; the Department of Canadian Heritage, Human Rights Program; and the Social Sciences and Humanities Research Council of Canada. We would like to thank each of these institutions for their support.

CHILDREN'S RIGHTS

Multidisciplinary Approaches to Participation and Protection

Introduction

TOM O'NEILL AND DAWN ZINGA

The promulgation of the 1989 Convention on the Rights of the Child is changing the way we think about children, and the fact that it is now the most widely ratified international covenant in history shows that much of the world is serious about those changes. This is something to be celebrated, for although many of the world's children continue to languish in conditions of poverty, disease, and conflict, we now have the tools that the CRC provides to improve their condition, and a global legal framework to redress those countries that do not comply. As formidable as this framework is, however, it is not itself enough to make children's rights a reality in children's lives. For that to happen, the concept of children's rights must take root in our everyday practices, in homes, schools, and institutions that care for children and youth.

Most of us are not specialists versed in the legal discourses of children's rights; we are scholars and researchers who share an interest in understanding how children's rights as defined in the CRC provide a framework for understanding the predicaments of particular children in a variety of contexts. Each of us shares a vital concern for children and youth who have been disadvantaged, exploited, or oppressed by the inequities of the adult world. For us, the notion that children have rights is both a means by which to measure this inequity and a call for action that is first and foremost in the best interests of children. The children we discuss are found in diverse places; Romanian orphanages, Nepalese schools, Canadian courts, classrooms, or other care facilities; they could all use the aid of the Convention in various ways, as victims of abuse, violence, bullying, or neglect. But for us, one of the most sage functions of the Convention is to remind the adult world that children are, or ought to be, participants in the societies that shape them. A consistent theme that emerges from this book is that we do not advocate for children's participation rights near well enough, that in addition to the many articles that protect children and ensure adequate provision for them, the CRC contains measures of child participation that protectors and providers frequently overlook.

A rights-based approach to understanding children and youth ought to be multidisciplinary. The preamble to both the 1989 Convention on the Rights of the Child and its 1959 forebear, the Declaration of the Rights of the Child, states that children require special protections and provisions because of their 'physical and mental immaturity'. There is much even in that seemingly basic premise that needs to be unpacked: How are children physically and mentally immature? What is the relationship between the two? How is 'immaturity' to be defined? Who is empowered to give such a definition? These questions, and the many more that arise as one begins to read the Convention, can only be answered from a common boundary that exists between physical, social, scientific, and critical/interpretive disciplines. This volume is situated at that boundary, across which anthropologists, educators, child and youth care advocates, psychologists, and sociologists exchange ideas, argue, and occasionally collaborate. If we offer no firm answers to those questions, it is because they have no universal, supra-historical answer, something that those who framed the Convention also had the wisdom to recognize.

In her autobiography, Margaret Mead, the anthropologist who did so much to make children and youth a focus for professional ethnographic study in the 1920s and 1930s, lamented the demise of an ambitious plan to build a multidisciplinary team to study the cultures of the South Pacific when the Second World War interfered. After the war, her efforts to revive the plan floundered on emerging disciplinary divisions that proved intractable: 'Social scientists – cultural and social anthropologists, social psychologists, and sociologists – were working in a kind of crazy tandem in which the traces had been cut' (1972, p. 201). The authors of this volume work in a similar tandem, but our intention is to lay a foundation for dialogue that the theoretical, practical, and political implications of children's rights demands. We are under no illusion that this dialogue will tie us together again in the way that Mead envisioned, but we do contend that in the multiple perspectives offered in this volume there is a potential for finding common ground.

A World of Children's Rights

The 1989 Convention on the Rights of the Child was a product of its time, and a document negotiated among various political, cultural, and religious interests. Those who treat the Convention as a universal code would do well to remember that it was not written in stone upon some desert mountaintop; it is, like every other human creation, socially constructed and subject to interpretation. To be effective, the CRC had to be written in such a way as to promote universal standards while allowing for national and cultural variation. As a result, the CRC is the most widely adopted international covenant in the world, ratified by 140 countries. Children's rights scholar Michael Freeman (2007) has quipped that only two countries have not ratified the CRC, 'Somalia, because it has no government, and the United States, because it does.' Somalia did not have a functioning government to sign the Convention when it was presented in 1989, and the United States has so far failed to ratify it because of the unilateral orientations of the legislative branch of its government (Mason, 2005). Though broadly ratified around the world, the number of declarations, reservations, and objections to the Convention show that the world does not accept it as a monolithic code. Canada, for example, reserves the right not to apply article 21 on adoption in the child's best interests when it 'may be inconsistent with customary forms of care among aboriginal peoples in Canada' – a hypocritical reservation in a country that doesn't do nearly enough to eliminate child poverty, a problem particularly associated with aboriginal reserves. In another example, Iran 'reserves the right not to apply any provisions or articles of the Convention that are incompatible with Islamic Laws,' that is, CRC articles apply only so long as they do not come into conflict with Islamic sharia law. These examples show that the interpretation of the Convention is contested even among those who agree on its basic principles.

The CRC has been criticized on many fronts, with some critics complaining that the document is founded on individualist, Western conceptions of childhood that are not shared the world over (see Burr, 2002; Boyden & de Berry, 2004), while other critics are dissatisfied with what they view as the half-way measures that neither are enforceable nor go far enough (see Melchiorre, 2004). Kristina Anne Bentley has recently argued that the CRC is grounded upon a 'halcyon fantasy' of a universal childhood based on Western conceptions of childhood as a period to be protected from the harsh realities of adult life (2005, p. 121). We, however, find that the universality of CRC is minimal, and that a careful reading of it reveals a highly nuanced document that is inclusive of multiple voices and perspectives. Jaap Doek, chairperson of the Committee of the Rights of the Child, urges everyone to engage in a careful reading of the document and claims that it is a text rich in both meaning and application (2006).

The four chapters in the first part of this volume explore the implications of children's rights in a variety of international contexts, each addressing the universality of rights for children in specific predicaments. Tom O'Neill's chapter on the participation of children in a Maoist insurgency in Nepal shows that universal definitions of 'the child' are too easily forgotten in time of war. Rather than take the view that children are mere victims of adult aggression, O'Neill notes that the Maoist insurgency in Nepal has exposed a tension between the need to protect children from the harmful effects of warfare and the recognition that some children, for a variety of personal or ideological reasons, volunteer to participate in violent political change. Child soldiers betray Western notions of childhood innocence and vulnerability as problematic and idealistic universal standards to uphold during violent political upheaval. O'Neill argues that the CRC should not be used to champion unrealistic conceptions of childhood, but rather that it contains pragmatic tools that the international community can use to hold both guerilla and government leaders accountable for their actions.

Many children in countries affected by rapid economic and political change find themselves in the predicament of being abandoned by their parents and being placed in institutional care. In their chapter, Lucy Le Mare, Karyn Audet, and Karen Kurytnik show that Romanian orphans, often minority 'Roma' children, have been not only abandoned but also neglected and systematically abused by child welfare agencies set up by the state to care for them. The CRC, in article 8, protects the national and cultural identity of children and exhorts states to ensure that it is re-established if a child should be deprived of any aspects of his or her identity. Many contemporary critics charge that international adoption is just such a form of deprivation, but Le Mare, Audet, and Kurytnik argue that international adoption, in the contexts they describe, is in the child's best interests. Adopted children are rescued from the brutality of institutional care that places their development at risk, and are instead placed in an environment in which most of their basic needs are met. The 'best interests' principle, as described in article 3 of the Convention, is an important guideline that puts the interests of individual children first, superseding competing priorities that often arise from the application of the Convention; article 21, which specifically addresses the issue of international adoption, reiterates this principle in the strongest possible way.

Hans Skott-Myhre and Donato Tarulli take a different approach by questioning what children's rights are and where they are located. By taking an ontological approach to rights, Skott-Myhre and Tarulli question epistemological frameworks that locate rights within legal entities such as conventions, statutes, or acts of parliament and focus instead on rights being produced within the forms of daily life, that is, in the creative agency of children and youth. Their paper questions a fundamental assumption of children's rights discourse: that what distinguishes adults from children is their 'developmental maturity.' This concept has acquired scientific authority in modernist anthopology, psychology and sociology, but is increasingly questioned by postmodernist scholars who argue that such a binary distinction obscures much of the variation among individuals of many ages, as well as undervalues the creative potential of children and youth. Skott-Myher and Tarulli further argue that the modernist conception of the child is inexorably associated with the liberal-democratic state, a central figure in the CRC that is responsible, and accountable, for assuring children their rights. Their paper convincingly suggests that this conception of rights does not create a theoretical space in which the fundamental injustices of the nation state can be challenged, but rather encourages a view of the child as a subject of the state who can, at best, enjoy a limited form of participation in prescribed, appropriate sociality that does not challenge authority.

The last chapter in part 1 moves from questioning the very conceptualization of rights as existing in a legal framework posited by Skott-Myher and Tarulli to considering how children's rights are expressed within different countries. Dawn Zinga and Sherri Young's chapter focuses on the importance of context and cultural relevance in the adoption of the CRC into the laws and policies of the countries that have ratified it. They contend that the articles of the CRC will gain strength through their incorporation into the laws, policy, and jurisprudence of the countries that have ratified the treaty. This incorporation is an important part of the process and will take different forms in different countries. Incorporation of the CRC in each country provides a mechanism by which violations of children's rights can be dealt with domestically. Zinga and Young stress the importance of dealing with children's rights issues domestically, because not only does the CRC have no mechanism under which violations of children's rights can be heard and adjudicated, dealing with such issues domestically also requires that each country interpret the CRC. They see common barriers to education faced by children in both developed and developing countries; however, they demonstrate that these barriers have different contexts and cultural relevance that need to be taken into consideration. They are not arguing that the CRC does not provide the underlying principles and the essence of what children's rights should be, but rather that each country gives expression to those rights through its policies and politics. Zinga and Young also argue that while advocates and scholars should question how well a country enacts and addresses children's rights, such questioning should be done with an appreciation of context and not, as is often the case, by oversimplifying children's rights issues and viewing them through a Western perspective.

The centrality of the state in children's rights discourses is problematic because far too much responsibility can be placed on the state as the promoter and protector of children's rights. R. Brian Howe and Katherine Covell (2005) argue that Canada has not lived up to its obligation, under the Convention, to educate children about the CRC and their rights. While this criticism is sound, it is also perhaps intentionally naive; children's rights education in Canada is subsumed, at the federal level, under general human-rights programming which is the responsibility of the federal department Heritage Canada, whose programs 'promote Canadian content, foster cultural participation, active citizenship and participation in Canada's civic life, and strengthen connections among Canadians.' Children's rights programming, then, must compete with museums, the arts, multiculturalism, and sports for limited resources. Several key aspects of the CRC, such as health and education, moreover, are provincial responsibilities, and Canada's provinces have a checkered record when it comes to even acknowledging the importance of children's rights. Almost every country in the world poses similar political limitations to rights education, and on the practical application of children's rights in general.

Children's rights are far too important to be left to states alone to provide and protect them. Indeed, a consistent theme in this volume is that children are not enjoying their rights in a variety of contexts – children caught in the cross-fire of an insurgency, abandoned by their parents, robbed of educational opportunity because of social inequality or disability, or caught in the judicial system. While the workings of the U.N. Committee on the Rights of the Child through the frequent national reporting process described in the third section of the Convention is an important impetus to the reform of national legislation for compliance with the CRC, these children cannot wait for the effects of these changes to trickle down to them. The Convention, we contend, must be a tool for everyone who studies, works with, or cares about children and youth, in schools families, and institutions where those rights are either practised or ignored.

Protecting Children's Rights

The evolution of international standards to protect children is a product of global modernity, which makes the international consensus that is the basis of the CRC even possible; but this evolution is also more necessary because global modernity has proliferated conditions of child exploitation by redefining the functions of the family, kinship, and community. Industrial and post-industrial society requires autonomous individuals that some argue are an ideological premise for capitalist modernity (Horkheimer and Adorno, 1979), and a Western conception that marginalizes alternative and collective identities (Stephens, 1995; Boyden, 1997). The preamble of the CRC states that 'the child, for the full and harmonious development of his or her personality, should grow up in a family environment, in an atmosphere of happiness, love and understanding.' The 1989 Convention offers only a minimalist definition of what 'personality' entails. Gary Melton argues that 'rather than reading the term as it is used colloquially or psychologically, policymakers would be advised to think of personality as synonymous with "personhood," that is, as individual potential embedded in numerous cultural or ideological contexts' (2005, p. 922). A covenant to protect each child as an evolving person, with the right to be given the opportunity to fulfill his or her potential is a historically significant and progressive step.

Previous declarations of children's rights said little about child and youth agency, as the notion that children ought to have a measure of choice in matters of concern to them is comparatively recent. The 1989 Convention makes a significant contribution to the evolution of rights by recognizing children as individuals who are capable of forming (their) own views and who ought to be listened to by adults. This contribution is made specifically in article 12, which has no precedent in any previous declaration. This new understanding of children as bearers of participation rights is often in tension with notions of children as subjects to be protected. While some of the authors in part 1 considered the tension between protection and participation, the authors who focus on the question of protecting children fully examine that tension. Many of the authors in part 2 go further by examining not only the tension between protection and participation but also tensions between specific rights as outlined in the CRC and in other legal contexts.

In chapter 5, Candace Johnson addresses the tension between protection and participation from the perspective of children's rights to health care and the role of the family. Within this context, the pragmatic application of rights confronts a conception of children as dependents of their parents that fails to provide Canada's substantial minority of poor children with basic health needs. Johnson agrees with other authors in this volume who have argued that the translation of global commitments into domestic policy is often lacking in many ways. In particular, Johnson focuses on how Canada's health care policy conceptualizes children as the dependents of their parents and in doing so increases their vulnerability and can impede their ability to access health care. She addresses the conflict between protection and participation in her argument that Canada's health care policies do not allow for children's participation except as mediated through their families and, as a result, fail to protect children's right to fully access health care.

Marjorie Aunos and Maurice Feldman also directly address the tension between protection and participation, but do so by focusing on the question of when children should remain in their homes of origin and when the removal of a child is justified by the need to protect the child. Specifically, they address issues of protection as espoused by family and children's services when the removal of a child from the family of origin is considered owing to one or more parents having an intellectual disability. Their chapter concentrates on the potential conflicts between a child's right to protection and a child's right to family. The CRC highlights the importance of being raised in one's family of origin and construes removal from the family of origin to be an action of last resort, but Aunos and Feldman argue that in the case of parents who have an intellectual disability, Canadian systems do not uphold removal as a last resort but seem to consider it the preferred action.

The authors discuss how such a system impacts children's rights to family, to the preservation of their identity, and to protection from discrimination. They suggest that in the attempting to protect children, policy often impairs children's ability to participate in their own lives and families.

Frances Owen et al. show that the agency of disabled children is too often ignored, because their status as children is complicated by their mental or physical disability. They propose 'person-centred service planning' and rights education to ensure that the views of the disabled child are not systematically ignored. Their chapter explores the many ways that disabled children may be disadvantaged in such arenas as the justice system and social services. They argue that the disabled child is entitled to understand his/her rights and that those who work most closely with the child should also be educated not only about what the child's rights are but about how best those rights can be facilitated. From their perspective, protection has been a long-standing issue of much debate, but the consideration of participation has been severely under-represented and often misconstrued.

Kim Roberts and Angela Evans observe a similar tension between child participation and protection in the Canadian legal system. They address these tensions within the framework of alleged child abuse, as it seems that alleged victims of child abuse are particularly caught between protection and participation since they must operate within an adult-based judicial system wherein their rights are balanced with the rights of the accused perpetrator. Roberts and Evans argue that an ad-hoc approach works best when jurors are provided with knowledge about the developmental appropriateness of the methods used to include children in the legal process, thus interpreting the CRC through the lens of developmental science. It is their opinion that developmental science can help mediate this tension by teaching those within the justice system about the capacities of children at various ages and about how the system might best be adapted to balance children's rights to both protection and participation more effectively within Canadian judicial systems.

Weighing Protection and Participation Rights in Schools

The extension of participatory rights to children raises other difficulties. As the previous section has shown, there are many adult-based institutions from the health care system to social services and the judicial system that face challenges in addressing both the protection and participation rights of children. The protection of children seems easier to conceptualize and to implement than children's participation. This is partially due to the fact that children take an active role in participation and may do so in ways that are not easily anticipated by adult-based systems. In addition, Lee (1999) has argued that article 12 of the CRC contains within it an ambiguity about children's capacities that makes their participation in adult institutions problematic. Lee finds fault in the CRC in that it fails to provide a generalizable standard that institutions can rely on in order to process children through institutional systems, where deferral of the resolution of this ambiguity may bring undue stress to children. An institutional, 'one size fits all' policy risks imposing a universal conception of childhood that goes well beyond the minimal universality needed to make children's rights pragmatically achievable in a diverse world.

The CRC conveys three types of rights: rights of provision, such as the material resources for growth, education, and good health; rights of protection from exploitative labour, sexual abuse, discrimination/ persecution, and arbitrary state intervention; and rights of participation. The first two types come from a long tradition of rights discourse, dating from 1924, but participation rights are new and, we argue, remain largely unrecognized by much of the world community. They are also in tension with deeply rooted perceptions of children's subordinate social roles, 'family values,' and the dominant, and dominating, cultural model of childhood as a period of innocence set apart from the harsh realities of the adult world (see James & Prout, 1998). Children's participation in social life as advocated by the Convention contradicts long-standing and institutional biases against their participation. Our reading of the CRC suggests that resolving that tension is one of the main challenges for the future.

While part 2 of the volume dealt with tensions between protection and participation rights within social systems, the final part 3 examines how these tensions are embodied within educational contexts. Each chapter focuses on educational contexts in various ways, with some chapters offering a broad perspective while others focus on a particular issue within education. As many children spend a significant amount of time in educational contexts, it is not surprising that issues of protection and participation often come into serious conflict within schools.

Schools are also a context within which the three types of rights (provision, protection, and participation) are all applicable. While a school's primary responsibility is the provision of education, schools are also responsible for keeping children safe and for teaching children how to actively participate in society. According to the Standing Senate Committee on Human Rights (Adreychuk & Fraser, 2007), the CRC is not 'solidly embedded in Canadian law, in policy, or in the national psyche,' but education about the CRC for children may best be addressed through specific programming on children's rights within school curricula. The authors in part 3 consider how well schools rise to the challenge not only of educating children about their rights but also of upholding those rights within various educational systems. Like the standing committee, they have some questions about how well this is being done and suggestions about changes that would make upholding children's rights within educational settings more effective.

Educators are constantly challenged to think about children's rights in new ways and often struggle with balancing the rights of the individual with those of the student body or the staff and administration. Some of the most recent challenges have been related to the use of technology and the responsibility of the school therein. Cases of cyber-bullying that initiate off school property and inappropriate comments about teachers in media such as Facebook have challenged schools to define the balance between the right to freedom of speech (participation) and the right to protection from discrimination or persecution (protection).

Shaheen Shariff and Leanne Johnny open part 3 with a discussion of the issues that are central to considerations of children's rights within cyberspace and the responsibility that schools have to address those rights. Like Roberts and Evans, they concentrate on how best to balance rights when they come into conflict, and particularly on how protection and participation are to be addressed. Children's rights within cyberspace and the implications of cyber-bullying are receiving increasing media attention and yet are just beginning to draw legal attention. Shariff and Johnny discuss the paucity of legal precedents to draw upon in addressing cyber-bullying and how schools need to negotiate their responsibility for actions on and off school property. They contend that cyberspace poses jurisdictional issues, for though the actual entry of damaging information (threats or slanderous statements) by a student may occur in the privacy of his/her own home, it may have a significant impact on the school environment. Canadian courts have been clear that schools are responsible for providing positive learning environments and for addressing actions that poison such environments. However, what has been less clear is how to balance the student's right to participation and freedom of speech against protection rights. Shariff and Johnny contend that this area will demand extensive interpretation of the CRC, along with other policy and law. They consider the legal embodiment of children's rights and the challenge that remains when two or more legal rights come into direct conflict in this new space that schools must address.

Johanna van Vliet and Rebecca Raby focus on another contentious area within education when they tackle the question of children's rights to sexual health education. Unlike cyberspace, this area has been contentious for some time, but like cyberspace it features an inherent conflict between protection and participation rights. Van Vliet and Raby argue that children's rights to health, information, education, and citizenship training, as outlined in the Convention, support their access to comprehensive sexual health education. They explore how conceptions of childhood innocence impede the access that a child in Ontario, Canada, has to information about sexuality, and use the Convention to argue for improved education about sexuality so that children are able to make informed choices when those choices are inevitably made. They also address the shortcomings that the current curriculum has not only in addressing children's right to access but also in addressing other rights associated with sexual diversity and the changing sexual culture. Sexual health education is often seen to be controversial, but van Vliet and Raby argue that the CRC and other international documents can provide some direction in successfully addressing children's rights in this area.

Sheila Bennett, Don Dworet, and Manta Zahos also address curriculum and the provision of services within education. Like van Vliet and Raby, they focus on Ontario, but instead of looking at a particular area such as sexual health education, they focus on the provision of education for children with special needs. After outlining a historical account of how the rights of students with exceptionalities have not been addressed, they move on to a consideration of how well the Ontario system is currently addressing the rights and needs of such students. Bennett, Dworet, and Zahos consider the role of identification, programming, and the definition of achievement in terms of how these elements promote inclusion or create barriers to inclusion. They also examine the legal contexts that have supported the inclusion of students with disabilities and consider how the education system has responded to changes to the legal context. The authors see positive changes through educator training and parent involvement within the education system. In the case of special education, Ontario seems to be more effective in upholding children's rights and in having systems to address situations when protection and participation rights come into conflict.

Monique Lacharite and Zopito Marini also focus on the Ontario educational context, but from the perspective of considering how anti-bullying programs can be grounded within the democratic rights of students. They contend that by placing bullying within a rights context, children and young people, along with school personnel, can be engaged in a consideration of rights and of how to address the violation of someone's rights. They conceptualize bullying as a form of rights violations that schools are duty-bound to address, and argue that incorporating education about individuals' rights into primary intervention is an effective way to raise awareness about bullying and to stop it before it happens. The authors do not contend that such an approach would eliminate bullying altogether or remove the need for intervention, but instead assert that it would provide a better cognitive framework for children to understand bullying from a rights perspective and to actively manage how to balance conflicts between protection and participation rights. This is a unique approach that empowers children to critically apply their knowledge of rights to current social issues.

In a different vein, Rebecca Raby promotes another unique approach to participation in her consideration of the extent to which students participate in the construction of school codes of conduct and her argument that a deeper level of participation would also serve to better prepare youth for active citizenship and employment. Raby provides a powerful critique of the notion that rights are to be awarded only for good behaviour at schools in Ontario, a misconception that she argues leads to passive citizenship. Children who fail to follow school 'codes of conduct' that are based on a specific cultural ideal of orderly, productive, and asexual behaviour too often find that their rights to participation and education are violated. Her discussion neatly exemplifies the contested space between a child's right to participate in their own lives and the social impulse to contain children, a space that becomes even more problematic when children are forced to conform to social and cultural contexts to which they do not already belong. Raby brings us fill circle back to some of the most difficult issues in children's rights in terms of how we conceptualize these rights and the difficulty that adults have in upholding children's and young people's participation rights without having them overshadowed by either protection issues or adult conceptualizations of how children's participation rights should be expressed.

Conclusion

The contributors to this volume have all approached the Convention from different disciplinary backgrounds, but are in agreement that the Convention is a tool to be utilized and contextualized by individuals, institutions, communities, and nations. Many of us have also identified tensions that exist and continue to present challenges to the CRC's implementation. Even though the preamble of the CRC defines the child as any individual under the age of eighteen (unless state laws place the age of majority earlier), this threshold exists more on paper than in practice: there is no global definition of the 'child,' nor any universal conceptualization of 'childhood.' If the Convention had been stronger in imposing specific models of children's development, by appealing to scientific or political authority, then critics would have been correct in stating that the CRC was a hegemonic document. The Convention is not, however, in the business of imposing Western ideals; it a document that requires interpretation in a variety of circumstances, and can only be realized through our diverse uses of it.

In order for the Convention to protect children, however they are defined, it must become integrated into the policies and laws of the ratifying nations. The way the CRC is written facilitates its interpretation and adoption into diverse nations' laws and policies. The chair of the Committee on the Rights of the Child, Jaap Doek (2004), argues that various national and cultural contexts must be taken into account in setting priorities and pursuing goals related to the CRC, but also that by ratifying the CRC each nation has committed itself to achieving the general goals it outlines. All of us must struggle with resolving the tensions between how the CRC is interpreted and applied. These tensions must be faced, as the Convention's reporting procedures consistently remind nations of their obligations under the Convention and promote the CRC at the grass-roots level, in schools, welfare agencies, and justice institutions.

Most of the authors in this volume point out that a child's rights to participation pose an even greater challenge to the implementation of the CRC, particularly when it contradicts institutional interests in raising, educating, and disciplining children. We need not reach for an exotic example to illustrate this conflict drawn from another culture, as it is readily apparent much closer to home: in the ideology of the family that subordinates the interests of children, in educational institutions that trade off rights and responsibilities in an effort to enforce conformity, and in institutions that assume that the participation of handicapped children is cognitively untenable. Article 12 of the CRC is one of the most challenging to interpret, as it extends to children the right to be heard in matters that pertain to them, which adults must recognize in ways that contradict conceptions of children as passive and irrational, or as dangers to themselves and society. This not to uncritically avoid questions about children's social, emotional, or cognitive ability to act in their own best interests, but it does require that the answers address specific children and contexts, and not universal ideals. We view child participation as a fundamental basis for good citizenship, which will lead to an educated and aware public culture that can make the progressive changes the world so direly needs.

This volume is not meant to provide definitive answers any more than the CRC was written to define 'child,' 'childhood,' or 'family.' It has been written to anticipate the future's tensions, contradictions, and challenges. The multidisciplinarity of this book illustrates a variety of perspectives that illuminate these challenges from competing perspectives. It also underscores the need to cooperate across disciplines, because, as we have argued, the nature of children as beings in a period of profound growth and transition requires it. A rights-based perspective holds the promise of retying the traces of the social sciences that were severed long ago, but this volume also puts us on notice that this task may not be easy; mere invocations of multidisciplinary or interdisciplinary intentions ought not to distract us from engaging in sober debate when this arises. What we learn from those debates will challenge our own conceptualizations, our own prejudices, our own disciplinary hubris. It is our hope that interdisciplinary and multidisciplinary approaches will not only expose challenges and tensions, but will also provide the tools to address them.

REFERENCES

Adreychuk, R., & Fraser, J. (2007). *Children: The silenced citizens; effective implementation of Canada's international obligations with respect to the rights of children*. Final Report of the Standing Senate Committee on Human Rights. Ottawa.

Bentley, Kristina Anne (2005). Can there be any universal children's rights? *International Journal of Human Rights, 9*(1), 107–123.

Boyden, J. (1997). Childhood and the policy makers: A comparative perspective on the globalization of childhood. In A. James & A. Prout (eds.) *Constructing and reconstructing childhood: Contemporary issues in the sociological study of childhood*. London: Falmer Press.

Boyden, J., & de Berry, J. (2004). *Children and youth on the front line: Ethnography, armed conflict and displacement*. New York: Bergahan Books.

Burr, R. (2002). Global and local approaches to children's rights in Vietnam. *Childhood, 9*, 49–61.

Doek, J. (2006). *Keynote address*. Children's Rights and International Development: Research, Challenges and Change Conference, Ottawa, Ontario.

Freeman, M. (2007). *Children's rights and children's welfare*. Plenary address at Investment and Citizenship: Towards a Transdisciplinary Dialogue on Child and Youth Rights Conference, St Catharines, ON.

Horkheimer, M., & Adorno, T. (1979). *The dialectic of enlightenment*. New York: Verso.

Howe, R.B., & Covell, K. (2005). *Empowering children: Children's rights education as a pathway to citizenship*. Toronto: University of Toronto Press.

James, A., Jenks, C., & Prout, A. (1998). *Theorizing childhood*, New York: Teacher's College Press.

Lee, N. (1999). The challenge of childhood: Distributions of childhood ambiguity in adult institutions. *Childhood 6*(4), 455–474.

Mason, M. (2005). The U.S. and the international children's rights crusade: Leader or laggard? *Journal of Social History, 38*(4), 955–963.

Mead, M. (1972). *Blackberry winter: My early years*. New York: Touchstone Books.

Melchiorre, A. (2004). *At what age?* 2nd ed., Right to Education Project.

Melton, G.B. (2005). Building humane communities respectful of children: The significance of the Convention on the Rights of the Child. *American Psychologist, 60*(8), 918–926.

Stevens, S. (1995). *Children and the politics of culture*. Princeton: Princeton University Press.

United Nations (1989). *Convention on the Rights of the Child*.

PART ONE

A World of Children's Rights

1 The Dilemma of Child and Youth Participation in Nepal's People's War

TOM O'NEILL

Like the Vietnam War, the successes and failures of the Maoist insurgency in Nepal have been largely measured in body counts. The Informal Sector Service Centre (INSEC), a Nepalese human rights organization, publishes frequent tallies of numbers of dead, missing, and tortured, all organized into tidy categories of ethnicity, gender, occupation, and district. Thus, from February 1996, when the 'People's War' began, to March 2004 there were 9170 dead, or, as they neatly summarize, 3.16 deaths per day. The numbers of dead police officers, soldiers, agricultural workers, and Maoist insurgents among others were separately counted. INSEC's periodical bulletins have evolved over the course of the insurgency, reflecting the growing impact of the violence at all levels of Nepalese society. Its March 2004 bulletin introduced a new variable into the calculus; for the first time, the numbers of dead children was given (INSEC, 2004). The relative age of the victims is central to an emerging debate on the effects of war on children, and on the recruitment, conscription and 'abduction' of child combatants by the Communist Party of Nepal (Maoist) in particular that speaks to the very legitimacy of the conflict.

In this chapter I explore the implications that the 'People's War' has on Nepal's children and youth from the standpoint of their prescribed 'right' to protection from conflict, which comes into profound conflict with their right to political participation. Nepal's civil conflict is, as I write, increasing with an unpredictable momentum (even though Maoist leaders claim that theirs is a 'scientific revolution') that makes predictive statements difficult to make. Ethnographic accounts of the violence are sketchy and often laden with their own ideological assumptions, and though Nepal's media has enjoyed until recently some latitude in covering the conflict, it has been subjected to official censorship and threat from both the state and Maoist forces. State-ments made by the leadership of both are blatantly unreliable, all of which makes any assessment of the conflict tenuous at best. Using what I consider the best available descriptions of the 'People's War,' I am therefore limited to a reflection on the problem of child and youth recruitment into violent political conflict as both moral and epistemo-logical: moral because it calls into question the legitimacy of violence as a political tool and epistemological because it must address how we understand competing claims to political, cultural, and historical legitimacy.

It is somewhat obvious to state that the eight-year-old 'People's War' in Nepal has been a human rights disaster, with rights violations documented on both sides. But rights violations are not only a conse-quence of the insurgency; claims and counter-claims about violations are part of the arsenal of this political struggle. A fundamental issue in insurgency has always been the legitimacy of the nation state or the struggle against it, and in a world permeated with the discourse of universal human rights that legitimacy must be articulated through a language of rights that is not easily applied to intra-national armed conflict. Legitimate nation states provide the 'rule of law' that protects human rights, but non-state insurgencies that for all intents and pur-poses are performing state functions – law, taxation, and, central to my purposes here, raising military forces – are in an ambiguous position. While pressing the claim that the nation state is violating human rights, they all too often commit their own violations, citing the strug-gle itself as the principal reason. The NCP (M) strategy seems to have been to provoke rights violations on the other side in order to legiti-mate its insurgency, but its current efforts to recruit young combatants risks rendering the party vulnerable to international criticisms that may undermine its own claim to legitimacy.

A 'Zone of Peace'?

Since the beginning of the 'People's War' the insurgent leadership and the government of Nepal have twice suspended violence and attempted dialogue. One month after the last ceasefire broke down, in August 2003, insurgents held a cultural program at a remote school in Mudbara, Doti, in far Western Nepal. Sometime after the rebels can-celled all classes and assembled the students for a 'cultural program,' the Nepalese army struck, killing six insurgents and four students who were caught in the cross-fire. The insurgents' corpses lay in the open for a number of days before the army returned and buried them in the schoolyard. As one student commented afterwards, 'Neither side showed it cared about the student's lives ... Both used the school for their own purposes' (*Nepali Times*, 2003).

As a result of the incident, and others like it, several prominent children's rights organizations in Kathmandu joined to advocate that Nepalese schools be declared 'zones of peace,' and urged both sides in the conflict to refrain from disrupting schools. The oldest and most influential of these groups, Child Workers in Nepal (CWIN), took this a step further by declaring that 'regardless of the existing nature of the national crisis, children are a zone of peace' (CWIN, 2003). Though these declarations were relatively benign and politically impotent, they underscore the deliberate strategy of the CPN (M) to transform the education system through violent and coercive means as well as the disregard the Nepalese state consistently displays towards the people it claims to defend. Constructing schools and children as 'zones of peace' resonates with an earlier pre-insurgency campaign by the late King Birendra to declare Nepal a 'zone of peace,' a policy rooted in cold-war non-alignment and fashioned to draw international tourists to the Kingdom. The designation of Nepal as a 'zone of peace,' however, is contrary to its violent political birth and the frequent bloody confrontations among its ruling elites. King Birendra, the monarchical heir to this 'peaceful' kingdom, was himself assassinated in a near Shakespearean display of pathological rage by his own son in June 2001.

The CPN (M) proposes an interpretation of Nepalese history that is more consistent with this violence, and claims lineage to the largely unrecorded peasant rebellions against these elites that have frequently taken place throughout the country's history. A 1995 party document, 'Strategy and Tactics of Armed Struggle in Nepal,' disputes this national discourse of the Nepalese people as being inherently peaceful by invoking instead the Gurkha soldier, world renowned for 'fighting prowess, bravery and sacrifice.' According to the document, Gurkha soldiers are predominantly from Nepal's 'tribal cultures' that were forcibly integrated into the Hindu caste system by invading Brahmins over one thousand years ago (Maoism, 1995). The current ruling elites of Nepal – the *Brahmin* and *Chetris* castes who dominate in the royalty, government, civil service, and army, thus represent both a class and ethnic enemy that is the target of Maoist struggle. Though this some-what simplistic framework is authored, it must be said, by Brahmin revolutionaries, it is nonetheless a compelling narrative for Nepal's countless disenfranchised. The document goes on to describe how this feudal elite violently suppressed frequent insurrections and forced Nepal's indigenous populations to submit to subaltern status, epito-mized by the mercenary armies it raised to fight for the imperialist powers (Great Britain and India) who had a vested interest in main-taining Nepal as a docile buffer in the great game of Himalayan geopolitics. Maoist violence is thus seen as crucial, and justifiable, in the struggle against Nepal's 'feudal elites.'

The current 'People's War' was declared in February 1996, after Maoist ideologue Baburam Bhattarai submitted a list of forty wide-ranging and inconsistent demands to Nepal's democratically elected government. Four days before the deadline for the government to respond to the demands, insurgents struck at two unmanned police posts in mid-western Rolpa district, an area with a long history of political organization by breakaway communist parties. CPN (M) activity in Rolpa before 1996 had aroused several ham-fisted responses from the Nepalese police that resulted in many extra-judicial killings. Significantly, according to Maoist accounts of its 'People's War,' the first death was of an eleven-year-old boy, Dil Bahadur Ramtel, who was shot while attempting to protect his father from arrest by police (*The Worker*, 2000). Ramtel thus became a martyr to the insurgency; the martyrdom of children in the 'People's War' is a consistent theme in Maoist discourse, and a significant departure from discourses of chil-dren's rights that stress children's protection from armed conflict, and their victimization through it.

Continued police violence in Rolpa and other mid-western districts since 1996, particularly the disastrous 'Kilo Sera' operation of 1998, have exacerbated the conflict, and allowed the Maoist leadership to claim Nepalese state human rights abuses as justification for the growing insurgency. At the same time, the leadership has had to protect its legitimacy against charges of its own abuses, and has shown particular sensitivity to claims that it deploys child soldiers. In August of 2000, Amnesty International warned that Maoists had been reported as having abducted and recruited youths under the age of eighteen for service in Maoist militias; by the end of the month, the general secre-tary of the CPN (M), Pushpa Kamal Dahal (who goes by the nom-de-guerre 'Prachanda,' or the 'fierce one'), issued a statement denying the

Amnesty report, and stated that these allegations were false propaganda spread by the Congress government (Human Rights and the People's War, 2000). A Maoist journal later commented:

> Today most of the schools in PW affected areas have been converted into barracks thus depriving children their education. So much for their so-called care for children and their blabbering of human rights for children. CPN (M) on the other hand has been campaigning for free education for all children. In areas where People's Committees are functioning, no private schools have been allowed to function while Government schools are supervised by People's Committees. The have also removed the burden of learning archaic Sanskrit language. While they have been strictly forbidden to join people's armed force, they have been organized under Akhil Bal Sangathan, a children's organization which takes care of overall development of children, including their right to express solidarity with what they consider good, including People's War. In that respect many Dil Bahadur Ramtels will continue to come forward to defend what they consider is justice. Maligning such voluntary acts as forceful recruitment into people's armed force is to fall into psychological warfare trap directed against People's War and its cause. In this regard, UN organization like UNESCO and Human Rights Organization like Amnesty International should be particularly careful as to not fall pray [sic] to such disinformation campaigns. (*The Worker*, 2000)

Though denying that children were involved as combatants, the Maoist leadership acknowledges here that children are a political constituency ripe for political work. Indeed, though this statement charges the Government with occupying school grounds, it also makes it clear that schools are a site of political struggle; government-run schools are supervised by 'People's Committees' in insurgent base areas such as Rolpa, while in other parts of the country the All Nepal National Free Student's Union (Revolutionary) has repeatedly closed schools, and the shadowy Swayam Sevak Dal organization that it controls systematically intimidated teachers and students who opposed them. Students of schools caught in the fray of the insurgency are frequently abducted for ideological training, and both sides routinely construct defensive bunkers on school grounds. Maoist discourse really leaves one right open to children: the right to support the 'People's War.'

But perhaps the most significant admission here is that 'voluntary acts' of children, such as the martyrdom of Dil Bahadur Ramtel, will continue. Another Maoist leader, Krishna Bahadur Mahara, similarly denied that children under the age of eighteen were being recruited as combatants to the American Cable News Network in 2001. Interestingly, eighteen years of age is the threshold set by the 2000 'Optional Protocol to the Convention on the Rights of the Child on the Involvement of Children in Armed Conflict,' to which the Nepalese Government but not the CPN (M) is signatory. Recent developments indicate that Maoist insurgents are more dependent on young combatants, as in Maoist base areas most young men have migrated to India and abroad to avoid being caught between the Maoists and the security forces. Many villages under Maoist control have been left with only the elderly and children, and indications are that both are currently being recruited. Even if Mahara's explanation were plausible in that children may not be recruited into the crack People's Liberation Army – a highly trained and heavily armed guerrilla force that is kept in reserve for the infrequent major engagements with the Nepalese police or army, they certainly do participate in village-level 'militias' that police rebel-held areas, and are often deployed as additional forces that serve as messengers, sentries, and porters. This was extensively documented by reporters travelling to Rolpa for the staunchly independent *Nepali Times* in December 2004:

> On 19 September, Maoist leader Prachanda issued a statement in which he said that his party hadn't abducted innocent civilians and this was against party principles. That same day the Barachhetra Secondary School in Rolpa's Badachaur district was deserted.

> None of the 300 students came to class because the head of the people's government, Comrade Agni, had ordered that all children from Grade five and above would have to join a 'special militia training.' The parents refused to send their children to school.

The boundary between combatant and civilian in rural insurgencies is arbitrarily drawn by all sides; indeed, to speak of these categories at all imposes an archaic framework on intra-national conflict in the post-cold war era. The 'People's War,' though rooted in ideological and millenarian social vision, shares many qualities with ethnic conflicts elsewhere in the world in that the subjectivity of people themselves is a battleground, and for both the CPN (M) and the Nepalese state, children and youth are a particularly fertile population on which to inscribe conflicting meanings. For revolutionary purposes, moreover, a complete transformation of subjectivity is called for that is to be achieved through the cleansing empowerment of violence. Philippe Ramirez draws a direct link between Nepalese Maoist ideology and that of the Indian Naxalbari movement from which the CPN (M) drew inspiration. Revolutionary violence, according to this theory, has a dual purpose: the 'annihilation of class enemies,' police, landlords, moneylenders, and spies, and the new birth of men 'who will defy death, and will be free of all self interests' (Mazmundar, as cited in Ramirez 2004, p. 240).

The martyrdom of Dil Bahadur Ramtel is a paradigmatic narrative for Nepalese Maoism. According to Anne de Sales, an anthropologist whose research area includes the Rolpa district where the insurgency first started, the cult of martyrdom that has been elaborated by the Maoist leadership has its roots in a traditional Kham Magar sacrificial 'symbolic revitalization' that imbues violent death with revolutionary meaning. The sacralization of local landmarks in Rolpa as memorials to the martyrs of the revolution, such as the commemorative pillars that overlook the Kham Magar homelands, shows that 'revolutionaries do not think that it is sufficient to occupy space physically, but that they have to root it in a specific history of events in which the principal actors are locals' (2003, p. 85).

Not only does the cult of martyrdom appease the death of revolutionary ancestors, it also places an obligation on the living to set aside self-interest and be prepared for their own deaths. Baburam Bhattarai was asked by the liberal *Nepali Times* newspaper in 2001 whether the 'People's War' had been worth the high price in human lives, which had just exceeded two thousand officially recognized deaths. His answer is instructive:

> Though it is anachronistic to attach a 'price' tag to an epoch-making revolutionary process in terms of human casualties, we feel the 'price' paid by the Nepalese masses so far in the six years of the people's war has been rather on the lower side. Such 'prices' in genuine revolutions are paid in millions, and not in thousands. Do you remember the French Revolution? Considering the power and prestige gained by the poor and oppressed masses of the Nepalese countryside during the past six years, the 'price' paid for has been definitely worth it. (Bhattarai, 2001)

What is striking in this admission is the apparent disregard for the individual suffering that the poor and oppressed incurred through their sacrifices, and its displacement into a faith that widespread violence will eventually lead to 'power and prestige' for the oppressed masses. The conviction that meaningful social change will occur only through revolutionary war begs the question of the justification of armed rebellion, of means and ends; and the expectation that people will voluntarily embrace the sacrifice necessary for rebirth raises questions' about voluntarism, empowerment, agency, and socio-cultural structure. Both of those questions are further complicated here in that we are speaking about children and youth; a group defined in international children's rights discourses as only ambiguously participating in the social and political life of the societies that are charged with their protection, an ambiguousness that is exacerbated by the fact of political violence.

Innocence and Voluntarism

The Nepalese NGO Informal Sector Service Centre has provided an ongoing account of the effect that the Maoist insurgency in Nepal is having on people that allow activists and scholars around the world to witness the human rights catastrophe that has been unfolding since the insurgency began. From their Situation Report (July–September 2003) I cite the following documented examples of individual acts of violence committed by both sides on 9 September 2003:

> Dabal Bahadur Jaisi, 7, his parents Tek Prasad Jaisi, 31, Chandra Kala Jaisi, 29, grandfather Bishnu Prasad Jaisi, 51, of Bhatte Kali of Palchaur VDC-7, and Kitthi Dhami, of Achham Basti VDC-6 at the bordering areas of Achham and Doti districts were shot dead at Achham Basti VDC-8, by the security personnel on patrol on 9 September and thrown the dead bodies of the victims branding them 'terrorists.' The victims were on their way to their houses after harvesting paddy.

> Bhawana Sanjel, 7, of Ikudol VDC-3, was killed in a grenade blast by the Maoists on 9 September. The victim was playing in the corridor of her house. As a witness said, the grenade exploded when the Maoists being trained to blast carelessly threw which hit the child to death. The villagers had caught the Maoists but they managed to escape later.

The deaths of Dabal Bahadur Jaisi and Bhawana Sanjel occurred on the same day, during the period that followed the breakdown in peace talks in August and the refutation of a negotiated 'code of conduct' and resumption of military activities by the insurgents on 26 September. The labelling of Dabal Baisi and his families as 'terrorists' is consistent with the widespread practice of evading responsibility for the indiscriminate use of force, abduction, and battlefield 'justice' by State security forces (see Dixit, 2003 for a full discussion of this). Bhawana Sanjel's death cannot be narrated as 'martyrdom' by the Maoists because it was clearly accidental, but the cadres who committed the offence escaped and also evaded responsibility for their actions. What is particularly salient about these two cases, out of the 477 deaths documented by INSEC during that three-month period, is the 'innocence' of the victims and, in both cases, the fact that they were caught up in the crossfire of the 'People's War.' Children's innocence is an essential element of conceptions of modern childhood that underpin universal children's rights discourse, even though the universality of those conceptions can be questioned, a point to which I shall turn shortly. In a general sense, however, 'innocence' is itself a concept in question in the context of internal civil conflict.

State labelling of the insurgents as 'terrorists' notwithstanding, the 'People's War' is a conflict in which terror is brought to bear against the population by all sides. Security forces frequently torture captives, intimidate suspected Maoist sympathisers, or make opponents 'disappear,' and the media frequently indulges in lurid narratives of Maoist torture of 'spies,' 'class enemies,' and 'imperialists.' The veracity of these narratives is less important than is their effect of creating a 'culture of terror' that places the innocence of everyone in question (Taussig, 1984). Fellow villagers become potential Maoist activists or police spies, political activists on all sides become the targets for class warfare waged from the right and the left; from the perspective of the combatants, there is no innocence. Everyone, and in particular children and youth, are either held as potential activists or martyrs to a cause, or, conversely, as maturing enemies of the state. As Veena Das and Arthur Kleinman et al. observed about the 'new political geography of the world' that is characterized by numerous intra-national ethnic, religious, and ideological wars: 'The violence in these areas seems to belong to a new moment in history: it certainly cannot be understood through earlier theories of contractual violence or a classification of just and unjust wars, for its most disturbing feature is that it has occurred between social actors who lived in the same social worlds and knew or thought they knew each other' (2000, p. 1).

How 'new' these forms of violence are is open to question. Earlier conceptions of interstate, conventional warfare that pitted professional 'combatants' in contests of officially sanctioned violence may be based on a reading of history that did not detail internal struggles or colonial outrages; but the perspective that Das and Kleinman present usefully brackets questions of means and ends, or the notion that some forms of violence are more justifiable than others. Das and Kleinman call for ethnographers to be witnesses to both overt and structural violence, not to evaluate its legitimacy but to take a position against all forms of violence by describing how it empowers and deforms individual subjectivity, often at the same time. Insurgents may be pressed into action by powerful and often coercive external forces, but if individual action is understood solely as a reflex of those forces, 'then the issue of responsibility for atrocity or failure of witnessing is too easily sidestepped, and the potential for refusal or resistance is denied' (2000, p. 17). People also have their own motivations for violence, such as an aggrieved desire for social change, social status, personal revenge, or even a sustainable income, and our analysis of civil conflict must include these factors as well.

Gathering first-hand accounts of civil conflict is a risky affair for an ethnographer, but as civil conflict in the new world disorder engulfs field sites where ethnographers are already working, it is an issue that fewer and fewer of us can ignore. Anne de Sales's account of the early genesis of the Nepalese conflict in mid-western Rolpa is an attempt to locate the struggle in local cultural context, and concludes in part that the Kham Magars who are indigenous to it 'have found themselves fighting a war that is not theirs: they are just cannon-fodder for the two parties struggling over territory' (2003, p. 87). Despite this, the insurgents managed to firmly root their movement there by appealing to a nostalgia among young people for the idealized warrior past of their ancestors. In a more recent description of the progress of the 'People's War' in the central Dolakha region, Sara Sneiderman and Mark Turin (2004) describe the evolution of insurgency as it took hold among the Thangmi and Tamang ethnic minorities where the Maoists successfully organized a Jan Sarkar ('People's Government') by appealing to long-standing grievances against the structural violence of the Nepalese state. Their article is based on an interview with one 'young man from a village in Dolakha,' and, while their article can be faulted for generalizing this one subjectivity to the broader population in the district, it does describe how one young person becomes not only sympathetic to the Maoists, but makes their struggle his own.

Recruitment to political, religious, or communal violence by nation states or by non-state insurgencies is rarely either purely coercive or purely voluntary. Many ethnographic accounts of child combatants point out that children are not necessarily the passive victims of conflict, and also that they have diverse motivations in taking up arms beyond (or even despite) ideological influences. Paul Richards writes that young militia members in Sierra Leone often drifted to the rebels after the death of their parents, or out of revenge for a lost family member, while others he found to be motivated by 'access to education and employment, rather than oppression and one-party rule' (2002, p. 275). Conscription, voluntary recruitment, and even abduction for service are not discrete categories, but points along a continuum of behaviour that is culturally and historically variable. Many young people recruited by the Maoist forces are also drawn by revenge and outrage at the other side due to family losses, while others may be drawn because being a Maoist combatant is a means of significantly increasing personal prestige. Women, for example, fight alongside men in rebel units against not only the security forces, but against a culture that severely restricts gender rights (Gautam et al., 2003)

Ideological commitment, moreover, has been shown to be a protective factor that renders at least some children and youth resilient to the psychological trauma of conflict that impairs many others. The cult of martyrdom, for example, inscribes the death of family members with meanings that shape children's responses, as well as prescribing future behaviour and practices (see Punamaki, 1996). Predominant emphasis on the protection of children as victims of conflict, with all of the attendant stress and trauma associated with it, does not provide a sufficient framework for understanding child and youth participation in violent action. On the other hand, Nancy Scheper-Hughes (2000) warns that combatants are all too easily abandoned by their recruiters once the battle is over, and are left to reinterpret their own violence when the choice between fight or flight continues to limit their future possibilities. Young South African *skollies* organized to fight the apartheid regime by the Pan African Congress were abandoned by them after 1990, leaving them to prone to crime and widespread public disapproval. Once participants in revolutionary social change, they were transformed afterwards into criminal youth gangs. Scheper-Hughes's local account of how structural violence 'deformed' a whole generation of South African youth is an important antidote to Naxalbari notions of the cleansing and creative power of civil violence.

It is significant that in both de Sales's and Sneiderman and Turin's ethnographies of local insurgent contexts the youth of the Maoist supporters is referred to, but never questioned from a basis of children's rights. Sneiderman and Turin provide detail about the schools in Dolakha that were targeted by Maoist cadres for proselytization, and report that students were soon singing 'What good is an education when we can fight the people's war,' but again they fail to remark on this as a potential rights violation. The question is, of course, a complex one, for while the deaths of two seven-year-old children is without question the victimization of innocents, the knowing participation of children and youth in the insurgency is far more problematic. For at what age, or at what time in an individual's growing awareness of themselves as social actors, can we accept that their voluntary acts of violence in service of political, religious, or communal interests are autonomous and fully informed?

Are Children's Rights Relevant?

Given the social polarities generated by the conflict at the community level, these questions must be considered in a context that often presents children or youth with a limited choice: fight for or against the 'People's War' or, to escape the violence, flee to protected district towns, Kathmandu, or even India, where they are often separated from their families and unable to attend school. The popular view of human rights and child soldiers that holds the experience of combat to be detrimental to children's development often imposes definitions of a universal childhood that are not inherent in the legal discourse of universal rights. Michael Faulkner, for example, writes that children 'are dragooned, enticed and seduced into taking up arms and effectively sacrificing their innocence in the name of this or that motivation, based on decisions made by adults' (2001, p. 491). The notion that childhood is a time of innocence is derived from a specifically Western discourse, and as I stated above, it is barely applicable to contexts where both adults and children have been caught up in decades of intra-national violence. Popular representations of childhood 'innocence' as a social space to be protected from harmful external realities, as is assumed in the 'children as a zone of peace' campaign in Nepal, are of little relevance when that reality has already been overwhelmed. Moreover, such campaigns also obscure the extent to which young people are participating in the conflict for their own reasons.

A prevalent misconception of the concept of universal human rights holds that it is no more than a cover under which Western cultural hegemony is being extended throughout the world, and any cursory reading of how children's rights are understood at a popular level will only substantiate that misconception. Threats to cultural sovereignty and collective identity due to the individualistic nature of human rights statutes are also decried by social scientists; anthropologists, for example, opposed the U.N. Declaration of Human Rights in 1948 because of the universal goals of the document. Culture, they argued, is a relative concept, and the notion that there are universal rights that supersede cultural variability was seen as the imposition of Western, Euro-centric models of morality on others (see Preis, 1996). In her agenda-setting 1995 contribution *Children and the Politics of Culture*, for example, Sharon Stevens (1995) argues that the United Nations Convention on the Rights of the Child (CRC), the rights document that specifically codifies family and state obligations towards children, imposes the nuclear family as an ideal model to which children ought to be entitled. A reading of the actual document, however, does not suggest that the CRC imposes any definition of 'the family' whatsoever; on the contrary, the document, like the 1948 declaration, assiduously avoids making any definitions in order to be inclusive of the many cultures and nations that signed on to it.

The CRC describes in general the obligations that families and states have towards children and youth under the age of eighteen to act in 'the best interests of the child' at all junctures, and the preamble to the Convention demands that we provide for and protect children because the child, 'by reason of his physical and mental immaturity, needs special safeguards and care, including appropriate legal protection, before as well as after birth.' What is particularly problematic here is the notion of 'the child,' a universal concept that masks, to a degree, all of the variation in children's experience cross-culturally. If we look past such abstract concerns, however, the rationale that children, however they are defined, are vulnerable because of their physical and mental immaturity is a useful benchmark from which to consider their 'best interests.' Protecting children from the physical, social, and psychological risks to their optimal development is a central aim of the Convention, but ironically when it came to protecting children from the risks posed by violent conflict and warfare in article 38 (2), the document was equivocal, such that while protecting children and youth under the age of eighteen from other risks, it only explicitly forbade the recruitment of children under the age of fifteen out of deference to powerful objections by the international community. The weakness of article 38 (2) is an artefact of international negotiations on the 1989 Convention, wherein no consensus could be reached on the age of military service. These negotiations reflect a wider debate on what constitutes a child in a universal sense (Freeman, 2000).

Most states, including Nepal, are now signatories to the 2000 'Optional Protocol on the Involvement of Children in Armed Conflict' that harmonizes policy regarding children's recruitment to armed violence with the overall intentions of the Convention. In a sense, Nepal's signature on the Optional Protocol is a sign of the legal sovereignty that the CPN (M) is contesting, that is, the power and responsibility of the state to protect the rights of its citizens/subjects; their assurances that they abide by the same standards are meant to convince the international community that Nepal's 'new regime' is worthy of that power and responsibility. The Maoists are not challenging state sovereignty per se; they are intent merely on monopolizing that sovereignty themselves, in the name of the Nepalese people. It should be noted, following Foucault (1991), that populations are not only objects of state protection and welfare, they are also sources of state power. The CPN (M)'s sensitivity to criticism about child recruitment is in recognition of the growing global consensus against child soldiering that undermines its own legitimate recourse to a demographically predominant and valuable human strategic resource.

Arguments about rights, state sovereignty, and legitimacy do not however address the role that individual agency plays within the structures that shape and deform subjectivities. Another important element of the 1989 CRC is that children should have the right to free expression, particularly on matters that affect them, but article 12, which grants this freedom, tempers it with another equivocation: 'the views of the child being given due weight in accordance with the age and maturity of the child.' It is not clear how 'age and maturity' are defined, nor, for that matter, what constitutes 'free expression.' Does it extend to voluntary civil violence, if the aim of that violence ostensibly contributes to social transformation? To assume that children and youth cannot make this decision on the basis of their (young) age and (lack) of maturity begs the question of at what threshold we would find such a choice acceptable, and how such a threshold would be legally generalized to the world community.

Such questions ought not to be central when children and youth participation is being considered; that is to say, it is not sufficient to state that children and youth should be protected from civil violence because this is a convention of international law. Human rights scholar Michael Ignatieff (2001) warns against 'rights idolatry,' or the tendency to treat human rights as universally valid and existing beyond positive law. Human rights codes, he argues, are pragmatic and socially constructed agreements that arose out of the experiences of the Second World War, and he rejects any view of rights that claims or imposes any essential ontological basis for human rights. Pragmatically, then, we should protect children from civil violence because such violence can cause suffering to them, and to those around them, and international rights conventions are only useful insofar as they help us do this. We should also be clear that we are protecting individual children from oppressive social forces that put them at physical, social, or psychological risk, and not protecting children as a category from risks to their 'innocence.'

Human rights codes are not intended to define a universal social or moral 'good'; the 1948 Universal Declaration of Human Rights guarantees only what Isaiah Berlin calls 'negative liberty,' and not social justice broadly conceived. What is determined to be good about social life must be arrived at through the participation of people claiming and challenging those definitions, and human rights are best understood as tools to fight the arbitrary abuse and oppression meted out by cultures, societies, families, and any other collective entity, including, it is assumed, both state and non-state insurgent forces (Ignatieff, 2001). The equivocation of many of the articles of the Convention on the Rights of the Child are thus an unavoidable, even necessary recognition of the multiple ways that 'childhood' is experienced by children in changing social environments.

Nepal has long been defined by the structural violence of caste domination, poverty, and political repression. In this social environment the violence of the Maoist insurgency and state counter-insurgency has taken root, and now overshadows the few seeds of progress that have been sowed since 1990. In this environment the relevancy of human rights at even its most basic level is ignored at the local level – a casualty of war. For children and youth the stark choice between volunteering for the revolution or fleeing their homes to escape both state and Maoist oppression moots many of the ancillary rights granted in the CRC, such as a right to an education, to a safe, healthy community in which to grow, and even to be part of a family that provides basic needs. The relevancy of rights at the global level is thus all the more important. While recognizing that some young people may make that choice with their eyes open, those of us who can only watch as events unfold must bear witness to how the conflict transforms and deforms children's experience, and ensure that those responsible for violations are held accountable, whether those responsible are legitimate states or insurgencies that challenge that legitimacy.

Conclusion

Despite their protests of a few years ago, it is clear that the CPN (M) relies on young combatants in its insurgency against the state, and demographic factors indicate that the recruitment of even younger fighters will increase as the conflict intensifies. A recent Amnesty International report (2005) details the continuing indiscriminate killing of children by the state, and the increasing abduction, indoctrination, and recruitment of children and youth by Maoist forces that exposes them to the violent consequences of the conflict. The report points out that both sides are violating children's rights as defined by the CRC with impunity, and that the progress that Nepal has made in promoting children's rights since 1990 has been undermined by the intensity of the conflict.

In this chapter I have explored the dilemma of child and youth participation in revolutionary violence, and whether that participation can be legitimately tolerated. Efforts to declare children as a 'zone of peace' that are currently popular among some children's rights organizations ignore some of the central realities of the 'People's War.' 'Innocence' becomes a field of conflict in civil conflict; some innocent children are killed, while other 'innocents' kill. Maoist appeals to the value of sacrifice and martyrdom exploit the participatory impulses of Nepalese children and youth, and place them, one way or another, in the line of fire. A children's rights perspective ought to consider how children can be protected and invited to participate in social change at the same time; but when the means to that social change are violent, our analysis of the situation needs to consider how violence both transforms and deforms children's individual subjectivity. This is the challenge of a rights-based approach to children's participation in civil conflict.

REFERENCES

Amnesty International (2000). *Nepal: Maoists must end abductions, killing and the recruitment of child soldiers.* Retrieved June 15, 2004, from http://web.amnesty.org/library/Index/ENGASA310252000

Amnesty International (2005). *Nepal: Children caught in the conflict.* Retrieved June 15, 2004, from http://web.amnesty.org/pages/npl-260705

Bhattarai, B. (2001). *You will enjoy more democratic rights under the New Democracy than you are enjoying today.* Retrieved June 15, 2004, from http://insof.org/politics/130701_interview_baburam.html

Child Workers in Nepal, CWIN (2003). *Children are (a) zone of peace.* Retrieved June 15, 2004, from http://www.cwin- nepal.org/press_room/pressreleases/joint_statement_cic.htm

Das, V., Kleinman, A., Ramphele, M., & Reynolds, P. (2000). *Violence and subjectivity.* Berkeley and Los Angeles: University of California Press.

de Sales, A. (2003). Between ethnic claims and Maoism. In D. Thapa (Ed.), *Understanding the Maoist movement of Nepal.* Kathmandu: Martin Chautari Centre for Social Research and Development.

Dixit, K.M. (2003). The Nepali army's battle with the maobadis. In D. Thapa (Ed.), *Understanding the Maoist movement of Nepal.* Kathmandu: Martin Chautari Centre for Social Research and Development.

Faulkner, F. (2001). Kindergarten killers: Morality, murder and the child soldier problem. *Third World Quarterly, 22*(4), 491–505.

Freeman, M. (2000). The future of children's rights. *Children and Society, 14,* 277–293.

Foucault, M. (1991). Governmentality. In G. Burchell, C. Gordon & P. Miller (Eds.), *The Foucault effect: Studies in governmentality.* Chicago: University of Chicago Press.

Gautam, S., Banskota, A., & Machanda, R. (2003). Women in the Maoist insurgency in Nepal. In D. Thapa (Ed.), *Understanding the Maoist movement of Nepal.* Kathmandu: Martin Chautari Centre for Social Research and Development.

Human Rights and the People's War. (2000). *No recruitment of child soldier.* Retrieved on June 15, 2004, from http://www.humanrights.de/doc_en/archiv/n/nepal/news/020900_press_statement.htm

Ignatieff, M. (2001). *Human rights as politics and idolatry.* Princeton: Princeton University Press.

Informal Sector Service Centre, INSEC (2003). *Situation report (July–September 2003).* Retrieved June 15, 2004, from http://www.insec.org.np

INSEC (2004). *Human rights data*. Retrieved June 15, 2004, from http://
www.insec.org.np

Maoism. (1995). *Strategy and tactics of armed struggle in Nepal*. Retrieved June
15, 2004, from http://www.maoism.org/misc/nepal/worker3/
strategy.htm

Nepali Times. (2003). *This is not a school, it is a cemetery*. Retrieved June 15,
2004, from http://www.nepalnews.com.np/ntimes/issue169/
nation_2.htm

Nepali Times. (2004). *Giving children a fighting chance*. Retrieved June 15, 2004,
from http://www.nepalnews.com.np/ntimes/issue227/nation.htm

Preis, A. (1996). Human rights as cultural practice: An anthropological critique. *Human Rights Quartery, 18*(2), 286–315.

Punamaki, R. (1996). Can ideological commitment protect children's psychological well-being in situations of political violence? *Child Development 67*,
55–69.

Ramirez, P. (2004). Maoism in Nepal: Towards a comparative perspective. In
M. Hutt (Ed.), *Himalayan People's War: Nepal's Maoist rebellion*. Bloomington:
University of Indiana Press.

Richards, P. (2002). Militia conscription in Sierra Leone: Recruitment of
young fighters in an African war. *The Comparative Study of the Conscription
in the Armed Forces, 20*, 255–276.

Scheper-Hughes, N. (2000). After the war is over. *Peace Review, 12*(3), 423–429.

Sneiderman, S., & Turin, M. (2004). The path to jan sarkar in Dolakha district:
Towards an ethnography of the Maoist movement. In M. Hutt (Ed.),
Himalayan People's War: Nepal's Maoist Rebellion. Bloomington: University of
Indiana Press.

Stevens, S. (1995). *Children and the politics of culture*. Princeton: Princeton University Press.

Taussig, M. (1984). Culture of terror – space of death. Roger Casement's Puta-
mayo report and the explanation of torture. *Comparative Studies in Society
and History, 26*, 467–497.

United Nations. (1989). *Convention on the Rights of the Child*.

The Worker. (2000). *Human rights situation and children*. Retrieved June 15,
2004, from http://www.cpnm.org/worker/issue6/workers_6_issue.html

2 Protecting the Rights of International 'Orphans': Evaluating the Alternatives

LUCY LE MARE, KARYN AUDET, AND KAREN KURYTNIK

This chapter addresses the rights of abandoned and orphaned children drawing particularly on examples from Romania, Russia, and China. Specifically, we consider how well the rights of the child, as described in the 1990 United Nations Convention on the Rights of the Child (CRC), can be and typically are upheld in a variety of care arrangements, including institutional settings, foster care, and domestic and foreign adoptive homes.

Human Rights Watch (1998) estimates that worldwide several million children are being raised in residential institutions (orphanages), making this the most common care arrangement for international orphans. In Romania, Russia, and China combined, half a million is likely a low estimate of the number of children currently living in institutions. Here we argue that, in practice, institutional rearing infringes on several fundamental rights, including the right to development and, relatedly, the rights to health care, education, and protection from harmful practices such as abuse, neglect, and exploitation.

One alternative to institutional care is inter-country adoption. Although inter-country adoption potentially addresses many of the problems associated with orphanage rearing, it raises a different set of concerns. These include the child's right to identification with their racial, ethnic, or national group, to know the truth about their personal histories, and to not be bought or sold.

As a remedy to the potential for the abuse of rights inherent in both institutional care and foreign adoption, several organizations concerned with children's rights (e.g., Human Rights Watch, World Vision, USAID, and UNICEF) have recommended the development of foster care and domestic adoption programs within those countries that have large numbers of orphans. These goals, while laudable, have their own set of difficulties. In countries such as China, Russia, and Romania, social, economic, and cultural conditions typically necessitate that the development and implementation of domestic fostering and adoption programs will be a lengthy process that will not soon be able to meet the needs that exist now. Indeed, those same conditions have supported the orphanage systems within these countries.

Who Are the International Orphans?

The term 'orphan' is actually a misnomer when used in reference to the vast majority of children currently being reared in residential institutions, as nearly all have living parents. For example, of the children who reside in Romanian and Russian orphanages, it is estimated that 84 and 95 per cent, respectively, have living parents (American Council for Voluntary International Action, 2002; Human Rights Watch, 1998). A similar situation exists in China. Typically, institutionalized children have been abandoned by their parents. Hence, the term 'social orphan' is often used to refer to those children who currently populate the orphanages of eastern Europe, the former Soviet Union, and parts of Asia.

Reasons for child abandonment vary both within and between countries and are linked to a variety of social, economic, and political factors. In Romania, for example, under the dictatorship of Nicolae Ceausescu, strong pro-natal policies with negative constraints resulted in a high birth rate. This, coupled with widespread poverty and a view, actively promoted by the government, that the state was better able to rear children than the family, resulted in the relinquishment of children, often at maternity hospitals, being commonplace. Child abandonment continues to be prevalent in Romania, where it remains an acceptable, and often the only, option available to parents disadvantaged by poverty or their own institutional upbringing (UNICEF, 2005).

In Russia, the huge orphanage system was inspired by the Soviet philosophy favouring collective organization over individual care and an ideal similar to that found in Romania that the state could replace the family. According to Human Rights Watch (1998) most Russians who left their children in the care of the state during the late Soviet period did so for reasons of poverty, illness, and family problems. The substantial social and economic changes that came with the end of the Cold War caused increases in substance abuse, poverty, and disease in Russia, which in turn have perpetuated child abandonment. It is also the case in Russia that parents of infants born with physical or mental disabilities are often urged by hospital personnel to give up their babies.

Reasons for child abandonment in China are linked to the one-child policy, established in communist China in 1979 to limit population growth. In a culture that has traditionally valued males over females as providers, carriers of the family name, and those who care for aging parents, the one-child policy has resulted in the abandonment of tens of thousands of female babies annually (Rojewski & Rojewski, 2001). Children born with disabilities are also frequently abandoned so that parents may try again for a healthy son.

Institutional Rearing and the CRC

It is important to note that although the UN Convention on the Rights of the Child does allow for the institutional care of children, it is seen as a reasonable option only if other, family-based care arrangements are not possible. As stated in article 20, 'Such arrangements could include, inter alia, foster placement, kafalah of Islamic law, (or) adoption.' If one of these care settings cannot be found, article 20 indicates, orphans can be placed in 'suitable institutions for the care of children.' In theory, institutional care need not necessarily violate the rights of the child to any great extent, particularly if it is short lived. In practice, however, rights that are frequently threatened include those to development, health, education, and humane treatment.

Ideally, an analysis of children's rights within residential institutions would be based on systematic assessments of orphanage environments; however, the reader is cautioned that such studies are rare. With few significant exceptions (e.g., Groark, Muhamedrahimov, & Palmov, 2005), most reports are short first- or second-hand narrative impressions and perceptions. Although there is considerable consistency among these narratives, there are also some conflicting reports.

The Right to Development

Article 27 of the CRC recognizes 'the right of every child to a standard of living adequate for the child's physical, mental, spiritual, moral, and social development.' As pointed out by MacLean (2003), virtually all developmental scholars acknowledge that institutional care has some detrimental effect on child development. There are numerous features typical of institutions that can account for this.

The Physical Environment

It is well recognized that the physical environment in which children are raised affects their behaviour and overall development. Researchers have identified a number of physical features of homes that support the cognitive and social development of children. These include appealing developmentally appropriate decorations on walls in children's bedrooms, living space that is well lit and perceptually interesting, child access to all rooms, space that enables children free movement, and accessibility for children to developmentally appropriate learning materials including toys, paper, crayons or pencils, games, and books (Bradley, Caldwell, Brisby, Magee, & Whiteside, 1992).

Just as the physical environments of homes are important, so are the physical environments of group care settings. According to the National Association for the Education of Young Children (NAEYC, 1991), the quality of the physical space and materials provided in childcare settings affects the level of involvement of children and the quality of interactions among adults and children. Important variables include the amount, arrangement, and use of space, both indoors and outdoors as well as the availability of toys and other educational material. Early childhood environments that stimulate children's cognitive and social development typically include: sufficient well-designed indoor and outdoor space, many windows for natural light, availability of a variety of age-appropriate toys and equipment, a colourful and inviting atmosphere, and comfortable and safe furniture (Child Care Resource and Resource Unit, 1995).

In stark contrast to these recommendations are the dull physical environments that characterize many orphanages. The physical design and layout of institutions are generally not like a home environment. Many orphanages are situated in multi-storey buildings similar in design to standard hospitals or schools. Signs indicating the uses of particular spaces (for example, 'laundry,' 'kitchen,' 'who is on duty today,' and 'exit') only emphasize that these buildings are institutions and not a home (Sloutsky, 1997). Children typically have access to sleeping rooms that they can share with up to fifteen others and 'living' rooms where all other daily activities take place.

Orphanages that receive little financial support from local governments or foreign agencies can be extremely bleak places. Descriptions of some Romanian and Chinese institutions indicate that few toys, books, and educational materials are available for children's use and walls are colourless and barren. Play space, both indoors and out, can be minimal to non-existent. In contrast, in other institutions, notably those in some Russian cities, the physical environments appear to be stimulating and child-friendly. Toys and educational materials are present and there are well-equipped playgrounds. However, even in these settings the resources are not necessarily available for children's use. Several authors (Groark et al., 2005; Human Rights Watch, 1998) have described the peculiar institutional practice of displaying newly acquired developmental toys in places only accessible to the staff. Such practices have been observed in both Romanian and Russian orphanages. In other institutions, donations from foreign agencies are often locked in storage rooms.

Health Care and Nutrition

Medical care and nutrition are also frequently substandard in institutions. The reasons for this are complex and include inadequate funding, crowded living conditions, systemic discrimination against orphans, and not enough or inadequately trained staff. Human Rights Watch (1996; 1998) has described horrific situations in Chinese and Russian institutions concerning the health and nutritional status of orphans, and Ames (1990) described an equally disturbing situation in Romania in 1990. Indeed, reports from the 1990s on the health status of post-institutionalized children all pointed to the high risk for poor health associated with institutional rearing. Specifically, this work showed high rates of infectious disease and growth retardation in international orphans (Ames, Fisher, & Sovoie, 1994; Hostetter, Iverson, Dole, & Johnson, 1989; Hostetter, Iverson, Thomas, McKenzie, Dole & Johnson, 1991; and Johnson, Miller, Iverson, Thomas, Franchino, Dole, Kiernan, Georgieff, & Hostetter, 1992). The available evidence at that time indicated that the right of children to physical development (article 27) was compromised in orphanages in part by the failure of those institutions to uphold article 24 of the CRC, which highlights 'the right of the child to the enjoyment of the highest attainable standard of health and to facilities for the treatment of illness and rehabilitation of health.'

Institutions in which sick babies and children are starved and left to die without any intervention or care are hopefully now a thing of the past. Certainly, more recent reports from Russia (e.g., Sloutsky, 1997; St. Petersburg–USA Orphanage Research Team, 2005) and China (e.g., Homewood, 2002) indicate that attention to the health and nutrition of orphans in those countries has significantly improved. Nevertheless, even in some of the very best Russian orphanages, researchers have reported that over 50 per cent of the children show significant growth delays (St. Petersburg–USA Orphanage Research Team, 2005), which, given that they are well fed, may be indicative of psychosocial dwarfism, a condition whereby children raised under stressful circumstances fail to grow. Such findings clearly suggest that even in settings with good physical care, orphanage rearing may deny children the right to a standard of living adequate for typical physical growth.

The Caregiving Environment

For the purposes of this chapter, the caregiving environment refers to the quality and quantity of interactions that take place between caregivers and children in institutional settings. One indicator of the caregiving environment within institutions is the caregiver-to-child ratio. Descriptions of Romanian institutions immediately following the fall of the Ceausescu regime indicate ratios in the range of one caregiver for every 25–30 infants and toddlers (Ames, 1990). To provide a context in which to judge these numbers, consider that the maximum staff-to-child ratios recommended by the NAEYC (2004) are 1:4 for children under 12 months, 1:5 for children aged 12 to 24 months, 1:6 for children 24 to 30 months, and 1:7 for children aged 30 to 36 months. Since the early 1990s, with changes in domestic policies and financial and volunteer support from foreign organizations, staffing ratios have improved in many Romanian orphanages. However, appropriate staffing ratios do not necessarily guarantee good care. Groark et al. (2005) report that many Russian institutions 'provide adequate care by American standards with respect to ... adult contact hours, and staff:child ratios,' yet characterize the overall quality of treatment of the children there as 'substandard.' Similarly, Human Rights Watch

(1996) reported very desirable caregiver to child ratios (1:1–1:5) in Chinese institutions, where child abuse and death rates were alarmingly high.

Additional staffing factors that affect the quality of care received by institutionalized children include staff work hours, staff turnover, staff training, and institutional culture regarding caregiver behaviour. In Russia, for example, most staff work part-time and do long shifts of up to 24 hours. This means that the same caregivers are rarely available on contiguous days. Further, children are typically moved from one set of caregivers to another at approximately 9, 12, and 24 months or age. These conditions, combined with an average staff turnover rate of 30 per cent per year, can result in infants being exposed to between 60 and 100 different caregivers in their first two years.

Levels of staff training in Russian institutions, while inadequate by Canadian standards, are typically higher than those found in Chinese and Romanian orphanages. Russian caregivers usually have eight to ten years of general education, and some have a further two to four years of specialized training (equivalent to high school graduation). However, since training in infant and toddler care is rare, the direct-care staff in the Baby Homes essentially have no pre-service training specific to their occupation. A similar situation exists in Romania, where many caregivers have a basic general education but very few have specialized training in childcare, education, or development. Moreover, in Romania childcare staff also often include young women who themselves grew up in institutions. In addition to being untrained, by virtue of their institutional rearing these individuals were denied good caregiving models in their own formative years, leaving them wholly unprepared to take care of others.

Partly as a consequence of staffing patterns and physical environments, care in institutions tends to be highly regimented and not individualized. Daily activities are carried out in age (and often ability) groups. Care routines are scheduled and children eat, sleep, bathe, and toilet together according to the caregiving routine rather than on the basis of their individual needs. The following narrative is an amalgamation of descriptions of caregiving in orphanages. It is not a report of a particular institution, but rather combines various accounts (St. Petersburg–USA Orphanage Team, 2005; Tharp-Taylor, 2003; Ames, 1990, Sloutsky, 1997; Audet, personal communication, 2005) to give the reader a better sense of the culture of institutional care.

Caregivers tend to be socially and emotionally detached and limit their interactions with the children to routine caregiving chores, which take place in a rapid, business-like fashion. Little or no emotion, warmth, or affection is expressed. Caregiving is entirely adult-directed. Children are told what to do and when to do it. The views of children are not solicited. Children's discomfort in certain caregiving interactions, for example, while being fed, bathed, and/or dressed, is ignored. Conformity among the children is enforced. Child–child interactions are not monitored, hence aggressive behaviour is rarely redirected and positive peer interactions are not supported. Children with special needs often receive the least of what little adult attention is available. Caregivers report a reluctance to form relationships with the children.

The kind of care described above represents a huge departure from that generally recognized as necessary for positive (i.e., normative) developmental outcomes. Current theory and research indicate that healthy development requires a caregiving environment in which the child has early and on-going interactions with one or more constant, responsive, and nurturing adults (see Cassidy & Shaver, 1999 for reviews of this work). Caregivers should express sensitivity by reading the child's signals, providing timely and appropriate responses, and being physically and emotionally available during the whole childhood period. In these terms, the quality of care typical in institutional settings constitutes social and emotional deprivation (see Tharp-Taylor, 2003).

The importance of the institutional caregiving environment for children's development has been most clearly demonstrated in an intervention study conducted in Russian orphanages (Groark et al., 2005; St. Petersburg–USA Orphanage Research Team, 2005). For some time now there has been a growing body of empirical work addressing the impact of institutional rearing on children's development (e.g., Ames, 1997; Dennis, 1973; Goldfarb, 1943, 1945; Hodges & Tizard, 1989; Kaler & Freeman, 1994; Le Mare & Audet, 2006; Marcovitch et al., 1997; Provence & Lipton, 1962; Rutter & Team, 1998; see MacLean, 2003 for a review). An unavoidable problem with much of this work, because the orphanage environment is typically globally deficient, is that it does not elucidate what particular types of deprivation are responsible for the various developmental difficulties observed in the children. In contrast, the work conducted by the St. Petersburg–USA Orphanage Research Team has taken place in institutions where the physical environment, nutrition, and medical care are all good, but where the care-giving conforms to the institutional care culture as described above. Baseline data from the children in these settings indicated behaviours typical of institutionalized children where the deprivation is more global (see Ames, 1997), including a lack of social responsivity in babies and toddlers, stereotypy and self-stimulation behaviours, a lack of interest in toys, and, among older children, open aggression, avoidant behaviours, and indiscriminate friendliness. In short, this research demonstrates that the good physical environment in which these children were being raised was not enough to prevent atypical development.

Further evidence for the importance of the quality of the caregiving environment for children's development comes from data on the impact of interventions introduced by the St. Petersburg–USA Orphanage Research Team. Two interventions were implemented in the orphanage setting, which included training caregivers to provide socially responsive interactions with the children and making structural changes that reduced the number of different caregivers children experienced and increased the number of consecutive days that children had contact with two 'primary' caregivers. These interventions were designed to support each other in fostering responsive, warm, and caring relationships between children and caregivers, and their impact proved to be positive. Post-intervention, in both children and caregivers there was increased two-way conversations, animated and enthusiastic emotional responses, and positive social and language interactions. Taken together, the baseline and post-intervention data from this study clearly point to (a) the importance of the quality of the caregiving environment in supporting children's opportunities for normative development and (b) the inadequacy of the typical institutional setting in providing such opportunities.

The Right to Education

Article 28 of the CRC explicitly recognizes the right of children to education and several other articles are relevant to this right (see chapter 4, this volume). Specifically, article 28 stipulates equal opportunity for all children to take advantage of compulsory primary education, available secondary education, and educational and vocational information and guidance. Several features common to many orphanage settings run counter to these aims.

It is now widely accepted that in order for children to receive the full advantage of primary schooling, they need to begin that schooling with a number of prerequisite skills, which together constitute the construct of school readiness (Doherty, 1997). School readiness refers to the child's ability to meet the task demands of schooling, including such skills as being able to attend to and understand the teacher, get along with peers, and handle materials. Readiness, then, entails physical, social, emotional, and language competencies as well as those in the cognitive domain.

As described in the previous sections of this chapter, the early rearing environments typically found in orphanages are such that school readiness skills are unlikely to fully develop. For example, as noted, when early childhood educational materials are present in institutions, they are not always available for children to use. Even when such materials are available, because of the nature of caregiving in institutions, children typically do not receive the appropriate adult support to be able to benefit from using them. Consequently, once orphanage-reared children reach school age, they are typically less able to benefit from the schooling available than are children with more enriched early experiences. These contentions are supported by the work of Sloutsky (1997), who compared the cognitive and social-emotional development of institution- and home-reared Russian children in kindergarten. Sloutsky found that the institution-reared children displayed significantly lower levels of development in all areas assessed than did the home-reared comparison group. Moreover, the finding that, within the institutionalized group, performance was significantly related to length of institutional stay suggested that it was institutionalization, rather than any pre-existing characteristics of the samples, that largely accounted for the group differences.

Another concern is the fact that in many institutions the educational opportunities available to children are dependent on diagnoses they have received or their performance on screening tests. For example, in Chinese institutions, there has been a history of systematic assessments of children's cognitive ability whereby senior medical staff have made inaccurate diagnoses of mental retardation and other disorders. This evaluative process has contributed to perpetuating a widespread belief that abandoned children are mentally handicapped and therefore not capable of receiving an education (Human Rights Watch, 1996).

A similar evaluation system exists in Russia. There, children abandoned at birth are observed by Ministry of Health staff and given various developmental diagnoses partially based on knowledge of the child's family history. The social characteristics of the birth families of many orphans are seen as risk factors and can themselves result in a diagnosis of the child as 'delayed.' This diagnosis, along with the risk factors that contributed to it, is noted on the infant's record and can further negatively affect on the quality of care the infant receives. At the age of four, after several years of living in an institution, these orphans are given a one-time evaluation by the Ministry of Education to decide what educational opportunities they should receive. UNICEF (1997) reports that this results in approximately 15 per cent of the children living full-time in institutions being placed in facilities for the 'uneducable' where they receive no formal education. The 85 per cent that are deemed 'educable' generally attend regular Russian public schools for nine years, after which they can either go on to earn a secondary school diploma or leave school at the age of fifteen.

Other orphans in Russia receive education inside their institutions, and upon completion are eligible for further training in a trade such as carpentry, electricity, masonry, and stuffed-animal making (Human Rights Watch, 1998). Such in-house education also exists in Romania, where it appears that many children are pushed to learn their trade and search for work before completion of their schooling (Audet, personal communication, 2005).

In summary, in practice institutional rearing is antithetical to the goals of article 28. In orphanages many children are denied even a basic education because of developmental diagnoses that may or may not be accurate. By virtue of their institutionalization those children deemed educable begin school disadvantaged and tend to be streamed into various trades. Educational and vocational information and guidance appear to be very limited and higher education is out of reach for most of these children owing to the social and educational policies pertaining to them.

The Right to Not Be Abused

Article 19 of the CRC describes how appropriate social and education measures should be taken to protect children from all forms of abuse and neglect. Of course, there is considerable overlap between this provision and those for development, health care, and education as described in articles 27, 24, and 28, inasmuch as failure to adhere to these articles could qualify as abusive or neglectful conditions. In previous sections of this chapter we have already made reference to those forms of neglect that are common to orphanage settings. However, the potential for direct physical and sexual abuse within institutions is also of concern.

During the 1990s Human Rights Watch (1996, 1998) documented reportedly common examples of cruel, inhuman, and degrading treatment of children in Chinese and Russian orphanages that included verbal, physical, and sexual abuse. Quite possibly as a result of those reports, efforts have been made to curb the abusive treatment of institutionalized children. According to the St. Petersburg–USA Orphanage Research Team (2005), within Russian orphanages today abuse is considered a very serious matter and is not prevalent. Specifically, in their observations of Russian orphanages, these researchers found minimal evidence of harsh treatment and disciplining of children. However, these authors do caution that their findings may only pertain to the kind of institution they visited (for children without physical or mental deficiencies) and to caregiving practices when an observer was present.

Similarly, Sloutsky (1997) reports that within the Russian orphanages that took part in his study, regulations were in place specifically in order to reduce the likelihood of abuse occurring. To minimize sexual abuse, only female workers were employed by the institutions and interactions between staff and children were carefully controlled so that personal relationships did not develop. Behaviours such as communicating with children outside of caregiving routines, taking children home, or giving gifts were not allowed, partly to help prevent the occurrence of abusive practices. Unfortunately, these efforts, while potentially protecting children from abuse, are in some ways self-defeating as they significantly contribute to the social and emotional neglect of children. Even the practice of exposing children only to females limits their experience in a way that could be considered neglectful. As Sloutsky explains, 'Many children who have spent their entire childhood in an institution have never seen a male. Thus, the children expressed amazement that the researcher and one of the assistants were males ... The children did not understand what a beard or moustache was, what they were made from, or their purpose' (p. 137).

Recent reports on the prevalence of abuse within Chinese institutions are very difficult to find, but there are indications that the abusive practices described by Human Rights Watch (1996) are not as widespread as they once were. In one of the few recent reports Campbell (Johns Hopkins University, 2002) explains that the Chinese orphanage in which she volunteered 'wasn't as horrible as I thought it would be.' Indeed, she describes a caring and hard-working staff who were limited in what they could do because of money and staff shortages. Despite the good intentions of the staff, practices that were at best neglectful, but could be considered abusive, still occurred. For example, Campbell reports that infants were left in their cribs twenty out of twenty-four hours a day, and many had bedsores as a result. As a result of their deprivation the babies were socially unresponsive.

Provisions for Children with Disabilities

Article 23 of the CRC recognizes that 'a mentally or physically disabled child should enjoy a full and decent life, in conditions which ensure dignity, promote self-reliance and facilitate the child's active participation in the community.' While few children have their developmental needs met in institutions, orphans with disabilities typically receive the poorest care.

Disabilities in Russia are often viewed with revulsion and, therefore, on maternity wards parents are encouraged to give up their disabled newborns, including those with Down's syndrome, cerebral palsy, and correctable conditions such as club foot and cleft palate (Human Rights Watch, 1998). For example, in 1994, forty-four children were born with Down's Syndrome in St Petersburg, and all but two were sent to institutions (St. Petersburg–USA Team, 2005). Once taken to baby houses, disabled children are confined to cribs in lying-down rooms where they are deprived of individual attention and sensory stimulation.

In addition to receiving even lower levels of adult attention than non-disabled orphans, as a result of their segregation (St. Petersburg–USA Team, 2005) children with disabilities are not able to benefit from interacting with more able peers. Further, while there may be equipment available for children with disabilities (e.g., wheelchairs), observers report that it is used rarely, and caregivers do not compensate by holding children or moving them to locations where they can feel included in activities (St. Petersburg–USA Team, 2005).

In Chinese institutions, children with disabilities are also segregated from their peers. Unlike in Russia, where rehabilitative equipment is available, disabled Chinese orphans are given no such assistance. In addition, when medical situations arise, children with disabilities are at the bottom of the priority list for treatment and are therefore more likely to die than their non-disabled peers (Johnson, 2004).

In summary, the available evidence clearly indicates that the rights conferred on children through the CRC for opportunities for development, education, protection from abuse, and assistance for the disabled are not adequately upheld in the typical institutional setting. Faced with the realities of so many children needing homes and the large 'market' for adoptable children in North America and western Europe, numerous countries, including China, Russia, and Romania, opened their doors to inter-country adopters.

Inter-country Adoption

Since 1990 inter-country adoption has flourished as potential parents from wealthy countries have sought to adopt social orphans from countries that have recently experienced economic and social upheaval, such as Russia, Romania, and China. From Romania, for example, there were only thirty inter-country adoptions in 1989, yet in the following year, after the overthrow of Ceausescu, more than 10,000 children left that country. Similarly, although no Russian child was adopted abroad before 1990, Russia has recently been one of the largest suppliers of orphans to foreign parents worldwide. There are an estimated 34,000 international adoptions world wide per year, primarily from Asia and central and Eastern Europe (Kapstein, 2003). In Canada alone, the number of internationally adopted children has increased from 232 in 1988 to 1874 in 2001 (Adoption Council of Canada, 2004), while in the United States the number has increased from 9050 in 1991 to 19,237 in 2001 (Evan B. Donaldson Adoption Institute, 2002).

Article 21 of the CRC, which deals specifically with inter-country adoption, has been seen as an important step towards international cooperation on such adoptions. In 1993 the Hague Convention on the Protection of Children and Cooperation in Respect of Intercountry Adoption (hereafter referred to as the Hague Convention) took on the challenge of acting as the legal backbone for inter-country adoption. Under the auspices of the Hague Conference on Private International Law, the Hague Convention reaffirms the principles set out in the CRC and then focuses more specifically on measures to ensure that inter-country adoptions are made in the best interests of the child. Both international treaties, the CRC and the Hague Convention, recognize inter-country adoption as an acceptable means of childcare only if the child cannot be adequately cared for in his or her country of origin. Proponents of inter-country adoption argue that this position relegates inter-country adoption to being the care option of last resort (see Bartholet, 1993) and fails to uphold the spirit of the CRC as explicitly stated in article 21,which is to 'ensure that the best interests of the child shall be the paramount consideration.'

There is little doubt that inter-country adoption offers an alternative that better satisfies the CRC as concerns the rights that institutional rearing fails to uphold. Owing to the costs inherent in inter-country adoption, most adopters of foreign orphans are relatively well educated and have financial resources that enable them to provide home environments in which children have ready access to amenities and services that support development (Ames, 1997). For similar reasons, international adoptees typically have access to good nutrition, health care, and medical services in their new countries. As concerns caregiving, inter-country adoption offers a family-rearing environment in which children can receive individual attention and care in a stable and loving arrangement. Adoption by a family in a Western country gives international orphans access to free public education that, by virtue of their more enriched home lives, they will likely be more ready and able to benefit from than if they had remained institutionalized. Finally, in Western countries such as Canada and the United States, discrimination against the disabled is unlawful and medical, educational, and social services are readily available to 'ensure dignity, promote self-reliance and facilitate the [disabled] child's active participation in the community' (article 23).

Despite the popularity of inter-country adoption, it is a controversial practice that, it has been argued, threatens several rights of children, including the rights to preserve one's identity, including nationality, name, and family relations, and to be protected from practices such as the sale of or traffic in children.

The Right to Preserve One's Identity

Article 8 of the CRC recognizes 'the right of the child to preserve his or her identity, including nationality, name and family relations.' Moreover, when a child cannot be cared for by his or her family, the convention dictates that in finding alternate care arrangements, 'due regard shall be paid to the desirability of continuity in a child's upbringing and to the child's ethnic, religious, cultural and linguistic background' (article 20). Critics of inter-country adoption argue that it is unfair to separate children from their racial, ethnic, cultural, and national groups of origin and that the adoption of foreign children presents the risk that these children will be deprived of the opportunity to know and have access to their birth families. It has been claimed that this risk presents an infringement of the basic rights of these children, particularly in comparison with more advantaged children in their country of origin and children in their adoptive country. Indeed, loss of nationality, ethnic identity, and links to one's birth family are argued to constitute forms of deprivation in themselves (Bartholet, 1993).

A potential solution to the loss of identity that can accompany inter-country adoption is for adoptive families to expose children to and maintain links with their culture of origin. Although many adoptive parents prioritize teaching children about their cultural backgrounds, this is not always the case (Westhues & Cohen, 1998). For example, some parents believe that their adopted children should be raised to assimilate into their new country's mainstream culture. In such cases, parents make little effort to educate their child about her or his country of origin.

Motivated by research findings that adoptive children placed trans-culturally (Andujo, 1988) and trans-racially (Simon & Altstein, 1987; McRoy et al., 1982, 1984, 1991; Bagley, 1991) have a weaker sense of ethnic identity than those placed in families of similar ethnic or racial background, Westhues and Cohen (1998) sought to explore identity in international adoptees and how it related to their adoptive parents' efforts to make them aware of their backgrounds. These researchers found that the majority of their participants were comfortable with their racial and ethnic identities. However, based on the efforts of their parents to maintain links with the children's cultures of origin, the authors concluded that 'the right conferred on children through the UN Convention on the Rights of the Child ... to retain a linkage to their roots has not been adequately maintained for most of the young people in our study' (p. 51).

Supporters of inter-country adoption (e.g., Bartholet, 1993) argue that concern over the loss of roots for internationally adopted children ignores the realities of life in their countries of origin, where they would most likely be institutionalized, and places undue emphasis on the importance of the right to identity at the expense of the right to development. Research studies on the developmental outcomes of internationally adopted children show that they typically demonstrate huge developmental gains in the cognitive, physical, language, and social domains in the period shortly following the adoption (McMullan & Fischer, 1992; McMullan, 1993; Rutter & Team, 1998), but that a proportion of children continue to demonstrate persistent deficits in relation to developmental norms throughout childhood (Fernyhough, Audet, & Le Mare, 2002; Le Mare & Audet, 2002; Le Mare, Vaughan, Warford, & Fernyhough, 2001; Rutter, O'Connor, & ERA Study Team, 2004). In direct comparisons with domestically born, non-adopted children, post-institutionalized international adoptees as a group display significantly more problems in all developmental domains (Ames, 1997; Le Mare, Audet, & Kurytnik, 2005; Le Mare & Audet, 2002; Le Mare & Kurytnik, 2004; Le Mare, Vaughan, Warford & Fernyhough, 2001; Le Mare, Warford, & Fernyhough, 2001). It is important to point out however, that the problems of inter-country adoptees are most likely related to their pre-adoptive experiences and are not a result of inter-country adoption per se. This conclusion is supported by our work on children adopted from Romania by Canadian families. The Romanian Adoption Project consists of three groups of children: Romanian Orphans (RO), who were adopted to Canada from Romania after being abandoned at birth and spending a minimum of eight months in an institution; Early Adopted (EA) orphans, who also were adopted by Canadian families from Romania after being abandoned, but before they gained much institutional experience (that is, before four months of age); and Canadian Born (CB) children who are being raised in their birth families in Canada. Results of this longitudinal study have consistently shown that while the RO group has more problems in all developmental domains assessed than the CB group, the EA group is developing as well as the CB group. Given that the EA group shares inter-country adoption (as well as pre- and peri-natal history) with the RO group but does not share institutionalization with that group, the most reasonable explanation for the outcomes in the RO group is institutional experience (and not the experience of inter-country adoption). What is missing from the literature on the development of abandoned children is a well-designed comparison between abandoned children who remained in their countries of origin and those who were internationally adopted. Anecdotally, however, observations of young adults in

Romania who remained in institutions for their entire growing years indicate that those who were adopted from institutions by Canadian families, despite the challenges they face, are faring much better (Audet, personal communication, 2005).

The right to identity includes not only links with one's ethnicity, culture, and race but also knowledge of one's birth family. In the case of inter-country adoption, this issue is complicated by legal, political, and cultural differences among nations (Heimerle, 2003). Various nation states have divergent laws pertaining to anonymity and disclosure in adoption, and domestic politics and culture can determine whether the identity of birth parents is collected and preserved or never recorded at all. For example, in China, where legal relinquishment of a child is not possible, parents abandon children, often in places where there is a high likelihood they will be found, with no identifying information. Although this situation prevents the internationally adopted child from determining her birth parents' identity, it is important to point out that she would be no more likely to uncover that identity if she had stayed in China.

Another criticism of inter-country adoption related to the preservation of identity is the claim that growing up in a foreign land, particularly if it entails being in a racial minority, poses the risk of discrimination. Westhues and Cohen (1998) addressed this issue and found that the vast majority of international adoptees in their study reported having experienced racial or ethnic discrimination. Interestingly, they found no relationship between the experience of discrimination and comfort with one's own racial and ethnic background. However, these authors cautioned that this lack of association may have been due to the fact that the experience of discrimination was so pervasive within their sample. Again, however, in evaluating inter-country adoption in relation to other forms of care, one needs to consider the discrimination that abandoned children experience in their countries of origin. Numerous authors (e.g., Bartholet, 1993; Hollingsworth, 2003, Human Rights Watch, 1998) have made the point that abandoned children who remain in their home countries are at risk of suffering acute social discrimination and denial of rights, particularly in comparison with children who live with their families. At the outset, abandonment can attach a stigma to children that is associated with the assumption that such children must have deficiencies that caused their parents to forsake them. Hence, very often abandoned and orphaned children face a lifetime of discrimination by virtue of that status, which itself is in violation of the CRC. For example, article 2 prohibits discriminatory treatment and denial of rights on the basis of 'race, colour, sex, language, religion, political or other opinion, national, ethnic, or social origin, property, disability, birth or other status.' Human Rights Watch (1998) has argued that discrimination against a child because of abandonment 'could fall into the category of discrimination on the basis of social origin or even birth' (p. 34).

The Right to Be Protected from Neglect and Abuse

As seen in an earlier section of this chapter, protection from neglect and abuse is a right of children conferred by the CRC that is often violated in institutional settings. Some critics of inter-country adoption have used evidence of abuse in adoptive families as an argument for restricting the practice. Indeed, media headlines regarding several cases of deaths of international adoptees at the hands of their parents have created debate about whether to place a moratorium on international adoptions. In one such case in 2005, a mother in Chicago was convicted of involuntary manslaughter of her newly adopted son. Without discounting the horrifying nature of such cases, Pertman (2005) cautions that in reporting these cases the media are 'too often ill-informed and lack critical perspective, while the consumers of those stories too often don't have the experience or information to put events into context for themselves.' This handful of sensational cases make headlines, leaving the public unaware that the vast majority of the 24,000-plus annual inter-country adoptions by North Americans are successful, with the resulting families being as fulfilled as those formed in any other way (Adoption Council of Canada, 2004; Pertman, 2005).

This view has been echoed by others. For example, in response to media reports of an adoptive mother in Tennessee being charged with first-degree murder, aggravated child abuse, aggravated child neglect, and reckless homicide in the death of her twenty-month-old daughter from China, adoption medicine specialist David Douglass (personal communication, November 2005) commented:

> At the same time may we please highlight the thousands of thriving U.S. adoptees who would have languished in orphanages overseas and graduated with horribly high rates of suicide, prostitution, and criminal behavior? I think it's intuitive that life-expectancy (not to mention quality

of life!) for orphans climbs dramatically upon adoption in spite of these horrific murders that get all the attention. While working to eliminate these terrible murders, let's not fall prey to the press that only publicizes the negative and thus allow the image of international adoption to be sullied.

Indeed, arguing for a moratorium on inter-country adoption on the basis of a minuscule percentage of adoptive parents who are abusive is similar to suggesting a moratorium on childbirth because some birth parents hurt their children.

The Right to Be Protected from Being Sold or Trafficked

Article 35 of the CRC determines that all appropriate measures be taken 'to prevent the abduction of, the sale of or traffic in children for any purpose or in any form.' Although inter-country adoption by no means necessitates that any of these practices will take place, concern has been raised that allowing international adoption increases the risk that they will (Carro, 1994; Bartholet, 1993). There are numerous documented instances of baby trafficking and other such abuses, many of which took place before the Hague Convention.

Carro (1994) describes baby-trafficking scandals that have occurred in a variety of countries and, in particular, the high profile example of Romania in 1990/1. Following the overthrow and execution of Ceausescu in December 1989 and the subsequent Western media coverage showing thousands of abandoned children, requests from Americans, Canadians, and western Europeans looking to adopt babies inundated Romania. As Carro recounts, prospective parents soon learned of the poor physical health of most orphanage children and impoverished Romanian parents, with the assistance of baby brokers, quickly discovered that their consent to adopt could be sold for the equivalent of several years' earnings. 'What followed was a disgrace: poor birth parents willing to sell their children to the highest bidder, desperate adoptive parents willing to pay almost any price, black marketers profiting by bringing the two together, and journalists present to witness and record the transactions' (p. 138).

This scandal broke when Romanian state-run television showed three Rom (gypsy) children being sold to undercover journalists. Romanian officials responded quickly by forming a National Adoption Commission, which in short order suspended inter-country

adoptions and undertook a census of all orphanages, creating an official list of children who were eligible for adoption. New adoption
laws followed that required all adoptions to be processed through the
commission, which would only accept applications from approved
adoption agencies. The adoption of children abandoned for less than
six months was no longer allowed and private adoptions were
outlawed. What occurred in Romania illustrates what can happen
when countries in social, economic, and political turmoil open up for
foreign adoption.

Closely related to the sale of children is the issue of adoption agencies and intermediaries charging exorbitant fees for facilitating inter-
country adoptions. Such practices also are in strict violation of the
CRC, which indicates that states should 'take all appropriate measures
to ensure that, in inter-country adoption, the placement does not result
in improper financial gain for those involved in it' (article 21 (d)).

Clearly, the purchase of children from Romania and other countries
where black markets have emerged represents a contravention of the
CRC, and the Hague Convention reflects the lessons learned from
those shameful practices. The Hague Convention represents an important effort to support the rights of international orphans in their adoptions. Countries need to be vigilant in their enforcement of international laws that prohibit child trafficking and that govern the process
by which a child is removed from one family to be given to another. It
is important to reiterate, however, that while inter-country adoption
may encourage some unscrupulous individuals or organizations to
attempt to profit from either the sale of children or the facilitation of
adoptions, these practices are not inherent to inter-country adoption.
Further, as noted earlier, when one considers any care option for international orphans, it must be balanced with the alternatives. As Bartholet (1993) has argued:

International adoption represents an extraordinarily positive option for
the homeless children of the world, compared to all other realistic
options. Most of these children will not be adopted otherwise. They will
continue to live in inadequate institutions or on the streets. Foster care is
available only to a limited degree and sometimes results in little more
than indentured servitude. The homeless children who survive to grow
up often will face virulent forms of discrimination in their own country,
based on their racial or ethnic status, or simply on the fact they are ille-
gitimate or orphaned. (97–8)

This quote acknowledges domestic foster care and adoption (albeit not very optimistically) as alternatives to institutional rearing and inter-country adoption. The development of such domestic programs has been recommended and supported by numerous organizations, including Human Rights Watch, World Vision, Save the Children, and UNICEF. These options are seen as preferable because, in theory, they do not entail the risk of rights abuses associated with orphanage rearing or inter-country adoption. Domestic foster care and adoption potentially carry with them all the benefits of inter-country adoption (a loving home with individual care) without the concerns over rights to identity and protection from being sold.

Foster Care and Domestic Adoption

Although domestic foster care and adoption for abandoned children are potentially appealing care alternatives to institutionalization and foreign adoption, they also are not without problems and are open to critique. In China, Russia, and Romania unique cultural, economic, and social conditions have impeded the development of effective domestic systems to provide adequate alternatives to institutionalization. Common to all three countries are economic challenges to developing non-institutional domestic care systems. In Russia and Romania, adoption and fostering have, historically, not been part of the culture, while in China the preference for boys is an impediment to baby girls being taken in.

In Romania, a foster care system is now in place. Although new legislation in 1997 increased the allowance to foster parents to 150,000 lei per child per month (approximately $20 U.S.), there is still a reluctance on the part of many potential foster parents to take on responsibility for a child in such a difficult economic climate. In 1997 Romania actually took steps to expand the foster care system by creating the role of 'professional foster carer.' Professional foster carers are paid at the level of a basic-grade social worker and their period of service as foster parents counts towards their pension entitlement.

These efforts to support a domestic foster care program, while well intended, have nonetheless come under fire. The primary reason Romanian birth parents abandon their children is family poverty. Although foster parents are eligible for the childcare allowance, birth parents and members of a child's extended family are not. Hence, the government is willing to pay non-family members to care for a child but is not willing to support impoverished families so that they can keep their children. Moreover, concerns have been raised that these financial incentives will result in people becoming foster parents solely for the money (Dickens, 1999). With this concern comes the associated fear of the type of rearing conditions these newly employed foster parents will provide.

Further undermining the foster care and adoption systems in Romania are the attitudes of the public, professionals, and politicians towards orphans. Part of the unique cultural and social conditions within Romania stem from the strong historical discrimination against members of the Rom ('Gypsy') community, which has generally been overrepresented where orphaned and abandoned children are concerned. This has resulted in a widespread view that orphans are of Gypsy origin and are hence distasteful.

Also to be overcome within Romania is the long-standing attitudes that 'the state wants the children, [and that] the state can look after them' (Dickens, 1999). Beliefs such as these will obviously have to be challenged before effective and widespread foster and adoption systems can operate in place of institutions.

The situation in Russia is similar in many respects to that of Romania. As noted earlier, within Russia there is the long-held prejudice that all abandoned children are in some way 'defective' (Human Rights Watch, 1998). One source of this discriminatory assumption is the tradition of infants born with congenital defects being abandoned in local maternity wards under advice from the medical staff. Physicians advise parents to give up children with disabilities because they do not believe that such children can be helped by either attentive parents or programs (which largely do not exist anyway). The prevalent view is that disabilities are permanent and unalterable (incidentally, a view that was common among North American pediatricians as recently as 35–40 years ago). Consequently, healthy babies who are given up for financial or domestic reasons are often unfairly branded as 'defective.' Moreover, within Russia there is no established culture of adopting 'other people's children,' and people provide foster care primarily for the money (a problem we have in North America as well; see chapter 6 of this volume), which, as in Romania, stops if they adopt the child (personal communication, Robert McCall, 30 November 2005). These factors combined indicate that the development of non-institutional domestic child welfare options will be slow and will not quickly meet the needs of the thousands of Russian children currently without homes.

Within China, the economic situation is similar to that of Russia and Romania. Compounding this is the prevalent view within that society to favour males over females. This view results in not only the abandonment of baby girls but also the disinterest in fostering female children. Within China an extra barrier to domestic adoption is the one-child policy, which in most cases prohibits parents from adopting children if they already have a child of their own (Johnson, 2004). Some couples in China see the adoption of a child as a desirable way to enlarge a small family. However, in many cases, birth-planning officials will refuse the adoption and even take the adopted child away if they discover the situation after the adoption has taken place (ibid.).

Summary and Conclusions

The United Nations Convention on the Rights of the Child confers basic human rights on children and, in addition, some special children's rights that include the right to a name; the right to know and be cared for by one's parents; the preservation of identity; the right to education; and freedom from abuse and exploitation. It also imposes the obligation to support the child's development to its maximum potential. Ideally, these rights would apply equally to all the children of the world. Unfortunately, this is not the case. One particular group of children at high risk for rights abuses are the abandoned children of China, Russia, and Romania. In this chapter we have considered several alternative arrangements for the care of these children and evaluated the extent to which each arrangement can and typically does protect the rights of these children.

The most common care arrangement, institutional rearing, is clearly the least favourable option in that it often entails denying children the most fundamental right to opportunities for development, as well as rights to education and protection from neglect and abuse. Clearly, substitutes to institutional rearing must be found.

If the most favourable care arrangement is that which most closely adheres to the CRC's principles, then greater effort must go into supporting countries in creating and maintaining domestic foster and adoption programs. At the same time, however, support for children in institutions and inter-country adoption programs must not be abandoned. As discussed, cultural and economic factors in Russia, Romania, and China are such that successful domestic adoption and fostering programs will likely take a long time to develop. In the meantime, the children who are currently in institutions must not be forgotten. The work of the St Petersburg–USA Orphanage Team has clearly shown how relatively inexpensive interventions can improve the lives and developmental opportunities of children in orphanages. Such interventions should be taking place while domestic home care programs are being developed.

Inter-country adoption, under the rules of the Hague Convention, should also continue. To reduce the risk of international adoptees 'losing their roots' there is a need for prospective adoptive parents to be educated so that they can ensure their child's right to identity. Although it has been claimed that supporting inter-country adoption programs runs counter to the development of domestic programs, this is not necessarily so. As Bartholet (1993) has pointed out, foreign adoption programs have tended to increase awareness in the United States, Canada, and other 'receiving' countries of the problems of children in 'sending' countries. Inter-country adoption is thus likely to create a climate that is sympathetic to wide-ranging forms of support for children abroad. We have certainly seen this in the families in our study that adopted from Romania, as well as families who have adopted from Russia (Cournoyer, 2005), many of whom now actively support institutions and agencies in those countries.

In closing, we acknowledge that institutional care, domestic adoption and foster care, and inter-country adoption are all solutions (of varying desirability) to much deeper problems of social injustice. The universal upholding of children's rights to be raised in safe, healthy, and loving environments by their birth families (see chapter 7 this volume) and in their cultures of origin are goals we should be working towards. At the same time, however, we must recognize that for many children this cannot be a reality. For these children, our guide in evaluating care alternatives should be article 21, which states that 'the best interests of the child shall be the paramount consideration.'

REFERENCES

Adoption Council of Canada (2004). *Adoption statistics by country*. Retrieved November 28, 2005, from http://www.adoption.ca
American Council for Voluntary International Action (2002). Retrieved November 28, 2005, from http://www.interaction.org/newswire/detail.php? id=226

Ames, E. (1990). Spitz revisited: A trip to Romanian 'orphanages.' *Developmental Psychology Newsletter, 9*(2), 8–11.

Ames, E. W. (1997). *The development of Romanian orphanage children adopted to Canada.* Ottawa: National Welfare Grants.

Ames, E.W., Fisher, L., & Savoie, L. (1994). *Behaviour problems of Romanian orphanage children adopted to Canada.* Paper presented at the Thirteenth Biennial Meeting of the International Society for the Study of Behavioural Development, Amsterdam, Netherlands, June.

Bagley, C. (1991). Adoption of native children in Canada: A policy analysis and a research report. In H. Altstein and R.J. Simon (Eds.), *Intercountry adoption: A multinational perspective* (pp. 55–79). New York: Praeger.

Bartholet, E. (1993). International adoption: Current status and future prospects. *The Future of Children, 1,* 89–103.

Bouchard, P (1998). Training and work: Myths about human capital. In S. Scott, B. Spencer, & A. Thomas (Eds.), *Learning for life: Canadian readings in adult education,* Toronto: Thompson Educational Publishing, Inc.

Bradley, R.H., Caldwell, B.M., Brisby, J., Magee, M., & Whiteside, L. (1992). The HOME inventory: A new scale for families of pre- and early adolescent children with disabilities. *Research in Developmental Disabilities, 13,* 313–333.

Bredekamp, S., Knuth, R.A., Kunesh, L.G., & Shulman, D.D. (1992). *What does research say about early childhood education?* Retrieved November 30, 2005, from http://www.ncrel.org/sdrs/areas/stw_esys/5erly_ch.htm

Cassidy, J., & Shaver, P.R. (2002). *Handbook of attachment: Theory, research and clinical application.* New York: Guilford Press.

Carro, J.L. (1994). Regulation of intercountry adoption: Can the abuses come to an end? *Hastings International and Comparative Law Review, 18,* 121–155.

Child Care Resource and Resource Unit (1995). *Early learning and child care quality by design: Physical environment.* Retrieved November 18, 2005, from http://www.childcarequality.ca/sys/perv.html

Cournoyer, L. (2005). *The experience of parents in forming a relationship with their older adopted children from Russia or other former Soviet Union countries.* Unpublished master's thesis, Simon Fraser University, Burnaby, British Columbia, Canada.

Dennis, W. (1973). *Children of the crèche.* New York: Appleton-Century-Crofts.

Dickens, J. (1999). Family support in Romania and the UK: Different circumstances, similar challenges. *Children and Society, 13,* 155–166.

Dodds, P.F. (1998). *International adoption: Opening Pandora's box.* Retrieved August 9, 2005, from http://www.adopting.org/dodds.html

Doherty, (1997). *Zero to Six: The Basis for School Readiness.* Retrieved on November 18, 2005, from http://www11.sdc.gc.ca/en/cs/sp/sdc/pkrf/publications/1997-002557/SP-241-02-01E.pdf

Evan B. Donaldson Adoption Institute (2002). *International adoption facts.* Retrieved December 15, 2005, from http://www.adoptioninstitute.org/ Fact Overview/international.html

Fernyhough, L., Audet, K., & Le Mare, L. (2002). *Attachment of Romanian orphans 10 years after being adopted to Canada.* Poster presented at the biennial meeting of the International Society of the Study of Behavioural Development, Ottawa, August 2–6.

Goldfarb, W. (1943). The effects of early institutional care on adolescent personality. *Journal of Experimental Education, 12,* 106–129.

Goldfarb, W. (1945). Effects of psychological deprivation in infancy and subsequent stimulation. *American Journal of Psychiatry, 102,* 18–33.

Groark, C.J., Muhamedrahimov, R.J., & Palmov, O.I. (2005). Improvements in early care in Russian orphanages and their relationship to observed behaviors. *Infant Mental Health Journal, 26*(2), 96–109.

Heimerle, N. (2003). International law and identity rights for adopted children. *Adoption Quarterly, 7*(2), 85–96.

Hodges, J., & Tizard, B. (1989). IQ and behavioural adjustment of ex-institutional adolescents. *Journal of Child Psychology and Psychiatry, 30,* 53–75.

Hollingsworth, L.D. (2003). International adoption among families in the United States: Considerations of social justice. *Social Work, 48*(2), 209–217.

Holt International (2005). *Holt programs in China.* Retrieved December 1, 2005, from http://www.holtintl.org/china/chinaproj.shtml

Homewood, G.S. (2002). *Wilson Fellowship leads student to Chinese orphanages.* Retrieved November 18, 2005, from http://www.jhu.edu/~gazette/2002/ 04feb02/04wilson.html

Hostetter, M.K., Iverson, S., Dole, K., & Johnson, D. (1989). Unsuspected infectious diseases and other medical diagnoses in the evaluation of internationally adopted children. *Pediatrics, 83*(4), 559–564.

Hostetter, M.K., Iverson S., Thomas, W., McKenzie, D., Dole, K., & Johnson, D. (1991). Medical evaluation of internationally adopted children. *The New England Journal of Medicine, 325*(7), 479–485.

Human Rights Watch (1996). *Death by default: A policy of fatal neglect in China's state orphanages.* New York: Human Rights Watch.

Human Rights Watch (1998). *Abandoned to the state: Cruelty and neglect in Russian orphanages.* New York: Human Rights Watch.

Ionita, G., Audet, K., & Kurytnik, K. (2005). *The influence of social relationships on the development of social cognition in institutionalized children.* Poster presented at the Annual Meeting of the Jean Piaget Society, Vancouver, BC, June 2–4.

Johns Hopkins University Office of News and Information (2002, Feb. 4). *Undergrad gets an inside view of Chinese orphanage.* Retrieved from http://www.jhu.edu/news/audio-video/campbell.html

Johnson, D.E., Miller, L.C., Iverson, S., Thomas, W., Franchino, B., Dole, K., Kiernan, M.T., Georgieff, M.K., & Hostetter, M.K. (1992). The health of children adopted from Romania. *Journal of the American Medical Association, 268*(24), 3446–3451.

Johnson, K. (2004). *Wanting a daughter, needing a son: Abandonment, adoption, and orphanage care in China.* St Paul, MN: Yeong & Yeong Book Co.

Kaler, S.R., & Freeman, B.J. (1994). Analysis of environmental deprivation: Cognitive and social development in Romanian orphans. *Journal of Child Psychology and Psychiatry, 35*(4), 769–781.

Kapstein, E.B. (2003). The baby trade. *Foreign Affairs, 82*(6), 115–122.

Kurytnik, K. (2003). A longitudinal study of the intellectual and academic development of children adopted from Romanian orphanages. Education, Simon Fraser University, Vancouver, BC. Master's thesis.

Le Mare, L., & Audet, K. (2002). *Attentional abilities of Romanian orphans 10 years after being adopted to Canada.* Poster presented at the biennial meeting of the International Society for the Study of Behavioural Development, Ottawa, On, August 2–6.

Le Mare, L., & Audet, K. (2006). A longitudinal study of the physical growth and health of post-institutionalized Romanian adoptees. *Paediatrics and Child Health, 11*(2), 85–91.

Le Mare, L., Audet, K., & Kurytnik, K. (2005). *Temperament in children adopted from Romanian orphanages.* In Le Mare (Chair), Psychosocial growth of post-institutionalized adoptees: Findings from UK, Canadian, and American longitudinal studies. Paper symposium conducted at the biennial meeting of the Society for Research in Child Development, Atlanta, GA.

Kurytnik, K., Audet, K., & Le Mare, L. (2005). *A longitudinal study of service use in families of children adopted from Romanian orphanages.* In Le Mare (Chair), Psychosocial growth of post-institutionalized adoptees: Findings from UK, Canadian, and American longitudinal studies. Paper symposium conducted at the biennial meeting of the Society for Research in Child Development (SRCD), Atlanta, GA.

Le Mare, L., & Kurytnik, K. (2004). *Parenting practices, child behaviour, and parenting stress in families with children adopted from Romanian institutions.* Poster presented at the biennial meeting of the International Society for the Study of Behavioural Development (ISSBD), Ghent, Belgium, July 11–15.

Le Mare, L., Vaughan, K., Warford, L., & Fernyhough, L. (2001). *Intellectual and academic performance of Romanian orphans 10 years after being adopted to Canada.* Poster presented at the biennial meeting of the Society for Research in Child Development (SRCD), Minneapolis, MN, April 17–20.

Le Mare, L., Warford, L., & Fernyhough, L. (2001). *Peer relationships of Romanian orphans 10 years after being adopted to Canada.* Poster presented at the

Biennial Meeting of the Society for Research in Child Development, Minneapolis, Minnesota, April 19–22.

MacLean, K. (2003). The impact of institutionalization on child development. *Development and Psychopathology, 15*(4), 853–884.

Marcovitch, S., Goldberg, S., Gold, A., Washington, J., Wasson, C., Krekewich, K., & Handley-Derry, M. (1997). Determinants of behavioural problems in Romanian children adopted in Ontario. *International Journal of Behavioural Development, 20*(1), 17–31.

Martin, M. (2004). *Transracial adoption part II: How important is racial/cultural identity?* Retrieved December 4, 2005, from http://preconception.com/resources/articles/transracialpt2.htm

McMullan, S.J. (1993). *Cognitive development of children adopted from Romanian orphanages.* Unpublished master's thesis, Simon Fraser University, Vancouver, BC.

McMullan, S.J., & Fisher, L. (1992). Developmental progress of Romanian orphanage children in Canada. *Canadian Psychology, 33*(2), 504.

McRoy, R. (1991). Significance of ethnic and racial identity in intercountry adoption within the United States. *Adoption and Fostering, 15*, 53–61.

McRoy, R., Zurcher, L.A., Lauderdale, M.L., & Anderson, R.A. (1982). Self-esteem and racial identity in transracial and inracial adoptees. *Social Work, 27*, 522–526.

McRoy, R., Zurcher, L.A., Lauderdale, M.L., & Anderson, R.A. (1984). The identity of transracial adoptees. *Social Casework, 65*, 34–39.

National Association for the Education of Young Children, NAEYC (1991). *Physical Environment.* Retrieved November 22, 2005, from http://www.ncrel.org/sdrs/areas/issues/students/earlycld/ea1lk4-5.htm.

NAEYC (2004). *Staff/Child Ratios.* Retrieved November 28, 2005, from http://www.earlychildhood.org/stanards/ratios.cfm

Pertman, A. (2005, December 1). Improve adoption press coverage. *Christian Science Monitor.*

Provence, S., & Lipton, R.C. (1962). *Infants in institutions.* New York: International Universities Press.

Rojewski, J.W., & Rojewski, J.L. (2001). *Intercountry adoption from China: Examining cultural heritage and other postadoption issues.* Portsmouth, NH: Greenwood.

Rutter, M., O'Connor, T.G., & the English and Romanian Adoptees (ERA) Study Team (2004). Are there biological programming effects for psychological development? Findings from a study of Romanian adoptees. *Developmental Psychology, 40*(1), 81–94.

Rutter, M., & Team, E.S. (1998). Developmental catch-up and deficit following adoption after severe global early deprivation. *Journal of Child Psychology and Psychiatry, 39*, 465–476.

The St Petersburg–USA Orphanage Research Team (2005). Characteristics of children, caregivers, and orphanages for young children in St. Petersburg, Russian Federation. *Journal of Applied Developmental Psychology, 26*(5), 477–506.

Shoemaker, C.H. (2004). *Culture combo: Adopting a baby of different nationality.* Retrieved December 4, 2005, from http://iparentingadoption.com/resources/articles/differentculture.htm

Simon, Rita J., & Altstein, Howard (1987). *Transracial adoptees and their families: A study of identity and commitment.* New York: Praeger Publishers.

Sloutsky, V.M. (1997). Institutional care and developmental outcomes of 6- and 7-year-old children: A contextualist perspective. *International Journal of Behavior Development, 20*(1), 131–151.

Sparling, J., Dragomir, C., & Ramey, S.L. (2005). An educational intervention improves developmental progress of young children in a Romanian orphanage. *Infant Mental Health Journal, 26*(2), 127–142.

Tharp-Taylor, S. (2003). *The effects of social deprivation on children reared in foreign orphanages.* East Lansing, MI: National Center for Research on Teacher Learning. (ERIC Document Reproduction Service No. ED 475594.)

UNICEF (1997). *Children at risk in Central and Eastern Europe: Perils and promises.* Regional Monitoring Report No. 4. Florence: International Child Development Centre.

UNICEF (2005). Situation of child abandonment in Romania. Retrieved November 18, 2005, from http://www.unicef.org/romania/cauzele _abandon_jan05.exec_summary.pdf

Vorria, P.,Rutter, M., Pickles, A.,Wolkind, S., & Hobsbaum, A. (1998). A comparative study of Greek children in long-term residential group care and in two-parent families: I. Social, emotional, and behavioural differences. *Journal of Child Psychology and Psychiatry, 39*(2), 225–236.

Westhues, A., & Cohen, J.S. (1998). Ethnic and racial identity of internationally adopted adolescents and young adults: Some issues in relation to children's rights. *Adoption Quarterly, 1*(4), 33–55.

3 Becoming-Child: Ontology, Immanence, and the Production of Child and Youth Rights

HANS SKOTT-MYHRE AND DONATO TARULLI

> The child [does] not become; it is becoming itself that is a child.
> Gilles Deleuze and Félix Guattari, *A Thousand Plateaus*

Much of the current discourse of human rights unfolds within the landscape of epistemology. This is a discourse, more specifically, that addresses issues in the interpretation and implementation of human rights, as these rights are represented and codified in official, juridical forms, such as the United Nations Convention on the Rights of the Child (CRC). Several of the chapters in this volume pursue this epistemological tack (e.g., see Zinga and Young for a discussion of the various definitional issues that complicate the implementation of rights-based educational curricula). Discourses oriented towards such epistemological concerns are critical for furthering our understanding of the conditions under which codified rights prescriptions and ideals are instantiated in specific public policies that affect the lives of children and youth.

While such efforts to interpret, implement, and further our knowledge of child and youth rights proceed apace, however, discussions bearing on the ontological status of child and youth rights – indeed, on the ontological status of rights more generally – occupy a more marginal status in the human rights corpus. Evans (2005) notes that an implication of this muting of philosophical discourses is a disabling of 'our abilities to imagine new futures' (p. 1053). In response to this implicit call for greater philosophical reflection, and in the hopes of articulating a conception of child and youth rights that expresses 'another possible community and ... the means for another consciousness and another sensibility' (Deleuze & Guattari, 1986, p. 17), we offer an ontological conception of rights that points up the lived-experiential dimensions of people's efforts to live and act in accordance with their immanent potential.[1]

Setting the Stage

To pose the question of human rights as a question of ontology is to ask 'What are human rights?' or, to use a spatial metaphor, 'Where are human rights?' That is to say, since ontology is the study of the conditions of existence, we need to determine the conditions under which rights are produced or come into being. It would be our contention here that rights do not come into existence as a legal or juridical form; rather, they come into being in the moment of human action.

The question might well be asked, Why raise this issue of the ontological status of child rights in a work dedicated to the exploration and extension of a particularly powerful juridical production – namely, the CRC? Is our purpose to undermine the convention? Is it to question the legitimacy of epistemological readings of children's rights? Or is it perhaps to unsettle the official codification and extension of a common knowledge of what constitutes such rights? While these may indeed be some of the possible effects of an ontological exploration of children's rights as a production of international law, they are not our primary interest here. Instead, our intention is to interrogate the assumption that rights for children can be understood through the continued explication of their instantiation as a juridical form.

What we propose here is a foregrounding of rights as immanent potential; or put in another term, an examination premised on the assumption that rights both precede the law and are not produced by the law, but instead are self-produced by the very subjects to whom such rights are attributed. Such an assumption holds the possibility that rights exceed the capacity of law to contain or regulate them. We will argue, accordingly, that rights qua rights are produced within the forms of daily life of what Hardt and Negri (2005; Negri, 1991) and others (Virno, 2004), following Spinoza, have termed the 'multitude.' On this view, rights as daily life are composed out of the activities of

---

1 See also Hardt and Negri (2005) for an extensive treatment of the production of new forms of community and political subjectivity built out of the concept of the minority and the multitude.

lived experience of multiple bodies creating the world through their activities and actions.

In this sense, whenever life is lived as creative process, rights are produced by the acts of the living. In other words, the power and force associated with rights does not stem from their association with governments, their juridical codification, nor the ability to enforce such codes through military or police action. Indeed, we will argue that such contemporary political forms of force are entirely reliant upon and gain their power from the acts of children themselves. The codes and regulations of the juridical form are always secondary to the courageous acts of children who resist with their bodies the unwarranted incursions of adults into their lives. In other words, it is the bodies of children and their activities that produce children's rights, both through their overt acts of resistance, but perhaps even more importantly through their creative capacities to produce their world.

Spinoza (2000) argued that power is composed of the ability to act. That is to say that power lies in the realm of living capacity. The living capacity of child bodies, then – and not their inscription in law – composes the realm of children's power. This affirmation of lived creative capacity determines the force of the child, which we will argue has particular political possibility when reconceived outside the constraints of epistemology and the juridical. Rather than seeking the traditional assertion of child rights as an extension of the Enlightenment project of individual rights, then, we are proposing child and youth rights as immanent force. Such force is essentially the product of constitutive action that can be found, not within the confines of law or convention, but in the existential excess or surplus that inheres in the lived-experiential relations of force found in the lives of children and youth throughout the world.[2]

Rights and Modernist Discourses of Childhood

To rethink child rights as an ontological project means to step aside from the traditional models of modernity that produce and defend the liberal democratic politics of the nation state and the juridical. Such

2 See Negri (1996) and Hardt and Negri (2000, 2005) for a detailed exposition of the role of constitutive creative action by non-dominant subjectivities in producing social change and revolution.

contemporary modernist discourses hold assumptions about the child subject that define its status from an adult perspective rooted in a version of developmental maturity produced by the social sciences. These modernist discourses, we argue, utilize the same discursive frameworks of teleology and evolution to propose understandings of developmental categories such as child and youth. On this modernist view, rights differentially adhere to children and youth precisely in virtue of transcendent taxonomic determinations, such as maturity or age (see the chapters by O'Neill and Raby for a discussion of some of the ambiguities surrounding the notion of the 'child' as inscribed in the CRC). This delineation of life force into divisions of those who, on the basis of a selected number of arbitrary measures – for example, chronological age or certain perceptions of changes in the living form, such as puberty – are deserving of certain rights, such as 'play' (CRC, article 31) or freedom from the most insidious forms of labour exploitation (article 32), is in turn inscribed in laws or juridical codes premised on jurisdictional, universal, or cosmic dispensation – codes that privilege the static being of rights over their processual becoming or eventness.

This bestowal of rights on the basis of perceived biological differ- ence through time is premised in a view of childhood written from the outside by subjects who no longer identify as 'child.' This separation of adulthood and childhood produces a bifurcation in the structure of rights that, again, allows for a differential allocation of rights rooted in Western scientific notions of age. Such notions construct biological age as normative and universal across all bodies of a similar chronological duration. That is to say that all subjects who have been on the earth for six years are assumed to have completed certain normative tasks that differentiate them, not as singular bodies, but as a group of bodies with common characteristics. These common bodies are then allocated certain rights presumed to be inherent to any being labelled child or youth. For such beings, in other words, rights become qualities that adhere or inhere in the child or youth simply by virtue of their holding a certain socio-scientific-political status. This is the child of law who is 'given' certain rights out of the beneficence of adults and assured these rights by the force of law and government.

This universal child of the CRC holds an ambivalent status within the juridical and scientific codes that constitute it. In the first instance, the child subject is produced as holding within itself the capacity for individual agency and the assertion of the kind of free will accorded the individuated self of high capital. On the other hand, the child within the CRC is also produced as a thoroughly disciplined bourgeois political subject complete with all the social constructions of disciplinary modernity, including 'competent authorities,' 'competent supervision,' 'responsibilities,' 'legal guardians,' 'persons legally responsible,' 'national law,' and the family (see articles 1–9). The child has a right to all these forms of discipline including the right to have an identity constructed through those hallmarks of the liberal modern project: 'nationality, name and family relations as recognized by law' (article 8).

Child as Becoming Minority

This binary that constitutes the child of agency and child of discipline is often reconciled within the liberal democratic project through an appeal to the Hobbesian logic of rights and responsibilities. That is to say, the child, like the adult, must balance the right to full creative expression against the responsibility to the social whole. Indeed, this may have some merit in a system free of regimes of domination in which the responsibility to the social whole is actually that. Within the current regime of global capitalism, however, the juridical codification of rights and responsibilities cannot easily be teased apart from the dominant discourses that produce the subject as global commodity. Indeed, the very negotiations and compromises that constitute the CRC in its accessions to various discourses of adult power point out the difficulty of resolving the contradictions of the binary child through the Hobbesian solution.

To write the child in relation to human rights in a way that extends the creative capacities of the subject so as to explode the binary restrictions of the modernist discourse requires, for us, the necessity of writing the child as an entirely different sort of subject. To do this we need to step aside from a fixed teleological child set in chronological time and evolutionary trajectory. Instead, we would suggest a child of indeterminate being, that is, a child whose ontological force or power of existence is premised not on a definition of what a child is, but on an ethological definition of its function and capacities. This is to move from the binary definition of the child as *either/or* to a definition of the child as *both/and*. When seen in this way the child is released from the chronological sense of time that defines it as *either* child *or* adult, becoming *both* child *and* adult simultaneously. This is, of course, counterintuitive within the common-sense discourses of our age. Children are not adults and adults are not children. However, our intention here is not to induct children into the highly restrictive definitions of adulthood within modernity, nor to return adults to some originary point of Rousseauian innocent nature. It is instead to release both subjects from the dominant discourses that constitute them as separate and unequal in every way and to release the latent force of the idiosyncratic and unique constitutive capacity of every body across time and age.

To do this we propose that we abandon the transcendent child, the universal child, the child defined from the outside, or the child formed out of the juridical manifestations of the law. Such a child is inadequate to our liberatory impetus. We are instead interested in 'child' as immanent becoming, as ontological praxis, and/or, as Deleuze and Guattari (1987) have asserted, as that minoritarian subject that we must all become.

Lines of Force: Lines of Childhood

To rethink 'child' outside the modernist conception of the subject we must diverge from that figure contained within the individuated body, wherein agency resides as a private space inaccessible to any other. Indeed, we must abandon the most fundamental and inalienable of modern rights: the private ownership and control of one's own thoughts, which modernist thinking would have us believe belong to us even under the extreme duress of imprisonment and torture. No doubt, under such conditions perhaps our thoughts do revert to our own private possession. They do not originate there, however. Instead, as Foucault shows us again and again, all of our thoughts are derived from the social training we receive and are bounded by the social linguistic field into which we are born. Even the very concept of our 'self' is a social construct we adopt from the language that surrounds us like water surrounds a fish. Put in other terms, as Derrida (1976) would have it, 'there is nothing outside the text' (p. 158). This means that we cannot seek child rights in some idealized universal outside the social text; rather, we must return rights to being a product of what Marx (1978) referred to as 'real individuals, their actuality and the material conditions under which they live, both those which they find already existing and those produced by their activity' (149).

To reconceive child in this way we must reinsert the subject back into the social as both a product of the social text and as one that produces that text anew. In this regard, Deleuze and Guattari (1987) invite us to understand the link between the individual and the social in terms of a series of lines or forces rather than subjects and interiorized consciousnesses. The advantage of such a conceptual framework is that it does not begin with a prior, idealized form of the subject. Instead, it allows us to explore the ways in which subjects are formed and unformed in the relation between the singular and the social. In proposing child as a set of relations that extends a line of creative possibility, child is no longer bound as a fixed biological entity constrained by chronological time and measured according to the norms of group development. Rather, child becomes a set of capacities for action that form and unform bodies along trajectories that make and unmake an infinitude of idiosyncratic subjects across the social field.

In this regard, Deleuze and Guattari propose three kinds of lines that are of interest to us here: namely, molar lines, molecular lines, and lines of flight. The first line, the molar, is a line that seeks to create territories and boundaries through the binary production of *either/or*. This is the line that creates the binaries of man/woman, public/private, adult/child, and so forth. This kind of binary logic is foundational for producing modern identities such as the self, which is always in a binary relation to the other.

The second, molecular line introduces instability through creating openings, cracks, and fissures in the bounded spaces of the molar. It does this through forming relations and connections that go beyond the *either/or* logic of the binary into the *both/and* logic of multiple possibilities. As such it maps the potential for movement, destabilization, and transformation. In another term, it opens the frontiers that extend the boundaries of the molar line.

The two lines together make and unmake the world as we can *know* it. The molar line creates the certainty of a given definition and the molecular line disrupts that certainty and opens the realm of alternate definition. Once the alternate definition becomes a possibility, the molar line immediately seeks to define its boundaries and limits. Once the molar sets the boundaries and limits, the molecular line disrupts them again, and so on.

Where the molecular line simply establishes a clearing for potentially moving beyond rigid segmentations, the third, nomadic line – the line of flight – takes us to places beyond the territorializing reach of molar unities and either/or dualisms. Lines of flight are, by definition, forces of deterritorialization, mutation, and release, and as such may be understood as ever-present opportunities for political resistance and creative change: 'It's along this line of flight that things come to pass, becomings evolve, revolutions take shape' (Deleuze, 1995, p. 45). In this regard, lines of flight constitute the nomadic, experimental movement of multiplicities. This Deleuzian notion of multiplicities orients us to an ontology not of what *is* or what should *be*, but to an ontology of *becoming* – such becoming understood, again, as an escape from rigid dualisms (e.g., one is *either* child *or* adult).

In relation to the discourse of rights, the Deleuzo-Guattarian notion of lines of flight orients us not to what rights are, in any definitive or prescriptive sense, nor to what rights should be, for each of these understandings involves a reduction of the many to the one, of difference to identity; rather, rights conceived as lines of flight express the ongoing, creative, inescapably local and situated struggle to become other than what one might otherwise, and statically, be. As becoming, activity, movement, or process, rights inhabit the in-between spaces from which extant meanings, constraints, understandings, and ways of being are subject to constant transformation. This world of becoming produces the question of rights outside the set of fixed constraints designed to restrain abuse, exploitation, and oppression that must be regulated by state and juridical force. Instead, child rights become the assertion of the creative capacities of bodies of all ages.

Becoming Child: Becoming Everyone

Modernist discourses of development routinely position children as becomings: children are defined with a view to what they *will* become, and not in terms of their being here and now. This teleological, future-oriented depiction of children is foundational for the discourse of children's rights associated with early liberal theory. In this connection, Arneil (2002) writes that liberal theory depicts children as

> citizens in waiting, human beings who do not yet possess the necessary attributes of citizenship, namely reason, autonomy, and the capacity for having authority over oneself, but will possess them in the future. As such, children are potential bearers of rights, which they may exercise only when they have reached the age of reason. They are not ends in themselves but rather creatures in the process of development. (p. 70)

Critics' response to this image of children has consisted largely of efforts to foreground children's worth as beings-in-the-present. This emphasis on children's present worth – on their status as complete beings rather than incomplete becomings – resonates clearly with the contemporary discourse of children's rights, and in particular, as Arneil (2002) has noted, with the recognition of children's right to autonomy: 'Only through the notion of autonomy is the child given full expression as a "being" or citizen rather than a "becoming" or subject' (p. 80).

While we are sympathetic with efforts that seek to challenge and problematize the unique identification of children with the realm of becoming, it strikes us that the challenge is itself rooted in a molar, either/or ontology: one that sees childhood and adulthood as distinct categories; one in which the development of the child is reduced to an organic becoming into time, that is, a form of becoming that unfolds within the logic of binary oppositions and identitarian practices that see child and adult as fixed categories. On this view, the power of becoming is muted in its promise that the child must become *something in particular* – an adult or an autonomous citizen. In this instance, then, the meaning of becoming is constrained by its inevitable movement towards being.

How might we reconceptualize the movement of becoming? Deleuze and Guattari (1987) offer a view in which the power of becoming does not hinge on the actualization of an identity – on the passage into being in which one becomes *something* – but rather inheres in the force of change and movement itself, in the raw capacity to affect and be affected. Here, becoming has no object other than difference itself. This is becoming as a molecular power, as a potential to unsettle the molarity of fixed or developing identities. The latter, as Mozère (2002) reminds us, are in any event

> an illusion or even a trap insofar they prevent us being on the watch, seizing new ways to gain more freedom in the sense of Spinoza, of becoming somebody new, a process which is always an enrichment – that is gaining power of action. To reach the multiplicities that live in each of us, to discover ... all the possibilities a body can experience, it is necessary to abandon roles and statuses and consider life as an adventure or a workshop. (pp. 3–4)

Becoming as a molecular power, then, implies that existence is the site of an ineradicable multiplicity and unfinshedness, or again, in Spinozist terms, of an irreducible power to affect and be affected. Following Deleuze and Guattari (1987), this adventure-filled, multiple, unfinalizable journey might reasonably be called autonomy – the force of continuous variation that defines becoming itself.

In what, then, does becoming-child in particular consist? It is easy to fall into a molar logic here and say that becoming-child involves imitating or acting like a child, or perhaps even recovering something of our past. But if as we have argued becoming is a molecular power, a non-teleological, deterritorializing force, then becoming-child must be defined more negatively, as it were, which is to say as a resistance to that which pretends to fix child and adult as molar entities. Becoming-child articulates the nomadic movement beyond such binarily inscribed identities; indeed it is the refusal of identity as such. As 'a passage between things, a decoding that proceeds via a mutative interaction with the stigmatized term of a binary power relation' (Bogue, 1997, p. 109), becoming-child suggests a path between adult and child, a path that circumvents the essentialisms of age codes and undoes the power of adult norms of conduct. It is a path, moreover, that we are all – children and adults alike – called upon to traverse. As Mozère (2002) notes, children too

> have to invent and create the ways and means to hear, perceive and make use of the molecular forces that enable them to have access to 'becoming-child.' All children are specially skilled to do this because they are not yet totally corseted in stereotyped thinking or acting. But being assigned to the closed worlds of family and school (or education more generally), children are prevented the opportunity to explore, eventually to get lost in other worlds, to live other experiences, although they usually manage to find breaches and hidden paths. (p. 6)

In short, becoming-child has to do with the creation of new ways of being. It is for both adult and child a movement of transformation in which the molar identities of 'adult' and 'child' are abandoned in the interest of the infinite variation associated with the creative capacity to act.

Beyond Child Binaries: Towards the Multitude

For children and youth as creative force, the question of rights exceeds the function of the juridical. Rights are not dependent upon the law or the ability to petition the state for status. Instead, rights are produced through the capacities of living bodies as they go about their daily lives and encounter various regimes of power at both the local micro and macro levels of power. As Foucault (2003) points out, power as a dominant force has never really functioned in the monarchical model of a top-down centralized force. It works through what he called relations of force or, more simply, the ways in which bodies struggle to persist at the daily level. It is the ways in which these struggles come together to form the grids of power that produces the capacities for different regimes of dominance or liberation. In other words, the power to dominate does not originate from the top but arises from the bottom; not, however, as a determinate form but as tendencies towards forms of organization that might be organized into certain forms of governance.[3]

One of the liberatory possibilities that might well be produced within the forms of daily life is that of the 'multitude' (Hardt & Negri, 2000, 2005; Negri, 1991; Virno, 2004). The multitude is the power of each unique and singular body, in its form as creative force, working together with other bodies towards a common political purpose that enhances each body's process of becoming. The multitude operates without a dominant or centralized overarching form of governance. It is governed, instead, through a form of radical democracy produced by bodies in their creative struggle to become. The multitude eschews the Hobbesian vision of social life as a war of all against all that must be moderated and controlled through subjugation to a state form. In contrast, it extends the political thought of Spinoza, whose central question of why people seek their own servitude led him to propose a model by which that servitude might be ended and the creative force of life turned to its own ends, rather than to the continued appropriation by systems of dominance and exploitation.

For our purposes, this means that no form of life can be subjected to the rule of law as sanctioned by the state without being subjected to its discipline. Such discipline invariably compromises the creative possibility of what we have called here the force of the becoming-child of all ages. Of course, there are those who would argue that such creative force, if unregulated, would lead to all sorts of anarchic acts of cruelty and brutality. They might argue further, *à la* Hobbes, that without the

---

3   See Hardt and Negri 2005 for a nuanced treatment of the issue of tendency versus economic determinism in Marxist thought that has influenced our thinking here.

law and the state we would be lost in a world of mindless violence and depravity. We would argue that the law and the state have not put an end to violence, and certainly not depravity. The law and the nation state has at its disposal, in our current age, more force than at any other time in history, and yet violence is endemic and depravity without limit.

Perhaps it is time to look elsewhere for forms of governance other than the dubious protections and disciplines of the law under global capitalism. The multitude as a potential new form of politics is premised in the form of the becoming-child. In other words, childhood and the right to become child is not produced by the disciplinary structures of the academy or science, nor the legislative functionaries of the state or juridical, but through the acts of those beings becoming-child across the globe. For example, it is the sad reality in the inner cities of the United States that no number of metal detectors, police officers, or well-intentioned anti-gang curricula can provide a safe community for inner-city children. However, children and youth in collaboration and cooperation with each other and adults interested in creative collaboration for mutual ends, rather than discipline and control, can establish the kinds of gang truces and non-violent crews (such the Klown and Krump Dance crews in Los Angeles) that can bring a significant reduction in violence. This must be done through the actions of the youth and children themselves and cannot be done by anyone else, including the adults who act in collaboration with them. The right to a neighbourhood free of youth violence must be established through the acts of young people because it is through their actions that violence occurs and it will be through their alternative actions that violence will cease.

Similarly, then, adults must also look to their own actions and quit trying to control and discipline the actions of young people. If the actions of adults are producing a world in which violence begins to make sense for young people, adults must change that world. However, that change cannot come about through an appeal to the modes of discipline and control available to them through the state. Instead, they must change their own actions and cease to participate in the system that perpetuates such violence. Only then can we say they are truly collaborators with young people in changing the world. This common action becomes the multitude.

Becoming-child as multitude, through the acts of children, youth, and adults working together, is not only operable at the local level. It operates as well through and within the world of the global networks of force that constitute our world today. The becoming-child is produced across the globe in an infinitude of virtual and actual connections between bodies that produce new forms of music, politics, economies, and all other productions of idiosyncratic creative forces inherent in the effects of globalization.[4] This is the moment at which becoming-child extends the capacity of any individualized being into a network of becoming through a multiplicity of beings as creative force. Each becoming-child, in opening – through bodily action, shared thought, or cooperative praxis – an expression of creative force, both amplifies the terms of its own idiosyncratic expressive singularity and, through the developing network of children being produced through the politics of struggle, opens the networked form of the child as creative force against the regimes of domination and exploitation.[5] Within this network every action of becoming-child, whether chronologically adult or child, produces the possibility of further action; every action of creative force gives rise, in other words, to a field of infinite possibility.[6]

Becoming-child, as creative force, is certainly an act of resistance against the forces of constraint and discipline in the globalized world of what Hardt and Negri (2000) have termed 'empire.' It is more than that, however. It is also an act of independent creative democracy.

Many might call what we are proposing here an unrealizable, idealistic pipedream. They might argue that it does not have a chance against what common sense tells us is 'real' human nature. While there are many responses we might give to this doubt, there is one that may well be pertinent here. To begin with, the fact that we have a common-sense notion of 'human nature' ought to put us on guard immediately. As both Deleuze and Guattari (1987) and Foucault (1972) point out, we are born into a system of language and, concomitantly, into a world of 'common sense' that is formulated directly to serve the interests of the dominant regimes of power. In other words, the most commonly accepted ideas are quite likely to be ideas that extend the advantage of

---

4 For a full and extremely useful treatment of the notion of network in the context of a new politics see Hardt and Negri (2005).
5 See Hardt and Negri (2005) for an extensive treatment of the importance of cooperation for both current regimes of domination and a liberative politics of the multitude.
6 See Hardt and Negri (2005) for a very interesting example of youth networked in just such a way in their discussion of the White Overalls.

those who benefit from the way things currently operate. For example, it is 'common sense' that we must appeal to the state and its international associations for our rights. It is similarly common sense that such an appeal must work its way through a system of legal negotiation between states and among judiciary bodies. While we might be frustrated by the length of time this takes, we accept it as the order of things and count as progress each minute advance in the direction of equity. We would argue that such a process is neither foreordained nor the best or only way to organize a society. Indeed, it might be argued that the 'common sense' of such a system is designed to the advantage of those who profit from the exploitation of children and their families. The fact that we are engaged in the long and arduous negotiations of pleading with the world's nation states to grant children the right to a decent and minimum standard of life extends the period of time the dominant system of power can remain the same and benefit from its current system of exploitation and abuse. In fact, at the end of the day, such an appeal may well founder on the will of the nation state in its collaboration with global capitalist interests to enforce the very international convention to which it has agreed. This is not a problem of human nature, but the nature of the state as a failed idealistic and unrealistic project.

The multitude, as an alternative, does not rely on the state form for the production of rights, but extends the rights of all beings with each act of becoming-child. This production of rights is premised in a vision of a new world founded fully in the expressive capacities of life itself. Becoming-child as the creative impetus to express the idiosyncratic and fully networked realm of desire allows Spinoza's concept of the multitude to take another turn in its uneven and broken trajectory towards actual democracy.

For Spinoza, the multitude (*multitudo*) captured the inescapable, ineradicable persistence of plurality in forms of collective life. Spinoza proposed a dystopic politics of struggle and collision in which the infinite capacities of God (which he referred to as substance) as creative expression produced the world through the striving of all to persist in unmediated idiosyncratic variation. The political force or entity whose sovereignty was premised in the deployment of radical idiosyncratic difference in the service of common political projects was precisely what he termed the multitude.

For the becoming-child as multitude, child rights are produced in struggle and through the force of difference in service to the common desire of living beings. Such desire is produced as child and youth rights by the children of Soweto in their insistence on the right to have an adequate education and their willingness to place their lives and bodies on the line to establish this right; by the street children of Brazil and India who organize themselves into political units such as the Movimento Nacional de Meninos e Meninas de Rua or the Children's Parliament in India to assert their right to housing, employment, and food; by the rock throwers of Palestine who put their bodies up against tanks and armoured personnel carriers to assert their right to a national state; by the graffiti artists of Toronto who insist on the right to the creative expression of their art; by the Krump and Clown dancers of Los Angeles who take the structure of the gang and reconfigure it as a non-violent act of creative expression and in doing so produce their own right to a safe environment; and by the millions of other children who create, with their bodies, the becoming-child. Child rights are set into creative motion and productive flight each time a child or an adult abandons the molar identities of developmental difference and accesses the becoming-child, and hence the common becoming, of human life.

REFERENCES

Arneil, B. (2002). Becoming versus being: A critical analysis of the child in liberal theory. In D. Archard & C.M. Macleod (Eds.), *The moral and political status of children* (pp. 70–94). Oxford, Eng.: Oxford University Press.

Bogue, R. (1997). Minor writing and minor literature. *symploke, 5*, 99–118.

Deleuze, G. (1995). *Negotiations* (M. Joughin, Trans.). New York: Columbia University Press. (Original work published 1990)

Deleuze, G., & Guattari, F. (1986). *Kafka: Toward a minor literature* (D. Polan, Trans.). Minneapolis: University of Minnesota Press. (Original work published 1975)

Deleuze, G., & Guattari, F. (1987). *A thousand plateaus: Capitalism and schizophrenia* (B. Masumi, Trans.). Minneapolis: University of Minnesota Press. (Original work published 1980)

Derrida, J. (1976). *Of grammatology* (G. Spivak, Trans.). Baltimore: Johns Hopkins University Press. (Original work published 1967)

Evans, T. (2005). International human rights law as power/knowledge. *Human Rights Quarterly, 27*, 1046–1068.

Foucault, M. (1972). *Archaeology of knowledge* (A.M. Sheridan Smith, Trans.). New York: Pantheon. (Original work published 1969)

Foucault, M. (2003). *Society must be defended: Lectures at the College de France, 1975–1976* (M. Bertani & A. Fontana, Eds., D. Macey, Trans.). New York: Picador.

Hardt, M., & Negri, A. (2000). *Empire*. Cambridge: Harvard University Press.

Hardt, M., & Negri, A. (2005). *Multitude: War and democracy in the age of empire*. New York: Penguin.

Marx, K. (1978). The German ideology: Part I. In R.C. Tucker (Ed.), *The Marx-Engels Reader* (pp. 146–200). New York: Norton. (Original work published 1932)

Mozère, L. (2002). *Deleuze and Guattari's concept of the becoming-child as an antidote to the discourse of failing children*. Paper presented at Reconceptualizing Early Childhood Education Conference, Tempe, AZ.

Negri, A. (1991). *The savage anomaly: The power of Spinoza's metaphysics and politics* (M. Hardt, Trans.). Minneapolis: University of Minnesota Press.

Negri, A. (1996). Twenty theses on Marx: Interpretation of the class situation today. In S. Makdisi, C. Casarino, & R. Karl (Eds.) & M. Hardt (Trans.), *Marxism beyond Marxism*. New York: Routledge.

Spinoza, B. (2000). *Ethics* (G.H.R. Parkinson, Ed. & Trans.). Oxford, Eng.: Oxford University Press.

United Nations (1989). *Convention on the Rights of the Child*.

Virno, P. (2004). *A grammar of the multitude* (I. Bertoletti, J. Cascaito, & A. Casson, Trans.). Los Angeles: Semiotext[e].

4 Children's Right to Education: Contextualizing Its Expression in Developed and Developing Countries

DAWN ZINGA AND SHERRI YOUNG

A current challenge facing countries around the globe is to find ways of interpreting and implementing children's rights in a way that is culturally relevant and can become embedded in countries' policies and practices. This is particularly important in the case of education, as associated policies are influenced by perceptions of children and their roles within society. The United Nations' Convention on the Rights of the Child (CRC) recognizes children's right to education and specifies that education should be free to all children on an equal-opportunity basis. However, the CRC does not have a mechanism under which violations of children's rights can be heard and adjudicated. While violations could be addressed to the Human Rights Tribunal, it is evident that the articles of the CRC will gain strength through their incorporation into the laws, policy, and jurisprudence of the countries that have ratified the treaty. Through this incorporation, violations of children's rights would be dealt with on a domestic level based on the individual country's legal interpretation of the international treaty. In fact, a careful reading of the CRC and the comments offered by its committee indicate that the treaty was drafted to facilitate its incorporation into the legal structures of the signatory countries while balancing the fine line between being proscriptive and being broad enough to be adopted in culturally appropriate ways.

Skott-Myhre and Tarulli question what children's rights are and where they are located, conceptualizing rights as being enacted in daily living rather than in conventions, laws, and policy. In this chapter we argue that the CRC identifies and defines the essence of children's educational rights, while the expression of those rights or lack thereof are enacted in the policies, politics, and common practices of individual countries. We focus on the important role of rights within children's daily lives as well as the impact of laws, policies, and practices. While the CRC has been criticized for using a Western lens, the majority of its articles are open to other interpretive approaches. The issue we are identifying is the tendency for researchers and experts from developed countries to oversimplify children's rights issues and to view these issues through a Western perspective. We are not arguing that the CRC's committee has not been clear about the principles of the CRC; rather, we argue that contextualizing the barriers provides a better opportunity to move towards an effective implementation of children's rights within the diverse countries that ratified the treaty.

We critically examine the factors that affect the expression of children's right to education and focus on how these factors act as obstacles to equity in children's access to primary education in developed and developing countries. In particular, we will examine child labour, gender issues, and the provision of education for indigenous children in both developed and developing countries. We also focus on how governmental policy and sociocultural context, including cultural traditions and social constructions of 'childhood,' act as important contextual factors. This examination will demonstrate that developed and developing countries share some of the same challenges to free and equitable access to education, but that these challenges often take different forms because of contextual factors. The articles of the Convention provide common ground for examining how contextual factors influence the interpretation and implementation of children's right to education. This chapter provides a critical analysis of the issues and context within which children's right to education finds expression or is muted, and demonstrates the importance of incorporating the CRC into the laws, policies, and common practices of developed and developing nations through a culturally appropriate interpretation of its articles.

Education and the CRC

What exactly does the CRC have to do with education? According to Verhellen (1993), the CRC has a lot to do with education. He divided the Convention into three areas, namely: rights to education, rights in education, and rights through education. According to this division, and following the precedent set by Verhellen, Covell, and Howe (2005) identify articles 28 and 23 as providing rights to education. Article 28 provides children with the right to free primary education as well as the right to accessible secondary education and higher education where capacity permits. In addition, it charges state parties to reduce drop-outs, put measures in place to support regular school attendance, and utilize school discipline that is consistent with the tenets of the Convention. Article 23 (2) provides for the right of the child with disabilities to have accessible education. In terms of rights in education, Covell and Howe have listed articles 2, 12, 13, 14, and 15 as being applicable to educational contexts. The articles address freedoms of expression, thought, and religion as well as the right to non-discrimination and participation. The third area, rights through education, involves articles 29 and 42, which Covell and Howe contend apply directly to 'education in which children are able to know their rights' and thus they stress the need for children's rights education.

Melchiorre (2004) looks at education and the Convention from a slightly different perspective. She links the Convention's goal for universal education with the elimination of child labour. Thus, she emphasizes articles 28 and 32 as applying directly to children's right to education. Melchiorre is also concerned with the inconsistency of minimum ages both within and across countries and the related effect on education, specifically their relation to compulsory ages for education. While Melchiorre has some valid points, different interpretations and practices are the solution to embodying the CRC in the various ratifying parties' laws and customs.

It is important to consider which articles pertain to education and in what contexts they might apply. Context and interpretation are important, as each state party must identify when and how an article applies. The contextual factors within each nation will influence how the CRC is brought to bear. Scholars who examine the CRC have varying opinions on which articles apply to education. We contend that there are thirteen articles (see table 4.1) that are relevant to education and multiple interpretations on how those articles might apply: the eleven articles previously identified (Covell & Howe, 2005; Melchiorre, 2004; Verhellen, 1993) and an additional two articles, article 9 (right of the child to reside with his/her parents) and article 30 (right to culture, religion, and language), which we have added into consideration. There are other articles that might occasionally be applied within educational contexts, but these thirteen are the most relevant to education.

Negotiating children's rights is not easy within educational contexts. Many chapters within this volume examine various areas of dif-

Table 4.1 Summary of CRC articles relevant to education

Article	Description
2	Right to non-discrimination
9	Right to reside with parents
12	Right to participation
13	Right to freedom of expression
14	Right to freedom of thought, conscience, and religion
15	Right to freedom of association and to peaceful assembly
16	Right to privacy and right to protection from interference or attacks
23 (2)	Right to accessible education for children with disabilities
28	Right to education (primary education compulsory and free)
29	Description of the scope and principles of education
30	Right to culture, religion, and language
32 (1)	Right to protection from economic exploitation
42	Directive to make the principles and provision of the convention widely known to adults and children

ficulty within Canadian schools, namely: the right to sex education (van Vliet and Raby); cyber bullying and bullying within school grounds (Shariff and Johnny; Lacharite and Marini); the provision of special education (Bennett, Dworet, and Zahos); the question of participation in schools (Raby). Each considers how the articles are being interpreted according to Western ideals and considers how the context affects the interpretation and provision of rights. As there are numerous instances within this volume where rights within education are considered within developed-nations contexts, this chapter will focus more on the CRC and education in developing countries and then consider how this differs from developed countries as well as examining common themes. Like the other chapters that focus on education, we will consider the tension between protection and participation.

Education within Developing and Developed Countries

Education within developing and developed countries is challenged by a number of issues that vary depending upon the political, economic, and cultural contexts of a given country. Among developing countries, issues such as access to education, demand for education (both economic and family-based), quality of education, gender equity, urban and rural differences, and several other factors create challenges to universal primary education. These factors include children with disabilities (Persson, 2001), the role of ethnicity, the language of instruction (Abu-Saad et al., 1998; Dei, 2004; Hall & Peters, 2003; Johnson, 2000; Khan, 2001; Rao, Cheng, & Narain, 2003), war and conflict (Foy, 2003; Sri-Jayantha, 2002: International Save the Children Alliance, 2005), and displaced children (Jansen, 2005; International Save the Children Alliance, 2005). A closer examination of the expression that these issues find within the varied contexts of different countries is essential to appreciate the complex nature of education in developing countries.

Mehrotra (1998) examined ten developing countries (Republic of Korea and Malaysia in East Asia and the Pacific Region; Kerala state in India and Sri Lanka in South Asia; Cuba, Costa Rica, and Barbados in Latin America; Botswana, Mauritius, and Zimbabwe in sub-Saharan Africa) that universalized primary education at an early stage in their development process. These countries were identified as being the top in their respective regions. Each has state-supported basic social services, state-run education (primary level or above), health-sector interventions, and investment in basic education. The countries also share patterns of high public expenditure on education, equity of spending across levels of education such that primary is not neglected, minimum standards of quality, and an economic demand for education as much of the available employment requires at least some education. Direct education costs, language of instruction, and gender equity are other factors that Mehrotra identifies as important to the promotion of primary education.

In contrast, a study that examined education in the least-developed countries, as defined by the United Nations, found that the majority of the school buildings are not conducive to teaching or learning owing to the poor conditions (Postlewaite, 1998). Only 10 per cent of the schools identify running water, toilets, and electricity as the schools' most needed improvement. Some of the areas encountering these difficulties include, but are not limited to, Congo (Shapiro & Tambashe, 2001), Ethiopia (Admassie, 2003), Kenya (Buchmann, 2000), Nepal (Carney, 2003), and South Africa (Mbelle & Katabaro, 2003). For these countries discrepancies between urban and rural areas are often most disparate.

Developing countries have not cornered the market on children's rights violations within educational contexts. Developed countries continue to struggle with the responsibilities associated with ratifying the Convention. Some of these struggles are very different from those in developing contexts, while others are strikingly similar. One of the major differences is that developed countries already have the infrastructure and educational systems in place, so many rights issues become focused not as much on the physical provision of and access to education as on the qualities of the educational context. For example, the issue of allergies among school children has become contentious and an issue of balancing rights. In Ontario, the passing of 'Sabrina's Law' has identified the right of children who have anaphylactic allergies to certain provisions and protection within education settings, including measures to protect the children from exposure to allergens.

There are still issues related directly to article 28 in developed countries, particularly for indigenous children. There is also an issue with undocumented children receiving access to education. The U.N. Committee on the Rights of the Child (2005) clearly states that unaccompanied children should be given 'full access to education during all stages of displacement' without discrimination. Displaced children in the United States are recognized as having a right to education but this is still debated in courts and there is a fear that 'free education' would draw more cases (Jansen, 2005). In Sweden, undocumented children do not have a right to education under the law, but must first apply for asylum (Jansen, 2005).

Most issues are associated with the spirit of the Convention and the interpretation of its articles. As with developing countries, there is some difficulty in matching the universal policy and general principles of the Convention to individual countries' specific policies and practices (Lee, 1999). Developed countries struggle with protecting children and promoting their interests (Leonard, 2004). Participation in decision-making (article 12) often clashes with assumptions about children's incompetence, assumptions that are predominant in developed countries (Lee, 1999). Levison (2000) talks about children's lack of power and argues that 'protecting' children from labour has excluded children from paid work but not unpaid work, and this is a direct result of their lack of power. These issues of power, participation, and educational environment are significant factors in developed countries' violations of the Convention.

Child Labour

Any form of child labour has the potential to negatively impact children's right to education, while economic exploitation places their physical, mental, spiritual, moral, or social development and health at risk. Thus, child labour often acts in opposition to articles 28, 29, and 32 (1). However, children also have the right to their culture (article 30), and in many cultures labour within the family, including domestic and agricultural assistance, is a cultural norm. There is also the question of street children, orphans, displaced children, and trafficked children, who are often at higher risk for economic exploitation and are frequently required to ensure their own survival through some form of labour.

Article 32 (1) protects children from economic exploitation and from any work that is hazardous or interferes with their education, and yet it is estimated that one million children serve as labourers in small-scale mining and quarrying operations worldwide (International Labour Office, 2005). These children range in age from five to seventeen and work in dangerous conditions without access to adequate housing, food, or basic education. While small-scale mining operations are frequently located in remote areas, child labour is not restricted to such regions. In urban centres, street children work for subsistence wages, have little or no access to schooling (see Balagophalan, 2002; Duyan, 2005; and Epstein, 1996), and often report that the education they are offered is ill suited to their needs. Children are also employed as domestic servants (Rubenson, Van Ahn, Hojer, & Johansson, 2004; White, 2002) and work in manufacturing and trades (Balagopalan, 2002; Epstein, 1996). Work severely limits and often eliminates any chance these children have of obtaining education. Children working in urban centres may have more educational opportunities in proximity than rural children, but conversely may be less able to take advantage of such opportunities if they work.

Children in rural settings have few educational opportunities and those that they do are frequently undermined by agricultural and domestic work. Buchmann (2000) suggests that in Kenya, educational reform that addresses the discrepancy between educational outcomes and labour opportunities would be more effective than banning child labour or teaching parents about the importance of education. Admassie (2003) offers a similar perspective on child labour and contends that banning child labour or implementing trade sanctions are simplistic solutions. Such approaches to eliminating child labour do not account for factors such as the realities of subsistence economies or the needs of AIDS orphans to support themselves and any siblings. In addition, much of the work on child labour focuses on urban settings and on work that is in manufacturing or related areas, not on agricultural and household work.

In Ethiopia the laws for minimum ages for work and education (age seven) are not well enforced in rural areas, and enforcement targets formal employment arrangements while not addressing agricultural and informal arrangements (Admassie, 2003). Most children (80%) reported that they were participating in household or farm work by the age of seven, and almost all were participating by the age of ten, but only one out of every five was attending school. Admassie argues that while education is the best tool to prevent child labour and the best solution for improving the lives of and the opportunities for children in rural Ethiopia, families in subsistence economies do not see the benefit of education.

Many families feel it is important for children to gain life skills by working and do not see the benefits of education, especially since there is no immediate return on the investment for the family. Children who are assisting with agricultural and domestic work often make the difference between survival and starvation in subsistence economies and benefit the family if they are contracted out (formally or informally) to perform work for others. While education has some long-term benefits, it interferes with the immediate survival needs of many families. The indirect costs of schooling, such as loss of a child's labour domestically or outside the family, are an important deterrent to education.

Researchers (Admassie, 2003; Buchmann, 2000; Burke & Beegle, 2004; Dayioglu, 2005; Mehrotra, 1998; Satz, 2003) suggest that increasing the parental demand for education by making the economic outcomes associated with education more direct could counteract this challenge. Admassie (2003) argues that while agricultural and domestic work may get in the way of education, policies that ban child labour will not help. Rather, flexible schooling policies that take peak agricultural seasons into account and make schooling and labour compatible would be more effective and allow a movement towards reduced child labour. This approach should be embedded in a comprehensive and integrative approach that engages legal, social, and economic measures to balance the needs of families in subsistence economies and children's rights to education.

Satz (2003) agrees with Buchmann (2000) and Admassie (2003) that banning child labour is a simplistic solution that ignores the variation and complexity of child labour. Satz contends that child labour may be the symptom of a number of root problems, including poverty, poor education systems, and discrimination, among others. Therefore, banning child labour will not necessarily eliminate the problems or result in increased education. In addition, it is not clear whether or not child labour is 'an avoidable reality' for developing countries. Satz makes the point that banning child labour may open other alternatives for children that would be even worse, but miserable working conditions, abuse, and exploitation within labour contexts should not be tolerated.

Proponents of the 'avoidable reality' of child labour in developing countries should turn their attention to the reality of child labour in developed countries. While child labour is often seen to be a 'problem' of developing countries, it continues to be problematic in developed countries as well. It is true that developed countries have legislation against child labour and protective legislation governing young workers who have not yet reached majority. However, this has not solved the issue of child labour.

The United Kingdom provides an excellent example of how child labour continues to be problematic. Legislation in the United Kingdom restricts children under sixteen from working without parental permission. Children are also banned from working in dangerous jobs such as factory work, selling petrol, or slaughterhouse work (P.J. White, 2004) and there are age-specific maximum hours of work per week as well as bans on certain hours of the day such as early in the morning or late in the evening during school terms (Leonard, 2004). Thus, while the legislation can be understood to be preserving children's right to education by ensuring that work does not interfere with it, the same legislation can be seen as failing to uphold article 12, children's right to participation, by not involving children in the decision-making process and by preventing those below the age of sixteen from having access to income.

White (2004) claims that child labour legislation in the United Kingdom does not effectively protect children from abuses in the workplace such as excessive hours and conditions leading to accidents. He argues that under the current legislation children can be treated as a casual, part-time, and dispensable workforce and that children have been victims of preventable workplace accidents involving dangerous work, unsafe working conditions, or lack of supervision. In addition, Admassie (2003) makes the point that informal working arrangements fall outside the legislation on child labour.

Informal working arrangements include children's contributions to household work and work in family businesses, both agricultural and urban. Cohen (2001) looked at children's contributions to household labour in three sociocultural contexts, a village in southern India, a town in Norway and a city in Canada. According to Cohen, even in urban-industrial settings children's participation has become indispensable owing to the restructuring of households and society. Many researchers have found that children are engaged in household work (Cheal, 2003; Cohen, 2001; Orellana, 2001; Song, 1999; Valenzuela, 1999). Miller (2005) argues that, for the most part, children in developed countries do not spend significant amounts of time on household chores in comparison with estimates of the time children in developing countries spend. However, there are exceptions, as children in immigrant households often take on caregiving and other household tasks in addition to helping their families adjust to the new country (Orellana, 2001; Valenzuela, 1999).

Working in family-owned businesses is another way that children contribute economically. This is true of children in immigrant families where children's contributions are often seen as necessary to the family's survival, although such work is often cited as interfering with school responsibilities (Song, 1999; Yeh, 2005). While immigrant children may be at particular risk for working in family businesses, many other children work in family businesses in both urban (Rowland, 1996) and rural settings (Kim & Zepeda, 2004; Wallace, Dunkerly, Cheal, & Warren, 1994). In Great Britain children in farming families contribute in economically important ways to the work of the farm (Wallace et al., 1994), a practice that is also common in the United States and Canada. In a study of Wisconsin farming families, Kim and Zepeda (2004) found that children over the age of six make significant labour contributions to the family farm. They also noted that there are some similarities between developing and developed countries in terms of children's participation in family farms.

The relationship between education and work continues to be contentious regardless of whether it is taking place in developed or developing countries. Some argue that work and school are incompatible (e.g., Dayioglu, 2005), while others contend that some forms of labour, such as that associated with families, are not incompatible with education and do not see a ban on child labour as the only solution (Admassie, 2003; Buchmann, 2000; Buchmann & Hannum, 2001; Satz, 2003). The evidence from developed countries suggests that legislation on child labour does not do enough to protect children or facilitate their right to participation (Leonard, 2004; Levison, 2000; P.J. White,

2004). Families in both developing and developed countries continue to rely on children's labour contributions for family survival.

Gender Issues

While there are many similarities to be seen in child labour between developed and developing countries in terms of the central issues, gender issues differ more between developing and developed countries. In developing countries, girls' access to education is the primary concern and within that framework barriers to girls' access such as economic or sexual exploitation, war and conflict, and early marriage are significant factors. Since the vast majority of girls in developed countries have access to education in suitably equipped schools, gender issues in education tend to be more focused on equity issues and factors within the school environment that interfere with education. Furthermore, in developing countries, gender issues within education tend to be focused on girls. This is not necessarily the case in developed countries, where gender issues may include lack of parity for boys (Bradley, 2005) and safe school environments for children of all sexual orientations (D'Augelli, 2002; Rostosky, Owens, & Zimmerman, 2003).

The Convention makes no gender distinctions in its provision of children's rights. Article 2 makes the provision that all the rights contained in the Convention must be respected by the state without discrimination of any kind, including that based on gender. Culture, politics, and economics are the most frequently cited causes for gender inequity (Admassie, 2003; Alderman, Kim, & Orazem, 2003; Arnold & Bertone, 2002; Blackstrom, 1996/7; Coleman, 2004; Jensen & Thornton, 2003; McNaughton, 1999; Slaughter-Dafoe, Addae, & Bell, 2002; Tansel, 2002). As children have the right to culture, religion, and language (article 30), it would seem that at times the right to education could be in opposition to article 30.

Blackstrom (1996/7) claims the CRC does not adequately address the abuses faced by the female child in terms of health issues, attitudes that support infanticide and sex-selective abortions, female genital surgeries, domestic violence, and educational issues. Cultural issues (e.g., servile marriage, dowry murder), political issues (e.g., nationality if conferred by the dominant male, legal status of women in some countries), and economic issues (child labour, domestic servitude, sexual exploitation) are also areas of vulnerability for girls in many parts of the world. The right to education is particularly problematic for girls. Coleman (2004) argues that while many agree that educating girls is one of the most effective ways to boost economies, particularly in developing countries, failure to invest in girls' education is still evident in low literacy rates for girls. She notes that girls' literacy rates are problematic in southern Asia, Arab countries, and sub-Saharan Africa. The education of girls is often not valued and is frequently blocked by societal barriers. Girls may be seen as an economic liability and education is often considered unnecessary and as a potential impediment to a girl adopting her 'natural' place in society.

In many cultures, a girl's natural place is as a wife and mother. As marriage and schooling generally tend to be incompatible in many countries, early marriages negatively affect girls' educational opportunities (Blackstrom, 1996/7; Ikamari, 2005; Jensen & Thornton, 2003; McNaughton, 1999). In a survey of several developing countries, early marriage was associated with reduced education for girls and some girls only received one or two years of education before their marriage (Jensen & Thornton, 2003). McNaughton (1999) argues that girls' lower educational attainment is directly related to the conceptualization of the 'girl child' as having less value and occupying a more proscribed and restricted role in many cultures. This has been supported in more recent research that directly or indirectly examines gender inequity in education in various countries (see Admassie, 2003; Alderman et al., 2003; Arnold & Bertone, 2002; Coleman, 2004; Jensen & Thornton, 2003; Slaughter-Dafoe et al., 2002; Tansel, 2002). Geographic location is also important, as girls in rural areas frequently have even lower levels of educational attainment than girls in urban areas (see Admassie, 2003; Arnold & Bertone, 2002; Slaughter-Dafoe et al., 2002; and Tansel, 2002)

In rural Ethiopia, girls' participation in work is much higher than boys' rates of participation (Admassie, 2003). Many families see domestic work knowledge as being essential to girls' future roles as wives and mothers. Girls' lower school attendance rates may be connected to the tendency for girls to be caring for younger siblings, a form of labour that is incompatible with school attendance. In addition, girls move into their husbands' families upon marriage; therefore, investing in education for a girl is seen as only providing benefit for her future husband's family.

Gender equity issues in developing countries apply most directly to girls' right to education, and frequently undermine girls' access to quality education, in contravention of articles 28 and 29. The issues also bring other rights into question, such as the right to non-discrimination (article 2) and the right to participate (article 12). Frequently these rights come into conflict with article 30, the right to culture, religion, and language. The context for gender issues within education is different in developed countries, where parity also applies to boys and the school environment is at issue. While articles 29, 2, and 12 are important, other rights, such as the right to the freedom of expression, thought, and association (articles 13, 14, 15) and the right to privacy and protection from attack (article 16), play a larger role.

Issues with gender parity primarily apply to articles 2 and 29, and have frequently resulted in debates about the advantages and disadvantages that single-sex classrooms or schools offer boys or girls in developed countries (see Herr & Arms, 2004; Howes & Kaplan, 2004; Mulholland, Hansen, & Kamanski, 2004; Salomone, 2003; Schmuck, Nagel, & Brody, 2002; Tsolidis & Dobson, 2006). Salomone (2003) contends that schools often act to perpetuate stereotypical constructions of gender that can negatively affect educational performance. She also states that the efficacy of single-sex schooling is mixed, as there is data that supports it, but such support is often context-specific and by no means conclusive. Schmuck et al. (2002) argue that single-sex schools can be effective but the gender consciousness of the administrators, teachers, and students is more important in establishing gender parity in education for girls.

School environments have also come to the fore as a gender issue through evidence suggesting that schools are not safe and welcoming environments for children of all sexual orientations. This is a particularly contested area that may violate all the articles associated with gender issues (articles 2, 12, 13, 14, 15, 16, 28, and 29). An examination of nineteen secondary schools in the United Kingdom revealed that while approximately 65 per cent of the schools addressed sexual orientation within their formal policies, none of their anti-bullying policies mentioned sexual orientation (Adams, Cox, & Dustan, 2004). Illingworth and Murphy (2004) point out that lesbian, gay, and bisexual adolescent students often experience hostile school environments and may suffer discrimination not only from students but also from staff at their schools. Systemic discrimination is often present in both the formal curriculum taught and in the hidden 'moral' curriculum that may govern the school (Illingworth & Murphy, 2004, 11). Multiple researchers have identified school environments as problematic and discriminatory in their treatment of lesbian, gay, and bisexual students, and these researchers continue to underscore the need for change within schools to ensure that all children are provided with safe and welcoming learning environments (Adams et al., 2004; D'Augelli, 2002; Green, 2004; Illingworth & Murphy, 2004; Macgillivray, 2004; Peters, 2003; Rostosky, Owens, & Zimmerman, 2003).

In both developing and developed countries, the lack of safe environments outside the school context can lead to girls not having access to education. Arnold and Bertone (2002) examined the vulnerability of girls in Thailand and their exploitation within the sex trade. One of the most important elements they identified was the need to view Thailand through a culturally sensitive lens and not from a Western perspective. Western governments have to take some responsibility for this exploitation and have been doing so by working with the government of Thailand to ensure that Western governments press sexual-tourism charges against their own citizens. Thailand has made some progress in protecting girls from unwanted involvement in the sex trade, and offers education programs and vocational training options for girls recovered from the trade.

Challenges remain as there is an increasing trend for girls to be trafficked from areas surrounding urban centres. At particular risk are the hill-tribe girls of Northern Thailand, who are caught between Burma and Thailand. These tribes are denied citizenship in Thailand and their girls are at particular risk for sexual exploitation either in their home location or through trafficking into central Thailand. One of the few positive movements has been the creation of the New Life Centre by a Western non-governmental organization (NGO). The Centre provides at-risk hill-tribe girls with educational opportunities in a residential program modelled after a family environment.

The situation in Vietnam has a different context, but involvement in the sex trade is also effective in blocking girls' access to education. In Ho Chi Min City, young girls working as prostitutes report having little access to education and being drawn into prostitution through cultural and societal factors and expectations (Rubenson, Van Ahn, Höjer, & Johansson, 2005). While Vietnam has engaged in policy and programming to implement the Convention, the girls in this study did not benefit from any of the policies. They reported that poverty, lack of employment opportunities, and the responsibility to assist in the support of their families made prostitution a viable option. While the girls are frequently disdained by society and several reported hiding their occupations from their families, there is evidence that prostitution is privately accepted as an alternative to poverty in Vietnam. Evidence of this type of attitude has also been found in Thailand (Arnold & Bertone, 2002; Montgomery, 2001).

Work in the sex trade has also been seen as a viable option for girls in developed countries. Like developing countries, the sexual exploitation or abuse of children in developed countries significantly reduces their access to education. The rights of children to non-discrimination (article 2), protection from interference or attack (article 16), and protection from exploitation (article 32) are also contravened by sexual exploitation.

Some children working in the sex trade are trafficked from developing into developed countries (Roby, 2005), while others enter the sex trade in the developed country where they live (Tonkin, 1999). A Canadian study found that the average age of entry into the domestic sex trade is sixteen, most of the sexually exploited youth are female, 90 per cent had been physically or sexually assaulted, 80 per cent had been in the care of government agencies at some point, and education was one of the top three needs that the youth identified (Tonkin, 1999). Street youth who have no access or extremely limited access to education often cite sexual abuse as one of the primary reasons for opting to live on the street (Kidd, 2004). In addition, sexual abuse is frequently seen to have significant negative effects on children's ability to focus in school and, for some, to complete education (Delfos, 2001; Oates, Gray, Schweitzer, Kempe, & Harmon, 1995; Veltman & Browne, 2001).

The gender issues associated with children's right to education in developed countries share few similarities with those of prominence in developing countries. Given the variability between developed and developing countries, how can gender equity within education best be addressed? Blackstrom (1996/7) suggests that a stronger position by the CRC on the rights of girls would force countries to establish gender equity. However, such an approach would lend credence to claims that the CRC is a hegemonic document and would not be culturally sensitive. Myers (2001) contends that by articulating rights in terms of objectives and principles the Convention provides room for ratifying members to implement it in ways that are appropriate to their situation. Developing and developed countries need to work out culturally sensitive and contextually appropriate methods for upholding the CRC by ensuring that all children have access to education that is provided in safe and non-discriminatory environments within schools and that all children have safe environments outside school that are supportive of education and article 29.

Indigenous Children

> We are all visitors to this time, this place. We are just passing through.
> Our purpose here is to observe, to learn, to grow, to love ... and then we
> return home.
>
>   Australian Aboriginal Proverb

In developing and developed countries indigenous children face significant barriers to education and are rarely provided with the opportunities 'to observe, to learn, to grow' within educational contexts. Children in developed countries face some educational challenges owing to the shortfalls of dominant education frameworks, but Indigenous children's experiences within education bear striking similarities to those confronted by similar children in developing countries and not to other children within their home nations. Neither the letter of the articles nor the spirit of the Convention is upheld within indigenous education in either developing or developed countries. The CRC is contravened most heavily in the case of indigenous populations, which suffer significantly more rights violations than global non-indigenous populations. In particular, articles 2, 9, 12, 13, 14, 28, 30 and 32 (1), are frequently violated.

Although article 2 provides children with the right to non-discrimination, indigenous children are often subject to discrimination in educational contexts within both developing countries (see Abu-Saad et al., 1998; Foy, 2003; Mehrotra, 1998; and Office of the High Commissioner for Human Rights, 2001) and developed countries (Edwards, 2001; Gallagher-Hayashi, 2004; Foy, 2003; Neegan, 2005; Nicholls, 2005; St. Denis & Hampton, 2002; Whattam, 2003). Indigenous children may have to attend residential schools and not be able to live with their families for significant periods, a practice that calls article 9, children's right to reside with their families, into contention (Behera & Nath, 2005; Monárrez-Espino, Martínez, Martínez, & Greiner, 2004). While residential schools are now rare in developed countries, Australia and Canada share a disgraceful history of residential schooling that has been equated with cultural genocide (Edwards, 2001; Foy, 2003; Neegan, 2005; Nicholls, 2005; Smith, 2003; Van Krieken, 1999; Whattam, 2003; Young, 2004). The bonds between tens of thousands of indigenous children and their families were broken, with disastrous results (Canada, 1996; Van Krieken, 1999; Whattam, 2003). These children grew up to be adults not capable of passing their culture, history, or religion on to their children, a travesty being repeated in some developing countries.

Indigenous children's right to participate (article 12) is frequently disregarded, as these children often have no say in the educational processes to which they have limited or no access (Foy, 2003; Magga, 2005). On a similar note, their freedom of expression (article 13) and freedom of thought, conscience, and religion (article 14) are also frequently stifled by educational systems in developing countries that disregard their languages and customs (Abu-Saad et al., 1998; Aquino & Kirylo, 2005; Chang, 2005; Foy, 2003). Indigenous children in Canada and Australia also report feeling alienated, socially isolated, and painfully aware of the cultural disconnect between school and their home culture (Neegan, 2005; Nicholls, 2005; Powers, 2005; Van Krieken, 1999; Whattam, 2003).

Article 28 is most frequently in question, as indigenous children in developing and developed countries seem to have limited access to education and to be at greater risk for economic exploitation (article 30 (1)) (Arnold & Bertone, 2002; Foy, 2003). Similarly, the upholding of article 29 in developing and developed countries is frequently questionable, as the education that indigenous children receive may not be in accord with the scope and principles of education as outlined in the article and may also violate article 30 by not upholding indigenous children's right to culture, religion, and language (Abu-Saad et al., 1998; Aquino & Kirylo, 2005; Chang, 2005; Foy, 2003; Nicholls, 2005; Powers, 2005; Van Krieken, 1999).

Article 30 of the CRC demands that children have a right to retain and learn about their culture, religion, and language through the education system. In order to bring global education standards up to a level that would meet the CRC's specifications, these barriers must be eliminated. Culture and language are intertwined, and yet many children have no access to education in their mother tongue. There are approximately 6000 languages spoken around the globe, with 4000 to 5000 of the languages being spoken by indigenous peoples (Office of the High Commissioner for Human Rights, 2001). There are almost 2500 languages in danger of extinction, most of which are spoken by indigenous people (ibid.). Researchers who have examined the education of indigenous children in various countries, including India (Behera & Nath, 2005; Pattnaik, 2005b), Mexico (Monárrez-Espino et al., 2004), Paraguay (Aquino & Kirylo, 2005), South Africa (Singh, 2005), and Taiwan (Chang, 2005), stress the importance of the language of instruction and cultural relevance of the curriculum.

The lack of schooling offered in indigenous languages in developing countries poses a significant barrier to education and further erodes the cultural knowledge contained in indigenous language when the dominant language of instruction becomes more prominent among indigenous children (Aquino & Kirylo, 2005; Pattnaik, 2005a, 2005b). A lack of teachers who speak the local language not only makes it more difficult for children to learn in another tongue, it also leads to the eradication of indigenous languages (Aquino & Kirylo, 2005; Foy, 2003; Pattnaik, 2005a, 2005b). Minimal funding leads to a lack of trained teachers who can teach the children in their mother tongue. Unique teacher education can address this issue (Aquino & Kirylo, 2005; Mehrotra, 1998), but such programs are the exception not the norm. School classes are often taught in the dominant language, which teaches children that their language is not worth learning and that if they want to be intelligent and 'successful,' they must learn and use the dominant language.

Today, many Indigenous peoples in Canada, the United States, and Australia do not know the language of their ancestors. Many feel separated from their culture, through the disconnection from or loss of their ancestral languages, teachings, and customs (Van Krieken, 1999; Simpson & Clancy, 2005; Whattam, 2003). When Australia was colonized there were 250 indigenous languages, but 75 per cent of those languages are now lost; not only are they no longer spoken, but some were never recorded (Nicholls, 2005). Indigenous children in Canada who live off-reserve, with the exception of Inuit children, have very low indigenous language skills (Turcotte & Zhao, 2004). According to Foy (2003), those within indigenous communities find cultural irrelevance in the curriculum to be the biggest obstacle to learning for their children. An inadequate cultural dimension creates a non-conducive learning environment and frustration in students, who tend to leave school (Aquino & Kirylo, 2005; Foy, 2003). The effects of not offering education in language-appropriate or culturally relevant ways have also been clearly demonstrated in developed nations, where there is strong evidence that the educational systems are failing indigenous children. Canadian and American statistics report lower graduation rates and high drop-out rates (Bylsma & Ireland, 2002) as well as lower academic performance levels (British Columbia Ministry of Education, 2006; Powers, 2005) for indigenous students. In Canada, off-reserve indigenous children represent 32 per cent of the off-reserve population compared to their non-indigenous peers, who represent 18 per cent of the non-indigenous population. Yet, the high school completion rate for off-reserve indigenous children is 52 per cent compared to 74 per cent for non-Indigenous children (Turcotte & Zhao, 2004).

Indigenous education is further compromised by a lack of resources such as materials, inadequate structural facilities, and the distance between home and school for the children. Education is often conducted in dilapidated buildings, unsafe for children or adults (Abu-Saad et al., 1998; Carney, 2003; Foy, 2003; Mbelle and Katabaro, 2003; Postlewaite, 1998). Some children do not have accessible roads for walking to school, while many of those who do use roads are travelling routes that are dangerous (Foy, 2003). In reserve schools in North America, many facilities are failing and are unsuitable environments for teaching and learning. A 2001 U.S. Bureau of Indian Affairs budget report noted that many schools on reservations were structurally unsound or not of a sufficient size to house all the students (ibid,). Recently Kashechewan, a reserve in Northern Ontario, made national news when the media became aware of 'Third World conditions,' including unsafe drinking water, unsuitable housing, a high school contaminated with asbestos, and an elementary school condemned owing to poor conditions and mould (Strauss, 2006).

Foy (2003) has found some evidence of positive changes in the education of indigenous children in developing countries. Viet Nam now has programs that include the development of bilingual books in ethnic minority languages, indigenous teachers, and accelerated training programs for teacher candidates from remote regions. In northeast Russia there is a school, the Palana Teacher Training School, that prepares teachers to teach in both Russian and indigenous languages. Bolivia is working on providing pre-school education close to home in rural locations and has developed a national policy for Quechua and Aymara children. Education in Cambodia has shifted to make the school schedule compatible with seasonal agricultural rhythms, while Mexico and Thailand have instituted the use of mobile teachers. In Paraguay an institution dedicated to keeping the indigenous Guaraní language and culture alive through teacher training is making inroads in education (Aquino & Kirylo, 2005). In developed countries there are also positive changes, including a new charter school in Alberta, Mother Earth's Children's Charter School, that has the distinction of being the first indigenous charter school in Canada (Pearce, Crowe, Letendre, Letendre, & Baydala, 2005); a First Nations high school in North Battleford, Saskatchewan; and Edmonton, Alberta's Amisk-

waciy Academy, a high school where education is centred around aboriginal culture. These advances are beginning to address the issues that
have plagued the education of indigenous children, particularly in reference to articles 2, 9, 12, 13, 14, 28, and 30.

Clearly, it is not enough to offer educational opportunities to indigenous children around the world. Instead, all countries must promote a
higher level of commitment through funding to offer education that is
linguistically and culturally relevant, conducted in a safe facility by
well-trained and salaried teachers, and within a close proximity to
home. Magga (2005) stresses the importance of involving parents and
the indigenous community in the planning, delivery, and evaluation of
educational services. Developing and developed countries continue to
violate the rights of indigenous children. As articulated by the CRC, all
countries must strive to find ways of meeting their obligations to
indigenous children by ensuring that all children have the opportunity
'to observe, to learn, to grow.'

Conclusion

Children around the globe face many obstacles in their pursuit of education. In developing and developed countries many of the larger
issues are the same, but they have very different expressions. The challenge that confronts nations is how to navigate these obstacles so that
education is provided for children in ways that uphold the spirit of the
Convention within the contexts that are particular to a given nation
and in keeping with that nation's conceptualization of children and
childhood. The CRC is not about a proscriptive form of education any
more than it is about defining a particular form of acceptable 'family.'
The terminology of the Convention was written to allow for a fit
within all contexts.

The CRC has been criticized on many fronts, with some critics complaining that the document goes too far and does not take non-Western
traditions and beliefs into consideration (see Burr, 2002), while other
critics are dissatisfied with what they have interpreted as half-way
measures that are not enforceable and do not go far enough (see Melchiorre, 2004). What some of the critics of the CRC fail to appreciate is
that the committee was faced with an almost impossible task. Given
the cultural variations around the world and the differences in terms
of other contextual factors including development, economics, politics,
and religion, it is next to impossible to draft a convention that protects
'children.' Such critics should examine their own approaches to chil-

dren's rights issues and ask whether they might not be guilty of using a Western lens without considering cultural context.

The future education of the world's children depends upon nations taking responsibility for the challenges to education that exist within their own borders and addressing those challenges so that the spirit of the Convention becomes embodied within the policies and practice of the nation. Countries will also have to deal with the complex issues of protection and participation, as many countries are making significant progress on protection issues but are more challenged by children's participation. Similarly, developing and developed countries have made progress with article 28, but are still significantly challenged by article 29 (Scherer & Hart, 1999). The critical analysis of child labour, gender issues, and the education of indigenous children demonstrates that these challenges are pervasive and in need of attention. Children's rights related to education are not simple and may at time come into conflict with other rights. In addition, the context of a given country has a significant impact on how a given challenge can be successfully addressed. The face of education may differ from country to country, but the CRC provides a common thread that runs through education. Each country needs to take that thread and weave a pattern that speaks to its own people and culture while embodying the spirit and principles of the CRC within educational practice and policy.

REFERENCES

Abu-Saad, I., Abu-Saad, K., Lewando-Hundt, G., Forman, M.R., Belmaker, I., Berendes, H.W., & Chang, D. (1998). Bedouin Arab mothers' aspirations for their children's education in the context of radical social change. *International Journal of Educational Development, 18*(4), 347–359.

Adams, N., Cox, T., & Dustan, L. (2004). 'I am the hate that dare not speak its name': Dealing with homophobia in secondary schools. *Educational Psychology in Practice, 20*(3), 259–269.

Admassie, A. (2003). Child labour and schooling in the context of a subsistence rural economy: Can they be compatible? *International Journal of Educational Development, 23*, 167–185.

Alderman, H., Kim, A., & Orazem, P.F. (2003). Design, evaluation, and sustainability of private schools for the poor: The Pakistan urban and rural fellowship school experiments. *Economics of Education Review, 22*, 265–274.

Alderson, P. (2000). UN Convention on the Rights of the Child: Some common criticisms and suggested responses. *Child Abuse Review, 9,* 439–443.

Alexander, N.C. (2001). Paying for education: How the World Bank and the International Monetary Fund influence education in developing countries. *Peabody Journal of Education, 76,* 285–338.

Aquino, A., & Kirylo, J. (2005). Proyecto Kuatiañe'e. *Childhood Education, 81*(6), 349–354.

Arnold, C., & Bertone, A.M. (2002). Addressing the sex trade in Thailand: Some lessons learned from NGO's. Part I. *Gender Issues, Winter,* 26–52.

Ashraf, H. (2003). UN says global plan to help world's poorest is failing some nations. *The Lancet, 362,* 131.

Balagopalan, S. (2002). Constructing Indigenous childhoods: Colonialism, vocational education and the working child. *Childhood, 9*(1), 19–34.

Barnitz, L. (2001). Effectively responding to the commercial sexual exploitation of children: A comprehensive approach to prevention, protection, and reintegration services. *Child Welfare, 80*(5), 597–610.

Behera, D.K., & Nath, N. (2005) Aboriginal female children in Kanyashrams of Orissa, India. *Childhood Education, 81*(6), 321–326.

Blackstrom, K.M. (1996/1997). The international human rights of the child: Do they protect the female child? *The George Washington Journal of International Law and Economics, 30*(2/3), 541–582.

Bradley, G. (2005). Global higher education rankings issued. *Academe, 91*(4), 5–6.

British Columbia Ministry of Education. (2006). Aboriginal report 2005/06: How are we doing? Retrieved on October 15, 2007, from http://www.bced.gov.bc.ca/abed/perf2006.pdf

Buchmann, C. (2000). Family structure, parental perceptions, and child labour in Kenya: What factors determine who is enrolled in school. *Social Forces, 78*(4), 1349–1379.

Buchmann, C., & Hannum, E. (2001). Education and stratification in developing countries: A review of theories and research. *Annual Review of Sociology, 27,* 77–102.

Burke, K., & Beegle, K. (2004). Why children aren't attending school: The case of northwestern Tanzania. *Journal of African Economies, 13*(2), 333–355.

Burr, R. (2002). Global and local approaches to children's rights in Vietnam. *Childhood, 9,* 49–61.

Bylsma, P., & Ireland, L. (2002). *Graduation and dropout statistics for Washington's counties, districts, and schools: Final report, school year 2000–01.* Retrieved May 12, 2005, from http://www.k12.wa.us/dataadmin/reports/DG2000-01.pdf

Canada. Royal Commission on Aboriginal Peoples. (1996). People to people, nation to nation: Highlights from the report of the Royal Commission on Aboriginal Peoples.

Carney, S. (2003). Globalisation, neo-liberalism and the limitations of school effectiveness research in developing countries: The case of Nepal. *Globalization, Societies and Education, 1*(1), 87–101.

Chang, C.L. (2005). Translating policies into practice. *Childhood Education, 81*(6), 355–359.

Cheal, D.J. (2003). Children's home responsibilities: Factors predicting children's household work. *Social Behavior & Personality: An International Journal, 31*(8), 789–794.

Cohen, R. (2001). Children's contribution to household labour in three socio-cultural contexts: A southern Indian village, a Norwegian town, and a Canadian city. *Comparative Sociology, 42*(4), 353–367.

Coleman, I. (2004). The pay-off from women's rights. *Foreign Affairs, May/June*, 80–95.

Covell, K., & Howe, R.B. (1999). The impact of children's rights education: A Canadian study. *International Journal of Children's Rights, 7*, 171–183.

Covell, K., & Howe, R.B. (2005). *Empowering children: Children's rights education as a pathway to citizenship*. Toronto: University of Toronto Press.

D'Augelli, A.R. (2002). Mental health problems among lesbian, gay, and bisexual youths ages 14 to 21. *Clinical Child Psychology and Psychiatry, 7*(3), 433–456.

Dayioglu, M. (2005). Patterns of change in child labour and schooling in Turkey: The impact of compulsory schooling. *Oxford Development Studies, 33*(2), 195–210.

Dei, G.J.S. (2004). Dealing with difference: Ethnicity and gender in the context of schooling in Ghana. *International Journal of Educational Development, 24*, 343–359.

Delfos, M.F. (2001). The developmental damage to children as a result of the violation of their rights. In J.C.M. Willems (Ed.), *Developmental and autonomy rights of children: Empowering caregivers and communities*. Antwerp, Groningen, Oxford: Intersentia.

Duyan, V. (2005). Relationships between the sociodemographic and family characteristics, street life experiences and the hopelessness of street children. *Childhood, 12*(4), 445–459.

Edwards, P. (2001). *One dead Indian*. Toronto: Stoddart Publishing.

Epstein, I. (1996). Educating street children: Some cross-cultural perspectives. *Comparative Education, 32*(3), 289–302.

Foy, J.E. (2003). Ensuring the rights of Indigenous children. *Innocenti Digest, 11*, 2–32.

Fredrickson, G.M. (2002). *Racism: A short history*. Princeton, NJ: Princeton University Press.

Gallagher-Hayashi, D. (2004). Connecting with aboriginal students. *Teacher Librarian, 31*(5), 20–24.

Green, B.I. (2004). Discussion and expression of gender and sexuality in schools. *Georgetown Journal of Gender & the Law, 5*(1), 329–341.

Griffiths, M. (2000). Learning for all? Interrogating children's experiences of primary schooling in Mauritius. *Teaching and Teacher Education, 16*, 785–800.

Hall, B.G., & Peters, P.A. (2003). Global ideals and local practicalities in educational planning in Lima, Peru. *Habitat International, 27*, 629–651.

Hannum, E. (2002). Educational stratification by ethnicity in China: Enrollment and attainment in the early school years. *Demography, 39*(1), 95–117.

Herr, K., & Arms, E. (2004). Accountability and single-sex schooling: A collision of reform agendas. *Education Evaluation and Policy Analysis, 26*(3), 527–555.

Howes, A., & Kaplan, I. (2004). A school responding to its cultural setting. *Improving Schools, 7*(1), 35–48.

Ikamari, L.D.E. (2005). The effect of education on the timing of marriage in Kenya. *Demographic Research, 12*, 1–27.

Illingworth, P., & Murphy, T. (2004). In our best interest: Meeting moral duties to lesbian, gay, and bisexual adolescent students. *Journal of Social Philosophy, 35*(2), 198–210.

International Labour Office (2005). The burden of gold: Child labour in small scale mines and quarries. *World of Work, 54*, 16–20.

The International Save the Children Alliance (2005). *Child protection in emergencies*. Stockholm: Save the Children Sweden and The International Save the Children Alliance.

Jansen, M.H. (2005). *Children without protection in Europe*. Stockholm: Save the Children Sweden.

Jensen, R., & Thornton, R. (2003). Early female marriage in the developing world. *Gender and Development, 11*, 9–19.

Johnson, B. (2000). The politics, policies, and practices in linguistic minority education in the People's Republic of China: The case of Tibet. *International Journal of Educational Research, 33*, 593–600.

Khan, A. (2001). Education in East Jerusalem: A study in disparity. *Palestine-Isreal Journal of Politics, Economics, and Culture, 7*(1), 1–47.

Kidd, S. (2004). 'The walls were closing in and, we were trapped': A Qualitative analysis of street youth suicide. *Youth & Society, 36*(1), 30–55.

Kim, J., & Zepeda, L. (2004). When all work is never done: Time allocation in US family farm households. *Feminist Economics, 10*(1), 115–139.

Lee, N. (1999). 'The challenge of childhood: Distribution of childhood's ambiguity in adult institutions.' *Childhood, 6*(4), 455–474.

Leonard, M. (2004). Children's views on children's right to work: Reflections from Dublin. *Childhood, 11*(1), 45–61.

Levison, D. (2000). Children as economic agents. *Feminist Economics, 6*(1), 125–134.

Macgillivray, I.K. (2004). Gay rights and school policy: A case study in community factors that facilitate or impede educational change. *International Journal of Qualitative Studies in Education, 17*(3), 347–370.

Magga, O. (2005). Indigenous education. *Childhood Education, 81*(6), 319–320.

Mbelle, A., and J. Katabaro (2003). School enrolment, performance and access to education in Tanzania. Dar es Salaam, REPOA / Mkuki na Nyota.

McNaughton, G. (1999). Promoting gender equity for young children in the South and South East Asian region. *International Journal of Early Years Education, 7*(1), 77–84.

Mehrotra, S. (1998). Education for all: Policy lessons from high-achieving countries. *International Review of Education, 44*(5/6), 461–484.

Melchiorre, A. (2004). *At what age?* 2nd ed., Right to Education Project.

Miller, P. (2005). Useful and priceless children in contemporary welfare states. *Social Politics, 12*(1), 3–41.

Monárrez-Espino, J., Martínez, H., Martínez, V., & Greiner, T. (2004). Nutritional status of Indigenous children at boarding schools in northern Mexico. *European Journal of Clinical Nutrition, 58*, 532–540.

Montgomery, H. (2001). *Modern Babylon? Prostituting children in Thailand.* Oxford: Berghahn Books.

Monture-Angus, P. (1995). *Thunder in my soul: A Mohawk woman speaks.* Halifax, NS: Fernwood Publishing.

Mulholland, J., Hansen, P., & Kamanski, E. (2004). Do single-gender classrooms in coeducational settings address boys' underachievement? An Australian study. *Educational Studies, 30*(1), 19–32.

Myers, W.E. (2001). The right rights? Child labour in a globalizing world. *The Annals of the American Academy, 575*, 38–55.

Neegan, E. (2005). Excuse me: Who are the first peoples of Canada? Aboriginal education in Canada then and now. *International Journal of Inclusive Education, 9*(1), 3–15.

Nicholls, C. (2005). Death by a thousand cuts: Indigenous language, bilingual education programmes in the Northern Territory of Australia, 1972–1998. *International Journal of Bilingual Education and Bilingualism, 8*(2/3), 160–177.

Office of the High Commissioner for Human Rights (2001). *Leaflet no. 10:*

Indigenous peoples and the environment. United Nations, Geneva. See also http://www.unhchr.ch/html/ racism/indileaflet10.doc

Orellana, M.J. (2001). The work kids do: Mexican and Central American children's contributions to households and schools in California. *Harvard International Review, 71*(3), 366–389.

Oates, R.K., Gray, J., Schweitzer, L., Kempe, R.S., & Harmon, R.J. (1995). A therapeutic preschool for abused children: The Keepsafe Project. *Child Abuse & Neglect, 19*, 1379–1386.

Pattnaik, J. (2005a). Global challenges and efforts: An introduction. *Childhood Education, 81*(6), 314–318.

Pattnaik, J. (2005b). Issues of language maintenance and education of aboriginal children in India. *Childhood Education, 81*(6), 360–364.

Pearce, M., Crowe, C., Letendre, M., Letendre, C., & Baydala, L. (2005). Mother Earth's Children's Charter School in Canada: Imagining a new story of school. *Childhood Education, 81*(6), 343–348.

Persson, U. (2001). *Children with disabilities.* Stockholm: Save the Children Sweden.

Peters, A.J. (2003). Isolation or inclusion: Creating safe spaces for lesbian and gay youth. *Families in Society, 84*(3), 331–337.

Postlewaite, N. (1998). The conditions of primary schools in the least-developed countries. *International Review of Education, 44*(4), 289–317.

Powers, K. (2005). Promoting school achievement among American Indian students throughout the school years. *Childhood Education, 81* (6), 338–342.

Rao, N., Cheng, K., & Narain, K. (2003). Primary schooling in China and India: Understanding how socio-contextual factors moderate the role of the state. *International Review of Education, 49*(1–2), 153–176.

Reynolds, R.J. (2005). The education of Australian Aboriginal and Torres Strait Islander students. *Childhood Education, 82*, 31–36.

Roby, J.L. (2005). Women and children in the global sex trade: Toward more effective policy. *International Social Work, 48*(2), 136–147.

Rostosky, S.S., Owens, G.P., & Zimmerman, R.S. (2003). Associations among sexual attraction status, school belonging, and alcohol and marijuana use in rural high school students. *Journal of Adolescence, 26*(6), 741–751.

Rowland, M. (1996). Putting your kids on the payroll. *Nation's Business, 84*(1), 33–34.

Rubenson, B., Van Ahn, N., Höjer, B., & Johansson, E. (2004). Child domestic servants in Hanoi: Who are they and how do they fare? *The International Journal of Children's Rights, 11*, 391–407.

Rubenson, B., Hanh, L.T., Höjer, B., & Johansson, E. (2005) Young sex workers in Ho Chi Minh City telling their life stories. *Childhood, 12*(3), 391–411.

St. Denis, V., & Hampton, E. (2002). *Literature review on racism and the effects on aboriginal education*. Prepared for Minister's Working Group on Education Indian and Northern Affairs Canada, Ottawa.

Salomone, R. (2003). *Same, different, equal: Rethinking single-sex schooling*. New Haven, CT: Yale University Press.

Satz, D. (2003). Child labour: A normative perspective. *World Bank Economic Review, 17*(2), 297–309.

Scherer, L., & Hart, S.N. (1999). Reporting to the UN Committee on the Rights of the Child: Analyses of the first 49 State Party Reports on the education articles of the Convention on the Rights of the Child and a proposition for an experimental reporting system for education. *The International Journal of Children's Rights, 7*(4), 349–363.

Schmuck, P., Nagel, N., & Brody, C. (2002). Studying gender consciousness in single-sex and coeducational high schools. In A. Datnow & L. Hubbard (Eds.)., *Gender in policy and practice: Perspectives on single-sex and coeducational schooling*. New York: Routledge.

Schrage, E.J., & Ewing, A.P. (2005). The cocoa industry and child labour. *Journal of Corporate Citizenship, 18*, 99–112.

Shapiro, D., & Tambashe, B.O. (2001). Gender, poverty, family structure, and investments in children's education in Kinshasa, Congo. *Economics of Education Review, 20*, 359–375.

Simpson, L., & Clancy, S. (2005). Enhancing opportunities for Australian Aboriginal literacy learners in early childhood settings. *Childhood Education, 81*(6), 327–332.

Singh, A. (2005). A decade after South Africa's first democratic election. *Childhood Education, 81*(6), 333–337.

Slaughter-Dafoe, D.T., Addae, W.A., & Bell, C. (2002). Toward the future schooling of girls: Global status, issues, and prospects. *Human Development, 45*(1), 34–53.

Smith, A. (2003). Soul wound: The legacy of Native American schools, *Amnesty Now, Summer*, 14–16.

Song, M. (1999). *Helping out: Children's labour in ethnic businesses*. Philadelphia: Temple University Press.

Sri-Jayantha, Avis. (2002). *The impact of war on children in Sri Lanka*. Ilankai Tamil Sangram Association of Tamils in Sri Lanka in the United States. Retrieved December 2, 2005, from http://www.sangam.org/ANALYSIS/Children_1_28_03.htm

Stephens, S. (Ed.) (1995). *Children and the politics of culture*. Princeton, NJ: Princeton University Press.

Strauss, J. (2006). Broken homes. *Canadian Family, March*, 66–69.

Tansel, A. (2002). Determinants of school attainment of boys and girls in Turkey: Individual, household and community factors. *Economics of Education Review, 21*, 455–470.

Tonkin, R. (1999). *Our kids too. Sexually exploited youth in BC: An adolescent health survey.* Vancouver: McCreary Centre Society.

Tsolidis, G., & Dobson, I.R. (2006). Single-sex schooling: Is it simply a 'class act'? *Gender & Education, 18*(2), 213–228.

Turcotte, M., & Zhao, J. (2004). Well-being of off-reserve aboriginal children. *Canadian Social Trends, 75*, 22–27.

United Nations Committee on the Rights of the Child (2005). *General comment no. 6 – Treatment of unaccompanied and separated children outside their country of origin.* CRC/GC/2005/6.

Valenzuela, A. (1999). Gender roles and settlement activities among children and their immigrant families. *American Behavioral Scientist, 42*(4), 720–742.

Van Krieken, R. (1999). The 'stolen generations' and cultural genocide. The forced removal of Australian Indigenous children from their families and its implications for the sociology of childhood. *Childhood, 6*(3), 297–311.

Veltman, M.W.M., & Browne, K.D. (2001). Three decades of child maltreatment research: Implications for the school years. *Trauma, Violence, & Abuse, 2*(3), 215–239.

Verhellen, E. (1993). Children's rights and education. *School Psychology International, 14*(3), 199–208

Wallace, C., Dunkerly, D., Cheal, B., & Warren, M. (1994). Young people and the division of labour in farming families. *Sociological Review, 42*(3), 501–530.

Whattam, T. (2003). Reflections on residential schools and our future: 'Daylight in our minds.' *Qualitative Studies in Education, 16*(3), 435–448.

White, P.J. (2004, January 12). Where children come cheap. *Newstatesman,* 36–37.

White, S.C. (2002). From the politics of poverty to the politics of identity? Child rights and working children in Bangladesh. *Journal of International Development, 14*, 725–735.

Yeh, C. (2005). *Asian immigrant cultural negotiations across interpersonal contexts.* Paper presented at Multicultural Days: An International Perspective, Brock University, St Catharines, ON.

Young, S. (2004). *Anti-aboriginal racism in Canada: An examination of policy which maintains the status quo.* Master of Arts major research paper, Brock University, St Catharines, ON.

PART TWO

Protecting Children's Rights

5 Entitlement Beyond the Family: Global Rights Commitments and Children's Health Policy in Canada

CANDACE JOHNSON

The preceding chapters demonstrate that children's rights in Canada, as elsewhere, are indefinite and, in many cases, unfulfilled. Rights violations are especially egregious in times of conflict, as revealed by Tom O'Neill's study of children in Nepal. However, in times of peace and political stability, and in the most developed and democratic nations, children's rights are still neglected. While the clear normative promises of human rights, best expressed through the United Nations' Convention on the Rights of the Child (CRC), have given shape to domestic policy commitments, the ability of children to understand and claim those rights remains limited. The CRC has 'shed new light on government responsibility for ensuring that children no longer be the objects of decisions affecting them, but subjects taking an increasing role in these decisions as their capacity to do so evolves' (Tarantola & Gruskin, 2005, p. 225). However, as is the case with other human rights imperatives, there is a considerable amount of distance between philosophical positions and policy practice. And human rights promises and practices for children, as will be explained throughout this chapter, are particularly ambiguous owing to their dependency on families and the state and to their coincident lack of full citizenship rights. The evidence shows that children's rights are aimed at their protection and development, but not at their empowerment. These rights are citizenship rights in that they declare and protect the moral space of children, but they are not intended to foster and guide their present political actions. Children are viewed as *future* political partic-

The author wishes to thank Kayla Monteiro, MA student in political science, University of Guelph, for her excellent research assistance.

ipants. While they are children they have rights that ought to be respected by governments and their families, yet there seems to be no expectation that children recognize or exercise these rights on their own behalf.

This is not necessarily the human rights transgression that Hans Skott-Myhre and Donato Tarulli believe it to be (see chapter 3). Rights that protect and (future) rights to full political participation do not constitute a bad deal, especially when we take into consideration that most countries in the world are not liberal-democratic regimes, and therefore recognize neither (see chapter 4 in this volume for Dawn Zinga and Sherri Young's analysis of children's rights to education in developed and developing countries). But Skott-Myhre and Tarulli's point, well taken, is that Canada can do better.

In this chapter I examine the substance of children's rights in Canada with particular attention to the right to health care. My analysis supports the arguments of the other contributors to this section: that global commitments and domestic policy action are incongruous. I argue that both international human rights documents and Canadian policies frame and grant rights to children primarily as dependents of their parents, rather than as individual citizens. In the case of health care, this familial dependency model is further reinforced by the paucity of entitlements available specifically for children. Entitlement to services beyond what the universal system provides tends to be contingent on socio-economic status, and therefore channeled through social welfare policies. Such an approach increases the vulnerability of children, at the same time that policy rhetoric claims to recognize their value and importance as the future of the country.

Health Policy in Canada: Entitlement and Universality

Canada's universal health system has been successful in providing all Canadians with service and care on equal terms and conditions. Such an achievement has been a source of national pride and has served to distinguish Canada from the United States (Redden, 2002b; Smith, 1995; Tuohy, 1999). However, there are major problems with health service provision in both countries. In the United States, health insurance is provided through private markets. Governments intervene only to insure marginalized or 'deserving' groups: the elderly, the indigent, children of low income families, native peoples, veterans, and members of the armed forces. In Canada, health insurance is guaranteed to all people regardless of socio-economic status, gender, or other ascriptive characteristics. Yet, there are some serious gaps in this universal entitlement.

The legislation that establishes the standards for public health insurance, the *Canada Health Act* (CHA), applies only to 'medically necessary' hospital services and services provided by physicians. Pharmaceuticals, home care, and alternative service providers (personal care workers, chiropractors, and the like) fall outside the purview of the act (Deber, 1999). The advancement of medical technology makes unnecessary many traditional forms of care, which means that health services can, in many cases, be delivered outside of institutional settings. This reality, in addition to the rising rates of child poverty (Rice, 2002; Robson-Haddow, 2004) and an aging population, presents serious challenges to the Canadian public and to marginalized populations in particular (Redden, 2002a, 2002b).

According to UNICEF, Canada ranked nineteenth out of twenty-six OECD countries for child poverty in 2005; in 2007 Canada ranked twelfth out of twenty-six for child well-being, a more comprehensive measure (UNICEF, 2005; 2007). In its 2005 report, the organization explains that 'Despite a national all-party resolution made in 1989 committing the Government of Canada to "seek to eliminate child poverty by the year 2000," almost 15 per cent of Canadian children still live in relative poverty. In comparison, 11 of the OECD countries have a relative child poverty rate of less than 10 per cent; and four of these have a rate of less than five per cent' (UNICEF, 2005b). Further, the current challenges to welfare states and the universal social programs that are their defining features were not foreseen by policy makers and practitioners. Therefore, these new challenges, which include AIDS, new reproductive technologies, the burgeoning market in pharmaceuticals, and the recognition of the expanding needs of diverse societies, cannot always be well accommodated by existing arrangements. The universal health system by definition covers everybody and is perceived as successfully doing so (at least in a way that is superior to the patchwork of private and public provision that exists in the United States). As a result, there is insufficient attention paid to vulnerable groups and their needs.

In Canada, children's health needs are indirectly recognized within withering universal health commitments and through welfare programs. There is little policy that addresses children's health within the mainstream, universal series of health policies. Rather, policy commitments are often made to the most vulnerable children (in low income families or with disabilities) through social assistance programs or family welfare policy. In fact, many provinces have departments dedicated to policy development and service delivery for children and families.

Canada's approach to providing health services to a diverse population effectively balances social rights and individual rights. However, health policy concerning children is much closer to an individual protective or privacy model than a community protective or public health model. Community protective measures tend to be reserved for emergency situations (like outbreaks of TB or, more recently, Severe Acute Respiratory Syndrome in Toronto). There is a third dimension, to be explored in this paper, to add to the privacy–public health dichotomy, and that is rights-contingent groups, such as children, who are particularly vulnerable because their rights are largely contingent on rights guaranteed to, and claimed by, others (such as parents). Thus, the location of responsibility and, by extension, the existence of rights is critical to understanding and analysing the vulnerability of different groups of people and the public health and health policy measures available to address infection and inequality among them.

As explained in the introduction, this paper will examine the content of the right to health care for children in Canada and the state's capacity for recognizing that right. Such an investigation will reveal important information about the conceptualization of 'the child' (as individual or as situated within and constituent of a family) and its implications for public policy. It will also indicate something about the abilities of Canadian governments and the health system to respond to the needs of diverse and vulnerable populations. The global health agenda for children, evident in international human rights documents and development goals, has established an undeniable 'right' to health and well-being for children and, as such, important standards for national policy development. Each signatory to these documents determines how to recognize this right within difficult budgetary, ethical, and political circumstances.

Health and Human Rights

The current global agenda for health makes children a priority. The rights of children to health care are enumerated in such documents as the International Covenant on Civil and Political Rights, article 24, the U.N. Convention on the Rights of the Child, the Universal Declaration of Human Rights, articles 16 (3) and 25 (2), and The International Covenant on Economic, Social, and Cultural Rights, article 12 (2a) (these documents also contain normative declarations about education rights), and are expressed in the United Nations' Millennium Development Goals. These rights are protected, it is hoped, by individual signatory nation states, and to some extent (if only rhetorically) by the international organizations that have declared them. As with other human rights covenants, these are ethical standards rather than binding legal arrangements. Human rights violations are addressed primarily through informal mechanisms, such as international pressure and embarrassment, as well as through sporadic, multilateral or bilateral, sanctioning exercises.

These exercises tend to punish disproportionately 'offenders' in the developing world. The United Nations has admonished Canada for its record in recognizing aboriginal rights, and the United States is widely criticized by international organizations for its continued legalization and use of capital punishment, but neither country has been held accountable by these judgments. The governments of developing countries, however, are routinely made responsible, through economic or political sanctions, for their human rights abuses. One of the most obvious examples might be the economic embargo imposed on South Africa during apartheid.

The failure of states to recognize in practice global human rights commitments is particularly damaging for children. The rhetorical significance of the inclusion of children in human rights legislation is significant, but insufficient. In the sections that follow, I will explain global commitments to children's (human) rights and identify the gaps that remain between these promises and their fulfilment in practice. I will do this by examining the case of entitlement to health services in Canada.

The Status of Children in International Human Rights Documents

One of the main problems of policy development as it pertains to children is their dual status as individual citizens and members of families. This problem is also evident in the philosophical predicates of global health and human rights guarantees. While many chapters in this volume make a convincing case for consideration of children as unique moral agents, their dependency cannot be separated from their status. That is to say, children are not completely independent citizens who can or ought to act autonomously. Fortunately, the very substance of human rights, its protective purpose rather than, say, an enabling function, does not contradict this reality.

The International Covenant on Civil and Political Rights identifies the full range of civil and political rights that ought to be accorded to children as individuals. Article 24 is unequivocal:

1. Every child shall have, without any discrimination as to race, colour, sex, language, religion, national or social origin, property or birth, the right to such measures of protection as are required by his status as a minor, on the part of his family, society and the State.
2. Every child shall be registered immediately after birth and shall have a name.
3. Every child has the right to acquire a nationality.

Unlike the documents that deal with social rights (to be considered subsequently), these rights are distinctly procedural and formal in nature: they deal with status and access to other rights, privileges, and benefits of citizenship. Respect for social rights is contingent on respect for these civil and political rights.

The most comprehensive formulation of children's rights is the United Nations' Convention on the Rights of the Child. This document, ratified in 1989 by all countries except two (the United States and Somalia), makes it clear that

Children are individuals. They have equal status with adults as members of the human family. Children are neither the possessions of parents nor of the state, nor are they mere people-in-the-making. Governments are morally obliged to recognize the full spectrum of human rights for all children. Using the Convention's definition of children as all human beings being below the age of 18, a large portion indeed of the world's population must be considered. (UNICEF, 2005)

The CRC further recognizes that children constitute a 'special case' for human rights. Children are at the same time unique social contributors and especially vulnerable. According to UNICEF:

The healthy development of children is crucial to the future well-being of any society; Children start life as totally dependent beings; The actions – or inactions – of government impact children more strongly than any other group in society; Children's views are rarely heard and rarely considered in the political process; Many changes in society are having a disproportionate – and often negative – impact on children; The costs to society of failing its children are huge; The global trend of urbanization has taken an especially severe toll on children. (Ibid.)

The same UNICEF report explains that the CRC addresses this vulnerability in the following manner:

It spells out the basic human rights that children everywhere — without discrimination — have: the right to survival; to develop to the fullest; to protection from harmful influences, abuse and exploitation; and to participate fully in family, cultural and social life. Every right spelled out in the convention is inherent to the human dignity and harmonious development of every child. The Convention protects children's rights by setting standards in health care, education and legal, civil and social services. These standards are benchmarks against which progress can be assessed. States that are party to the Convention are obliged to develop and undertake all actions and policies in the light of the best interests of the child. (Ibid.)

Although the CRC seems to manage well, in its language, the unique situation of the child as a dependent rights bearer, other documents seem to privilege the view of children-as-responsibility-of-family over children as individual moral agents. It also implicitly insists on the social dimensions of human rights. For example, the Universal Declaration of Human Rights (UDHR) (Articles 16 (3) and 25 (2)), explicitly states that 'the family is the natural and fundamental group unit of society and is entitled to protection by society and the State.'

The protection for families that is afforded by this declaration is consistent with the view that children are the responsibilities of their families and their rights are exercised within the familial relationship of dependency, not independently. By protecting families, the declaration seeks to exalt familial relationships (although it does not define them) and secure families' abilities to protect and care for their members. It is significant that this group-based understanding of entitlement, rather than a more individualistic model, is fundamental to this human rights declaration.

The UDHR further demonstrates the social dynamic of human

rights claims, and widens the definition of family, declared above to be the fundamental unit of society. Article 25 (2) states that 'motherhood and childhood are entitled to special care and assistance. All children, whether born in or out of wedlock, shall enjoy the same social protection.' To be sure, all rights, at their foundations, are social protections that inform or create normative standards concerning the relationship between individuals, groups, and the state. That is to say, they declare what ought to be done and thereby set important standards for law and public policy formulation. The position that motherhood and childhood are entitled to special care and assistance might be widely accepted, but has been respected or recognized in very different ways in different contexts. This article obligates states to act, and thus provides a prescriptive dimension to the declaration of the family as the fundamental unit of society. Such prescriptions have been realized in public policy concerning maternity and parental leave, medical and dental care, entitlement to nutritional supplements, and tax credits, for example. In developing countries, the focus is on the fulfilment of basic needs (food, potable water, nutritional supplements, access to hospitals and clinics for birthing), whereas in developed countries public policy seems to focus on supplemental benefits for low income children and families. In Canada, as explained, there is a universal health system that provides service and care to all citizens regardless of wealth or income level, or ability to pay. Health benefits are not linked to employment, therefore entitlement to health care is not (for the most part) contingent on earning, and time out of the paid labour force (such as parental leave) does not affect ability to access health insurance or services. Provincial governments extend additional services to children in recognition of their vulnerability and importance as future social contributors. And in both developed and developing countries there is much done at local levels by public health units to promote healthy children and families.

Thus, the human right to health care is given substance by broader guarantees to mothers and children. It is also proclaimed in documents dedicated to social rights and global health goals. The International Covenant on Economic, Social, and Cultural Rights, article 12 (2a) enumerates the following rights:

1. The States Parties to the present Covenant recognize the right of everyone to the enjoyment of the highest attainable standard of physical and mental health.

2. The steps to be taken by the States Parties to the present Covenant to achieve the full realization of this right shall include those necessary for:
   a. The provision for the reduction of the stillbirth rate and of infant mortality and for the healthy development of the child;

Such indicators serve as important markers for the standard of living in a country. The ability of a health system to effectively provide care for pregnant women and children says a great deal about a society's level of development, commitment to equality and fairness, and capacities in technology and human capital. According to the Pan American Health Organization (PAHO), Canada's rates of stillbirth and infant mortality (the infant mortality rate for 2003 is five females and six males per 1000 live births) are among the lowest in the world, and the absolute lowest within its region of the Americas (WHO, 2005a; PAHO, 2005). However, as the Pan American Health Organization explains: 'Infant mortality rates vary substantially among the Canadian provinces and territories, with higher rates found in northern areas and in regions with a larger percentage of Aboriginal peoples; some Aboriginal populations experience infant mortality rates twice as high as the national rate' (PAHO, 2002, vol. 2, p. 126).

These figures provide evidence that the country is delivering on some human rights promises (overall rates of infant mortality are low), while violating others (commitments to equality, non-discrimination, and recognition for aboriginal peoples). It is much more difficult to measure 'healthy development of the child,' which would likely be demonstrated through multiple public policies, such as those relevant to health and education. In addition, the right to health for children is substantiated by the WHO's Millennium Development Goals. Set in 2000, these goals establish targets for progress concerning maternal and child health (WHO, 2005, p. 16–19). It should also be noted that many children's rights are contingent on, or bound within, rights for women (as childbearers, mothers, and caregivers). Taken together, these commitments demonstrate the centrality of health care and health rights to the exercise of other human rights, such as the right to live, work, vote, and own property.

These international human rights documents clearly indicate that there are health rights for children, although they are normative declarations, and perhaps morally binding (Canada is a signatory to all the declarations and covenants examined in this chapter), but not enforceable or formally sanctionable covenants. Further, there is evidence in the documents of respect for both family-centred and individual-protective models of human rights. Protection for families is not equivalent to deference: the documents seem to suggest that families are incontrovertible facts of dynamic human existence, and the protection of other human rights is often contingent on respect for family structures. However, responsibility for children's health and well-being is shared among families, communities, and states. Therefore, children as individuals, and as a sub-population, have relationships with states. In fact, all of these human rights documents recognize and insist on state (and not family) action in order to realize the rights of children.

At the state level, national goals are similarly important. As will be explained in the following sections, the Canadian federal government has set standards for the development of children, although the provinces have constitutional responsibility for creating specific policy. Policy responses include entitlements to additional services for children, and such entitlements differ widely from one province to the next. At the local level, which is under the purview of the provincial governments, there are numerous services aimed at improving maternal and child health through public health programs.

Children's Health Policy in Canada

In Canada there is little health policy that directly addresses the needs of children. Canada has a universal health system, which means that all citizens – children, adults, the elderly – are entitled to the same physician and hospital services. Such universality might render children's health policy unnecessary in the way that women's health policy might be unnecessary. If everyone in society is publicly insured for health services, then why should specific populations generate a need for 'differentiated' health policy? The very logic of universality seems to preclude this. By universal standards, no individual citizen or group of citizens is more important or deserving than any other. To the contrary, universal social programs, conceived as social rights, make benefits available to all citizens on equal terms and conditions, regardless of wealth or income level (Marshall, 1964). Benefits are delivered according to medical need, not the ability to pay for services, or membership in one sub-population or another.

Health care in Canada is an area of exclusive provincial jurisdiction, and each province has developed its own health system. Although there is considerable interprovincial consistency, programs and services differ from one province to the next (see table 5.1). This is especially true for children, in that provincial governments have responded to the vulnerability of children (in terms of both stage of life and degree of dependency within families) with additional policy entitlements. Most of these differential entitlements are delivered in the form of dental and optometric services, and either through the universal program or income-contingent benefits. For example, regular eye examinations for children are covered by provincial insurance plans in British Columbia and Manitoba (for children under 19), Saskatchewan, Quebec (for children under 18), Ontario (for children under 20), and Nova Scotia (for children under 10). In Prince Edward Island, Quebec, and Newfoundland preventative dental services are provided for all children aged three to 16 (PEI) and under 10 (Quebec) or 13 (Newfoundland). All provinces have numerous services (optometric, dental, pharmaceutical, mental health) that are available to children in low income families (in some instances these benefits are tied to social assistance eligibility; in others, benefits are determined by different eligibility thresholds). Childhood immunizations are covered in all provinces.

Intergovernmental Frameworks for Early Childhood Development

As is evident from the preceding description of provincial programs for child health, there are no national standards directly pertaining to children's health. The involvement of the federal government in this area, through Health Canada (rather than indirectly through transfer payments made to the provinces), is limited to health promotion and maintenance campaigns: warnings about drug recalls, information on the dangers of smoking, alcohol, and drugs, and on nutritional targets, recommendations for physical activity levels, and guidelines for immunizations.

In 2000 the Federal/Provincial/Territorial Council on Social Policy Renewal released the final version of its Children's Agenda. The policy, which is properly considered to be national but not federal, makes many formidable rhetorical commitments to improving the welfare of children and their families. The policy document states:

> The Government of Canada has made helping children and their families a priority of its long-term commitment to a better quality of life. Healthy

Table 5.1 Provincial programs and services

Province	Dental coverage	Optometric (regular eye exams)	Child immunizations
Ontario	No basic dental covered	**Under 20** – 1 exam per year covered	All basic childhood immunizations covered
Manitoba	No basic dental covered	**Under 19** – one complete routine eye exam allowed every two years	All basic childhood immunizations covered
Alberta	No basic dental covered	**Under 19** – 1 complete exam, 1 partial exam, and 1 diagnostic procedure per year covered	All basic childhood immunizations covered
Saskatchewan	No basic dental covered; if receiving family benefit – coverage of basic services until age 18	**Under 18** – 1 exam per year covered; basic eyeglasses covered if receiving family health benefit	All basic childhood immunizations covered
Quebec	**Under 10** – Exam is covered once a year; after age 10 not covered	**Under 18** – 1 exam per year covered	All basic childhood immunizations covered
Nova Scotia	**Under 10** – Preventative dental covered (once a year); if receiving community services, coverage continues (social assistance)	**Under 10** – 1 exam every two years covered	All basic childhood immunizations covered

children, secure families and vibrant communities are all essential in defining quality of life in Canada.

Current evidence suggests that the early years of childhood are especially vital to a child's development and future ability to learn. Promoting early childhood development can have long term benefits that extend throughout children's lives.

The Government of Canada plays a major role in supporting Canadian families and their children *through strong income support*. (Canada 2000; emphasis added)

Table 5.1 (*continued*)

Province	Dental coverage	Optometric (regular eye exams)	Child immunizations
Prince Edward Island	**Ages 3–16** – Basic dental covered; pay $15, max. $35/year for child; pay 20% of treatment cost if required; if income below $30,000, gov't. will cover the 20%	No examinations covered	All basic childhood immunizations covered
Newfoundland	**Under 13** – Basic dental covered; if receiving social assistance, basic dental coverage provided from ages 13–17	No examinations covered	All basic childhood immunizations covered
New Brunswick	No basic dental covered	No examinations covered	All basic childhood immunizations covered
British Columbia	No basic dental covered Dental care for children available for those who qualify for premium assistance (adjusted net income below $28,000, combined) until children reach age 18, up to max of $700	**Under 19** – 1 exam per year covered	All basic childhood immunizations are covered

The National Children's Agenda was the initial iteration, the foundation, of the shared vision for Canada's children. It has been built upon in rhetorical ways (see Canada, 2004: *A Canada Fit for Children*). It has also resulted in the creation of concrete policy frameworks, the first of which was the September 2000 federal/provincial/territorial Early Childhood Development Agreement. In this multilateral framework, the provinces and the federal government agreed in principle to develop or enhance a range of programs for early childhood care and development, including 'promoting healthy pregnancy, birth, and infancy; improving parenting and family supports; strengthening early childhood development, learning and care; and strengthening community supports' (Canada 2005). The federal government committed to transfer '$3.2 billion between 2001 and 2008 to provinces and territories to support their investments in early childhood development programs and services' (ibid.), as well as to fund and develop a parallel early childhood program for aboriginal children.

This multilateral framework provided the context for a number of specific, bilateral agreements between the federal government and particular provincial governments. These agreements continued to target low socio-economic status populations, although many of the programs offered universal benefits (such as standards for child care). Some of the most promising components included the promotion of early childhood development through learning activities and environments in child care facilities, and the creating and enhancing of programs for special-needs children. Most of these programs were negotiated by, and intended to be delivered through, social services departments. However, one of the first major policy decisions of Stephen Harper's Conservative government (elected in 2006) was the cancellation of the existing agreements and funding for the Children's Agenda, which has created even greater uncertainty in this policy field.

Nonetheless, the federal initiatives, as developed over a period of thirteen years by Liberal governments, demonstrate two important trends, which are not likely to be reversed by a Conservative federal government. The first is that rhetorical commitments to the improvement of children's health and welfare are strong and are consistent with the evidence and with widespread beliefs about early childhood development. Few people would challenge the idea that children are our future, or disagree that the early years of a child's life constitute a critical, formative stage. The second trend is that measures for the improvement of children's health and welfare are targeted at children in low income families and are channelled through social assistance and income maintenance programs rather than health programs per se. Thus, there are two main constituencies for national children's health policy: (1) children in low income families (LIFs) and (2) aboriginal children and their families. The latter is a unique case because aboriginal peoples are within the constitutional jurisdiction of the federal government and have unique health needs. The important topic of aboriginal children's health is not addressed here, as the focus is on health services delivered by the provinces.

The children's health policy field is fractured and inconsistent and does not fit exclusively within the arena of health policy. Rather, children's health care is created and developed indirectly through social assistance or income maintenance policies. To be sure, this policy area is closely, if not inextricably, related to health. It is well known that socio-economic status (SES) has a profound effect on health. Poorer people tend to have worse health than richer people. In part, this is explained by limited access to those products and services not provided under the public insurance plan (such as pharmaceuticals and dental care). But there is another dimension of this effect. Health, it seems, is affected by relative economic disparity or income distribution within societies. In other words, in societies that have a wide polarization between the rich and poor, that have a substantial gap between the highest and lowest SES, health indicators are worse for those of low SES and for society as a whole (Farmer, 1999; Wilkinson, 1994). Therefore, if a society is concerned about health and children, then it must also be concerned with inequality.

Moreover, children's health should be of particular concern because children, much more so than adults, are constrained by their circumstances. Children cannot change jobs or work additional hours to pay for uninsured health services. They cannot move to a better environment. They do not vote, which means that they are not political actors on their own behalf. They are, for better or worse, stuck in their families and cannot exercise much choice. As a result, superior moral status tends to be accorded to children – they are innocent and deserving because they are fully dependent on the circumstances of their families – and they ought to be protected by the state from the negative consequences of those circumstances.

Further, general intuitions about choices and circumstances do not seem to hold for children. Many people would agree that an able-bodied person who chooses not to work does not deserve, or ought not to be entitled to, compensation for his or her joblessness. For children, the element of choice is absent from moral consideration, and deservedness or entitlement is linked to or extracted from their powerlessness. The traditional view, or conservative rejoinder to this view of children's innocence, is that children are the responsibility of their parents, who exercise choice and discretion on their behalf. The state is not obligated to provide for children – families are. However, this view is being replaced with a more individualistic policy orientation in both Canada and the United States. There seems to be a shift under way (Brooks & Miljan, 2003) from the family-centred view that children are the responsibility of their parents to the view that children are individuals and as such should develop or have access to a relationship with the state that is independent of their family unit.

In part, this shift is a response to changing configurations of the family; there are more single-parent families and blended families, for instance. The changing of family structures means revisiting ideas about obligations and the ways in which each individual (child or adult) is contained or not contained within families, societies, and the state. Evidence of this shift in understanding and consequent policy pertaining to children, health, and inequality can be found by examining social-assistance and income-maintenance policy in Canada.

The political value of social-assistance and income-maintenance policy is clearly inferior to that of health care. As Carolyn Tuohy explains, 'Canadian social policy presents a puzzle. On the one hand, it comprises a relatively niggardly set of policies directed at income security – notably public pensions and social assistance ... On the other hand, Canada has adopted a system of national health insurance that is both generous and outstandingly popular' (Tuohy, 1993, p. 275). At the time of Tuohy's assessment, her forecast was as follows: 'In the income maintenance arena ... where policies on balance enjoy neither the popular nor the elite support accorded to medicare, the prospects for erosion and fragmentation in a decentralized system appear greater' (ibid., p. 302). Since then, social assistance and income maintenance policies, including components directed at children, have developed in a direction consistent with Tuohy's evaluation. This policy field has been further devalued as a result of continued changes to the fiscal arrangements between the provinces and the federal government. In 1995 the federal government introduced the Canada Health and Social Transfer (CHST), which combined funding for health care, post-secondary education, and social assistance. What this meant for social assistance was that federal funds to the provinces for welfare spending would no longer be made through a shared-cost program (the Canada Assistance Plan [CAP]), but through a block grant. Provinces would receive less money and would have to set priorities among three social policy areas. To no one's surprise, health care fared the best and social assistance the worst. With the federal government's reduced role came greater provincial policy variance. With lack of uniformity in income distribution came, as could be predicted, greater inequality. As James Rice explains:

The shift from CAP and EPF to the CHST means that provinces no longer need to provide support to people 'in need' regardless of their category. They can now decide to provide benefits to some groups and not to others. Many provinces have tightened their regulations regarding single unemployed males. Some have tightened their regulations regarding mothers with children. Others have introduced the requirement that applicants meet mandatory work conditions before receiving social assistance. (Rice, 2002, p. 114)

In short, social welfare policy does not provide a reliable pattern of services for all children who might need them or be entitled to them. This is the result of weak political commitment and insufficient resource allocation by both the federal government and the provinces. The variability produced is threatening to children in low income families and to the Canadian population in general (in that the situation creates greater inequality). It also violates Canada's human rights commitments.

Children's Rights and the *Canadian Charter of Rights and Freedoms*

The preceding section examined the manner in which children's entitlements to health care are recognized in or marginalized through policies in both the health and welfare policy sectors. In this section I examine the degree to which children's rights can be articulated and determined, not in contingent ways (in relation to socio-economic status, for instance), but in unequivocal terms through court decisions. Of particular political importance are those that consider various claims against the rights guaranteed by the *Charter of Rights and Freedoms*.

The courts are significant because they offer children an important avenue for participation in the democratic process (which excludes them in other activities, such as voting). The decisions of courts in *Charter* cases are binding on governments, which means that they shape policies. In recent years, the courts have been involved in decision making concerning the distribution of health care across populations. In some of these cases, notably *B. (R.) v. Children's Aid Society of Metropolitan Toronto* and *Auton (Guardian ad litem of) v. British Columbia (Attorney General)*, the health and fundamental human rights in question involved children.

In *B. (R.) v. Children's Aid Society of Metropolitan Toronto*, the courts were asked to decide on the constitutionality of the intervention of the Children's Aid Society in overriding parental rights (as well as individual rights to religious expression and practice). The parents of S.B., a month-old infant who required intensive medical care, refused to consent to a blood transfusion for their baby on religious grounds (the parents are Jehovah's Witnesses). The Children's Aid Society of Metropolitan Toronto was granted temporary custody of S.B. so that the blood transfusion could be administered, if necessary. The intervention was aimed at protecting the health and interests of the infant. The parents objected, claiming that such an intervention breached their freedom of religion as guaranteed in the *Charter*. A series of court cases ensued.

The Supreme Court of Canada decided that the intervention of the Children's Aid Society did not constitute a violation of the parent's rights, which are not conferred in absolute terms but subject to the 'reasonable limits' of a free and just society. Furthermore, on the matter of a parent's fiduciary rights, the court determined the following:

> The right to nurture a child, to care for its development, and to make decisions for it in fundamental matters such as medical care, are part of the liberty interest of a parent. The common law has long recognized that parents are in the best position to take care of their children and make all the decisions necessary to ensure their well-being. This recognition was based on the presumption that parents act in the best interest of their child. Although the philosophy underlying state intervention has changed over time, most contemporary statutes dealing with child protection matters, and in particular the Ontario Act, while focusing on the best interest of the child, favour minimal intervention. In recent years, courts have expressed some reluctance to interfere with parental rights, and state intervention has been tolerated only when necessity was demonstrated, thereby confirming that the parental interest in bringing up, nurturing and caring for a child, including medical care and moral upbringing, is an individual interest of fundamental importance to our society.
>
> While parents bear responsibilities toward their children, they must enjoy correlative rights to exercise them, given the fundamental importance of choice and personal autonomy in our society. Although this liberty interest is not a parental right tantamount to a right of property in children, our society is far from having repudiated the privileged role parents exercise in the upbringing of their children. This role translates into a protected sphere of parental decision-making which is rooted in the presumption that parents should make important decisions affecting

their children both because parents are more likely to appreciate the best interests of their children and because the state is ill-equipped to make such decisions itself. While the state may intervene when it considers it necessary to safeguard the child's autonomy or health, such intervention must be justified. (S.C.R. 317–18)

As explained, such a justification was compelling in this case. The state's intervention is legitimate when the child's 'autonomy or health' is at risk. Parental responsibility, then, is expected to be all-encompassing for children, although not 'tantamount to a right of property.' This view is reflected in the policies discussed concerning universal health care and supplementary benefits for children of families receiving social assistance. State action is confined to extreme necessity; benefits are not granted to children as a group.

This approach/orientation is also reflected in *Auton (Guardian ad litem of) v. British Columbia (Attorney General)*. In this case, parents of autistic children sought provincial funding for ABI/IBI therapy, an early treatment for autism. The Supreme Court of Canada overturned the BC Supreme Court's decision to require the provincial government to compensate the families for the denial of the treatment, which it believed to be an infringement of basic equality rights. On appeal, the Supreme Court of Canada determined that the BC government's decision to deny funding for the service was not discriminatory because the treatment was not considered a 'core service' and was not provided by official 'health care practitioners,' both key conditions of provincial legislation. The scheme whereby some non-core services were funded was by its nature partial, therefore exclusions were to be expected and were in accordance with the purposes of the plan itself.

This case is significant to the study of children's rights for a few reasons. First, it demonstrates that children are rights bearers, and have access to the court system, which can be considered a direct mode of political participation. The *Charter* enumerates fundamental individual and, in some cases, group-based rights, and in so doing expands the rights dialogue in Canada. This national rights orientation, as with global human rights guarantees, is considered to be of particular importance to marginalized groups. However, the case also indicates that there is no constitutional preference for children's rights over the rights accorded to all individual Canadian citizens. Children, as a vulnerable group, have no special status. Their rights are human rights, no more and no less. This view recognizes the worth of children by according them the same rights accorded to adults, at the same time that it confirms their dependency on their families (in this case for paying for treatment that is not funded by the provincial health plan).

Conclusion: The Global Agenda and National Implementation

The aim of the human rights guarantees examined in the first part of this chapter is to provide access to basic health care for children in all parts of the world, although the assumption seems to be that these rights need recognition in the developing world in particular, and that developed countries have an obligation to assist in achieving that end. In many developed countries, however, there are human rights needs concerning the health of children that are not being met. In countries with universal health systems, such as Canada, children are assumed to be accommodated within the pattern of universal entitlement, so there are few programs targeted specifically at that population. However, in recent years, as universal systems have had to ration services and restrict entitlement, it has become apparent that children constitute a particularly vulnerable population.

If Canada is going to continue to fulfil its international human rights commitments, then a more deliberate and nationally consistent approach is required. In order to reduce the inequality that bears negatively on health, programs for children will have to be developed within the field of health policy proper. That is to say, additional programs and services for children should be addressed through the universal health system rather than as a series of income-contingent supplementary benefits through social-welfare or income-maintenance policies. Such a prescription seems to demand that children are regarded as individual rights-bearers or citizens, nurtured, cared-for, and raised within families. Consequently, children's rights to health care should not be completely dependent on the capacities and capabilities of their families. Provincial programs reflect this belief, and current approaches might be sufficient if social welfare policy were a higher political priority. As it stands, however, children's access to vision care, prostheses, dental services, and prescription drugs is contingent on family circumstances and (income-based) state provision. As child poverty rates increase, there is no indication that governments are going to restructure priorities so that policy action matches need. Moreover, changing configurations of family challenge old notions of care and responsibility. If children's human rights are to be taken seriously, then entitlements must be consistent among jurisdictions and fully recognized regardless of circumstances; they must be conceived and addressed beyond the family, irrespective of wealth or income level. This is to argue for differential entitlement for children as a marginalized population that requires not just greater protection, but greater benefits delivered through health policy. This pattern of distribution is not currently reflected in public policy trends, yet seems to be consistent with global human rights commitments concerning children. The Harper government's recent announcement of the establishment of targets for health care wait times for children is a step in the direction of international and national policy congruency. It remains to be seen whether policy and rights for children will progress further in this direction.

REFERENCES

Auton (Guardian ad litem of) v. British Columbia (Attorney General), 2004 SCC 78, [2004] 3 S.C.R. 657.

B. (R.) v. Children's Aid Society of Metropolitan Toronto, [1995] 1 S.C.R. 315.

Brooks, S., & Miljan, L. (2003). *Public Policy in Canada: An Introduction*. Toronto: Oxford.

Canada (2005). Human Resources and Social Development Canada. 'Investing in our future: Government of Canada reports on progress in early childhood development. February 28. Retrieved March 3, 2006, from http://www.sdc.gc.ca/en/cs/comm/sd/news/2005/050228a.shtml

Canada (2004). *A Canada fit for children: Canada's plan of action in response to the May 2002 United Nations Special Session on Children*. Ottawa: Human Resources and Social Development Canada.

Canada (2000). *Supporting families and children: Government of Canada initiatives*. Sept. 20. http://www.socialunion.ca/nca_e.html. Retrieved March 3, 2006

Deber, R. (1999). The use and misuse of economics. In M. A. Somerville (Ed.), *Do we care? Renewing Canada's commitment to health*. Montreal: McGill-Queen's University Press.

Farmer, P. (1999). *Infections and inequalities: The modern plagues*. Berkeley and Los Angeles: University of California Press.

Johnson, C. (2006). Health as culture and nationalism in Cuba. *Canadian Journal of Latin American and Caribbean Studies*, 31(61), 91–113.

PAHO (2005). *Health Situation in the Americas: Basic Indicators*.

PAHO (2002). *Health in the Americas*. Vols. 1 and 2.

Redden, C J. (2002a). *Health care, entitlement and citizenship*. Toronto: University of Toronto Press.

Redden, C.J. (2002b). Health care as citizenship development: Examining social rights and entitlement. *Canadian Journal of Political Science, 35*(1), 103–125.

Rice, J. (2002). Being poor in the best of times. In B. Doern (Ed.), *How Ottawa spends*. Oxford: Oxford University Press.

Robson-Haddow, J. (2004). *The key to tackling child poverty: Income support for immediate needs and assets for their future*. Ottawa: Caledon Institute for Social Policy.

Smith, M. (1995). Retrenching the sacred trust: Medicare and Canadian federalism. In F. Rocher & M. Smith (Eds.), *New trends in Canadian federalism*. Peterborough: Broadview Press.

Tarantola, D., & Gruskin, S. (2005). Children confronting HIV/AIDS: Charting the confluence of rights and health. In S. Gruskin, M. A. Grodin, G. G. Annas, & S. P. Marks (Eds.), *Perspectives on health and human rights*. New York: Routledge.

Tuohy, C. (1999). *Accidental logics: The dynamics of change in the health care arena in the United States, Britain and Canada*. New York: Oxford.

Tuohy, C. (1993). Social policy: Two worlds. In M. Atkinson (Ed.), *Governing Canada: Institutions and public policy*. Toronto: Harcourt Brace Jovanovich.

UNICEF (2005a). *Convention on the Rights of the Child*. Retrieved September 25, 2005, from http://www.unicef.org/crc/crc.htm

UNICEF (2005b). *Child poverty rates failing to improve in richest countries: Canada ranks 19th out of 26 OECD nations*. Retrieved October 6, 2006, from http://www.unicef.ca/news/displayNewsItem.php?id=119.

UNICEF (2007). *Child poverty report*. Retrieved March 27, 2007, from http://www.unicef.org/media/files/ChildPovertyReport.pdf

United Nations (1948). *Universal Declaration of Human Rights*.

United Nations (1966a). *International Covenant on Civil and Political Rights*.

United Nations (1966b). *International Covenant on Economic, Social, and cultural rights*.

United Nations (1989). *Convention on the Rights of the Child*.

Wilkinson, R. (1994). The epidemiological transition: From material scarcity to social disadvantage. *Daedalus, Fall*, 61–78.

WHO (2005a). *Canada health indicators*. Retrieved September 25, 2005, from http://www3.who.int/whosis/country/compare.cfm?country=CAN&indicator=MortChildMale,MortChildFem ale&language=english

WHO (2005b). *Health and millennium development goals: Keep the promise*. Geneva: World Health Organization.

6 There's No Place Like Home: The Child's Right to Family

MARJORIE AUNOS AND MAURICE FELDMAN

'The family is the basic unit of society and as such should be strengthened. It is entitled to receive comprehensive protection and support ... All institutions of society should respect children's rights and secure their well-being and render appropriate assistance to parents ... so that children can grow and develop in a safe and stable environment and in an atmosphere of happiness, love and understanding, bearing in mind that in different cultural, social and political systems, various forms of family exists.

UNICEF, *A World Fit for Its Children*

This quote comes from the United Nations Special Session on Children held on 8–10 May 2002, which was meant as a follow-up to the Convention on the Rights of the Child (CRC), adopted twelve years earlier. In this session, leaders from around the world reiterated that families should be provided with assistance and protection, as they are the first and primary unit in which children grow, learn, and develop (CRC, 1990, Preamble). Based on the spirit of the CRC, we see that promoting the rights of children partly means supporting the rights of families, as long as this is in the best interests of the child.

Introduction

Families are the cornerstone of most societies, and it is generally accepted that children do best growing up with their birth parents. Sometimes, a child's right to live with his or her birth parents is removed, because the child is being abused or neglected by the parents, or is at risk for maltreatment. In these cases, articles 3, 9 and 19 of the Convention are clear – decisions should be made in the best interests of the child and to protect him or her from abuse or neglect. Indeed, the right to be protected from harm and be raised in a safe, secure and stimulating environment sometimes conflicts with (and is seen as superseding) the right to maintain relationships with one's biological family (article 9; Quebec Youth Protection Act, 2002).

Despite the potential conflict between the child's right to protection and right to family, many youth protection acts maintain (as does the CRC) that the break-up of the natural family is the last resort, and that reasonable efforts should be made to provide supports to parents so that their children can remain with them in a secure and nurturing environment (CRC, articles 9, 18, 27; UNICEF, 2002). Unfortunately, sometimes it may be difficult to support a child's right to be with his/her biological parents when those parents present problems that may put the child at risk for maltreatment. Several types of parental conditions are thought to be risk factors for inadequate parenting, including substance abuse, mental illness, criminality, and intellectual disabilities. Parents with low IQs (referred to as intellectual disabilities – ID), for example, have been seen for decades as having more impediments to parenting than other parents owing to their cognitive limitations (Aunos & Feldman, 2002). In this chapter we will highlight the impediments to and supports for the child's right to family, using parents with ID as the model. Following the general guidelines of the CRC, we will begin by discussing the rights of children and see how these apply to children of parents with ID. We will also discuss parenting rights and supports for parents with ID. Then we will highlight the obstacles that the current system, itself, creates to stifle family preservation. Finally, we will present evidence-based interventions that help parents to support their children, so that the child's right to family is achieved whenever possible.

Parents with ID

Before beginning our discussion of children's rights to be with their families when there are concerns about the parents' capabilities, we will first briefly describe parents with ID. According to the newest definition of the American Association on Intellectual and Developmental Disabilities (AAIDD, previously known as AAMR) (Luckasson et al.,

2002), a person is diagnosed with intellectual disability if the person (1) has significant cognitive limitations – i.e., two standard deviations (plus or minus 5 points due to measure error) below the mean of the normative sample on standardized intelligence tests, (2) has significant limitations in adaptive skills as measured by a valid test, and if (3) these limitations occurred before the age of eighteen years. In other words, a person with a diagnosis of ID will often present difficulties in the areas of communication, academics, vocational skills, community living skills, problem-solving abilities, abstract reasoning, generalization, and social judgment (Éthier, Biron, Boutet, & Rivet, 1999; Whitman & Accardo, 1990).

Based on the AAIDD definition, persons with ID are a heterogeneous group. In other words, depending on the availability of supports and their personal characteristics, persons with ID can present different difficulties and strengths at different times of their lives. This new definition places an emphasis on the availability and adequacy of supports that allow the person to function independently in the community and take responsibilities (e.g., work, parenting).

Persons with ID who become parents are also a heterogeneous group, although most are usually able to care for themselves in the community with minimal supports (Booth & Booth, 1993; Feldman, 2002). Persons with ID who are less capable (e.g., require 24-hour support) usually do not have the opportunity to procreate or their children are removed at birth because it is quite clear that these individuals are not capable of looking after their own needs independently, let alone those of a child. Following the AAIDD definition, each parent with ID presents with strengths and difficulties, but their limitations and abilities may change and develop depending on circumstances (e.g., life stressors, stigma) and the available supports present at different moments of their lives (Feldman, 2002; Luckasson et al., 2002).

Children's Rights

Children of parents with ID have the same rights as any other children. They have the right to be adequately cared for, to be physically and mentally stimulated, to receive affection, and to be protected from any harm (Tymchuk, 1998). As mentioned in chapter 8 below, different articles of the CRC correspond to the rights of children in regard to their family and upbringing. This section will link the rights of children, the difficulties parents with ID face in respecting those rights, and how appropriate supports can help parents with ID in providing those rights to their children.

The Right to an Adequate Standard of Living

Article 27 of the Convention highlights the need and right of every child to receive appropriate care and stimulation in terms of his/her physical, mental, and social development. Parents with ID are often presumed to be less competent than parents without a disability and their children are often taken away at birth (Booth, 2000; Tymchuk & Feldman, 1991). These parents are seen as having difficulties in raising their children and providing an adequate environment that favours their child's development. But they also have the ability to learn the skills necessary to parent (Feldman, 1994). Several evidence-based parenting programs designed specifically for parents with ID have been validated over the past twenty-five years (e.g., Feldman, 1998; Llewellyn, McConnell, Russo, Mayes, & Honey, 2002; McGaw, Ball, & Clark, 2002; Tymchuk & Andron, 1992). It is quite clear from these studies that when programs take into account effective ways of teaching and supporting persons with ID, the parents can learn the complexities of parenting (although ongoing training may be needed to address new skills as the child ages) and provide an adequate standard of living to their family.

The Right to Live in an Adequate Physical Environment

Article 27 implies that the physical environment in which children live and develop needs to be enriched with stimulation and follow acceptable standards. Although these 'acceptable standards' are not clearly defined in the CRC, one can hypothesize that an acceptable environment includes elements such as its cleanliness, the provision of safety measures and accessibility to food and appropriate clothing.

According to some studies, the home environment provided by parents (mostly mothers) with ID is less adequate than that provided by parents who do not have an ID (Feldman, 1994; Feldman & Walton-Allen, 1997; Keltner, 1994). Providing a safe environment is somewhat difficult for parents with ID (Campion, 1995). These studies indicate that unsafe environments may be related to the lack of education parents with ID have about physical hazards and the protections needed when you have children. Following structured interventions, however, the safety of the home environment of parents with ID contained fewer potential hazards and fewer unsafe incidents occurred (Tymchuk, Hamada, Andron, & Anderson, 1990, 1993).

The Right to Live in a Nurturing Environment

Providing a safe and secure physical environment is primary, but article 27 also states that children need access to a positive caregiving environment and consistent interactions with their parents (and other caregivers) to promote their development. Although they may have difficulty expressing verbal and physical affection, most parents with ID love their children (Feldman, Sparks, & Case, 1993; Mandeville & Snodgrass, 1998). These parents want the best for their children: a good neighbourhood, home, education, friends, employment, and a family of their own (Mandeville & Snodgrass, 1998). Many of these parents know they need support to raise their children, but they want to be treated as adults and as parents (Booth & Booth, 2004; Mandeville & Snodgrass, 1998; Strike & McConnell, 2002).

Children of parents with ID are at a higher risk of developmental, language, and academic delays, and of emotional and behavioral problems (Feldman, Case, Towns, & Betel, 1985; Feldman & Walton-Allen, 1997; Lalande, Éthier, Rivest, & Boutet, 2002; Llewellyn, McConnell, Honey, Mayes, & Russo, 2003; Llewellyn, McConnell, Russo, Mayes, & Honey, 2002; McConnell, Llewellyn, Mayes, Russo, & Honey, 2003; McGaw, Ball, & Clark, 2002; O'Neill, 1985; Pixa-Kettner, 1999; Whitman & Accardo, 1990). Despite this increased risk, many children of parents with ID have no cognitive deficits or delays (Aunos et al., 2004; Feldman & Walton-Allen, 1997; Gath, 1988; Keltner, Wise, & Taylor, 1999; Morch, Skår & Andresgård, 1997; O'Neill, 1985).

Although a propensity for low intelligence in their offspring may be partly inherited, parents with ID (before intervention) tend not to engage in the kinds of parent–child interactions that stimulate child development (Feldman, Case, et al., 1985, 1998; Slater, 1986). Mothers with ID tend to be inconsistent, more directive, and more restrictive in their interactions with their children (Aunos et al., 2004). In particular, they often do not engage in warm, responsive, and stimulating interactions (Feldman, Sparks, & Case, 1993; Tymchuk & Andron, 1992). Results from specific programs where parents were taught interactional skills and use of positive reinforcement show that parents with

ID learned to engage in more positive interactions with their children (Feldman, Sparks, & Case, 1993; Keltner, Finn, & Shearer, 1995; Tymchuk & Andron, 1992; Slater, 1986). Importantly, following parental participation in an educational program, their children had significant developmental gains in language and social skills (Feldman, Sparks, & Case, 1993; Slater, 1986; Tymchuk & Andron, 1988).

Parents with ID are distressed that they cannot support their children in regard to their cognitive abilities and school work (Mandeville & Snodgrass, 1998). They know they especially need help in that area of child development. Article 27 does state that parents have the responsibility to provide conditions favourable to the child's development, but within the parents' own abilities and financial resources. Parents with ID realize their limitations in that area but cannot afford private tutors, for example, as most parents with ID are living under the poverty line. Again, article 27 foresees these difficulties and clearly mentions that in a case like this, the state should assist parents in providing adequate care through public assistance and the development of support programs.

The Right to Appropriate Health Care and Nutrition

A child needs to have appropriate health care and balanced nutrition in order to grow and develop in a healthy way. Article 24 of the Convention seeks to ensure that this fundamental right is respected for every child. Often parents with ID have inadequate knowledge of first-aid procedures, recognition of child illnesses, nutrition and feeding (Feldman, 1994; Tymchuk, 1992; Tymchuk, Hamada, Andron, & Anderson, 1990). Generally, parents with ID are not mal-intentioned towards their children; rather, they lack knowledge and experience with children and most lack adequate parenting role models from their own childhood (Crain & Millor, 1978; Glaun & Brown, 1999; Taylor et al., 1990; Tymchuk & Andron, 1990).

Available generic child-care informational materials and services are not adapted to the understanding and learning styles of parents with ID (Llewellyn, McConnell, Honey, Mayes, & Russo, 2003). Take, for instance, ubiquitous prenatal classes that cover many skills and subjects and usually assume that participants can read the informational materials provided. There is seldom any follow-up or adaptation to support parents in generalizing teachings in their natural environments or even in concretely practising skills. Interestingly enough, the CRC mandates, that in sections (d), (e) and (f) of article 24, governments, 'ensure appropriate pre-natal and post-natal health care for mothers,' that parents be 'informed ... and supported in the use of basic knowledge of child health and nutrition, ... hygiene ... and the prevention of accidents,' and that governments should develop such services to inform parents.

Supporting parents with ID in acquiring knowledge in nutrition and health care (and applying it to 'real' situations) has demonstrated positive results. With behavioural instructional methods and *in-vivo* practice situations, parents have learned basic childcare skills (Feldman & Case, 1997, 1999; Feldman, Case, & Sparks, 1992; Feldman, Ducharme, & Case, 1999) and how to provide a safe and secure environment (Feldman & Case, 1997; Llewellyn, McConnell, Honey, Mayes, & Russo, 2003; Tymchuk, 1992). Parents can even learn these skills using self-directed learning materials specifically geared to their learning style (Feldman, 2004). Moreover, their children have benefited from these teachings. For example, some malnourished children have gained weight after their parents were taught feeding and nutrition skills (Feldman, Garrick, & Case, 1997). Thus, as parents become more proficient through appropriate supports and teaching methods, their children's development and their health benefit, which in turn increases the likelihood of family continuance (Feldman et al., 1992; Feldman et al., 1993).

The Right to Education

Parents with ID know their own limitations and know that it is very hard for them to help their children with their homework, for example, and to stimulate cognitively their children as they age (Booth & Booth, 2004; Mandeville & Snodgrass, 1998; Strike & McConnell, 2002). They also, as mentioned earlier, do not have the financial resources to provide private help or tutorship to support their children. Nonetheless, children have the right to education, including early intervention (article 28). In the United States the Head Start program and Early Head Start (Smith, 1995) are two programs that were developed for at-risk, low-income families to enhance optimal development in their children. These programs have been demonstrated as being effective in attaining this goal. It is not clear whether children of parents with

ID benefit from Head Start–type interventions. Two more intensive, experimental pre-school programs did find improvements in the IQs of children of parents with ID (Garber, 1988; Ramey & Ramey, 1992). Offering a similar program specifically for children of parents with ID would respect articles 27 and 28, related to ensuring the development of children and their right to education.

The Right to Be Protected from Abuse and Neglect

Articles 19 and 20 of the Convention provide guidelines to ensure that children are protected from physical, emotional, and sexual abuse, or neglect. Those two articles also state that social programs should be implemented with families to ensure that those rights are respected and, if outside supports are not enough to protect children, that children be removed from the abusive or neglectful environment.

Many children of parents with ID are referred to Youth Protection Services because of concerns of potential or actual parental neglect and lack of supervision (Morch, Skår, & Andresgård, 1997; Ray, Rubenstein, & Russo, 1994). There is actually an over-representation of parents with ID in court systems (Booth, Booth, & McConnell, 2005; McConnell, Llewellyn, & Ferronato, 2000). Mostly, parents with ID are referred to youth protection more for reasons of neglect than for having been abusive towards their children (Glaun & Brown, 1999; Taylor et al., 1990; Tymchuk & Andron, 1992). When neglect is suspected, it is not related to a parent's lack of motivation, but rather, sometimes, a lack of knowledge of particular skills or the effect of other impending factors, such as increased stressors, depression, exploitation, and poverty (Feldman, 2004). Skill training programs are quite effective in improving basic child-care skills to minimize neglect (Feldman, 1994). When a child is abused, the perpetrator is often the (non-handicapped) male partner (Ronai, 1997). Leaving an abusive partner is difficult for any woman, especially when that woman has limited supports, as many mothers with ID do (Feldman, Case, & Sparks, 1992). Mothers with ID who were able to leave their abusive partner following the intervention of youth protection did not have their children returned despite the fact that the mother had no part in the abuse of the children, and was often being abused herself (Aunos et al., 2004; Booth & Booth, 2002).

The Right to Stay with One's Birth Family

The Convention also highlights the importance of being raised by one's own parents (and removal of the child as the last resort), as long as the best interests of the child are respected (articles 3, 9, 18, and 27). Despite the Convention and the considerable evidence that parents with ID can raise their children (albeit sometimes with specialized supports), recent surveys of custody decisions show that a disproportionate number of parents with ID still have their children taken away, often on the basis of presumed (rather than demonstrated) incompetence (Booth, Booth, & McConnell, 2005; Llewellyn, McConnell, & Ferronato, 2003). Although one must exercise caution in comparing different studies from different countries, it is possible that the percentage of parents losing their children may have decreased over the past twenty years from about 80 per cent (Schilling et al., 1982; Taylor et al., 1986; Feldman, Case, & Sparks, 1992) to about 50 per cent (Booth, Booth, & McConnell, 2005; Llewellyn, McConnell, & Ferronato, 2003). Nonetheless, many parents with ID lose their children; they are thirty to sixty times more likely to have their children appointed to youth protection services than any other parent (Booth & Booth, 2004). Parenting rights often are terminated without actual evidence of maltreatment and without attempts to provide appropriate supports and services (Booth & Booth, 1997, 2005; Llewellyn, McConnell, & Ferronato, 2003; Sackett, 1991; Samra-Grewal, 1999). Parents involved in specialized support programs show a much lower rate of child removal (Feldman, Case, & Sparks, 1992; Feldman, Sparks, & Case, 1993).

The Right to Preserve One's Own Identity

The Convention respects the importance of knowing one's family and keeping relationships with family members (article 8). In the case of a child who is separated from his or her parents, states should ensure that family relationships are maintained (as long as this is in the best interest of the child) (article 9). Like other children, children of parents with ID generally want to live with their 'real' parents (Booth & Booth, 1997). Some even report being closer to and feeling safer with their mothers with ID than with their fathers without ID (Booth & Booth, 1997; Ronai, 1997). As adults some may express positive feelings towards their parents, but they remain ambivalent over the way they were raised (Booth & Booth, 2000; Ronai, 1997). While appreciating the dire circumstances under which their parents tried to raise them (e.g., poverty, limited social supports, exploitation and stigmatization), the offspring also felt betrayed that their parents did not give them a better life and protect them from abuse (Ronai, 1997). In most cases, the offspring report that supportive others in their lives (e.g., grandmother, family friend, social service worker) made a significant positive impact on their quality of life (Booth & Booth, 1997; Ronai, 1997).

Nonetheless, between 34 per cent and 80 per cent of the children of parents with ID are placed in foster care, and up to 6 per cent of children of parents with ID have been adopted (Whitman & Accardo, 1990; Aunos et al., 2004; Booth & Booth, 1993, 1994; Feldman, Sparks, & Case, 1993; Mirfin-Veitch, Bray, Williams, Clarkson & Belton, 1999). Usually, placement occurs at birth, an early school age (i.e., six years old), or the early teenage years (Aunos et al., 2004; Morch et al., 1997). Often, no specific interventions are made in order to preserve their relationship between the children and their birth parents. Often, no explanations are given to parents as to why child removal was chosen over the provision of family supports (Booth & Booth, 2004).

The Right to Be Protected from Discrimination

Children's rights should be respected without discrimination, including being protected from discrimination brought on by a parent's disability (article 2). Persons with ID often have a history of stigmatization and discrimination (see chapter 13). When they become parents, their children, unfortunately, often suffer from such stigmatization and discrimination along with their parents (Perkins, Holburn, Deaux, Flory, & Vietze, 2002). The over-representation of parents with ID in court systems with a lack of evidence of abuse or neglect in most cases are only some examples of how that discrimination is expressed in real situations (Booth, Booth, & McConnell, 2005; McConnell, Llewellyn, & Ferronato, 2000). Court reports stereotypically portray parents with ID as being out of touch and grossly incompetent. Often the assessment methods used to reach these conclusions (that too often result in the child being removed) are inappropriate (e.g., based primarily on an IQ test and some hypothetical questions) or not even described (Tymchuk & Feldman, 1991; Swain & Cameron, 2003). More balanced and humanitarian alternatives are available (Aunos & Feldman, 2007a).

Although many would agree that parental competence is a social construct based on society's values and normative standards, it is often not well defined (Booth & Booth, 1993). Most jurisdictions fail to adequately and clearly define 'good parenting,' and as a result, vague and shifting criteria lend themselves to discriminatory application (Booth, 2000; Greene, Norman, Searle, Daniels, & Lubeck, 1995; McConnell & Llewellyn, 2000; Spencer, 2001). Indeed, the guidelines may be based on the assumption that a parent with ID simply cannot parent, period. For instance, a commonly used Canadian parent-capacity assessment explicitly assumes that a parent having ID per se necessarily has significant child-care deficits (Steinhauer, 1991). In the absence of a clear definition of competent parenting, parent-capacity assessments rely on the assessor's clinical judgment and biases (Aunos & Feldman, 2007a; Booth et al., 2005; Gelles, 2000; Mandel, Lehman, & Yuille, 1994; McConnell & Llewellyn, 2000; Munro, 1999). Sometimes the assessor may have no or limited knowledge or experience in working with and assessing competence in persons with ID, and too much weight is placed on the parent's IQ score (Booth, 2000; Campion, 1995; Tymchuk & Feldman, 1991; Spencer, 2001). Furthermore, although often used in parental competence hearings, it has been argued that the presence of a diagnosis of ID does not solely constitute legal grounds for removal of children, nor is adequate parenting a function of intelligence (Azar, 2002; Booth & Booth, 1993; Tucker & Johnson, 1989).

A second problem with the current system is that parents with ID often are held to stricter standards, owing in part to ambiguous definitions of parental competence, presumptions of incompetence, discriminatory attitudes, impoverished living conditions, and overzealous scrutiny (Booth & Booth, 1997, 2004; McConnell & Llewellyn, 2000). When the children are placed, it is often because of a perceived risk of maltreatment owing to the parent's presumed inability to adequately care for children. Frequently, no evidence is presented of actual maltreatment or of the provision of services and supports *appropriate for parents with ID* to increase their competence (Feldman, 2002; Tymchuk & Feldman, 1991; Swain & Cameron, 2003).

A third critique of the system is that unlike the reality for the rest of us, parents with ID are judged based on their potential to raise children on their own without supports (Booth et al., 2005; McConnell &

Llewellyn, 2000). Thus, the very need for support and services is often interpreted as evidence of the parents being 'dependent' on others and thus not being able to care for their children, thereby justifying the termination of parenting rights. This discriminatory practice creates a double bind for some parents with ID. If they admit they need help, then this admission could be used to justify attitudes that these individuals are not capable of parenting. On the other hand, if the parents reject needed services, then they are accused of not understanding the complexities of child-rearing and their own limitations in doing so; that response, too, is taken as evidence that they should not raise children.

Respecting Children's Rights and Supporting Families

Although there exists no prevalence rates of children born to parents with ID or of how many of these children are referred to youth protection in Canada, estimates in other countries show that around 60 per cent of children of parents with ID are referred to youth protection services (Booth et al., 2005; McConnell, Llewellyn, & Ferronato, 2000; Ray et al., 1994), with between 30 and 80 per cent of children of parents with ID placed out of the home (Booth, 2000). Although decisions to place children are taken to respect children's best interests, these decisions are not without any repercussions on the children's lives.

The severance of family ties is not without problems that may, in fact, be worse than trying to maintain the child at home (with appropriate supports and supervision). For instance, foster placements may result in child emotional and behavioural dysfunction that can last into adulthood (Cook-Fong, 2000; Steinhauer, 1991). Some children may develop lifelong feelings of abandonment, rejection, guilt, and anxiety over having been separated from their biological parents. Furthermore, the emotional and financial costs of foster care may greatly exceed efforts to keep the family together and the child protected (Cook-Fong, 2000; Mandel et al., 1994; Sackett, 1991).

On the other hand, there are documented beneficial effects in maintaining the family unit. Having a close, secure, and continuing emotional bond with their natural parents helps children develop their identity and helps them with their social adjustment and self-esteem (Booth & Booth, 1997). Many children who are placed want to have regular contacts or want to live with their biological families (Chapman, Wall, & Barth, 2004; Sackett, 1991). This need to keep contact with and know their natural family is mentioned and respected in the Convention (article 8).

Many families headed by parents with ID may require supports in raising their children or keeping incontact with them. They even may ask to be adequately supported to raise their children (Mandeville & Snodgrass, 1998; Strike & McConnell, 2002).

The CRC has several articles that highlight the importance of family supports in respecting children's rights. Article 4, for example, implies the need to assess social services and all systems that provide supports to families. This article also implies that governments have the responsibility to ensure that adequate funding is provided to those services that support families and responds to children's rights. Article 5 places the overall responsibility on governments to assist families in their role of raising children. This article implies (as do articles 18 and 27) that the state should provide families with essential supports and services that would help parents meet the physical, emotional, social, and intellectual needs of their children. Of course, supports should be in place in the natural family as long as it is in the best interests of the child (articles 19 and 20).

Protecting Children

Competence-Based Family Assessment

It is often assumed that most of the problems faced by the children of parents with ID are due to inadequate parental care. In turn, parental incompetence is blamed on the parent's cognitive limitations. Many authors now recognize, however, that many factors (common to the lives of persons with ID) in addition to, or instead of, low IQ adversely affect the parenting of persons with ID (Booth & Booth, 1994; Feldman, 2002; McConnell & Llewellyn, 2000; Tymchuk & Keltner, 1991).

Indeed, parents with ID face an inordinate number of obstacles to being effective parents and maintaining their parenting rights (Booth & Booth, 1994, 1997). These 'pressures' can undermine their ability to cope as parents. Many of these pressures are not unique to parents with ID and also affect the parenting abilities of parents without ID who are referred to youth protection (Booth & Booth, 1993). These impediments include, to name but a few, a history of ongoing victimization, exploitation, discrimination, and stigmatization; poverty; social isolation; lack of positive spousal and social support; poor physical health; mental health issues; and child health, developmental, and behaviour problems. According to certain authors, one of the main obstacles is the system itself – a system that blames the victim instead of providing necessary and appropriate supports that would allow the children to stay with their parents (Booth, 2000; Booth & Booth, 1997; Sackett, 1991). Not surprisingly, many parents with ID despair that the system is against them and they distrust (and are reticent to work with) youth protection and other workers (Aunos & Feldman, 2007b).

To account for the multitude of factors that may impinge on the par- enting capacity of parents with ID, Feldman (2002) developed an inter- actional model that looks at the interrelationships of potential risk and resilience factors. Other authors and researchers have also outlined the risk factors and advantage profiles of parents with ID (Tymchuk & Keltner, 1991).

What is noteworthy about Feldman's model is that it provides a framework for a more comprehensive and fair assessment of parenting competence in parents with ID. This model is based on ecological-transactional child outcome models developed by Bronfenbrenner (1979), Belsky (1984), Sameroff & Chandler (1975), and others. The model hypothesizes that cognitive limitations are but one of many factors that should be examined when evaluating parental competence in this population. This model accounts for variables such as social factors (e.g., stigmatization, discrimination), life history (e.g., a history of abuse, poor parent role models), socio-economic status (e.g., poverty, unemployment), parental health (e.g., chronic health prob- lems, depression), social support, and child characteristics (e.g., devel- opmental delay, behaviour problems) as moderating parental compe- tence of parents with ID.

Research is emerging that supports aspects of this model. Aunos et al. (2004) showed that mothers with ID are in the lowest percentile for physical and mental health status. Tymchuk (1993) had also demon- strated that mothers with ID have more symptoms of depression than mothers without ID who are of the same socio-economic status. Clearly, a parent suffering from physical and/or mental health prob- lems will find it difficult to provide optimal childcare. For instance, the negative effects of parental depression on parenting and child out- comes have been well documented (Downey & Coyne, 1990; Lovejoy, Graczyk, O'Hare, & Neuman, 2000; Taylor et al., 1990). Parents with ID also report significant stress and low levels of social support (Booth & Booth, 1993; Feldman, Léger, & Walton-Allen, 1997; Llewellyn, 1990), which were negatively correlated (Feldman, Varghese, Ramsay, & Rajska, 2002). Indeed, parents' satisfaction with supports was significantly correlated with their positive interactions with their children (Feldman, Varghese, et al., 2002). These findings illustrate the numerous factors that relate to parent and child outcomes and the interconnectedness of these variables as described in Feldman's (2002) model.

In that respect, a more equitable system would mandate that parenting assessments be comprehensive, taking into account the family's impediments and supports, and including *in vivo* observations of childcare skills (Aunos & Feldman, 2007b; Booth & Booth, 2004, 2005; Feldman, 2002; Tymchuk & Feldman, 1991). With such assessments, recommendations should be made regarding supports and services that may allow the child to remain with (or be returned to) the family and to no longer need protection (Aunos & Feldman, 2007a; Sackett, 1991). Youth protection laws and the CRC also agree that reasonable efforts should be made in providing counselling or any other type of supports to parents, when needed (articles 4, 18, 27; Greene et al., 1995).

Competence-Based Supports for Families

Multiple or inappropriate foster-care placements are detrimental to a child (Steinhauer, 1991). Studies regarding Intensive Family Preservation programs show positive results in keeping families together (Landy & Munro, 1998). As many factors seem to influence the parenting and coping skills of parents with ID, interventions should focus on increasing their abilities and decreasing the environmental pressures they face (Booth & Booth, 1997).

As illustrated above in different sections, many parenting programs have been developed and validated for parents with ID. The evidence-based interventions tend to be competence-based – that is, they objectively assess the family's strengths and needs and design interventions to address the needs (Feldman, 1994). Specific programs attempt to (a) increase parenting skills to target health, safety, and developmental needs of children and (b) decrease the environmental pressures that parents with ID face every day (Booth & Booth, 1997). The Parents Together program (Booth & Booth, 1999, 2003), for example, attained these two objectives by offering formalized group meetings focused on the specific needs and demands of parents with ID. Other programs, such as Step-By-Step Child-Care (Feldman & Case, 1993), focus more on developing specific childcare skills for parents of children aged zero to five years old. This evidence-based program provides workers with guidelines and checklists in order to facilitate the assessment, teaching, and evaluation of parenting skills (Feldman, 1998). It also offers self-instructional pictorial workbooks that allow parents to learn skills on their own (Feldman, 2004). Other programs aim more at enhancing parents' knowledge regarding safety measures and how to promote health in their children (Llewellyn, McConnell, Russo, Mayes, & Honey, 2002; Tymchuk, 2006). Evidence-based interventions to teach parenting skills to parents with ID rely on behavioural techniques such as task analysis, pictorial prompts, modelling, practice, feedback, and reinforcement (Aunos, 2000; Feldman, 1994, 1998).

The 'Two-Generation' Program for Children and Families

The 'Two-Generation' program model developed for Head Start and Early Head Start in the United States (Smith, 1995) offers a promising model for families where the parents have ID. As stated earlier, this model originally provided comprehensive services for at-risk, low-income families. The goal of a 'two-generation' program is to not only enhance optimal development in the children, but also to ensure that the family has the supports to do so. A focus on improving the quality of life and abilities of the parents is included.

What would a two-generation model look like for families headed by parents with ID? In many ways the nominal services and supports would be similar to what any low-income, at-risk family would need. These services could be divided up into those with a primary emphasis on the child and those with an emphasis on the parents and the family unit. Child supports would include (a) promotion of development though parent education, placement in a specialized pre-school (or high-quality day care), support in school, tutoring, provision of adequate nutrition and health care, and (b) protection, supervision, and crisis response, as needed. Intensive pre-school programs result in positive outcomes in the intellectual development of children of parents with ID (Garber, 1988; Lemieux, 2001; Ramey & Ramey, 1992).

The parental and family supports of a two-generation program could include (a) financial support, (b) a competence-based support network, (c) academic and vocational upgrading, (d) personal counselling, (e) transportation (especially in rural areas), (f) education on nutrition and health care, (g) housing, (h) advocacy support, and (i) crisis support (e.g., in the event of illness, eviction, abuse, loss of income). There are likely many more supports not listed above that would be needed for individual families.

Agency Collaboration

In order to make a two-generation program model work, either one (super) agency provides all the needed services or (more typically) multiple agencies collaborate and coordinate their services around the family. Unfortunately, it is common for parents with ID to have many workers from different agencies that do not coordinate their services. Each of these workers makes his or her own assessment of the family's needs and situation. Each of these workers also follow a certain mandate and have a certain role, weather it be that of youth protection or offering support to parents. Youth protection workers, for example, have the main mandate to protect children's rights and ensure that they are raised in a safe and non-abusive environment. Alternatively, workers from agencies whose mandate it is to support the rights of adults with ID in the community may strongly support their client's right to be a parent and identify supports to do so. Added to the mix are members of the family's natural support system (e.g., other family members, friends, neighbours) who are also giving advice and support to the parents, usually independently of each other and the service providers. Collaboration among all would allow for greater respect for children's rights to be protected and grow in a safe and nurturing environ-ment and parents' rights to be supported (Booth & Booth, 2005). The rationale of a two-generation program is to respect children's rights within the family system, when possible, and not to see family rights as impeding children's rights (Matava, 1994).

The many involved workers' mandates, opinions, priorities, and intervention plans may be in conflict. This state of affairs can become very confusing and stressful to parents with ID (Strike & McConnell, 2002). The effective collaboration of support and service partners in a two-generation program allows attending to the dual objectives of protecting children while supporting parents. In such a collaboration, partner agencies and the parents would design a process to derive consensus on priorities and objectives, and then determine which services would provide the most appropriate supports to the family in an efficient manner (Gilson, Bricourt, & Baskind, 1998; Lemieux, 2001). Agreements could be established whereby youth protection gradually withdraws supervision (if the child is at home) or slowly returns the child to the home (if the child had been removed) as the agencies and parents reach agreed-upon measurable objectives that place the child at decreased risk. These actions require considerable trust between agencies and the consent of the parents and agencies to share information.

Conclusion

In this chapter we have examined the child's right to be raised by his or her birth parents when there are concerns about the parent's competence to care for and protect the child. Although protection of the child is paramount (articles 19 and 20), the Convention clearly states that in order for the child to remain in the family and be safe, the parents have the right to be supported in their parenting role, as needed (articles 4, 5, 7, 8, 18, and 27). We noted how many of the child's rights are placed at risk when parents lack capacity. However, we also indicated how children's rights can be violated when they are removed from the home without any attempts to provide adequate and appropriate family supports.

In particular, children of parents with ID are at high risk for being removed, even when there is little direct evidence of child maltreatment. Their parents are simply judged as being incapable based on their low IQ or a label, although many factors, in addition to the parent's cognition limitations, play a role in determining parenting abilities. Evidence-based interventions exist that demonstrate that parents with ID can learn to be better parents and that their children benefit from intervention, too. Many of these families do not have access to these services before the child is removed. Future research should focus on ways of reducing the high prevalence of family discontinuance in these families. To reach this goal may require a change in society's attitudes towards parents with ID to reduce discriminatory parent-capacity assessments and custody decisions. In recognition of the very real risks some of these children face and of the parents' needs to improve their parenting abilities, more research is needed on adapted Family Preservation and Two-Generation intervention models that would allow the children to exercise their rights to be raised in safe and nurturing home environments.

REFERENCES

Aunos, M. (2000). Les programmes de formation aux habiletés parentales pour des adultes présentant une déficience intellectuelle. *La revue internationale de l'éducation familiale, 4,* 59–75.

Aunos, M., & Feldman, M. (2002). Attitudes on sexuality, sterilisation and parenting rights of persons with intellectual disabilities. *Journal of Applied Research on Intellectual Disabilities, 15,* 285–296.

Aunos, M., & Feldman, M. (2007a). Assessing parenting capacity in parents with intellectual disabilities. In C. Chamberland, S. Léveillé, and N. Trocmé (Eds.), *Des enfants à protéger, des adultes à aider: Deux univers à rapprocher* (pp. 223–240). Sainte-Foy: Presses de l'université du Québec.

Aunos, M., & Feldman, M. (2007b). Parenting by persons with an intellectual disability. In I. Brown and M. Percy (Eds.), *A Comprehensive Guide to Intellectual and Developmental Disabilities* (pp. 593–603). Baltimore, MD: Paul H. Brookes Publishing Co.

Aunos, M., Goupil, G., Feldman, M. (2004). Mothers with intellectual disabilities who do or do not have custody of their children. *Journal on Developmental Disabilities, 10,* 65–79.

Azar, S.T. (2002). Family research and the law: Can family research help Solomon? Contributions and challenges. In J.P. McHale & W.S. Grolnick (Eds.), *Retrospect and prospect in the psychological study of families* (pp. 283–320). Mahwah, NJ: Lawrence Erlbaum Associates.

Belsky, J. (1984). The determinants of parenting: A process model. *Child Development, 55,* 83–96.

Booth, T. (2000). Parents with learning difficulties, child protection and the courts. *Representing Children, 13,* 175–188.

Booth, T., & Booth, W. (1993). Parenting with learning difficulties: Lessons for practitioners. *British Journal of Social Work, 23,* 459–480.

Booth, T., & Booth, W. (1994). Working with parents with mental retardation: Lessons from research. *Journal of Developmental and Physical Disabilities, 6,* 23–41.

Booth, T., & Booth, W. (1997). *Exceptional childhoods, unexceptional children: Growing up with parents who have learning difficulties.* London, UK: Family Policies Studies Centre.

Booth, T., & Booth, W. (1999). Parents together: action research and advocacy support for parents with learning difficulties. *Health and Social Care in the Community, 7,* 464–474.

Booth, T., & Booth, W. (2000). Against the odds: Growing up with parents who have learning difficulties. *Mental Retardation, 38,* 1–14.

Booth, T., & Booth, W. (2002). Men in the lives of mothers with intellectual disabilities. *Journal of Applied Research in Intellectual Disabilities, 15*, 187–199.

Booth, T., & Booth, W. (2003). Self-advocacy and supported learning for mothers with learning difficulties. *Journal of Learning difficulties, 7*, 165–193.

Booth, T., & Booth, W. (2004). A family at risk: Multiple perspectives on parenting and child protection. *British Journal of Learning Disabilities, 32*, 9–15.

Booth, T., & Booth, W. (2005). Parents with learning difficulties in the child protection system: Experiences and Perspectives. *Journal of Intellectual Disabilities, 9*, 109–129.

Booth, T., Booth, W., & McConnell, D. (2005). The prevalence and outcomes of care proceedings involving parents with learning difficulties in the family courts. *Journal of Applied Research in Intellectual Disabilities, 18*, 7–17.

Bronfenbrenner, U. (1979). Contexts of child rearing: Problems and prospects. *American Psychologist, 34*, 844–850.

Campion, M.J. (1995). *Who's fit to be a parent?* Florence, KY: Taylor & Frances/ Routledge.

Chapman, M.V., Wall, A., & Barth, R.P. (2004). Children's voices: The perceptions of children in foster care. *American Journal of Orthopsychiatry, 74*, 293–304.

Cook-Fong, S.K. (2000). The adult well-being of individuals reared in family foster care placements. *Child & Youth Care Forum, 29*, 7–25.

Crain, L.S., & Millor, G.K. (1978). Forgotten children: Maltreated children of mentally retarded parents. *Pediatrics, 61*, 130–132.

Downey, G., & Coyne, J.C. (1990). Children of depressed parents: An integrative review. *Psychological Bulletin, 108*, 50–76.

Éthier, L.S., Biron, C., Boutet, M., & Rivet, C. (1999). Les compétences parentales chez les personnes présentant des incapacités intellectuelles: État de la question. *Revue francophone de la déficience intellectuelle, 10*, 109–124.

Feldman, M.A. (1994). Parenting education for parents with intellectual disabilities: A review of outcome studies. *Research in Developmental Disabilities, 15*, 299–332.

Feldman, M.A. (1998). Parents with intellectual disabilities: Implications and interventions. In J. Lutzker (Ed.), *Child abuse: A handbook of theory, research, and treatment* (pp. 401–419). New York: Plenum.

Feldman, M.A. (2002). Parents with intellectual disabilities and their children: Impediments and supports. In. D. Griffiths & P. Federoff (Eds.), *Ethical dilemmas: Sexuality and developmental disability* (pp. 255–292). Kingston, NY: NADD Press.

Feldman, M.A. (2004). Self-directed learning of child-care skills by parents with intellectual disabilities. *Infants & Young Children, 17*, 17–31.

Feldman, M.A., & Case, L. (1993). Step-by-step guide. Unpublished document. Toronto: Surrey Place.

Feldman, M.A., & Case, L. (1997). Effectiveness of self-instructional audiovisual materials in teaching child-care skills to parents with intellectual disabilities. *Journal of Behavioral Education, 7*, 235–257.

Feldman, M.A., & Case, L. (1999). Teaching child-care and safety skills to parents with intellectual disabilities via self-learning. *Journal of Intellectual and Developmental Disabilities, 24*, 27–44.

Feldman, M.A., Case, L., & Sparks, B. (1992). Effectiveness of a child-care training program for parents at-risk for child neglect. *Canadian Journal of Behavioural Science, 24*, 14–28.

Feldman, M.A., Case, L., Towns, F., & Betel, J. (1985). Parent education project I: Development and nurturance of children of mentally retarded parents. *American Journal of Mental Deficiency, 90*, 253–258.

Feldman, M.A., Ducharme, J.M., & Case, L. (1999). Using self-instructional pictorial manuals to teach child-care skills to mothers with intellectual disabilities. *Behavior Modification, 23*, 480–497.

Feldman, M.A., Garrick, M., & Case, L. (1997). The effects of parent training on weight gain of nonorganic-failure-to-thrive children of parents with intellectual disabilities. *Journal on Developmental Disabilities, 5*, 47–61.

Feldman, M.A., Léger, M., & Walton-Allen, N. (1997). Stress in mothers with intellectual disabilities. *Journal of Child and Family Studies, 6*, 471–485.

Feldman, M.A., Sparks, B., & Case, L. (1993). Effectiveness of home-based early intervention on the language development of children of parents with mental retardation. *Research in Developmental Disabilities, 14*, 387–408.

Feldman, M.A., Varghese, J., Ramsay, J., & Rajska, D. (2002). Relationship between social support, stress and mother–child interactions in mothers with intellectual disabilities. *Journal of Applied Research in Intellectual Disability, 15*, 314–323.

Feldman, M.A., & Walton-Allen, N. (1997). Effects of maternal mental retardation and poverty on intellectual, academic, and behavioral status of school-age children. *American Journal on Mental Retardation, 101*, 352–364.

Garber, H.L. (1988). *The Milwaukee Project: Preventing mental retardation in children at risk*. Washington, DC: American Association on Mental Retardation.

Gath, A. (1988). Mentally handicapped people as parents. *Journal of Child Psychology and Psychiatry, 29*, 739–744.

Gelles, R.J. (2000). How evaluation research can help reform and improve the child welfare system. *Journal of Aggression, Maltreatment & Trauma, 4,* 7–28.

Gilson, S.F., Bricourt, J.C., & Baskind, F.R. (1998). Listening to the voices of individuals with disabilities. *Families in society: The Journal of Contemporary Services, 79,* 188–196.

Glaun, D.E., & Brown, P.F. (1999). Motherhood, intellectual disability and child protection: Characteristics of a court sample. *Journal of Intellectual and Developmental Disabilities, 24,* 95–105.

Greene, B.F., Norman, R., Searle, M.S., Daniels, M., & Lubeck, R.C. (1995). Child abuse and neglect by parents with disabilities: a tale of two families. *Journal of Applied Behavior Analysis, 28,* 417–434.

Keltner, B. (1994). Home environments of mothers with mental retardation. *Mental Retardation, 32,* 123–127.

Keltner, B., Finn, D., & Shearer, D. (1995). Effects of family intervention on maternal–child interaction for mothers with developmental disabilities. *Family & Community Health, 17,* 35–49.

Keltner, B.R., Wise, L.A., & Taylor, G. (1999). Mothers with intellectual limitations and their 2-year-old children's developmental outcomes. *Journal of Intellectual & Developmental Disability, 24,* 45–57.

Lalande, D., Éthier, L.S., Rivest, C., Boutet, M. (2002). Parenthood and mental retardation: A pilot study / Parentalité et incapacités intellectuelles: Une étude pilote. *Revue francophone de la déficience intellectuelle, 13,* 133–154.

Landy, S., & Munro, S. (1998). Shared parenting: Assessing the success of a foster parent program aimed at family reunification. *Child Abuse & Neglect, 22,* 305–318.

Lemieux, C. (2001). The challenge of empowerment in child protective services: A case study of a mother with mental retardation. *Families in Society, 82,* 175–185.

Llewellyn, G. (1990). People with intellectual disability as parents: Perspectives from the professional literature. *Australia and New Zealand Journal of Developmental Disabilities, 16,* 369–380.

Llewellyn, G., McConnell, D., & Ferronato, L. (2003). Prevalence and outcomes for parents with disabilities and their children in an Australian court sample. *Child Abuse & Neglect, 27,* 235–251.

Llewellyn, G., McConnell, D., Honey, A., Mayes, R., & Russo, D. (2003). Promoting health and home safety for children of parents with intellectual disability: A randomized controlled trial. *Research in Developmental Disabilities, 24,* 405–431.

Llewellyn, G., McConnell, D., Russo, D., Mayes, R., & Honey, A. (2002).

Home-based programmes for parents with intellectual disabilities: Lessons from practice. *Journal of Applied Research in Intellectual Disabilities, 15,* 341–353.

Lovejoy, M.C., Graczyk, P.A., O'Hare, E., & Neuman, G. (2000). Maternal depression and parenting behavior: A meta-analytic review. *Clinical Psychology Review, 20,* 561–592.

Luckasson, R., Borthwick-Duffy, S., Buntinx, W.H.E., Coulter, D.L., Craig, E. M., Reeve, A., Schalock, R.L., Snell, M.E., Spitalnik, D.M., Spreat, S., Tassé, M.J. (2002). *Mental retardation: Definition, classification, and systems of supports* (10th ed.). Washington, DC: American Association on Mental Retardation.

Mandel, D.R., Lehman, D.R., & Yuille, J.C. (1994). Reasoning about the removal of a child from home: A comparison of police officers and social workers. *Journal of Applied Social Psychology, 25*(10), 906–921.

Mandeville, H., & Snodgrass, P. (1998). Helping parents be parents. *Impact, 11,* 2–3.

Matava, M. (1994). The implications of parenting standards in child protection: A paradox in disability policy. *Policy Studies Journal, 22,* 146–151.

McConnell, D., & Llewellyn, G. (2000). Disability and discrimination in statutory child protection proceedings. *Disability & Society, 15,* 883–895.

McConnell, D., Llewellyn, G., & Ferronato, L. (2000). *Parents with a disability and the NSW Children's Court.* Report of the Family Support and Services Project. Sydney, Australia: University of Sydney.

McConnell, D., Llewellyn, G., Mayes, R., Russo, D., & Honey, A. (2003). Developmental profiles of children born to mothers with intellectual disability. *Journal of Intellectual & Developmental Disability, 28,* 122–134.

McGaw, S., Ball, K., & Clark, A. (2002). The effect of group intervention on the relationships of parents with intellectual disabilities. *Journal of Applied Research in Intellectual Disabilities, 15,* 354–366.

Mirfin-Veitch, B., Bray, A., Williams, S., Clarkson, J. & Belton, A. (1999). Supporting parents with intellectual disabilities. *New Zealand Journal of Disability Studies, 6,* 60–74.

Morch, W.T., Skår, J., & Andresgård, A.B. (1997). Mentally retarded persons as parents: Prevalence and the situation of their children. *Scandinavian Journal of Psychology, 38,* 343–348.

Munro, E. (1999). Common errors of reasoning in child protection work. *Child Abuse & Neglect, 23,* 745–758.

O'Neill, A.M. (1985). Normal and bright children of mentally retarded parents: The Huck Finn Syndrome. *Child Psychiatry and Human Development, 15,* 255–268.

Perkins, T.S., Holburn, S., Deaux, K., Flory, M.J., & Vietze, P.M. (2002). Children of mothers with intellectual disability: Stigma, mother-child relationship and self-esteem. *Journal of Applied Research in Intellectual Disabilities, 15,* 297–313.

Pixa-Kettner, U. (1999). Follow-up study on parenting with intellectual disability in Germany. *Journal of Intellectual & Developmental Disability, 24,* 75–93.

Quebec Youth Protection Act (2002). R.S.Q. Chapter 34.1. Retrieved from http://www.canlii.org/qc/laws/sta/p-34/20051019/whole.html

Ramey, C.T., & Ramey, S.L. (1992). Effective early intervention. *Mental Retardation, 30,* 337–345.

Ray, N.K., Rubenstein, H., & Russo, N.J. (1994). Understanding the parents who are mentally retarded: Guidelines for family preservation programs. *Child Welfare, 73,* 725–743.

Ronai, C.R. (1997). On loving and hating my mentally retarded mother. *Mental Retardation, 35,* 417–432.

Sackett, R.S. (1991). Terminating parental rights of the handicapped. *Family Law Quaterly, 25,* 253–298.

Sameroff, A.J., & Chandler, M. (1975). Reproductive risk and the continuum of caretaking causalty. In F. Horowitz (Ed.), *Review of child development research* (Vol. 4, pp. 157–243). Chicago: University of Chicago Press.

Samra-Grewal, J. (1999). Custody and access evaluations: Issues for mental health professionals conducting assessments with mentally disordered or mentally retarded parents. *Expert Evidence, 7,* 85–111.

Schilling, R.F., Schinke, S.P., Blythe, B.J., & Barth, R.P. (1982). Child maltreatment and mentally retarded parents: Is there a relationship? *Mental Retardation, 20,* 201–209.

Slater, M.A. (1986). Modification of mother–child interaction processes in families with children at-risk for mental retardation. *American Journal of Mental Deficiency, 91,* 257–267.

Smith, S. (1995). *Two generation programs for families in poverty: A new intervention strategy.* Westport, CT: Ablex Publishing.

Spencer, M. (2001). Proceed with caution: The limitations of current parenting capacity assessments. *Developing Practice, Winter,* 16–24.

Steinhauer, P.D. (1991). *The least detrimental alternative: A systematic guide to case planning and decision making for children in care.* Toronto: University of Toronto Press.

Strike, R., & McConnell, D. (2002). Look at me, listen to me, I have something important to say. *Sexuality and Disability. Special Issue: Parents with disabilities, 20,* 53–63.

Swain, P.A., & Cameron, N. (2003). 'Good enough Parenting': Parental disability and child protection. *Disability and Society, 18,* 165–177.

Taylor, C.G., Norman, D., Murphy, J., Jellinek, M., Quinn, D., Poitrast, F., & Goshko, M. (1990). Diagnosed intellectual and emotional impairment among parents who seriously mistreat their children.

Tucker, M.B., & Johnson, O. (1989). Competence promoting versus competing inhibiting social support for mentally retarded mothers. *Human Organization, 48,* 95–107.

Tymchuk, A.J. (1992). Do mothers with or without mental retardation know what to report when they think their child is ill? *Children's Health Care, 21,* 53–57.

Tymchuk, A.J. (1994). Depression symptomatology in mothers with mild intellectual disability: An exploratory study. *Australia and New Zealand Journal of Developmental Disabilities, 19,* 111–119.

Tymchuk, A.J. (1998). The importance of matching educational interventions to parent needs in child maltreatment: Issues, methods, and recommendations. In J.R. Lutzker (Ed.), *Handbook of child abuse research and treatment. Issues in clinical child psychology* (pp. 543–560). New York: Plenum Press.

Tymchuk, A.J. (2006). *The Health and Wellness program: A parenting curriculum for families at-risk.* Baltimore, MD: Paul H. Brookes Publishing.

Tymchuk, A., & Andron, L. (1988). Clinic and home parent training of a mother with mental handicap caring for three children with developmental delay. *Mental Handicap Research, 1,* 24–38.

Tymchuk, A.J., & Andron, L. (1990). Mothers with mental retardation who do or do not abuse or neglect their children. *Child Abuse & Neglect, 14,* 313–323.

Tymchuk, A., & Andron, L. (1992). Project parenting: Child interactional training with mothers who are mentally handicapped. *Mental Handicap Research, 5,* 4–32.

Tymchuk, A., & Feldman, M.A. (1991). Parents with mental retardation and their children: Review of research relevant to professional practice. *Canadian Psychology, 32,* 486–494.

Tymchuk, A.J., Hamada, D., Andron, L., & Anderson, S. (1990). Home safety training with mothers who are mentally retarded. *Education and Training in Mental Retardation, June,* 142–149.

Tymchuk, A.J., Hamada, D., Andron, L., & Anderson, S. (1993). Training with mothers who are mentally retarded to make their home safe: A replication. *Journal of Practical Approaches to Developmental Handicap, 17,* 9–15.

Tymchuk, A.J., & Keltner, B. (1991). Advantage profiles: A tool for health care professionals working with parents with mental retardation. *Pediatric Nursing, 14,* 155–161.

UNICEF. *A world fit for its children*. (2002). New York. Retrieved www.unicef
  .org
United Nations. (1989). *Convention on the Rights of the Child* (CRC).
Whitman, B.Y., & Accardo, P.J. (1990). *When a parent is mentally retarded*. Baltimore: Paul H. Brookes Publishing.

7 Human Rights for Children and Youth with Developmental Disabilities

FRANCES OWEN, CHRISTINE TARDIF-WILLIAMS,
DONATO TARULLI, GLENYS MCQUEEN-FUENTES,
MAURICE FELDMAN, CAROL SALES, KAREN STONER,
LEANNE GOSSE, AND DOROTHY GRIFFITHS

> Patterns of injustice throughout the world have prevented people with
> disabilities from participating in the same way as those without disabili-
> ties. Science, medicine, economics, and government policy – in both the
> national and international sphere – have rationalized and justified selec-
> tive participation, entitlement, and rights.
>
> Rioux, 2003, p. 314

Throughout history, children and youth with disabilities have been
rejected from society and subjected to a different standard of treatment
regarding their rights. However, the past half-century has witnessed
the adoption of the United Nation Declaration of Human Rights (1948),
the United Nations Declaration on the Rights of Mentally Retarded
Persons (1971), and the Declaration on the Rights of Disabled Persons
(1975). Although most Canadians have come to assume the protection
of rights and freedoms as articulated in declarations and conventions
of law, including the *Canadian Charter of Rights and Freedoms* of 1985
(Brabeck & Lauren, 2000), the rights of children and youth with intellectual disabilities to live in their family homes, to have access to education or educational support systems, and in some cases to life-saving
medical treatment remain issues of controversy.

In this chapter we will explore the historical, theoretical, and pragmatic issues related to the human rights of persons with intellectual
disabilities, with particular emphasis on developments in the Canadian setting. A brief historical analysis will provide a context for
understanding the theoretical, pragmatic, and ideological underpin-
nings that drive current practice in the emerging field of rights advo-

cacy for persons with intellectual disabilities, including the movement towards community living, self-determination, person-centred service delivery, and self-advocacy. The chapter will conclude with a discussion of the systemic and pragmatic barriers to the achievement of rights and a consideration of policy, procedure, and programmatic enterprises that have been employed to actualize the achievement of rights protections. In this latter section, research-based evidence will be used from the *3Rs* Niagara Community University Alliance (Brock University and Community Living Welland-Pelham) to illustrate this evolving practice (Griffiths et al., 2003; Owen, Griffiths, Stoner, Gosse, et al., 2003; Tarulli et al., 2004).

Historical Relevance of the Issue of Rights of Children and Youth Who Have Intellectual Disabilities

Herr believed that 'in a perfect world, one would need to go no further than the elegant phrases contained in the Universal Declaration of Human Rights' (2003, p. 119), which was adopted in 1948 following the Second World War. In this monumental agreement, 'the equal and inalienable rights of all members of the human family' were articulated and persons with disabilities were ensured the right to an adequate living standard.

This declaration followed a period of time in history when human freedoms and dignity and the security of the citizens of the world had been shattered. Amongst the many Holocaust victims, children and youth with intellectual disabilities formed a significant, yet generally silent and unknown group. Hitler referred to these children and youth as 'useless eaters,' who consumed the product of the nation without contributing to its wealth and prosperity. Under his regime, children with intellectual disabilities were identified and sent to institutions, where they were denied life-saving medical treatment or subjected to passive or active euthanasia (i.e., allowed to die from denial of nutrients or eliminated through the gas chambers). Propaganda convinced some families that it was kinder to kill children with a disability than to allow them to suffer such a life; physicians in Nazi Germany were rewarded for their contributions to this social elimination program (Scheerenberger, 1983).

In Canadian history, children and youth with intellectual disabilities were also subjected to social policy decisions that by today's standards would be considered unthinkable. They were subjected to medical experimentation, substandard living conditions, and, involuntarily, sterilization. They were also overmedicated and victimized through abuse, neglect, or cruel and unusual punishment. By the 1970s, Canada supported the United Nations Declaration on the Rights of Mentally Retarded Persons and the Declaration on the Rights of Disabled Persons.

The *Canadian Human Rights Act* (1977) prohibited service providers from discrimination on many dimensions, including physical or mental disability. In 1978 the Canadian Human Rights Commission was established to provide a process for preventing discrimination through education, to promote understanding of rights and the mechanisms for protection, and to restore rights when discrimination had occurred. Indeed, in 1985 Canada became the first nation in the world to declare within its constitution the right to equal protection and equal benefit of the law to persons with disabilities (Rioux & Frazee, 1999) and to guarantee protection against discrimination for all citizens, including those with a disability (Neuman, 1984). In Canada, persons of all ages and abilities are guaranteed equal rights; and all other laws in Canada must 'meet the standard set out in the Charter' (Rioux & Frazee, 1999, p. 60).

Canadians with intellectual disabilities have since experienced more than a quarter-century of equal rights and freedoms, which has produced significant positive changes in the lives of children and youth with intellectual disabilities. Flynn and Lemay (1999), in reviewing the changes in social policy regarding persons with intellectual disabilities for the previous quarter-century, note that there has been enormous improvement in the field since the formulation and adoption of the principles of normalization. Normalization requires that services make provisions that afford individuals with disabilities the same opportunities in life as non-disabled persons have available.

Despite these changes and advances, however, critical issues of human rights continue to be raised and debated within our society. In a recent decision, Supreme Court of Canada Justice LaForest noted: 'It is an unfortunate truth that the history of people with disabilities in Canada is largely one of exclusion and marginalization. People with disabilities ... have not generally been afforded the "equal concern, respect and consideration" that ... the Charter demands' (Accreditation Ontario, 2000, p. 33).

Advocates often question why the rights of children and youth with disabilities continue to be challenged in a society that so openly declares equality of rights. O'Neill (1996) poses a discourse in regards to children's rights that has direct applicability to children and youth who have intellectual disabilities. She suggests that there are

> good reasons for caution in using the rhetoric of rights to think about ethical issues on children's lives ... The discourse of rights is an entirely legitimate descendent of older discussions of obligation and justice, of virtue and happiness, which have been ubiquitous both in popular and in philosophical discussion ... However, the legitimacy of the discourse of rights becomes problematic when it aspires to become the sole or fundamental ethical category. (p. 35)

From a constructivist position, O'Neill argues that, within the discussion of fundamental rights, there must also be a discussion of obligations. Two issues related to the field of intellectual disabilities emerge from this discourse. First and foremost is the challenge between the rights of the child or youth with an intellectual disability and the obligations of the care providers (child-rearing or educational providers) to protect the child or youth and to provide adequate support, guidance, and nurturance. O'Neill describes this challenge in terms of obligations. Universal obligations, she notes, are those that represent perfect obligations, applicable to all children and youth, such as freedom from abuse and neglect. These represent fundamental rights. Other perfect obligations are those held as a result of the relationship with specified children and youth, as defined in the role of care-provider or educator. Yet a third set of obligations are socially or institutionally specific and represent an imperfect obligation. In today's society, such an imperfect but fundamental obligation would be that of treating all children in a kind and considerate manner.

The second, related issue pertains to the perspective of agency of personal rights and receipt of rights. Children and youth with intellectual disabilities have less agency in the recognition, realization, and exercise of their rights than their non-disabled peers. 'The history of services for people with disabilities reveals many examples of less than equal treatment in relation to rights' (Accreditation Ontario, 2000, p. 1). Today's society cannot base the restriction of rights and privileges simply upon the disability. However, rights restrictions routinely occur for persons with intellectual disabilities and are often justified as protection for the individual or others, or even, occasionally, on less defensible grounds, such as the prevention of immorality or offence to others.

As noted above, much of the disempowerment of children and youth with intellectual disabilities has been the result of social oppression. However, some persons with intellectual disabilities may be unavoidably, and in some cases completely, dependent upon others and, as such, have less power in their lives. As O'Neill (1996) claims, 'It is not surprising that oppressors often try to suggest that they stand in paternal relation to those whom they oppress; in that way they suggest that the latter's dependence is natural and irremediable and their own exercise of power a burden which they bear with benevolent fortitude' (p. 37). Schultz (1996) similarly cautions that when care-providers justify decisions of power because 'they know what's best,' the system degenerates to the point where 'needs' become separated from 'rights' and where providers do things *for* people rather than *with* them.

Manifesto rights, those enshrined in laws and declarations, cannot be claimed unless or until practices and institutions are established that recognize those rights and establish a system in which restrictions or violations of those rights can be addressed (O'Neill, 1996). 'Mere insistence that certain ideals or goals are rights cannot make them into rights; but a proleptic rhetoric of rights may be politically useful in working to set up institutions that secure positive rights that constitute (one possible) realization of fundamental imperfect obligations' (ibid., p. 36).

The scope of rights restrictions of persons with intellectual disabilities remains largely unknown. Moreover, with rare exception where Charter challenges have been claimed, there is no universal mechanism to monitor and review rights restrictions that may be imposed within the systems for persons with intellectual disabilities in Canadian service agencies (Tarulli et al., 2004). One recent study has explored the nature of rights restrictions within a community residential agency. At the request of an agency seeking to conduct an internal evaluation of its own service, Griffiths et al. (2003) interviewed seventy-four individuals with intellectual disabilities living in community residential programs (group homes, specialized group homes, family homes, semi-independent living). Their findings showed that individuals supported within the community living programs reported restrictions in four distinct rights domains: (1) access and autonomy, (2) relationships and community supports, (3) safety, security and privacy, and (4) control and decision-making. Parallel questionnaires given to primary and support staff showed that staff placed greater emphasis on *control and decision-making* and *access and autonomy* issues. Part-time staff also noted some restrictions in *safety, security, and privacy* rights. However, none of the staff expressed concerns about rights restrictions in the area of *relationships and community supports*, which were the paramount concerns of the supported individuals. These data were used by the agency to initiate a Rights, Respect, and Responsibility (*3Rs*) focus within their service setting that included policy changes, development of a Human Rights Facilitation Committee to review all possible infringements, and *3Rs* training for all management, staff, and individuals supported by the agency. The *3Rs* project will be discussed in more detail below.

Challenges to the Rights of Children and Youth with Intellectual Disabilities

In this section we explore eight of the fundamental rights guaranteed to all Canadians under the *Canadian Charter of Rights and Freedoms* (1982). We will discuss the challenges presented by the actualization of these rights for people with intellectual disabilities both traditionally and in current practice. The following rights will be explored:

1 Right to equal treatment without discrimination
2 Freedom of opinion and expression
3 Freedom of peaceful assembly and association
4 Right not to be subjected to cruel or unusual treatment or punishment
5 Right to be secure against unreasonable search or seizure
6 Right to life, liberty, and security
7 Right to not be deprived of life, liberty, or security, except in accordance with the principles of fundamental justice
8 Right to equal protection and equal benefit of the law

1 Right to Equal Treatment without Discrimination

Discrimination can appear in many forms. In our society, children and youth with intellectual disabilities experience discrimination in the very manner in which we choose to describe them. 'Language is a reflection of how people in a society see each other' (Blaska, 1993, p. 25). Historically, children with intellectual disabilities were described in ways that would now be viewed as pejorative and devaluing. The term 'disability' itself implies the deprivation of an ability or fitness that disqualifies the person from some aspect of life (Asch, Gosten, & Johnson, 2003). Within our society, the terms for disability or handicap have the associated stigma of undesirability, burden, pity, and even villainy (ibid.). This stigmatizing vocabulary reinforces the trappings of paternalism that are often misused to mask unacceptable faces of power. Again, as O'Neill (1996) notes, 'It is not mere metaphor, but highly political rhetoric, when oppressors describe what they do as paternalistic' (p. 37). In regard to language usage, what we wish to note here is that, traditionally, the personhood of children and youth with disabilities has been afforded a secondary status, with the 'disability' assuming a primary descriptive role, as in expressions such as the 'disabled child.' In some measure, current language redresses this problem by referring to the child, youth, or person first, with reference to the individual's disability appearing in a secondary position, as needed, to add clarity.

Labelling and categorizing persons with intellectual disabilities has been the tool of segregationists. Historically, children and youth with disabilities were identified using IQ tests, labelled in accordance with their test performance, and 'placed' in certain educational streams based on this label. In the past century, designations by level of intelligence would determine whether institutionalization in provincial facilities would occur. Today, this type of categorization is often used to determine school placements. Since the 1970s, the education of children and youth with intellectual disabilities has become the responsibility of the local boards of education; previously, parent Associations for the Mentally Retarded (now called Associations for Community Living) operated schools using volunteers and donations to fund their efforts. The schools for children and youth with disabilities were typically segregated.

A movement towards the integration of children and youth with disabilities into mainstream schools often resulted in self-contained classrooms within schools, although some school boards moved to a more inclusive approach whereby children and youth were fully included into regular classes within their home schools. In the 1980s and 1990s some parents whose children were still segregated in either special schools or self-contained classrooms began to file complaints with the Human Rights Commission on the basis of discrimination. The cases have not been uniformly judged, some receiving positive outcomes, some not, and still others having decisions reversed in later judgments. In general, however, the judgments have not had a widespread impact on regulating non-discriminatory practices in the school system. Individual boards of education interpret the policies on inclusion in very different ways and implementation is far from universal.

Even today, parents, educators, researchers, and policy-makers continue to disagree on the most appropriate educational setting for providing special education to children and youth who have disabilities (Fuchs & Fuchs, 1994; Gartner & Lipsky, 1987; Kauffman, 1993). This disagreement and debate continues despite research findings indicating that full inclusion of children and youth who have disabilities within general-education classrooms can avoid some of the harmful effects of exclusion from regular classroom settings (for meta-analytic reviews, see Carlberg & Kavale, 1980; Wang & Baker, 1985–6), and that students can benefit socially and emotionally from more inclusive educational placements (Wiener & Tardif, 2004). Exclusion is often detrimental to children and youth who have disabilities; for example, they may feel lonelier and more depressed because they do not spend as much time with their peers who do not have disabilities (Stainback & Stainback, 1996). The self-concept or self-esteem of excluded students who have disabilities may also be at risk owing to their identification as having special needs and their separation from the regular classroom (Leondari, 1993). Further, as a result of increased opportunities to make friends with peers who do not have disabilities, children and youth who have disabilities often benefit socially and emotionally from more inclusive education placements (Stainback & Stainback, 1996).

In short, the regular classroom can provide a frame of reference for more normative and successful friendships and social interactions. Students with disabilities who are placed in more inclusive educational settings are likely to feel less stigmatized, be better liked and accepted, and have more friends and more positive self-perceptions than students with disabilities who are segregated in special-education classrooms (Gartner & Lipsky, 1989; Stainback & Stainback, 1996). These findings underscore the need for a stronger movement towards providing all children and youth who have disabilities with equal opportunities to interact with peers without disabilities in regular educational settings. This is particularly imperative if educators are to prepare children and youth with disabilities to successfully negotiate the social situations they will no doubt encounter in the *real world* – the very same social situations encountered by their peers who do not have disabilities.

2 Freedom of Opinion and Expression

Despite the gains seen in developed countries in the areas of prevention and early identification of disabilities in infancy and early childhood, the United Nations has estimated that 'in many developing countries 90% of disabled children will not survive beyond 20 years of age, 90% of intellectually impaired children do not survive beyond 5 years of age, and only 3% get education beyond the basic minimum' (Lansdown, 1998, p. 221). Lansdown describes the life of institutionalization and deprivation of the most basic human needs faced by children in the hundreds of thousands. Children with disabilities 'are perhaps amongst those most vulnerable to abuse and neglect by adults with responsibility for them, and least able to assert their rights on their own behalf' (p. 222).

Despite their desperate circumstances, children who have disabilities often remain invisible to the eyes of those setting public-policy agendas (Lansdown, 1998). They may also be functionally invisible, or at least limited in their ability to communicate needs, such as that for protection from abuse, by virtue of functional difficulties in self-expression (Oosterhoorn & Kendrick, 2001). Nevertheless, articles 12 and 13 of the U.N. Convention on the Rights of the Child refer to children's rights to receive information and their right to express themselves (Cavet & Sloper, 2004). In their review of the literature, Cavet and Sloper found strong evidence of children with a variety of disabilities seeking respect for their opinions. 'One criterion of quality in services from a disabled child's point of view is having the opportunity to make real choices' (p. 282).

However, the voice of persons with intellectual disabilities was silent in much of the twentieth century, as children and youth with intellectual disabilities were segregated and invisible within society. Moreover, within the institutional society, there was an expectation that persons with intellectual disabilities should be largely compliant in their behaviour, that they should follow the rules and dictates of the staff and institutional personnel. Indeed, non-compliance was often met with sanctions and punishment. One of the most common programs to emerge in the 1970s was 'compliance training,' whereby children were taught to unconditionally follow the instructions of persons in authority. The concepts of choice and self-determination for children with intellectual disabilities did not emerge in the field until the 1980s. In this regard, one of the turning points was a study conducted by Carr (1977), in which he demonstrated that much of the 'challenging behaviour' observed in children with intellectual disabilities had identifiable functions, such as escape or gaining attention. Other authors have argued that the challenging behaviour of children with intellectual disabilities has a communicative intent (Donnellan & La Vigna, 1990). Thus, although voice and choice had been denied these children, many were achieving these functions through the use of behaviours such as aggression or self-injury (cf. Parr, 2005).

The field has shifted radically in the past few decades owing to the recognition that most challenging behaviour has function and meaning for the individual, and that the key to effective treatment lies in understanding that function and meaning (Carr, Horner, et al., 1999). Today, the standard for behavioural support and intervention for children with intellectual disabilities requires that a full biopsychosocial assessment, including a functional assessment, be conducted before the application of any intervention. The practice is now based on understanding why the challenging behaviour is occurring and, where possible, eliminating the factors that are prompting the behavior, and/or teaching the individual an alternative way to achieve the same function (i.e., escape, gain attention, or communicate). Consistent with this understanding, Beauchamp and Childrenss (1994) note that to respect autonomy is to acknowledge a person's right to hold views, to make choices, and to take actions based on personal values and beliefs. The field, it seems, is shifting from one of control and paternalism to self-determination.

In recent years within the field of intellectual disabilities, this emphasis on self-determination is perhaps most evident in the growing recognition of the importance of person-centred planning (Smull & Parsley, 2003). In effect, this planning approach allows persons to determine their lifestyle preference and to determine 'what is important to the individual and what is important for the individual' (ibid., p. 185). As Smull and Parsley elaborate:

> This is not to say that the preferred lifestyle of a person with an intellectual disability is always controlling. A balance is still needed. Many people with intellectual disabilities have health and safety needs that must be addressed. Many are vulnerable to abuse, neglect, or exploitation. The state has a legitimate interest in protecting these individuals. The state also has legitimate concerns regarding the expenditure of its resources. A new balance is therefore needed. One way to strike this balance is through a process that considers (1) the desired lifestyle of the individual, (2) the health and safety needs of the individual and others, and (3) the resources available to support the individual. (p. 194)

Although the person-centred planning approach has led to persons with mild and moderate levels of intellectual disability gaining greater control over their lives, the lifestyle decisions for persons with more significant intellectual disabilities may still be more determined by issues of health and safety (Smull & Parsley, 2003).

3 Freedom of Peaceful Assembly and Association

'Freedom of association is a right that is violated for individuals with developmental disabilities living in institutional settings, or any residential placement where a person has no opportunity to express a preference as to where or with whom s/he wishes to live' (Rooke, 2003, p. 19). We would add that the right of association is also called into question when children and youth with intellectual disabilities are denied inclusion in mainstreamed systems such as schools in their natural neighbourhood. It has been argued that children who are denied access to neighbourhood schools are being denied opportunities to make friends and gain valuable associations (Brown et al., 1989). Conversely, in the pursuit of social role valorization of persons with intellectual disabilities, advocacy agencies have discouraged children and youth from taking part in segregated programs, such as Special Olympics. These advocates suggest that programs that congregate children and youth with disabilities do not promote the social value of persons with disabilities. This message, however, suggests a situation in which children and youth with intellectual disabilities are being denied the right of assembly and association with their peers with a disability because it does not support the advocacy movement.

4 Right Not to Be Subjected to Any Cruel or Unusual Treatment or Punishment

The Canadian Charter guarantees freedom from both cruel or unusual treatment and cruel or unusual punishment. In the 1980s, a debate in the field emerged over the use of aversive and punitive procedures to manage or modify the behaviour of children and youth with intellectual disabilities. These punishment procedures included, but were not limited to, physical and chemical restraint, isolation, and aversive conditioning, including faradic stimulation (contingent electric shock). In 1984 the *Ontario Child and Family Services Act* declared that treatment for children must follow the least restrictive or disruptive course of action that is available and appropriate. Accordingly, the use of such procedures must be put to the test before consideration as viable options. The test used in criminal law for cruel or unusual treatment was laid out in 1984 (*R. v. Langevin*) and can be articulated in terms of the following questions: Is the treatment without therapeutic value or does it go beyond what is necessary to achieve a legitimate treatment aim? Can it be applied on a rational basis according to set standards? Is there an adequate alternative? Would the treatment be unacceptable to a large segment of the population, violate public standards of decency or propriety, or degrade human dignity and worth?

In 1988 Weagant and Griffiths argued that the non-voluntary use of contingent electric shock and other such aversive approaches would be contestable under the *Charter of Rights and Freedoms*. Their arguments were threefold. First, they suggested that the use of such a technique is proscribed under section 12 of the Charter, which states that 'everyone has the right not to be subjected to any cruel and unusual treatment or punishment.' Second, they argued that sufficient consent could never be obtained for such a technique because it is not a therapeutic procedure. Third, they claimed that since current practice in the field would suggest aversives such as shock are not the least restrictive course of action available, and because these techniques may be nothing more than punishment, the use of these techniques might also arguably be in violation of section 7 of the Charter, which guarantees the right to life, liberty, and security, except in accordance with the principles of fundamental justice.

Feldman (1990) discussed the need to balance freedom from harm and the right to effective treatment. He presented arguments from both camps. The group representing the right to effective treatment (Van Houten et al., 1988) has maintained that the right to treatment is just as important a right as freedom from harm and that children with intellectual disabilities should not be discriminated against because of their disability. This camp argues that society should not withhold life-saving surgery because a child with intellectual disabilities may not be able to understand that a surgeon will be cutting open his/her body. It also argues that one cannot judge a treatment in isolation; rather, one must judge whether the treatment, despite its potentially unpleasant aspects, would actually reduce the overall harm experienced by the child. The most obvious example is severe self-injurious behaviour, in which children with intellectual disabilities have a greater risk of engaging than children without intellectual disabilities. Advocates of the right to treatment argue that if a treatment such as contingent electric shock results in a child no longer smashing his or her head against a wall 100 times a day or gouging out chunks of skin, is not the treatment worth it? The use of contingent shock, they argue, replaces the more restrictive alternative of full restraint to protect the child from self-harm, and perhaps even death. The freedom-from-harm position, elucidated by Weagant and Griffiths (1988) and others, is described cogently above. For his part, Feldman offers a compromise position: namely, that the least intrusive model should always be followed, but restrictive/intrusive procedures could be made available as a last resort under controlled conditions. Feldman anticipated that recent advances in non-intrusive positive behavioural interventions make the use of aversive techniques less and less necessary, even for treating severe behaviour problems like self-injury and aggression in children with intellectual disabilities (Feldman, Condillac, et al., 2002).

5 Right to Be Secure against Unreasonable Search or Seizure

Individuals with intellectual disabilities living in congregate residential programs have been denied personal possessions, or personal possessions have been withheld and access to them has been controlled by others. Personal items have been used as program reinforcement or removed as punishment. In addition to the history of seizure related to interventions, people who have intellectual disabilities may feel pressure about the security of their personal possessions by virtue of living in communal settings, such as group homes. In the 3Rs survey described above, one of the two questions that contributed statistically most heavily to the safety, security, and privacy factor was 'This individual is worried about his/her things being stolen' (Griffiths et al., 2003, p. 30).

6 Right to Life, Liberty and Security

Although Canadian law dictates that any citizen has a right not to be deprived of life, liberty, or security except in accordance with the principles of fundamental justice, some have argued that many children and youth with intellectual disabilities have endured gross violations of this right in the form of euthanasia and murder. Within the field, institutionally grounded practices such as sterilization, abortion, denial of life-saving medical treatment, and genetic engineering have come under attack for the real and potential threats they pose to this fundamental set of rights (e.g., Hollander, 1989; Rioux, 2003; Sobsey, Donnellan, & Wolbring, 1994; Ticol, 1996).

Historically, children and youth with intellectual disabilities were subjects of the eugenics social movement, as conceived by Goddard (1920). The eugenics advocates sought to purify the human race from elements that reduced the intellectual and social-welfare capacity of society. This movement led to widespread sterilization laws that legally and permanently ensured that thousands of young people with intellectual disabilities would not procreate. The movement was based on the belief that persons with intellectual disabilities would give birth to children who were disabled, and since disability, mental health risks, and criminality were all considered interrelated, the fabric of society would be protected through sterilization laws. Although the theory had many scientific flaws, the practice of eugenics continued throughout much of North America until the 1970s.

Advocates for the rights of persons with intellectual disabilities have also criticized certain contemporary medical practices for the rights violations they perpetuate. For example, amniocentesis – a routine medical procedure, particularly for women who are older – is used to determine if the fetus might develop Down syndrome. In some circumstances, the practice may be used to prepare a parent to be informed about how to best care for and understand the needs of their newborn child with Down syndrome, while in others the parents, so advised, may choose abortion. On the other hand, in recent years an increasing number of family members and individuals with disabilities have sued physicians who did not identify the disability before birth. These 'wrongful life' legal arguments imply that the person should never have been allowed to be born. Within the field of disability studies, such arguments present a challenge to rights advocates who have traditionally defended the value of life – however defined – in and of itself.

In Canada, rights advocates also point to the unsettling number of incidents where parents have been accused of the murder or attempted murder of their children with intellectual disabilities, in some cases claiming they are performing euthanasia. Tracy Latimer's case is exemplary in this regard (Parker, 2001). Advocates clearly and vehemently oppose these practices, and warn that the message they convey to society recalls the underlying message of the eugenics movement: that the individual with a disability, the family of that person, and society would prefer that this person was not born and that disability does not exist in our society.

Within certain segments of the disability-studies community, concerns about the disregard for the life of children with intellectual disabilities extend to current work in the exploration and discovery of the human genome. The Human Genome Initiative promises great potential for understanding the nature of diverse disabling conditions and enhancing the potential for improved quality of life for many persons with disabilities (Griffiths & Watson, 2004). However, critics of the project have argued that this potential scientific benefit to persons with disabilities does not come without a counterbalancing risk to the same population. More specifically, concerned advocates have countered that as the knowledge of the genetic location of various disabling conditions becomes known, this information may be applied either to enhance the quality of life of persons with disabilities or to introduce a new eugenics movement to eliminate individual persons with disability or to eliminate a disability from society altogether. Advocates fear that once the genetic etiology of a specific disability can be identified through genetic counselling or in utero, families could be pressured to choose to avoid pregnancy, to abort a fetus with a disability, or to alter the genes of the fetus to eliminate the disability. The pressure for such outcomes may come from many sources: personal, economic, professional, societal, and even governmental (Asch et al., 2003). The science of the human genome project could therefore conceivably be used, argue its critics, to eliminate the life of children with disabilities, thus serving as a new form of eugenics.

Last in the discussion of the right to life is the concern that persons with intellectual disabilities may be denied appropriate medical treatment and support. 'There is a tremendous amount of work to be done in order that children with disabilities in Canada receive medical treatment as would any other child' (Blanchet, 1995, p. 71). Clinicians have long since noted that persons with intellectual disabilities often have medical challenges that have been neglected or undiagnosed (Ryan, 2001).

In some cases the neglect is due to ignorance, a lack of communicative skill with persons who have disabilities, or 'diagnostic overshadowing' (Reiss, Levitan, & Szyszko, 1982), whereby the disability is used to account for other medically based symptoms. In some cases, however, the neglect is intended. For example, in 1983, the spinal-fluid shunt of six-year-old Stephen Dawson became blocked. His parents were convinced by the professional presiding over the case to allow the child to die rather than repair his shunt because his quality of life was deteriorating. If it had not been for local advocates and the ruling by Justice McKenzie to override the parental and medical decision,

Stephen would have been denied life-saving medical intervention (*Re S.D., 1986*).

This case is not an isolated situation. As Blanchet (1995) notes:

> In examining the issues affecting the rights of children with disabilities to medical treatment, one serious problem is the 'No Code' practice. In this practice, it is decided, often before a child requires life-saving or any other medical intervention, that the child will not receive any treatment except comfort measures or that no resuscitation will take place in the event of cardiac arrest. Children *(with disabilities)* are subject to this practice in ambulance services, in hospital emergency wards and in intensive care units. (p. 74)[1]

The practice of intentional medical neglect is based on the 'conscious or unconscious value judgments made by professionals about the quality of life of people with a disability, particularly those with severe disabilities' (Blanchet, 1995, p. 75). Wolfensburger (1989) also noted that medical organizations oppose restrictions on the 'privatized death-making of impaired newborns' (p. 63). The value of the life is also weighed against economic concerns where treatment is costly or requires a decision of deservedness. The latter situation has been observed with the case of Terry Urquhart, a young man with Down syndrome who required a heart transplant and was initially refused on the basis not of medical compatibility or viability but of deservedness. He later was granted the transplant when the refusal of treatment was challenged legally by the family (*Welland Tribune*, 13 April 1995).

Limitations on access to health care resources are not restricted to life-and-death decisions. Despite the greater likelihood of people with intellectual disabilities having health problems than the general population (U.S. Department of Health and Human Services, 2002), there are pervasive international concerns about the availability of and access to health-promotion and intervention services for them, both in regard to their general health needs as well as those needs specific to their disability (Lennox & Kerr, 1997). Feldman, Owen, et al. (2005) have argued for the need to develop and test educational programs to

---

1   In Ontario, Do Not Resuscitate orders are honoured by licensed health care practitioners only. Unlike the situation described in Blanchet (1995), paramedics may not honour DNR orders and are required to treat patients (Guru, Verbeek, & Morrison, 1999).

provide health self-advocacy training for people with intellectual disabilities. Since people who have intellectual disabilities have a greater likelihood of needing medical care than people without such disabilities, the issue of health self-advocacy is especially important. For example, Garth and Aroni (2003) interviewed children with cerebral palsy about their experiences of communication in a medical setting. This study confirmed the importance of a supportive partnership between families and physicians. Mothers indicated that continuity in medical care gave physicians a better understanding of their child as a whole person, which leads to better communication. The authors quote one mother who said: '"Even though ... he [the child] mightn't understand it all but she [the general practitioner] still makes an effort by not talking baby talk but by talking to him at the level she thinks he will understand"' (p. 572).

From the eugenics movement to the Holocaust, to current and emerging practice in the scientific community, the controversy of the right to life of children and youth with intellectual disabilities has been and continues to be a matter of debate and differing practice in our society.

7 Right to Not Be Deprived of Life, Liberty or Security, Except in Accordance with the Principles of Fundamental Justice

From the beginning of the last century until the 1970s, people with intellectual disabilities were provided services to protect them and society from perceived threats associated with their disability. However, 'whenever others determine how another will live, personal liberty is likely to be restricted' (Smull & Parsley, 2003, p. 190).

The right to liberty and security is also implicated in the practice of making personal decisions for persons with intellectual disabilities, such as placement decisions (Rooke, 2003). Rooke suggests that these rights are violated as long as individuals with intellectual disabilities are not given choice as to where they wish to live, noting that, as Accreditation Ontario reported, the Supreme Court of Canada has ruled that security includes the 'psychological integrity inherent in being in control of what happens in one's life' (as cited in Rocke, 2003, p. 20). Although the U.N. Convention on the Rights of the Child clearly articulates that 'no child shall be deprived of his or her liberty unlawfully or arbitrarily' (article 37b), institutionalization of children and youth with intellectual disabilities has been standard practice. Like children who have been detained through inappropriate legal interventions, historically children with intellectual disabilities who have been institutionalized have been deprived of their liberty and of free access to the community without appropriate legal protections.

Another area in which youth with intellectual disabilities have been denied control is that of sexuality and, in particular, reproductive rights. The reproductive rights of persons with intellectual disabilities have historical civil-law significance. In the previous century, the reproductive control of young persons with intellectual disabilities resulted in institutionalization, mass sterilization, intrusive reproductive research involving castration, and even mass murder (Scheerenberger, 1983). Until the 1970s, children and youth with intellectual disabilities were sterilized, including 'boys and girls 11 years of age' (ibid., p. 226). At the Michener Centre in Red Deer Alberta, for example, young males with Down syndrome were the targets of intrusive research involving castration, despite the fact that males with nonmosaic Down syndrome are typically infertile (Pringle, 1997).

It is no wonder, therefore, that in the past few decades there have been two landmark civil cases involving persons labelled as intellectually disabled with regard to issues of reproduction and sterilization. The case of *R. v. Mrs. Eve* (1986), heard by the Supreme Court of Canada, protected Eve's right to not be subjected to non-therapeutic sterilization, a procedure requested by her mother. The court decided that although third-party (*parens patriae*) consent may be appropriate for some procedures, such an irreversible and intrusive procedure that affected bodily integrity could not be provided under *parens patriae*. In the more recent case of *Muir v. Alberta* (1996), Muir brought legal action against the Province of Alberta for forced sterilization conducted when she was a child residing at the Michener Centre in Red Deer. The suit was won on the grounds that the decision to sterilize was not justified according to the statute (*Alberta Sterilization Act*) and that a proper process was not followed. Other suits followed.

Despite the legal and legislative 'precedents, nontherapeutic sterilizations without consent are still being performed in this country' (Blanchet, 1995, p. 74). There remains a general lack of information and confusion about non-therapeutic sterilization among physicians regarding the law and the interpretations of the procedure's definition. Moreover, because of prevailing bias among some physicians, persons with intellectual disabilities are more likely to receive more invasive interventions when they present with typical gynecological issues (Blanchet, 1995).

8 Right to Equal Protection and Equal Benefit of the Law

Relatively little attention has been paid to children and youth with intellectual disabilities who are participants within Canadian criminal and civil courts (Marinos & Griffiths, 2005), yet compared to other groups of children and youth their involvement in the justice system occurs at a disproportionately higher rate. Children and youth with intellectual disabilities become entangled in the court process for the same range of complex cognitive, social, emotional, and economic reasons as do non-disabled persons. The life experiences of individuals with intellectual disabilities are associated with vulnerability to become both perpetrators and victims of certain crimes (Conley, Luckasson, & Bouthilet, 1992; Griffiths & Marini, 2000).

Individuals with intellectual disabilities have a greater likelihood of experiencing victimization from crime, yet these crimes often go unreported (Sobsey, 1994; Wilson & Brewer, 1992). Persons with intellectual disabilities experience a rate of crime that is four to ten times in excess of that experienced by non-disabled persons (Sobsey, Lucardie, & Mansell, 1995). The more significant the disability, the more likely the crime will remain unreported (Wilson & Brewer, 1992). Moreover, the victimization of persons with intellectual disabilities is often perpetrated within the very system in which they are supported and by the individuals empowered to support them (Luckassson, 1992; Sobsey & Varnhagen, 1988).

The following quotes collectively describe the current challenges to the rights of child victims who have disabilities:

> It somehow seems more okay to abuse an imperfect child, or someone who really doesn't know what is going on, or is powerless. Disabled children are powerless in many respects – if they can't move, they can't talk. If they can't hear ... (Musuda & Ridington, 1990, as cited in Doe, 1995, p. 49)

> Yet we have a long way to go in extending to children who are victims the human rights we offer to defendants. Children with disabilities, especially those who cannot talk, are not being given full access to this potential protection. Children with disabilities are considered 'prosecution-proof' victims. That means the offender can almost be guaranteed that there will be no prosecution or punishment because the child cannot communicate what happened, cannot name the offender, cannot describe

the situation and may never have access to justice, all because of communication gaps between them and the legal system. (Doe, 1995, p. 51)

Another challenge to children and youth with disabilities arises if
and when they become involved with the justice system as an accused
person. When a child or youth with an intellectual disability commits
a crime, it is generally less severe than any committed by a non-disabled person (Day, 1997); however, the child or youth with an intellectual disability is more likely to be apprehended, confess to the crime,
incriminate himself or herself, be led by the interviewer, plead guilty,
and waive rights without full comprehension of the process, and is less
likely to plea bargain or appeal a judgment, understand the implications of their statements, or be able to afford appropriate legal defense
(Abel & Rouleau, 1990; Brown & Courtless, 1971; McGee & Menolascino, 1992; Moschella, 1982; Murphy, Coleman, & Haynes, 1983; Santamour & West, 1978).

Once within the judicial system, young victims or those accused find
it difficult to gain full access to criminal-justice provisions. Marinos &
Griffiths (in press) argue that the ability of the person with an intellectual disability to fully participate and benefit from the legal system is
multifaceted and includes the following considerations:

1 The identification of persons with intellectual disabilities in the
   courtroom for the purpose of providing both any assessment
   required for accommodations and supports and skills needed for
   engaging in court proceedings.
2 The implications of a low IQ or mental age, and the relationship
   between intellectual disability, memory, and the person's ability to
   be a witness in court or provide testimony.
3 The implications for interaction of the child or youth with intellectual disabilities within the judicial process and strategies to enhance
   the retrieval process.

Emerging Practice in the Field of Intellectual Disabilities

Within the field of intellectual disabilities, there are two prevailing
approaches to the formulation of the concept of disability: individual
pathology (biomedical or functional approaches) or social pathology
(environmental or rights-outcome approaches) (Rioux, 2003). When
compared to the prevailing concepts of equity (equal treatment, equal

opportunity, or equal outcome), the implications for discrimination across these divergent formulations vary significantly. Canadian law requires equal treatment, a concept based largely on a biomedical model. As such, the premise of equal treatment provided by rights recognizes the social responsibility to protect the individual from the ill effects of a disability through state protection. Other models, either individual or pathological, that see the disability as either functional or environmentally caused, pose a concept of equal opportunity as an issue of right, leading to compensatory privilege and the provision of services to minimize the disabling condition. Lastly, an emerging concept is based on the entitlement of the right to an equal outcome. This concept of equality takes a distinctive rights-outcome approach and envisions rights outcomes as determined by the status of well-being, where well-being is measured by citizenship (Rioux, 2003).

The challenge in adopting a human rights and well-being approach to the field of disability is that it would require examination both of the structures and systems in which persons with intellectual disabilities are served and, more specifically, of the range of opportunities and the conditions within these structures and systems that facilitate or impede those opportunities (Rioux, 2003). This examination has major implications for the policy and practice of service delivery and support.

In recent years, Canadians have gained a growing awareness of the need to develop proactive policies to ensure that the rights of people with intellectual disabilities are respected. Many of the community-based service agencies in Canada that support children and youth with intellectual disabilities fall under the funding umbrella of provincial ministries, such as those for community and social services, and are sponsored by the Canadian Association for Community Living (CACL) and its provincial and local affiliates, or through family and children's services. Although there are overarching provincial guidelines, most agencies determine their own policies and procedures for practice. Similarly, educational opportunities play a vital role in the support of children and youth with intellectual disabilities; these services are provided locally, with general guidelines being established within the education act and policies being locally determined. While the model of decentralization provides opportunities for agencies to create locally appropriate policy, at the same time it creates enormous inconsistency within the system in terms of the opportunities provided.

In most cases, challenges to rights violations for persons with intellectual disabilities arise not from any dispute with the legal or philosophical affirmation of rights in principle, but rather from the practice (economic, social, and cultural aspects) of how the exercise of rights is measured. The interrelatedness of these two aspects of rights (Rioux, 2003) was recognized for the first time in 1991 at the Convention of Rights of the Child. Rioux notes that the practices of rights 'have to be organized in a manner that enables individuals to participate in decision making. They have to permit the development of a human rights model and indicators of compliance that incorporate both structural and individual properties' (p. 314).

As in Canada, Australians living in the State of Victoria who have disabilities are guaranteed the same rights as all other citizens of that country. Young and Quibell (2000) emphasize that enshrinement of rights in law does not guarantee meaningful community inclusion. They cite concerns that rights legislation has been used to ensure minimum services but is limited in producing broad-based social change and protection from abuse. They further argue that 'negative rights' protections tend to be applied only after a right has been violated. A focus on negative rights does not promote examination of the systemic factors that contribute to rights violations, and strategies are necessary to ensure respect for rights.

Young and Quibell argue that a major failure in both the U.S. and State of Victoria models is that responsibility for ensuring that the rights of people with disabilities are respected is often left to others. The citizens with intellectual disabilities themselves are frequently left to rely on others to speak for them. The focus on rights has emphasized individual autonomy and the law over the fundamental need for human beings to understand one another: 'Rather than acting as atomistic individuals, people should attempt to understand each other, to "do each other justice." In this way, we come to terms with who people are, where they come from, and what they need' (p. 758). A commitment to this view moves people from perceiving justice as existing only in law to a focus on meaningful interaction and dialogue one with another, and to hearing people's personal narratives.

Service providers have a responsibility to both affirm and protect the rights of the persons they support. This can be accomplished through education, by establishing processes that will ensure that individuals have the same opportunities as non-disabled persons to exercise their rights, and by removing barriers to the exercise of those rights (Accreditation Ontario, 2000).

Rights Education: The Need for a Systemic Approach

Young and Quibell's point is that rights are not sufficient; understanding is necessary and understanding is facilitated by meaningful dialogue. However, for this to be real, participants in the dialogue must have access to their own voice, a voice that can be strengthened by making people aware of their rights and then providing them with a supportive forum in which to exercise them. During the course of the *3Rs: Rights, Respect and Responsibility Project* referred to earlier in this chapter, a man described the challenges he faced in persuading those around him that he wanted to make choices about his own medication. He described the long dialogue in which he engaged with powerful others in his life. No social analysis could be as powerful for those who witnessed this recounting and the sheer joy he expressed when, at the end of his story, he exclaimed exultantly that the outcome for him was 'No more pills!' This personal narrative was transformational for those who witnessed it.

Understanding the first-person lived experience of those struggling with issues such as those expressed by this man requires a broad systemic focus and education to help people who have intellectual disabilities to be heard in a meaningful and systemically impactful way. It is this commitment to a systemic view that inspired the development of the *3Rs: Rights, Respect and Responsibility Project* (Griffiths et al., 2003, Owen, Griffiths, Stoner, Gosse, et al., 2003). This ongoing action-research project focuses on rights-awareness education in the context of the need for respect and responsibility for self and others. It examines rights in relationships and in an everyday context. The education program promotes the ability to identify rights violations and an awareness of strategies that can be used to redress them. To promote understanding and the potential for generalizing training to the home environment, the *3Rs* project has produced an interactive CD-ROM that includes human-rights scenarios portrayed by volunteer actors who have disabilities. The results of preliminary testing show that participants demonstrated a significant change in their ability to identify rights violations and ways they could be remediated following training that was provided using either a classroom format or the interactive CD-ROM (Owen, Griffiths, Stoner, Vyrostko, et al., 2004).

Educating people with disabilities about the nature of human rights and how they can be applied in daily life is necessary, but not sufficient, to ensure a rights-promotion culture. For that to happen, it is necessary to embed the rights education in a broad system of supports that includes those who, by virtue of their access to resources and their organizational position, are able to facilitate responses to expressed rights concerns. This includes parents, sibling caregivers, educators, medical personnel, and community agency staff.

Caregiver Training and a Systemic Response

Before responsible rights-awareness education can be provided in a school or community agency context, it is necessary to ensure that the organization has committed itself to provide an environment that will support the rights it espouses and, at a practical level, that it has established a mechanism to monitor reported rights limitations, restrictions, and infringements. This is no small task. As in the case of ensuring children's participation in decision-making (Shier, 2001), organizations must enshrine this commitment in policy and in practice. In the case of the education program developed through the *3Rs Project*, organizations undertaking the program must commit to the adoption by their board of directors of a rights statement and to having their staff trained in these principles before the education program is provided to the people supported by the organization. The absence of such a broad systemic commitment could lead to abuse if a person makes a complaint that does not receive an appropriate response (Owen, Griffiths, Stoner, Gosse, et al., 2003).

The *3Rs Project* advocates that each participating organization have access to a Rights Facilitation Committee consisting of members of the organization's administration and staff, with community representatives from various relevant disciplines. The function of this committee is to review and recommend responses to rights concerns brought forward by people supported by the community organization, their care-providers, and families. In addition, staff working in community agencies must be trained first so that they are aware of the material the people they support will be learning, and will be equipped to respond appropriately.

Families have their own particular concerns related to human rights. In a pilot study of thirty-four participants designed to gather information about the human rights concerns of families with children or adult members with intellectual disabilities, families who have a member living in a community residential service, and families who support individuals with intellectual disabilities through the Family Home Program, Penic (2004) found that families had human rights concerns in the following areas: (a) diagnosis and treatment; (b) issues related to the educational system; (c) issues in the employment of persons with ID; (d) sexuality and sterilization; and (e) the availability of supports for families including funding, information, and recreation for children. Parent advocacy groups exist in Canada and around the world to help parents address such issues, and to advocate for systemic change (Reyes, 1999).

Self-Expression and Active Participation in Decision-Making

The new shift to a person-centred approach to service delivery is dependent on participation by each individual in his or her life decisions. Shier (2001) has proposed a model for facilitating children's full participation in decision-making about their lives in accordance with the United Nations Convention on the Rights of the Child (article 12.1). He suggests a five-tiered model of participation: '1. Children are listened to; 2. Children are supported in expressing their views; 3. Children's views are taken into account; 4. Children are involved in decision-making processes; 5. Children share power and responsibility for decision-making' (p. 110). As with person-centred planning, Shier's model challenges organizations to develop policies that ensure children's full participation in decisions about their lives.

This is not to say that the expressed preferences of children and youth are the sole basis on which decisions about their lives are based. All relevant factors, including their preferences, must be considered. 'A sound policy is to look for areas where, weighing up all the potential risks and benefits, it is appropriate for children to share power and responsibility for decisions, then to make this happen in a supportive environment' (Shier, 2001, p. 115). The determination of risks and benefits is, of course, extraordinarily complex. Adults' conceptions of childhood tend to determine their perception of children's autonomy. Cavet and Sloper (2004) argue that there is evidence supporting the ability of children with various disabilities to participate in decision-making about their lives 'if they are asked in an appropriate way and offered the right support' (p. 284). The 'right support' includes the following: multi-media approaches; suitable communication aids; using a variety of sources to get to know the child; approaches that are individualized and responsive to each child's age, gender, and ethnic background; flexibility regarding the manner in which children participate; confidential participation; and a child-centred approach that makes participation in decision-making fun. While this approach is encouraging, the authors admit that they found little research focused on the participation of children with profound cognitive impairments.

Adoption of a person-centred approach demands that families and other caregivers examine their willingness and ability to create an environment and a system of supports that promotes full participation by children who have intellectual disabilities, no matter how technically challenging that task may be. Full participation must also be based in an awareness of human rights.

Summary

Internationally, there has been a long and painful history of abuse, abandonment, depersonalization, and neglect in the lives of children and youth with disabilities of all kinds and intellectual disabilities in particular. It is only relatively recently that children and young people with intellectual disabilities have been afforded the rights that other citizens have come to take for granted. Of particular importance is the right to active participation in decisions about the care they receive and the activities in which they engage. While this is a complex area for children who do not have a disability, for those who do, the balance of the need for protection with the right to self-determination is far from clear. It is mitigated by the conceptions of childhood and disability held by those in positions of power: family members, care-providers, educators, medical personnel, and others. Lack of information about their rights and difficulty in self-expression can prevent children and young people with intellectual disabilities from being active participants in decisions that change their lives. Emerging trends in the field of services for people with intellectual disabilities reflect an increasing commitment to person-centred service planning and systemically grounded human-rights awareness education.

REFERENCES

Accreditation Ontario (2000). *Enhancing the rights and personal freedoms of people with disabilities.* Algoma Mills, ON: Author.
Abel, G.G., & Rouleau, J. (1990). The nature and extent of sexual assault. In W.L. Marshall, D.R. Laws, & H.E. Barbaree (Eds.), *Handbook of sexual assault* (pp. 9–21). New York: Plenum Press.

Asch, A., Gostin, L.O., & Johnson, D.M. (2003). Respecting persons with disabilities and preventing disability: Is there a conflict? In S.S. Herr, L.O.
Gostin, and H.H. Koh (Eds.), *The human rights of persons with intellectual disabilities: Different but equal* (pp. 319–346). Oxford, UK: Oxford University Press.

Beauchamp, T., & Childrenss, J. (1994) *Principles of biomedical ethics* (4th ed.).
Toronto: Oxford University Press.

Blanchet, A. (1995). The right to medical treatment. In Roeher Institute (Ed.),
As if children matter: Perspectives on children, rights and disability. Toronto,
ON: Roeher Institute.

Blaska, J. (1993). The power of language: Speak and write using 'person first.'
In M. Nagler (Ed.), *Perspectives on disability*. Palo Alto, CA: Health Markets
Research.

Brabeck, M.M., & Lauren, R. (2000). Human rights as a moral issue: Lessons
for moral educators from human rights work. *Journal of Moral Education,
29*(2), 167–183.

Brown, B.S., & Courtless, R.F. (1971). *Mentally retarded offender.* Washington,
DC: National Institute of Mental Health.

Brown, L., Long, E., Udvari-Solner, A., Davis, L., VanDeventer, R., Ahlgrem,
C., Johnson, F., Gruenewald, L, & Jorgensen, J. (1988*). The home school: Why
students with severe intellectual disabilities must attend the schools of their broth-
ers, sisters, friends and neighbors.* Madison: University of Wisconsin-Madison
and Madison Metropolitan School District.

Canadian Charter of Rights and Freedoms: A Guide for Canadians (1982). Ottawa:
Minister of Supply and Services Canada.

Carlberg, C., & Kavale, K. (1980). The efficacy of special versus regular class
placement for exceptional children: A meta-analysis. *Journal of Special Education, 14*, 25–52.

Carr, E.G. (1977). The motivation of self-injurious behaviour: A review of
some hypotheses. *Psychological Bulletin, 84*, 800–816.

Carr, E.G., Horner, R.H., Turnbull, A.P., Marquis, J.G., McLaughlin, D.M.,
McAtee, M. I., Smith, C.E., Anderson Ryan, K., Ruef, M.B., Doolabh, A., &
Braddock, D. (1999). *Positive behavior support for people with developmental
disabilities: A research synthesis.* Washington, DC: AAMR.

Cavet, J., & Sloper, P. (2004). Disabled children's participation in decision-
making. *Children & Society, 18*, 278–290.

Conley, R.W., Luckasson, R., & Bouthilet, G.N. (1992). *The criminal justice
system and a developmental disability: Defendants and victims.* Baltimore: Paul
H. Brookes Publishing.

Constitution Act 1982. Part I – Canadian Charter of Rights and Freedoms. Section
15(1).

Day, K. (1997). Clinical features and offence behaviour of mentally retarded sex offenders: A review of research. In R.J. Fletcher & D. Griffiths (Eds.), *Congress proceedings: International congress II on the dually diagnosed.* New York: NADD.

Doe, T. (1995). Access to justice and children with disabilities. In Roeher Institute (Ed.), *As if children matter: Perspectives on children, rights and disabilities* (pp. 49–56). Toronto, ON: Roeher Institute.

Donnellan, A.M., & LaVigna, G.W. (1990) Myths about punishment. In A.C. Repp. A.C. & N.N. Singh (Eds.), *Perspectives on the use of nonaversive and aversive interventions for persons with developmental disabilities* (pp. 30–57). Sycamore, IL: Sycamore Publishing Co.

Feldman, M. (1990). Balancing freedom from harm and right to treatment for persons with developmental disabilities. In A.C. Repp, & N.N. Singh (Eds.), *Perspectives on the use of nonaversive and aversive interventions for persons with developmental disabilities* (pp. 261–271). Sycamore, IL: Sycamore Publishing Co.

Feldman, M., Condillac, R.A., Tough, S., Hunt, S., & Griffiths, D. (2002). Effectiveness of community positive behavioral intervention for persons with developmental disabilities and severe behavior disorders. *Behavior Therapy, 33*(3), 377–399.

Feldman, M., Owen, F., Griffiths, D., Tarulli, D., Tardif, C. Mcqueen-Fuentes, G., Atkinson, L., Fedoroff, P., & Lunsky, Y. (2005). Facilitating health care and mental health care access for persons with intellectual disabilities: One element of systemic change. *The NADD Bulletin, 8(4)*, 71–76.

Flynn, R.J., & Lemay, R.A. (1999). Normalization and social role valorization at a quarter-century: Evolution, impact and renewal. In R.J. Flynn & R.A. Lemay (Eds.), *A quarter century of normalization and social role valorization: Evolution and impact* (pp. 3–16). Ottawa: University of Ottawa Press.

Fuchs, D., & Fuchs, L.S. (1994). Inclusive schools movement and the radicalization of special education reform. *Exceptional Children, 60*, 294–309.

Garth, B., & Aroni, R. (2003). 'I value what you have to say.' Seeking the perspective of children with a disability, not just their parents. *Disability & Society, 18*, 561–576.

Gartner, A., & Lipsky, D. (1987). Beyond special education: Toward a quality system for all students. *Harvard Education Review, 57*, 367–395.

Goddard, H. (1920). *Feeble-mindedness: Its causes and consequences.* New York: MacMillan.

Griffiths, D., Owen, F., Gosse, L., Stoner, K., Tardif, C.Y., Watson, S., Sales, C., & Vyrostko, B. (2003). Human rights and persons with intellectual disabilities: A method for a community-based organizational self-evaluation. *Journal on Developmental Disabilities, 10*(2), 25–43.

Griffiths, D., & Marini, Z. (2000). Interacting with the legal system regarding a sexual offence: Social and cognitive considerations for persons with developmental disabilities. *Journal of Developmental Disabilities, 7*, 77–121.

Griffiths, D., & Watson, S. (2004). Demystifying syndromes associated with developmental disabilities. In D. Griffiths & R. King (Eds.), *Demystifying syndromes*. Kingston, NY: NADD.

Guru, V., Verbeek, P.R., & Morrison, L.J. (1999). Response of paramedics to terminally ill patients with cardiac arrest: An ethical dilemma. *CMAJ, 161*(10), 1251–1254.

Herr, S. S. (2003). From wrongs to rights: International human rights and legal protection. In S.S. Herr, L.O. Gostin, and H.H. Koh (Eds.), *The human rights of persons with intellectual disabilities: Different but equal* (pp. 115–150). Oxford, UK: Oxford University Press.

Hollander, R. (1989). Euthanasia and mental retardation: Suggesting the unthinkable. *Mental Retardation, 27*(2), 53–61.

Kauffman, J. M. (1993). How we might achieve the radical reform of special education. *Exceptional Children, 60*, 6–16.

Lansdown, G. (1998). Practice and implementation: The rights of disabled children. *International Journal of Children's Rights, 6*, 221–227.

Lennox, N.G., & Kerr, M.P. (1997). Primary health care and people with intellectual disability: The evidence base. *Journal of Intellectual Disability Research, 41*, 365–372.

Leondari, A. (1993). Comparability of self-concept among normal achievers, low achievers and children with learning difficulties. *Educational Studies, 19*, 357–371.

Luckasson, R. (1992). People with a developmental disability as victims of crime. In R.W. Conley, R. Luckasson, & G.N. Bouthilet (Eds.), *The criminal justice system and mental retardation: Defendants and victims*. Baltimore: Paul H. Brookes Publishing.

Marinos, V., & Griffiths, D. (2005). Persons with intellectual disabilities and their participation in the courtroom. Ottawa: National Judicial Institute.

Marinos, V., & Griffiths, D. (in press). Persons with intellectual disabilities and the law. In F. Owen & D. Griffiths, *Rights and intellectual disability*. Publisher to be determined.

Masuda, S., & Ridington, J. (1990). *Meeting our needs: An access manual for transition houses*. Toronto: DisAbled Women's Network Canada.

McGee, J., & Menolascino, F.J. (1992). The evaluation of defendants with mental retardation in the criminal justice system. In R.W. Conley, R. Luckasson, and G.N. Bouthilet (Eds.), *The criminal justice system and mental retardation: Defendants and victims* (pp. 55–77). Baltimore: Paul. H. Brookes Publishing.

Moschella, S. (1982). The mentally retarded offender: Law enforcement and court proceedings. In M.B. Santamour & P.S. Watson (Eds.), *The retarded offender*. New York: Praeger.

Muir v. Alberta, [1996] 4 W.W.R. 177, 132 D.L.R. (4th) 695, (Alta. Q.B.).

Murphy, W.D., Coleman, E.M., & Haynes, M. (1983). Treatment and evaluation issues with the mentally retarded sex offender. In J. Greer & I. Stuart (Eds.), *The sexual aggressor: Current perspectives on treatment*. New York: Van Nostrand Reinhold.

Neuman, E. (1984, February 14). Human rights and the nursing home resident. Address to the Institute on Nursing Home Care, Toronto, ON.

O'Neill. O. (1996). Children's rights and children's lives. In R. E. Ladd (Ed.), *Children's rights re-visioned: Philosophical readings*. Scarborough, ON: Nelson Canada.

Oosterhoorn, R., & Kendrick, A. (2001). No sign of harm: Issues of disabled children communicating about abuse. *Child Abuse Review, 10*, 243–253.

Owen, F., Griffiths, D., Stoner, K., Gosse, L., Watson, S., Tardif, C.Y., Sales, C., & Vyrostko, B. (2003). Multi-level human rights training: The first step to changing systems. *Journal on Developmental Disabilities, 10*(2), 43–64.

Owen, F., Griffiths, D., Stoner, K., Vyrostko, B., Tardif, C., Tarulli, D., McQueen-Fuentes, G., Sales, C., Feldman, M., & Gosse, L. (2004). Multimedia technology in human rights training for individuals supported by community agencies. Unpublished presentation at annual conference of National Association for Dual Diagnosis Conference, Vancouver, BC.

Parker, S. (2001). Latimer's lethal legacy. *The Report Newsmagazine, 28*, 18.

Parr, A. (2005). The deterritorializing language of child detainees: Self-harm or embodied graffiti? *Childhood, 12*, 281–299.

Penic, L. (2004). Parent concerns for the human rights of individuals with intellectual disabilities. Unpublished honours thesis, Brock University, St Catharines, ON.

Pringle, H. (1997, June). Alberta Barren. *Saturday Night, 112*(5), 30–36, 70, 74.

R. v. Langevin (1984), 9 C.R.R. 16 (Ont. C.A.).

Re Eve (1986), 31 D.L.R. (4th) 1 (S.C.C.).

Re S.D., [1986] 3 W.W.E. 597 (B.C. Prov. Ct.), [1983] 3 W.W.R. 618 / (B.C. Sup. Ct.)

Reiss, S., Levitan, G.W., & Szyszko, J. (1982). Emotional disturbance and mental retardation: Diagnostic overshadowing. *American Journal of Mental Deficiency, 86*(6), 567–574.

Reyes, E.I. (1999). Parents, families and communities ensuring children's rights. *Bilingual Review, 24*, 53–62.

Rioux, M. (1996). Reproductive technology: A rights issue. *Entourage, Summer*, 5–7.

Rioux, M.R. (2003). On second thought: Constructing knowledge, law, disability and inequity. In S.S. Herr, L.O. Gostin, and H.H. Koh (Eds.), *The human rights of persons with intellectual disabilities: Different but equal* (pp. 319–346). Oxford, UK: Oxford University Press.

Rioux, M.R. & Frazee, C.L. (1999). Rights and freedoms. In I. Brown & M. Percy (Eds.), *Developmental disabilities in Ontario*. Toronto, ON: Front Porch Publishing.

Rooke, J. (2003). Reaching one's potential: A discussion of individual human rights and people with developmental disabilities in Canada. *Journal on Developmental Disabilities, 10*(2), 15–24.

Ryan, R. (2001). *Handbook of mental health care of persons with developmental disabilities*. Quebec, QC: Diverse City Press.

Santamour, W., & West, B. (1978). *The mentally retarded offender and corrections*. Washington, DC: U.S. Department of Justice.

Scheerenberger, R.C. (1983). *A history of mental retardation*. Baltimore: Paul H. Brookes Publishing.

Schultz, G.S. (1996). Taxonomy of rights: A proposed classification system of rights for individuals with mental retardation or developmental disabilities. *Journal of Developmental and Physical Disabilities, 8*(3), 275–285.

Shier, H. (2001). Pathways to participation: Openings, opportunities and obligations: A new model for enhancing children's participation in decision-making, in line with Article 12.1 of the United Nations Convention on the Rights of the Child. *Children & Society, 15*, 107–i17.

Small, M.W., & Parsley, L. (2003). Liberty, due process and the pursuit of happiness. In S.S. Herr, L.O. Gostin, & H.H. Koh (Eds.), *The human rights of persons with intellectual disabilities: Different but equal* (pp. 185–199). Oxford, UK: Oxford University Press.

Sobsey, D. (1994). *Violence and abuse in the lives of people with disabilities: The end of silent acceptance?* Baltimore: Paul H. Brookes Publishing.

Sobsey, D., Donnellan, A., & Wolbring, G. (1994). Reflections on the Holocaust: Where did it begin and has it really ended? *Developmental Disabilities Bulletin, 22*, 120–135.

Sobsey, D., Lucardie, R., & Mansell, S. (1995). *Violence and disability: An annotated bibliography*. Baltimore: Paul H. Brookes Publishing.

Sobsey, D., & Varnhagen, C. (1988). *Sexual abuse, assault, and exploitation of people with disabilities*. Ottawa: Health and Welfare Canada.

Stainback, S. & Stainback, W. (1996). *Inclusion: A guide for educators*. Baltimore: Paul H. Brookes Publishing.

Tarulli, D., Tardif, C.Y., Griffiths, D., Owen, F., McQueen-Fuentes, G.,

Feldman, M.A., Sales, C., & Stoner, K. (2004). Human rights and persons with intellectual disabilities: Historical, pedagogical and philosophical considerations. *Encounters in Education, 56,* 161–181.

Tricol, M. (1996). The human genome project: A challenge for the new millennium. *Entourage, Summer,* 10–12.

United Nations. (1989). *Convention on the Rights of the Child.*

U.S. Department of Health and Human Services (2002). *Closing the gap: A national blueprint to improve the health of persons with mental retardation.* The Report of the Surgeon General's Conference on Health Disparities and Mental Retardation, 5.

Van Houten, R., Axelrod, S., Bailey, J.S., Favell, J.E., Foxx, R.M., Iwata, B.A., & Lovaas, O.I. (1988). The right to effective behavioral treatment. *Journal of Applied Behavior Analysis, 21*(4), 381–384.

Wang, M.C., & Baker, E.T. (1985–1986). Mainstreaming programs: Design features and effects. *Journal of Special Education, 19,* 503–521.

Weagant, B., & Griffiths, D. (1988). Legal advocacy and the use of aversives. In G. Allan Roeher Institute (Ed.), *The language of pain: Perspectives on behaviour management* (pp. 115–130). Toronto, ON: G. Allan Roeher Institute.

Welland Tribune (1995, April 13). Down's victim awaits transplant.

Wiener, J., & Tardif, C.Y. (2004). Social and emotional functioning of children with learning disabilities: Does special education placement make a difference? *Learning Disabilities Research & Practice, 19,* 20–32.

Wilson, C., & Brewer, N. (1992). The incidence of criminal victimization of individuals with an intellectual disability. *Australian Psychologist, 2,* 1114–1117.

Wolfensburger, W. (1989). The killing thought in the eugenic era and today: A commentary on Hollander's essay. *American Association on Mental Retardation, 27,* 63–65.

Young, D.A., & Quibell, R. (2000) Why rights are never enough: Rights, intellectual disability and understanding, *Disability & Society, 15*(5), 747–764.

8 Protecting the Rights of Alleged of Child Abuse in Adult-Based Ju Systems

KIM P. ROBERTS AND ANGELA D. EVANS

The U.N. Convention on the Rights of the Child asserts that states parties are obligated to protect children from abuse, neglect, and maltreatment by establishing 'effective procedures for ... identification, reporting, referral, investigation, treatment, and follow-up of instances of child maltreatment ... and, as appropriate, judicial involvement' (article 19). Establishing what effective procedures entail has proved to be a difficult dance for countries with adult-based, adversarial judicial systems such as Canada, the United States, the United Kingdom, and Australia. Jurors in child abuse trials, for example, sometimes rely on the child's distressed demeanour to conclude that abuse did take place (see Golding, Fryman, Marsil, & Yozwiak, 2003). Reducing children's trauma in the judicial system, therefore, may prevent successful prosecution in child abuse trials. Other chapters in this volume address the difficult issues that arise when the Convention is applied in legal situations (e.g., Shariff and Johnny's chapter on cyber-bullying). In this chapter we specifically evaluate what procedures exist for the *investigation* of child abuse within the context of adversarial judicial systems, and how they address children's rights.[1]

Key characteristics of investigations involving child witnesses are identified and evaluated with respect to how they attempt to fulfil the obligation to provide effective procedures for the investigation of child abuse. Essentially, we outline the developmental profile of child witnesses with respect to these judicial requirements and show that many

---

1 In contrast to adversarial justice systems, some countries such as Germany and the Netherlands function with inquisitorial systems that do not have any juries. Instead, decisions are made by appointed panels of experts and judges. For current purposes, however, 'adversarial justice systems' will be abbreviated to 'justice systems.'

current practices are not effective procedures because children are
expected to reach adult standards of evidence rather than standards
that better match their developmental levels. A critical analysis of judicial systems is presented with particular emphasis on the adult standards expected of children in these contexts, and the requirement to
balance children's rights with those of defendants. We then assess
modifications that have been made in Western judicial systems that
attempt to enhance the court testimony of alleged victims of child maltreatment. In sum, the chapter explores some of the complexities inherent in protecting children's rights (particularly those in articles 3, 12,
19, and 36 of the CRC) while also ensuring that children can participate
in a fair, judicial process in cases of child maltreatment. While some
progress has been made in protecting children's rights through courtroom modifications, these modifications are experienced by only a
small percentage of children in the system. We conclude that greater
emphasis needs to be placed on the development and training of
interview protocols that are developmentally normed. Enhancing the
quality of investigative interview procedures will allow a greater percentage of children the opportunity to describe their experiences in
ways that adequately reach judicial standards. In this way, children's
rights are protected (because the investigation process is effective, as
required by article 19), as are defendants' rights as outlined by judicial
systems are also protected (because they can still contest children's evidence).

Background

Article 12 of the United Nations Convention on the Rights of the Child
states that the child who is capable of forming his or her own views
has the 'right to express those views freely in all matters affecting the
child, the views of the child being given due weight in accordance
with the age and maturity of the child.' Further, the convention states
that children must be 'provided with the opportunity to be heard in
any judicial ... proceedings affecting the child.' Applied to the case of
children who have been abused or maltreated, children essentially
have the right to 'tell their story.' On first glance, this seems to com-
plement the requirements of justice systems given that the main evidence in many instances of crimes against children, such as sexual
abuse, is the alleged victims' testimony about what occurred. Sexual
abuse cases, in particular, are notorious for the lack of physical or

medical evidence (e.g., Lamb, Sternberg, Esplin, Hershkowitz, Orbach, & Hovav, 1997). Many victims do not disclose abuse until some time has passed, when little physical evidence remains. Further, there are typically few witnesses to the abuse. Thus, children's ability to accurately recount the details of their abuse is central to successful prosecution. It seems that investigators, prosecutors, and the United Nations are in agreement as to what child witnesses can be encouraged to do.

Despite such agreement, prosecution of child abuse requires more than children simply giving narratives of their experiences. In any given investigation, there are a number of details that must be specified with exactitude to fulfil the requirements of the justice system, such as the temporal and spatial context of the incidents, the exact actions, the order of actions, and so on (Poole & Lamb, 1998; Wilson & Powell, 2001). For example, probing the time at which an incident took place gives an alleged perpetrator fair opportunity to provide an alibi. Although it is well established that children can have remarkable memories of their experiences (see Hudson, Fivush, & Kuebli, 1992), some of the concepts probed in investigative interviews are beyond the developmental capacity of the youngest victims. Failure to report such details or errors in reporting can adversely impact the credibility of child witnesses and may affect the likelihood of prosecution.

As well as aspects of the investigation, children face challenges within the whole environment of the justice system, particularly within the courtroom. In addition to simply lacking knowledge of the justice system (Saywitz, Jaenicke, & Camparo, 1990), children face scrutiny with respect to their understanding of the need to tell the truth (because it is assumed that they may be more likely to lie than adults; Talwar & Lee, 2002), and are challenged by legalese (the complex nature of legal sentence construction combined with the use of terminology specific to the court; Saywitz et al., 1990). Participation in legal proceedings may, on the face of it, be fulfilling children's rights to express their views (article 12); on deeper examination, however, children are potentially denied their rights to tell their stories because of the strict parameters within which the justice system operates.

The justice system was not created with children in mind, yet prosecution of crimes against children must operate within the system. As a result, children are held to adult standards of testimony and judicial procedure, sometimes without regard to children's developmental profiles. Substantial progress has been made in courtrooms around the world to accommodate child witnesses (e.g., the use of screens so that children do not have to face the defendant; see Bala, Lee, & McNamara, 2001 and Myers, 1996). Yet children still face barriers to recounting their experiences accurately. The inherent conflicts between the child's right to protection and the child's right to participation are also addressed in other chapters in this volume (see Raby; Shariff and Johnny; and Zinga and Young). As we will see in the current chapter, addressing the developmentally inappropriate aspects of the justice system is complicated by the need to also address the rights of alleged perpetrators and the need to fulfil judicial standards.

In the first section, we address the developmental profile of children's memories as a function of how their reports are elicited. In the second and third sections, we identify two examples of judicial standards that can be particular challenges for children. In the second section, we evaluate children's ability to report key forensic details, particularly in light of the judicial requirement to recall the temporal context of abusive incidents. In the third section, we address the developmental profile of children's memories of repeated experiences given that at least 50 per cent of allegations involve repeated abuse. Finally, we examine developmental issues in the justice environment (e.g., children's understanding of the oath). In each section, we consider how the justice system considers children's development and their rights. We conclude with suggestions for a research agenda in the area of children's rights in the justice system, coupled with specific recommendations to ensure that children's rights are respected while the mandate to protect children is fulfilled.

Elicitation Techniques in Child Abuse Investigations

There is now a substantial body of knowledge demonstrating that children can provide detailed and accurate narratives of traumatic and non-traumatic experiences (e.g., see a recent review by Pipe, Lamb, Orbach, & Esplin, 2004). Whether children *will* provide such high-quality testimony, however, is dependent on the elicitation techniques employed by their interviewers. We first review scientific findings on how different elicitation techniques affect the quality of children's memory reports, and then turn to an examination of elicitation techniques used in the justice system in cases of child sexual and physical abuse.

In general, older children report more information about a given event than younger children do. In a well-cited study, for example,

Goodman and Reed (1986) asked children and adults to recall an incident with an unfamiliar man. Three year olds reported less information than did six year olds, and the six year olds reported less information than did adults. When memories were probed with specific questions to see whether the children *recognized* information from the event, however, the six year olds were as accurate as the adults, although the three year olds still remembered less information than the other groups. These results have been replicated many times (e.g., Gee, Gregory, & Pipe, 1999; and Roberts & Blades, 1999) and show that children often remember more information than they are able to report in response to general recall prompts such as 'Tell me what happened.'

Although children can answer recognition questions well, there is an important caveat that leads to the recommendation that such recognition questions be avoided if possible in the field of child abuse investigations. Numerous laboratory studies have shown that, while children can accurately answer recognition questions that contain details that actually occurred, children can be inaccurate when questions contain false information (e.g., 'Did he have a red jacket?' when there was no red jacket; see Ceci & Bruck, 1995, for a review). In contrast to lab studies, it is not possible in the field to know whether a given recognition question contains an accurate or inaccurate detail. Indeed, the main point of investigative interviews with alleged child victims is to ascertain what may have happened. Thus, alleged child victims may be swayed to provide inaccurate testimony if recognition questions are relied on as the main questioning technique, because the probability of introducing inaccurate details is raised with the use of recognition prompts.

If recall prompts such as 'Tell me what happened' elicit accurate but sparse accounts from children, how can children exercise their rights to tell their story (article 12) and how can the obligation to provide effective investigation procedures be fulfilled (article 19)? Research in the lab and in the field has shown that children can, in fact, be trained to respond informatively to general recall prompts. Children who practised answering recall prompts during a rapport-building phase subsequently gave more complete reports of their abuse than did children for whom rapport was established using recognition prompts (Sternberg, Lamb, Hershkowitz, Yudilevitch, Orbach, Esplin, & Hovav, 1997). Importantly, the style of rapport building did not adversely affect the accuracy of children's reports in a lab study (Roberts, Lamb, & Sternberg, 1999). In other studies, the use of recall-based prompts elicited more key forensic information from alleged sexual abuse victims than did the use of recognition-based prompts (Orbach, Hershkowitz, Lamb, Esplin, & Horowitz, 2000), even with children as young as three years old (Sternberg, Lamb, Orbach, Esplin, & Mitchell, 2000). Thus, recall prompts are the most effective way to elicit detailed testimony provided children have been trained in responding to such prompts. Although inaccurate reports can also be given in response to recall prompts, for example, when children have been exposed to highly suggestive procedures (e.g., Ceci, Loftus, Leichtman, & Bruck, 1994), children are given better opportunities to accurately recount their experiences when interviewed with recall prompts.

Despite the clear advantage of recall versus recognition prompts, an examination of interviewing practices in child sexual and physical abuse investigations reveals that most interviews incorporate recognition prompts as the primary interview method (e.g., Cederborg, Orbach, Sternberg, & Lamb, 2000; Davies, Westcott, & Horan, 2000; Myklebust & Laurence, 2000; Sternberg, Lamb, Hershkowitz, Esplin, Redlich, & Sunshine, 1996). These results are found despite investigative interviewers taking pains to receive training in child development and best interviewing practices, and despite interviewers' efforts to use recall prompts (Pipe et al., 2004). Indeed, an anecdotal observation by the first author is that the desire to implement best practices to protect alleged child victims is one of the most striking observations when working with front-line interviewers. Thus, there is a bottleneck in funnelling knowledge into practice. What has become clear is that effective interviewing is dependent on continuous feedback and evaluation of interviews (e.g., Lamb, Sternberg, Orbach, Hershkowitz, Horowitz, & Esplin, 2002; Warren, Woodall, Hunt, & Perry, 1996). This evaluation process takes time and intensive supervision, but is highly effective in enabling children (even pre-schoolers) to provide detailed accounts of their experiences. For example, in Israel, structured interviews incorporating open-ended questions are consistently used, and have been found to lead to a high rate of disclosure (Hershkowitz, Horowitz, & Lamb, 2005).

The above analysis showed that effective interviewing practices are not the norm, despite an international consensus on appropriate child interview techniques. Thus, one can argue that 'effective procedures ... .for the investigation ... of child maltreatment' (article 19) may be in place in principle, but not in practice. One reason why interviewers may be guiding children's testimony with recognition prompts rather than encouraging children to describe their experiences in their own words is that key forensic details the justice system requires (e.g., the temporal and spatial context of incidents) . Such details can determine the charges laid against perpetrators as well as provide case information that is later the subject of debate in the courtroom. Because of the way that the justice system operates, then, investigative interviewers must sometimes directly probe for this information if children have not volunteered the information spontaneously. We now turn to an examination of children's ability to provide these case-specific details.

The Temporal Context of Abusive Incidents

There are common elements across different countries in information that is critical to successful investigation of child abuse. As well as an accurate account of the exact actions that took place, investigators need to elicit as best they can information about the timing, duration, frequency, and location of the behaviour (Wilson & Powell, 2001). Accurate retrieval of such information involves some understanding of concepts such as time and space, as well as measurement and comparison skills. Indeed, even without the memory demands of an investigative interview, temporal and spatial judgments can be difficult for young children (i.e., three to six year olds). In this section we focus on children's ability to provide *temporal information* about their experiences, because this information can be critical for prosecution and there is a body of knowledge that can inform us on the development of this ability.

A child sexual abuse case was recently held in California and the defendant, Alex Avila, was not convicted. One member of the jury commented that the defendant was acquitted because the child witness could not specify how many times the abuse had occurred (Lyon, 2002). In Australian courts children must specify the time or temporal context of each incident as part of the 'particularization' requirement (*S v. R.*, 1989). Children's understanding of temporal concepts is limited, however, until about age eight.

Research on children's understanding of time has shown that competence is achieved in some domains before others. Children as young as four years old, for example, can correctly sequence major aspects of a day (e.g., breakfast, lunch, dinner; Friedman, 1990), but have difficulty sequencing a single occurrence of a repeated event (Powell, Thomson, & Ceci, 2003). Sequencing events of the day in backwards order is not possible until about age six (Friedman, 1990), thus investigative interviewers, judges, and attorneys are more likely to elicit accurate responses from child witnesses by asking *What happened next?* or *What happened after that?* than by asking *What happened before that?*

Although some young children can make gross judgments of time, it is only at about age six that children can directly locate events in their correct time frame. For example, in Friedman's (1991) study, 70 per cent of children aged four could identify which of two events was most recent (when given one event that occurred a week ago, and one that was seven weeks prior), but they could not identify the day of the week, the month, or the season of the older event. Although children aged six and eight were able to temporally locate the event better than chance, only 39 per cent of the six year olds and 63 per cent of the eight year olds could specify the time of the event to within two days of when it occurred.

Even when children regularly use temporal words in their speech (e.g., 'We went to the park *yesterday*'), it is important for investigative interviewers to probe for further information using recall prompts. This is because children's comprehension typically lags behind their production of linguistic terms. Children aged three, for example, use the word 'yesterday' to mean any day that is not the present. In another example, a three year old who was told that his birthday was 'tomorrow' asked hopefully the following day, 'Is today tomorrow?' Thus, young children can operate with a temporal lexicon before full understanding of it is achieved.

Despite age differences in linguistics and in the ability to localize events, all of the children in Friedman's (1991) study were able to identify the general time of day that the event occurred (e.g., lunch time) and all recalled contextual details from the time of the events (e.g., the location of the events). Furthermore, children's errors showed that they have a general sense of time that could be useful in the effective investigation of crimes against children. For example, children were more likely to misattribute an event that happened on a school day to another school day, rather than a weekend day. Thus, children can accurately recall contextual details from an event even though they may not be able to use conventional time scales to exactly locate them, and they are able to contextually locate events with respect to meaningful aspects of their lives. This further underscores the age-appropriateness of using recall-based techniques when questioning child witnesses: it gives children the opportunity to report contextual details that may enable the events to be localized in time without the need for children to explicitly identify their time. Finally, children aged four to nine years can recall details of events that happened at a specific and meaningful time in the past (e.g., Halloween, child's birthday, last summer), which again showsthat children can provide forensically relevant information when questions are framed and formatted in an age-appropriate style (Friedman, 1992).

The level of specificity required regarding temporal details varies by jurisdiction. In some cases, protection by the legal system can only proceed if children can specify the time of alleged incidents; in other cases, however, such as when children have provided detailed accounts of incidents but without being able to exactly specify temporal information, one must ask whether such stringent and adult-based standards unfairly discriminate against child victim-witnesses. The question 'Has the child been abused?' becomes one of 'Is the child able to temporally specify the abuse?' and there is debate as to whether the latter question fulfils the obligation to provide effective procedures for the investigation and prosecution of abuse (article 19). As is outlined in the next section, reaching current standards of evidence is particularly difficult for children in cases of repeated abuse.

Eliciting Memories of Repeated Experiences

Although some jurisdictions allow prosecution to proceed with a general account of the alleged abuse, such as in some cases where a child has been repeatedly abused (Poole & Lamb, 1998), the norm in most cases is that the child must provide detailed information (e.g., describe when, who, where, and specific actions) for each separate alleged incident (e.g., S v. R., 1989). Children who are asked about multiple abusive incidents in forensic interviews will often describe individual incidents with generic phrases like 'the same as last time' or 'he always does it like this,' which demonstrates the highly repetitive nature of many children's sexual abuse experiences. Research on children's memories of non-abusive events shows that, after repeated experience of the event, children establish a 'general event representation' whereby characteristics that are common across the occurrences are well remembered and are used to structure recall (see Hudson, Fivush, & Kuebli, 1992). Even three year olds can develop such sophisticated 'scripts' and produce accurate and organized accounts of events (Fivush, Hudson, & Nelson, 1984; Nelson, 1986;

Powell, Roberts, Ceci, & Hembrooke, 1999). In other words, children can accurately recall general features that do not vary across repeated occurrences.

The ability to form scripts readily can be an advantage when children experience an occurrence that deviates in some way from the usual experience. In a study by Farrar and Goodman (1992), for example, children participated once or three times in a staged event (the standard event) and then participated in an additional event that contained features that deviated from the prior event(s). The seven year olds (but not the four year olds) in the study were better able to accurately recall features of the deviation event if they had experienced the standard event three times (and thus had built up a script of the event) than were children who had experienced the standard event just once (and thus had not built up a script).

As well as having some knowledge of research on children's recall of atypical details, it is also of relevance to child abuse investigations to know at what age children can accurately recall specific details when those details vary slightly *each time* an event is experienced (e.g., a child may be abused when a particular relative visits ,but the exact nature of the abuse differs each time). Recalling details that varied during each incident is more difficult than recalling details that were identical each time. Powell, Roberts et al. (1999), for example, asked five- to six-year-old children to recall the fourth occurrence of a repeated event. They found that children remembered an impressive 96 per cent of details that were identical across the occurrences, but just 35 per cent of details that had varied. Despite poor recall of the 'variable' details, children's errors were illuminating: 61 per cent of the errors came about in recalling the corresponding details in the other occurrences (e.g., recalling a puzzle of a clown juggling [from the third occurrence] rather than a puzzle of a clown on a bike [from the fourth occurrence]). Interestingly, these errors were more common than incorporating false information that had previously been suggested by interviewers (accounting for 9 per cent of the errors) and reporting details that had never taken place in any of the four occurrences (3 per cent of the errors).

Research on children's memories of repeated experiences, then, shows that children can accurately remember many of the features of the events but may be confused as to which details occurred in which specific incidents. Importantly, these findings resonate with those reported in the clinical literature about children who have experienced repeated traumatic events (Terr, 1991, 1994). Thus, children are most likely to be confused when the events are similar to each other, and when there has been a long delay before recall (e.g., Lindsay, Johnson, & Kwon, 1991; Roberts & Blades, 1999; Roberts & Powell, 2005). Children's credibility in instances such as these can be threatened because their confusion between incidents is sometimes used to cast doubt on their entire testimony. The research discussed above provides no evidence to support this practice: children's memories for repeated experiences rarely included false information (Powell, Roberts, et al., 1999). Hence, children who have been abused the most, and who may remember the events better than children who have been abused just one time, may be those least likely to see successful prosecution of their abuse. This raises the issue of whether expecting children to adhere to adult standards is simply unreasonable in cases of repeated abuse. Indeed, even adults are more confused between similar than dissimilar events (e.g., Lindsay et al., 1991; Roberts & Blades, 1999), make script-driven errors (Bower, Black, & Turner, 1979), and can be suggestible (e.g., Warren & Lane, 1995), though the absolute number of these errors is typically lower than that produced by children (see Ceci & Bruck, 1999). Nonetheless, it may be that the children who have been victimized the most are also the ones whose task in the justice system is most difficult.

The Justice System

'The justice system can be intimidating, overwhelming, and confusing.' Many adults would concur with that statement; how much more frightening might it then be for children implanted into an archaic system? In the following section, we have selected two aspects of the court system that pose challenges for children and for which there is a reasonable body of research assessing their impact: the courtroom environment and the oath to tell the truth.

With an increased number of children testifying in court there is a growing concern about the effects on child victims of taking the stand. Both short- and long-term effects of testifying on child victims have been documented. Specifically, children who took the stand exhibited more behavioural disturbances than non-testifiers, especially after testifying numerous times (Goodman, Taub, Jones, & England, 1992). In addition, long-term mental health was negatively affected by a number of factors such as children's age at the time of testifying, the severity of abuse, and the number of times children testified (Quas, Goodman, Ghetti, Alexander, Edelstein, Redlich, Cordon, & Jones, 2005). Thus, many children are further victimized by participating in court proceedings. This calls into question the implementation of article 3 of the U.N. Convention, whereby children have the right for parties to act in their 'best interests.'

Despite the trauma of court proceedings, however, children still have the right to be heard (article 12). Indeed, many children who were *not* given the opportunity to testify suffered poor mental health and maintained negative attitudes towards the justice system, especially if the perpetrator received a lenient sentence (Quas et al., 2005). Although children have the right to express their views regarding whether to testify (article 12), prosecutors sometimes make the final decision based on their knowledge of the court system. Thus, decisions about whether children should testify are sometimes based on judicial considerations designed ultimately to protect children by gaining convictions against perpetrators, rather than on children's desire to testify. Providing children with the opportunity to be heard can clearly result in both positive and negative consequences.

The court system is not regularly using the available innovative techniques that can reduce children's stress when testifying (Quas et al., 2005; Bala, Duvall-Antonacopoulos, Lindsay, Lee, & Talwar, in press). The use of such techniques as closed-circuit television, screens, and video-recorded evidence can minimize the impact of children's stress when testifying (Bala et al., 2001). Currently, the right to be heard and the right to be protected are not always working together in the justice system.

Witnesses testifying in court are required to take an oath to promise to tell the truth. There has been considerable debate about whether children are 'competent' to take such an oath and whether the competency exam has any bearing on whether child witnesses will tell the truth or lie. As children age, they are more likely to tell lies in order to conceal bad behaviour (Lewis, Stanger, & Sullivan, 1989; Talwar & Lee, 2002). Talwar and Lee, for example, found that only half of the three year olds in their study lied to conceal their bad behaviour, yet the majority of older children lied. Children also become more convincing liars with age because they learn to control their verbal and non-verbal behaviours in order to better conceal their lies. Although children as young as three can conceal their lies through non-verbal behaviours, they fail to control their verbal behaviour. By around the age of eight, children's lies are barely detectable by adults (Talwar & Lee, 2002). Therefore, although three year olds may not understand the concepts of truth and lies, they are less likely to lie and less skilled in their telling of lies than are older children.

In North America children are required before testifying in court to complete a competency exam assessing their understanding of truth and lies and to establish their moral standards of telling the truth (Bala et al., 2001). Once children's competency is established they will be asked prior to testifying to promise to tell the truth. However, recent evidence suggests that the discussion of truth and lies in a competency test has less impact on actual truth-telling than the simple act of prom-ising to tell the truth. In fact, it has been shown that children's under-standing of truth and lies has little impact on their truth-telling (Talwar, Lee, Bala, & Lindsay, 2002). As a result of psychological research on truth-telling, however, Canadian courts have now abol-ished the need for children to undergo a competency test (Bala et al., in press). The new amendments to Bill C-2 came into effect in early 2006. In short, the bill states that a child under the age of fourteen is presumed to have the capacity to testify, and the burden of proving otherwise is now placed on the defence. Children must continue to promise to tell the truth, but these new amendments allow children who were previously excluded, but were capable of testifying, to now take the stand.

Thus, research on children's lying and truth/lie discussions has resulted in simple recommendations in some jurisdictions that better fulfil children's right to 'effective procedures ... for judicial involve-ment' (article 19). It remains to be seen how the revisions to Bill C-2 in Canada affect the judicial process.

Summary and Conclusions

Children have the right to effective investigation of crimes committed against them (Article 19), and parties have the responsibility to put effective investigatory procedures in place. The research reviewed in this chapter shows that children have the capacity to be informative witnesses in cases of child sexual and physical abuse. However, there are some judicial requirements (e.g., specifying the temporal context of incidents, discriminating between multiple incidents, competency tests) that may exceed the capacity of some young witnesses. Ques-tions about the likelihood of abuse are superseded by questions about whether children can meet judicial standards to prosecute the abuse. Hence, the burden to protect children from abuse is partly dependent on the developmental capacities of abused children themselves.

There is clearly tension and conflict between the rights outlined in Articles 3 (best interests), 12 (freedom of expression), 19 and 36 (child protection) and children's involvement in the justice system. In this chapter, we identified two specific conflicts: (1) Children's right to be protected from maltreatment sometimes conflicts with the requirements of the justice system for children to provide adult-style testimony; (2) Defendants also have rights and these often conflict with children's rights. The two conflicts are somewhat related.

Protection of children through the legal system is possible by following existing legal procedures, yet many procedures serve adults well but are not well matched to children's unique cognitive and emotional capacities. Children are held to adult standards of testimony by being required to provide articulate, detailed accounts containing key contextual information particular to individual crimes. These standards are required so that defendants have opportunities to defend themselves when wrongfully accused. Given the severe consequences of child abuse convictions, it is important to maintain a justice system that is fair and just and where innocent people are able to protect their innocence. Respecting defendants' rights, however, sometimes prevents children's rights from being exercised or, at least, fully executed.

Many of the issues inherent in these conflicts stem from a naive view of children's capacities. Actual jurors have cited a child's apparent lack of temporal knowledge as a reason to acquit a defendant (Lyon, 2002), and defence attorneys sometimes use complex language when questioning child witnesses (Westcott, 1995). Assumptions are made, then about the cognitive and linguistic capabilities of child witnesses. Mock jury studies have shown that child witnesses are judged to be less honest and credible when children do not present themselves in ways consistent with jurors' expectancies about victims of child abuse (Regan & Baker, 1998). For example, Regan and Baker found that mock jurors judged distressed child witnesses to be more credible than witnesses who were not distressed. Defendants are considered to be 'innocent until proven guilty' and so child victims are required to meet standards of testimony that show beyond a doubt that the alleged crimes occurred. Thus, children who are unable to provide incident-specific information may be judged to be not credible, even though research shows that children can provide detailed and honest accounts of their experiences even if they cannot specify individual incidents (Roberts & Powell, 2001). Similarly, when children have difficulty responding to questions phrased in legal language (e.g., 'Did you not say that the defendant ... ?'), it does not indicate that their reports are inaccurate (Saywitz & Nathanson, 1993).

The resolution of the conflicts between upholding children's rights while maintaining defendants' rights hinges on debates about whether the standards of testimony can be relaxed for children without unfairly impinging on defendants' rights. An assumption that all testimony from children is accurate is not appropriate, as seen in the overturning of many of the convictions in high-profile daycare cases in the 1980s (see Ceci & Bruck, 1995). Further, over twenty years of research has carefully outlined the precise factors that affect the accuracy of children's reports of their experiences (see Pipe et al., 2004). By drawing on this research, it is possible to employ techniques that maximize the amount of accurate information children can report about their experiences. The more information children can report, the more opportunity there is for corroboration. Thus, it may be possible to follow up details provided by children to determine the likely guilt of defendants without recourse to adult standards and while protecting defendants' rights to a fair trial. Such testimony is only possible, of course, if children are interviewed in developmentally appropriate ways using open-ended interviewing techniques.

Several recommendations have developed from the review above. While substantial progress has been made to accommodate child witnesses in the courtroom, improvements in investigative procedures will likely protect a greater number of children. Thus, our recommendations focus mainly at the investigative stage. As even young children can provide informative accounts of their experiences, we endorse the recommendation from many agencies worldwide to elicit children's accounts by using recall-based elicitation techniques as much as possible. Investigative interviewers have a daunting responsibility to elicit accurate and complete accounts from children and need support in terms of time and training to be able to conduct good interviews. It is our argument that effective procedures for the investigation of abuse (article 19) must necessarily involve intensive and ongoing training and supervision of expert child interviewers.

The temporal context of events can sometimes be deduced from contextual information that children provide even when they are too young to provide exact temporal information. The use of recall-based interviewing protocols will help, but a wider dialogue must be initiated to determine what standards of temporal identification are required in different cases, especially in cases where children can provide otherwise articulate accounts of their experiences.

Human brains (adult and juvenile) process large amounts of repetitive information by extracting general details (Nelson, 1986). Discriminating between similar incidents can be a difficult task but one that does not necessarily encourage completely false information to intrude into memories (Powell et al., 1999). Recently, several groups of researchers have embarked on the difficult task of developing protocols that train children to discriminate between multiple incidents (e.g., Cameron & Roberts, 2005; Poole & Lindsay, 2001; Thierry & Spence, 2001). These protocols are in their infancy, but hopefully recommendations can soon be made for investigative interviews. For now, a major aim of researchers could be to educate the legal system on the way that memory works and what children (and adults) are capable of recalling after multiple experiences. It may be time to discuss whether the requirement to discriminate between multiple incidents is an inappropriate standard for cases involving child witnesses.

Many of these recommendations focus on improving the chances that child witnesses can provide testimony according to the standard currently required by courts (e.g., encouraging the use of recall-based elicitation techniques to maximize the completeness of reports). But how fair is it to place full responsibility on children to protect themselves, and how can this right to protection be reconciled with children's rights to participation? We argue that the legal system also has the responsibility to protect children involved in judicial proceedings. Researchers can help by educating judges, lawyers, front-line interviewers, and so on, about the developmental profile of children in the cognitive, social, and moral domains. Judges can educate jurors and prevent developmentally inappropriate techniques in the courtroom. Accurate expectations of what children at different ages and under different circumstances can reasonably accomplish may be better indicators of child credibility than current yardsticks (e.g., see Brady, Roberts, & Giardino, 2005).

Finally, most of the research in this chapter has been concerned with the capacities of children aged three to ten. There is a body of research on adolescents' understanding of their rights that has not been discussed here, but which shows that adolescents have limited understanding of, and do not invoke, their rights (e.g., Abramovitch, Peterson-Badali, and Rohan, 1995; Grisso, 1980). As well as further research in the area of children's understanding of their rights and their ability to protect those rights, it would also be informative to see more research on the eyewitness capacities of adolescents (Poole & Lindsay, 2001).

In sum, children's disclosures of abuse can be the start of a long and arduous journey to protect children from their aggressors. Children are key players in this journey and play a vital role in the justice system. To fulfil their rights as outlined in the U.N. Convention, we must be willing to strike a balance between fair expectations of children at different developmental levels and the need to maintain a fair and effective justice system.

REFERENCES

Abramovitch, R., Peterson-Badali, M., & Rohan, M. (1995). Young peoples' understanding and assertion of their rights to silence and legal counsel. *Canadian Journal of Criminology, 37*, 1–18.

Bala, N. (1999). Child witnesses in the Canadian criminal courts: Recognizing their capacities and needs. *Psychology, Public Policy, and Law, 5*, 323–354.

Bala, N., Duvall-Antonacopoulos, K., Lindsay, R.C.L., Lee, K., & Talwar, V. (in press). Bill C-2: A new law for Canada's child witnesses. *Criminal Reports.*

Bala, N., Lee, J., & McNamara, E. (2001). Children as witnesses: Recognizing their capacities, needs and experiences. *Journal of Social Distress & the Homeless, 10*, 41–68.

Bower, G.H., Black, J.B. & Turner, T.J. (1979). Scripts in memory for text. *Cognitive Psychology, 11*, 177–220.

Brady, A., Roberts, K.P., & Giardino, A. (2005). The developmental aspects of the young child in child maltreatment cases. In A. Giardino & R. Alexander (Eds.), 'Child maltreatment: A clinical guide and reference' (3rd Ed.) (pp. 343–366). St Louis, MO: GW Medical Publishing, Inc.

Cameron, S.C., & Roberts, K.P. (2005). 'I remember, I just can't remember where': Training children to discriminate between memories of highly similar events. Manuscript submitted for publication.

Ceci, S.J., & Bruck, M. (1995). *Jeopardy in the courtroom*. Washington, DC: American Psychological Association.

Ceci, S.J., Loftus, E.F., Leichtman, M.D., & Bruck, M. (1994). The possible role of source misattributions in the creation of false beliefs among preschoolers. *International Journal of Clinical and Experimental Hypnosis, 42*, 304–320.

Cederborg, A.C., Orbach, Y., Sternberg, K.J., & Lamb, M.E. (2000). Investigative interviews of child witnesses in Sweden. *Child Abuse & Neglect, 24,* 1355–1361.

Davies, G.M., Westcott, H.L., & Horan, N. (2000). The impact of questioning style on the content of investigative interviews with suspected child abuse victims. *Psychology, Crime & Law, 6,* 81–97.

Farrar, M.J., & Goodman, G.S. (1992). Developmental changes in memory. *Child Development, 63,* 173–187.

Fivush, R., Hudson, J., & Nelson, K. (1984). Children's long-term memory for a novel event: An exploratory study. *Merrill-Palmer Quarterly, 30,* 303–316.

Friedman, W.J. (1990). Children's representations of the pattern of daily activities. *Child Development, 61,* 1399–1412.

Friedman, W.J. (1991). The development of children's memory for the time of past events. *Child Development, 62,* 139–155.

Friedman, W.J. (1992). Children's time memory: The development of a differentiated past. *Cognitive Development, 7,* 171–187.

Gee, S., Gregory, M., & Pipe, M.E. (1999). 'What colour is your pet dinosaur?' The impact of pre-interview training and question type on children's answers. *Legal and Criminological Psychology, 4,* 111–128.

Golding, J.M., Fryman, H.M., Marsil, D.F., & Yozwiak, J.A. (2003). Big girls don't cry: The effect of child witness demeanor on juror decisions in a child sexual abuse trial. *Child Abuse & Neglect, 27,* 1311–1321.

Goodman, G.S., & Reed, R S. (1986). Age differences in eyewitness testimony. *Law and Human Behavior, 10,* 317–332.

Goodman, G.S., Taub, E.P., Jones, D.P., England, P., Port, L.K., Rudy, L., & Prado, L. (1992). Testifying in criminal court: Emotional effects on child sexual assault victims. *Monographs for the Society for Research in Child Development, 57,* 1–142.

Grisso, T. (1980). Juveniles' capacities to waive Miranda rights: An empirical analysis. *California Law Review, 68,* 1134–1166.

Hershkowitz, I., Horowitz, D., & Lamb, M.E. (2005). Trends in children's disclosure of abuse in Israel: A national study. *Child Abuse & Neglect, 29,* 1203–1214.

Hudson, J.A., Fivush, R., & Kuebli, J. (1992). Scripts and episodes: The development of event memory. *Applied Cognitive Psychology, 6,* 483–505.

Lamb, M.E., Sternberg, K.J., Esplin, P.W., Hershkowitz, I., Orbach, Y., & Hovav, M. (1997). Criterion-based content analysis: A field validation study. *Child Abuse and Neglect, 21,* 255–264.

Lamb, M., Sternberg, K J., Orbach, Y., Hershkowitz, I., Horowitz, D., &

Esplin, P.W. (2002). The effects of intensive training and ongoing supervision on the quality of investigative interviews with alleged sex abuse victims. *Applied Developmental Science, 6,* 114–125.

Lewis, M., Stanger, C., & Sullivan, M.W. (1989). Deception in 3–year-olds. *Developmental Psychology, 25,* 439–443.

Lindsay, S.D., Johnson, M.K., & Kwon, P. (1991). Developmental changes in memory source monitoring. *Journal of Experimental Psychology, 53,* 297–318.

Lyon, T.D. (2002). *Child maltreatment and the law: Avila's acquittal.* Paper presented at the annual meeting of the American Psychological Association.

Myers, J.E.B. (1996). A decade of international reform to accommodate child witnesses. *Criminal Justice & Behavior, 23,* 402–422.

Myklebust, T., & Laurence, A. (2000). The current state of police interviews with children in Norway: How discrepant are they from models based on current issues in memory and communication? *Psychology, Crime & Law, 6,* 331–351.

Nelson, K. (1986). *Event knowledge: Structure and function in development.* Hillsdale, NJ: Lawrence Erlbaum Associates.

Orbach, Y., Hershkowitz, I., Lamb, M.E., Esplin, P.W., & Horowitz, D. (2000). Assessing the value of structured protocols for forensic interviews of alleged child abuse victims. *Child Abuse & Neglect, 26,* 733–752.

Pezdek, K., & Roe, C. (1995). The effects of memory trace strength on suggestibility. *Journal of Experimental Child Psychology, 60,* 116–128.

Pipe, M.E., Lamb, M.E., Orbach, Y., & Esplin, P.W. (2004). Recent research on children's testimony about experienced and witnessed events. *Developmental Review, 42,* 404–468.

Poole, D.A., & Lamb, M.E. (1998). *Investigative interviews of children.* Washington, DC: American Psychological Association.

Poole, D.A., & Lindsay, D.S. (2001). Children's eyewitness reports after exposure to misinformation from parents. *Journal of Experimental Psychology: Applied, 7,* 27–50.

Powell, M.B., Roberts, K.P., Ceci, S.J., & Hembrooke, H. (1999). The effects of repeated experience on children's memory. *Developmental Psychology, 35,* 1462–1477.

Powell, M.B., & Thomson, D.M. (1996). Children's memory of an occurrence of a repeated event: Effects of age, repetition, and retention intervals across three question types. *Child Development, 67,* 1988–2004.

Powell, M.B., & Thomson, D.M. (1997). Contrasting memory for temporal-source and memory for content in children's discrimination of repeated events. *Applied Cognitive Psychology, 11,* 339–360.

Powell, M.B., Thomson, D.M., & Ceci, S.J. (2003). Children's memory of recurring events: Is the first event always the best remembered? *Applied Cognitive Psychology, 17,* 127–146.

Quas, J.A., Goodman, G.S., Ghetti, S., Alexander, K.W., Edelstein, R., Redlich, A.D., Cordon, I.M., & Jones, D.P.H. (2005). Childhood sexual assault victims: Long-term outcomes after testifying in criminal court. *Monographs of the Society for Research in Child Development, 70,* v–127.

R. v. B. (G.) [1990] 2 S.C.R. 30.

Regan, P.C., & Baker, S.J. (1998). The impact of child witness demeanor on perceived credibility and trial outcome in sexual abuse cases, *Journal of Family Violence, 13,* 187–195.

Roberts, K.P., & Blades, M. (1999). Children's memory and source monitoring of real life and televised events. *Journal of Applied Developmental Psychology, 20,* 575–596.

Roberts, K.P., Lamb, M.E., & Sternberg, K.J. (1999). Effects of timing of postevent information on preschoolers' memories of an event. *Applied Cognitive Psychology, 13,* 541–559.

Roberts, K.P., & Powell, M.B. (2001). Describing individual incidents of sexual abuse: A review of research on the effects of multiple sources of information on children's reports. *Child Abuse & Neglect, 25,* 1643–1659.

Roberts, K.P., & Powell, M.B. (2007). The roles of prior experience and the timing of misinformation on children's event memories. *Child Development, 78,* 1137–1152.

S v. R. (1989), 168 CLR 266.

Saywitz, K.J., Jaenicke, C., & Camparo, L. (1990). Children's knowledge of legal terminology. *Law & Human Behavior, 14,* 523–535.

Saywitz, K.J., & Nathanson, R. (1993). Children's testimony and their perceptions of stress in and out of the courtroom. *Child Abuse and Neglect, 17,* 613–622.

Sternberg, K.J., Lamb, M.E., Hershkowitz, I., Esplin, P.W., Redlich, A., & Sunshine, N. (1996). The relation between investigative utterance type and the informativeness of child witnesses. *Journal of Applied Developmental Psychology, 17,* 439–451.

Sternberg, K.J., Lamb, M.E., Hershkowitz, I., Yudilevitch, L., Orbach, Y., Esplin, P.W., & Hovav, M. (1997). Effects of introductory style on children's ability to describe experiences of sexual abuse. *Child Abuse & Neglect, 21,* 1133–1146.

Sternberg, K.J., Lamb, M.E., Orbach, Y., Esplin, P.W., & Mitchell, S. (2001). Use of a structured investigative protocol enhances young children's responses to free-recall prompts in the course of forensic interviews. *Journal of Applied Psychology, 86,* 997–1005.

Talwar, V., & Lee, K. (2002). Development of lying to conceal a transgression: Children's control of expressive behaviour during verbal deception. *International Journal of Behavioural Development, 26*, 436–444.

Talwar, V., Lee, K., Bala, N., & Lindsay, R.C.L. (2002). Children's lie-telling to conceal a parent's transgression: Legal implications. *Law and Human Behaviour, 28*, 411–435.

Terr, L. (1991). Childhood traumas: An outline and overview. *American Journal of Psychiatry, 148*, 10–20.

Terr, L. (1994). *Unchained memories: True stories of traumatic memories, lost and found.* New York: HarperCollins.

Thierry, K.L., & Spence, M.J. (2002). Source-monitoring training facilitates preschoolers' eyewitness memory performance. *Developmental Psychology, 38*, 428–437.

United Nations. (1989). *Convention on the Rights of the Child.*

Warren, A.R., & Lane, P. (1995). Effects of timing and type of question on eyewitness accuracy and suggestibility. In M. S. Zaragoza, G.C.N. Hall, R. Hirschman, & Y.S. Ben-Porath (Eds.), *Memory and testimony in the child witness* (pp. 44–60). Thousand Oaks, CA: Sage Publications Inc.

Warren, A., Woodall, C.E., Hunt, J.S., & Perry, N.W. (1996). 'It sounds good in theory, but ...': Do investigative interviewers follow guidelines based on memory research? *Child Maltreatment, 1*, 231–245.

Westcott, H.L. (1995). Children's experiences of being examined and cross-examined: The opportunity to be heard? *Expert Evidence, 4*, 13–19.

Wilson, C., & Powell, M.B. (2001). *A guide to interviewing children.* Crows Nest, Australia: Allen & Unwin.

PART THREE

Weighing Protection and Participation
Rights in Schools

9 Child Rights in Cyber-Space: Protection, Participation, and Privacy

SHAHEEN SHARIFF AND LEANNE JOHNNY

Young people ... do not see the Net as a distinct entity or environment. It is simply one more space in which they live their lives – connecting with friends, pursuing interests, figuring out what it means to be a teenager and a grown-up. Questions that asked how the Internet has changed their lives did not seem to resonate. To them, the Net has become wallpaper, seamlessly blending with the social spaces they inhabit in the real world. And one of its draws is the way it provides them with a window into a teenaged or adult world that is otherwise closed to them.

Steeves Wing (2005)

In the recent *United Nations World Report on Violence against Children* (Pinheiro, 2006) it was noted that bullying in schools has become a growing problem, especially within the North American context. While educators have been grappling with this issue for a number of years, the rapid increase in cellphone and computer use among youth has made this matter increasingly more complex. For example, cyber-bullying has emerged as a covert form of verbal and written harassment, conveyed by adolescents and teens through electronic mediums such as cellphones, text messages, web-cams, offensive websites, chat rooms, and email. It can include websites that are specifically constructed with the purpose of putting down, insulting, and teasing a classmate; photographs taken on cell phones that are modified and sent to an infinite audience; web-cams that do the same; MUD rooms where students adopt virtual identities and abuse others; and chat rooms where gossip and rumours are spread – the list is endless (Harmon, 2004; Leishman, 2002; Chu, 2005). As young people develop social relations in cyberspace, researchers have found a disturbing increase in cyber-bullying (Li, 2005; Shariff & Strong-Wilson, 2005). This raises a number of unprecedented legal considerations for schools, especially with regard to the privacy, protection, and participation rights of children.

The Canadian government is signatory to the Convention on the Rights of the Child (1989). Scholars such as Howe and Covell (2000) have argued that schools, as institutions of government, have a legal obligation to respect and uphold the rights of children articulated within this legal instrument. One of the most groundbreaking aspects of the CRC is the participatory rights that it ascribes to youth (Cohen, 2002), which include the right for young people to express themselves freely through any medium of communication such as cellphones and computers (article 13). Numerous scholars have argued that respect for the participation rights of children in educational contexts is central to the cultivation of democratic virtues (see, for example, White, 1996; Howe & Covell, 2005; Johnny, 2005). For instance, in another chapter, Raby highlights the foundational role that these rights play in the promotion of active citizenship. We certainly agree with this point and concur that, schools should take greater strides to educate children about these rights. However, as we will discuss, there are certain limitations that must be placed on student expression, especially when it comes to cyber-bullying. For instance, the Convention states that children have the right to be free from discrimination (article 2) and abuse (article 19), which places a duty on educators to maintain a safe school environment where all students are free to learn without fear of harassment and intimidation. We posit that cyber-bullying poses a serious threat to this objective. In this regard, we argue that educators must balance the participation rights of young people with their duty to protect the interests and safety of their students in both physical and virtual spaces.

In this chapter we consider legally sound and rights-based approaches for responding to cyber-bullying. We begin with a brief description of the key legal and educational concerns it presents for schools. These are delineated elsewhere (Shariff & Gouin, 2005; Shariff, 2005; Shariff & Johnny, 2007), together with research findings on cyber-bullying, its prevalence, and its impact on emotional health and learning. Excerpts from those papers are reiterated here briefly, as they provide the background and context for our discussion of the legal issues. We then consider cyber-bullying as it relates to the Convention on the Rights of the Child. We highlight the inherent tension that exists between children's rights to protection and participation, with a view to informing how schools might interpret and apply the Convention when responding to acts of online violence and harassment among classmates. We also consider the legal status of the Convention in Canada and the extent to which it places an obligation on educators to protect children from cyber-bullying.

In the next section, we turn to the Canadian legal landscape. We focus our attention on the privacy rights and fundamental freedoms of students as protected under the *Canadian Charter of Rights and Freedoms* (1982) and human rights jurisprudence. Pending the development of legislation relating to the legal boundaries of protection in cyberspace and specific legal and policy directives from governments and courts, we look to established law to extrapolate guidelines that will help schools navigate the blurred boundaries between the protection and participation of students in cyberspace.

We conclude our paper by suggesting that schools and university preparation programs collaborate with Internet safety experts such as the Media Awareness Network in Canada, and NetSafe (an Internet safety group in New Zealand). These organizations have begun to develop online programs based on comprehensive, scholarly research findings (MNet, 2000, 2005; NetSafe, 2005). We propose that university faculties of education, school boards, and schools work with such organizations to lobby and network with governments, police forces, health care organizations, technology providers, and parents. Given the enormity and complexity of online communications and related legal considerations, it is important that schools have maximum support and access to well-researched online educational programs that are developed in collaboration with Internet experts. Such an approach shows greater promise to protect students and educate them in socially responsible electronic discourse.

Finally, we advocate that knowledge about children's rights, as articulated in both international and national laws, be incorporated into university professional development programs to equip prospective educators with an understanding of their legal obligations to students. We propose that innovative approaches to school policy and practice informed by critical pedagogy, social justice, and leadership theories that are congruent with both children's rights and Charter principles show greater promise of protecting and educating young people in a world of new technologies. In this regard, we recommend responses to cyber-bullying that would be both educational and reasonably justified under section 1 of the Charter and articles 3 and 28 of the Convention.

Cyber-Bullying and Key Concerns for Schools[1]

When bullying occurs (during physical, verbal, or virtual social interactions among schoolmates) several conditions are present. First, bullying is always unwanted, deliberate, and relentless. It can be distinguished from friendly teasing and horseplay when it establishes a power imbalance between perpetrator(s) and victims(s). Second, victim blame appears to justify the social exclusion of certain children from their peer group (Artz, Riecken, MacIntyre, Lam, and Maczewski, 2000; Katch, 2001). For example, victims might be excluded for their race, gender, or different looks; for their sexual orientation, or simply for appearing to be gay (see, e.g., *Jubran v. North Vancouver School Distr.*, 2002); for their clothes, accent, or appearance; for being intelligent or gifted and talented; for having special needs or disabilities (Glover, Cartwright, & Gleeson, 1998).

Preliminary research discloses that 99% of teens use the Internet regularly; 74% of girls aged twelve to eighteen spend more time in chat rooms or doing instant messaging than in doing homework; one in every seventeen children is threatened on the Internet; and one in four youth aged eleven to nineteen is threatened via computer or cellphone (Leishman, 2002). A recent survey of 3700 American middle-school students disclosed that 18% had experienced cyber-bullying (Chu, 2005). A similar Canadian study of 177 middle-school students in Calgary, Alberta, revealed that 23% of respondents were bullied by email, 35% in chat rooms, 41% by cellphone text messaging, 32% by known schoolmates, 11% by people outside their school, and 16% by multiple sources including schoolmates (Li, 2005). Importantly, 41% did not know the identity of their perpetrators. MNet (2005) found that 9% were bullied over the Internet and 2% on cellphones. Incidentally, they noticed that younger children more frequently reported cyber-bullying. The number of children who use instant messaging and communicate with friends increases from 28% in grade 4 to 73% in grade 7.

---

1 Variations of this profile have also been presented in Shariff & Guoin (2005); Shariff & Johnny (2005); and Shariff & Strong-Wilson (2005).

Cyber-bullying has only recently begun to gain attention as a serious form of online social cruelty. Consequently, while the above statistics provide some insight, there is still a dearth of established or long-term research and scholarship in this area as new problems emerge with rapidly evolving new technologies. Most of the data currently available reflect the experiences and habits of adolescents rather than young children. It is likely that researchers have focused on adolescents because there is a significant increase in the number of young people who use communications technologies at the middle-school level. As we saw in the preceding statistics, there is some variation in the findings of different studies. For example, Chu (2005) found that only 18 per cent of adolescents experience cyber-bullying, while a similar study in Alberta found that the figure is more likely around 41 per cent. There are several variables that could account for these differences, such as increased access to technology in certain areas. Nationwide studies might help to clarify the exact number of children who are experiencing cyber-bullying. A collaborative study is currently under way in Quebec and British Columbia to conduct qualitative research in six to eight high schools (grades 7–9). In the meantime, the current data, although somewhat scant, provides evidence that cyber-bullying affects a significant number of youth. This presents several key concerns for schools.

Teachers and principals find it difficult to monitor students' hateful comments about classmates, gossip about and intimidation of victims, and inflammatory, racist, sexist, and homophobic threats and slurs. This is because cyber-bullying typically occurs outside supervision boundaries, often on home computers, outside school hours. Anonymity is another challenge. Perpetrators are shielded by screen names that protect their identity. Moreover, verbal forms of harassment in both physical and virtual spaces are often the most difficult to detect. Although cyber-bullying begins anonymously in the *virtual* domain, it has a spillover effect in schools that creates an unsafe atmosphere within the physical learning environment. The consequences can be psychologically devastating for victims, and socially detrimental for all students. Victims fear unknown cyber-perpetrators among their classmates. Moreover, cyber-bullying detracts *all* students (victims, bystanders, and perpetrators) from concentrating on schoolwork. This atmosphere makes all students feel unwelcome and unsafe (Shariff, 2004; Shariff & Strong-Wilson, 2005).

Support for perpetrators is another concern. Research on general bullying finds that 30 per cent of bystanders support perpetrators instead of victims (Salmivalli, Lagerspetz, Bjorqvist, Osterman, & Kaukiainen, 1996; Boulton, 1993). The longer it persists, the more bystanders join in the abuse, increasing the power imbalance between victim and perpetrators. Isolation renders victims vulnerable to continued abuse, and the cycle repeats itself. In cyberspace (especially on the Internet) this power imbalance between victim and perpetrator(s) is magnified as the medium allows for an infinite number of bystanders who support the instigator(s) of the abuse. Consider, for example, David Knight's experience. David became a victim of cyber-bullying when his classmates created a website (where he was labelled a homosexual pedophile) with the sole purpose of recording insults against him. David was interviewed in a CBC broadcast and said (Leishman, 2002): 'Rather than just some people, say 30 in a cafeteria, hearing them all yell insults at you, it's up there for 6 billion people to see. Anyone with a computer can see it ... And you can't get away from it. It doesn't go away when you come home from school. It made me feel even more trapped' (1).

What might begin in the physical school environment as friendly banter can quickly turn into verbal bullying that continues in cyberspace as covert psychological bullying. The difference in cyberspace is that hundreds of perpetrators can get involved in the abuse, and classmates who may not engage in the bullying at school can hide behind technology to inflict the most serious abuse. Power imbalances between victims and perpetrators are intensified by the extent of the audience available to aggressors. Racist, sexist, or homophobic statements and compromising sexual photographs (emailed in confidence to friends) can be altered and sent to unlimited audiences once relationships sour (Harmon, 2004). Cyberspace facilitates relentless bullying by increasing the numbers of peers.

Finally, a significant amount of online harassment is gender-driven, sexual, or homophobic (Shariff & Gouin, 2005). For example, research shows that cyber-bullying occurs more frequently in the lives of girls. This point is best exemplified in an Alberta study of middle-school children which disclosed that boys owned up to cyber-bullying more frequently and girls were more often victimized (Li, 2005). Adam (2001) reports as many as one out of three female children reported having been harassed online in 2001 alone. These findings are supported by Herring (1999), who reports that among children, girls appear to be targeted twice as much as boys.

In addition to its gendered nature, cyber-bullying also takes the form of sexual harassment. This can include virtual rape (Dibell, 1993) and cyber-stalking (Adam, 2001; Spitzberg & Hoobler, 2002; Tavani & Grodzinksy, 2002). Barak (2005) explains that verbal sexual harassment includes offensive sexual messages from harasser to victim, and gender-humiliating comments and sexual remarks. Passive verbal sexual harassment often includes offensive nicknames and online identities for perpetrators such as 'wetpussy' or 'xlargetool.' By comparison, active graphic gendered harassment can include unwanted pornographic content through email or posting in online environments. For example, Herring (2002) observes that 25 per cent of Internet users aged ten to seventeen were exposed to unwanted pornographic images in the past year. In addition to sex and nudity, 8 per cent of the images involved violence.

In some cases sexual threats play out as physical bullying in schools (Shariff, 2005). However, even when the threats remain online, Biber et al. (as cited in Glaser and Kahn, 2004) discovered that online misogynist comments, including unwanted sexual and gender harassment and sexual coercion, were rated as *more threatening and harassing*. The researchers suggest that the online discourse medium may *intensify* perceived harassment, instead of lessening it. This implies that the physical school environment can become very frightening for victims who may not know the exact identity of their perpetrator(s) but are aware that they are school- or classmates who might carry out their threats in school hallways, playgrounds, or even classrooms.

For example, the blurred lines between electronic and actual space resulted in the suicide of one Canadian teenager. Dawn Marie Wesley committed suicide when her classmate uttered a threat 'You're f.....g dead!' She believed these words would be followed through. Her perpetrator was convicted of criminal harassment. The court observed that despite the perpetrator's vehement denial that she meant to kill Dawn, the victim's perceived threat to her safety amounted to actual harm (*R. v. D.W. and K.P.D.*, 2002). Herring (1999) agrees that online behaviour that leads to assault against the physical, psychological, or emotional well-being of an individual or group in effect constitutes an actual form of violence.

We would argue, further, that this behaviour also significantly impairs victim rights, especially when they are aware that the perpetrators are from their school or institutional environment. As we have

explained, cyber-bullying creates a hostile physical school environment where students feel unwelcome and unsafe. In such an atmosphere, equal opportunities to learn are greatly reduced (Kapell, 2005;
Willard, 2003; Shariff & Strong-Wilson, 2005). The pressure on schools
to protect children and provide safe learning environments (both
physical and virtual) leads us to consider three important issues: (1)
whether children have unfettered rights to online free speech; (2) the
extent to which schools have an obligation to intervene; and (3) the
rights of victims to protection, from cyber-abuse so that they have
equal opportunities to learn without fear for their safety. The following sections address the tensions between free speech, protection, and
privacy rights. Our objective is to extrapolate standards that will
guide schools to navigate through the issues and dilemmas outlined
here.

Cyber-Bullying and the Convention on the Rights of the Child

Schools, as public institutions, are subject to a range of legal obligations. The first obligation rests in their role as agents of the Canadian
government and their corresponding duty to uphold human-rights
agreements that Canada has ratified such as the Convention on the
Rights of the Child (1989). There are several articles within the Convention that are relevant to schools. Most notably, children have
rights to an education on the basis of equal opportunity (article 28);
they have rights to equal treatment without discrimination (article 2);
they are guaranteed participatory rights (article 12), including rights
to freedom of expression (article 13), religion (article 14), and association (article 15); and, importantly, adults must act in the best interests
of children (article 3). While all the rights in the Convention are inter-
dependent, and foundational to the proper care and development of
children, at times these rights can conflict with one another. For
instance, scholars such as Almog and Bendor (2004) note that there is
an unclear relationship between article 3, which places a paternalistic
duty upon adults to protect children and act in their best interests,
and sections of the Convention that provide children with civil liberties and, hence, a degree of autonomy and choice. The tension lies in
determining the amount of autonomy young people should be
afforded and, moreover, whether intervening in the civil liberties of

children, such as their right to freedom of expression, is in fact in their best interests.

Protection versus Participation in Education

In the educational context, there is much evidence to support the idea that respect for rights that provide young people with freedom and autonomy are central to the cultivation of democratic virtues (see, for example, Howe & Covell, 2005; Devine, 2002; and Reich, 2002; Levinson, 1999). This is largely because when schools, as small models of society, provide structures that encourage young people to exercise their rights, they at the same time engage in a process of education – young people learn to value their rights and they develop the skills and attitudinal dispositions that are central to democratic citizenship (Johnny, 2005). The importance of respecting freedom of expression in the school environment has been established in law. For example, the landmark American case *Tinker et al. v. Des Moines Independent Community School District* (1969) involved three students who were suspended because they wore black armbands to school as a silent form of political protest against the Vietnam War. They had ignored school administrators' warnings not to wear them. They sued the school district under the freedom-of-expression provisions of the First Amendment. The court ruled in favour of the students, stating the famous dictum that '[i]t can hardly be argued that either students or teachers shed their constitutional rights to freedom of speech or expression at the schoolhouse gate' (p. 506).

Canadian courts have taken a similar stance. For instance, *Lutes v. Board of Education of Prairie View School Division No. 74* (1992) involved a student from Saskatchewan who was disciplined by his vice-principal for singing *Let's Talk about Sex* – a popular song among youth that had been banned by the school district. Chris and his mother took this issue to court, arguing that his punishment was unjustified because the school officials had violated his right to freedom of expression as protected under the *Canadian Charter of Rights and Freedoms* (Watkinson, 1999). The courts upheld the claims of the appellant, noting that the song did not contain any offensive lyrics but rather carried an important message about safe sex and AIDS.

While it is clear that North American courts have recognized the importance of extending certain democratic values into the school environment, both the Convention and the judiciary recognize that there are limits that must be placed upon student speech. The Convention states that expression may be subject to certain restrictions in order to respect the rights and reputations of others, and to protect public order and morals (article 13). When it comes to cyber-bullying this point is significant. As previously mentioned, although cyber-bullying begins anonymously in the *virtual* environment, it creates a hostile physical school environment. Arguably, students feel unsafe when educators fail to maintain proper order. In such an environment, equal opportunities to learn are greatly reduced. Moreover, when bullying or violence of any sort is tolerated within the school, it poses challenges to the general moral framework under which our public institutions operate. Considering that bullying is often associated with larger intersecting and interlocking systems of oppression grounded in racism, sexism, homophobia, and ableism (Razack, 1999; Shariff & Strong-Wilson, 2005), it is crucial to consider the extent to which schools protect children from discrimination when they ignore bullying between students.

Even the judge in *Tinker* (1969) noted that, while students may express their opinions, no matter how controversial, their expression must not *materially* or *substantially* interfere with the requirements of appropriate discipline in the operation of the school or express opinions that collide with the rights of others. Arguably, this rationale is rooted in a somewhat protective doctrine that subjects the civil rights of children to their educational and developmental needs (Almog & Bendor, 2004), but it does not mean that schools can arbitrarily restrict student speech. For instance, in the Canadian context, when schools adopt policies that infringe upon the rights of students, it is incumbent on education officials to convince the court that their policy is necessary to protect the safety interests of the student population (Mackay & Burt-Gerrans, 2005). We posit that when it comes to cyber-bullying, school policies that aim to prevent offensive and violent online expression may be in the best interests of student safety and protection. In other words, while schools should encourage socially responsible forms of expression, and this includes expression using different forms of technology, educators may need, under certain circumstances, to restrict these rights (in both physical and virtual spaces) in order to foster a safe and orderly school environment. Free expression must be balanced with the impact of such expression on the rights, safety, and personal well-being of individuals or groups in society.

Legal Implications of the U.N. Convention[2]

While it is clear that cyber-bullying poses a serious threat to the education rights of children, what is less evident is whether Canadian educators have a legal obligation to protect the rights of children as articulated in the Convention on the Rights of the Child. In the Canadian context, studies have shown that few teachers are aware of child rights and most provinces have not adopted the teaching of the Convention into their official curriculum (Covell & Howe, 2001a). This problem is exacerbated by the fact that our government has been sluggish in its attempts to fully implement the Convention into domestic policy and law. It is here that we must question not only the extent to which the Convention, as a legal instrument, is actually binding within the Canadian legal framework but also what implications its legal legitimacy may have for schools and their responsibilities to address cyber-bullying.

For examining the legal status of the Convention one landmark case provides insight into how Canadian courts apply this international instrument within the domestic sphere. In *Baker v. Canada* (1999) the Supreme Court questioned whether international agreements ratified by Canada but not implemented into domestic law can be interpreted and applied in legal disputes (Human Rights Internet, 2004a). More specifically, this case involved a woman, Marvis Baker, who had entered Canada as a visitor and remained working illegally for almost eleven years after her arrival. When the minister of citizenship and immigration ordered her deportation, Baker disputed the request given that her Canadian-born children still depended upon her financially and emotionally. She argued that the minister of citizenship had not considered the best interests of her children pursuant to article 3 of the United Nations Convention on the Rights of the Child. In its final ruling the Supreme Court held that the Convention did not have binding application in Canadian law. However, it also acknowledged that 'the values reflected in international humanitarian rights law may help inform the contextual approach to statutory interpretation and judicial review' (as cited by Human Rights Internet, 2004a). Thus, while the courts are not bound by the Convention, they may still draw upon its principles to inform their decisions.

---

2   Variations of this legal framework have also been presented in Johnny (2005).

In the Baker case the courts found that the immigration officer had not given due weight to the best interests of Baker's children and the appeal was allowed. As noted by Knop, this case demonstrates that international human-rights law can be used in the interpretation of domestic legislation (as cited in Human Rights Internet, 2004a). What does this mean for schools? If we consider that the Convention was used to interpret the *Immigration Act*, we might assume that it could be used in the interpretation of other statutory laws, such as provincial education acts. In other words, while the Convention may not be legally binding, it could be used to inform educational policy and practice (Johnny, 2005). In relation to cyber-bullying this ruling is crucial, because it shows that the best interests of the child should guide the actions of government officials. Therefore, when it comes to cyber-bullying, it is plausible that the courts would expect teachers also to defend the best interests of children by protecting them from, and educating them about, online abuse and other forms of digital harassment and danger.

Based on this ruling, it is also plausible that educational statutes and policies related to violence should reflect the rights of children. Unfortunately, when it comes to cyber-bullying, many schools still adopt zero-tolerance policies that are not only minimally effective but also have a tendency to restrict the rights of students. For example, research suggests that while schools state their intent to have inclusive and democratic policies, in reality many school administrators prefer to implement zero-tolerance policies that originate in a military model emphasizing punishment. Students who engage in bullying or cyber-bullying might be suspended under such policies. DiGuilio (2001) and Giroux (2003) argue that although the perpetrating student is out of the way for a few days (and, it could be argued, *material and substantial disruption* of learning is dealt with quickly), this does nothing to advance the educational mission of the school. In fact, a recent study conducted by the Ontario Human Rights Commission (2007) suggests that the *Safe Schools Act* (2001), adopted by the Ministry of Education to prevent violence, may have a disproportionate impact on students from racial minority groups and students with disabilities. This raises serious questions about the extent to which zero-tolerance policies that aim to prevent violence in schools actually infringe upon the equality and educational rights of certain children.

As we discuss later in this chapter, educational responses that address the root of violence, which could involve numerous intersecting and interlocking barriers of oppression for students grounded in racism, sexism, homophobia, and ableism (Razack, 1999; Shariff & Strong-Wilson, 2005) are the best approaches to dealing with cyber-bullying. Moreover, rather than adopting reactive responses, adults can encourage young people to participate in their own protection and safety. For instance, a recent MNet (2005) study reports that when children as young as age nine were asked about safety concerns on their use of the Internet, they wanted to learn how to authenticate sources. Moreover, 78 to 83 per cent of children in grades 7 to 11 expressed that children two years younger than they should be protected from hate sites, violence and gore sites, on-line pornography, bullying, and harassment (MNet, 2005, p. 11). The study notes that girls were more likely to think about protecting other children. This suggests that children from a very young age can be responsible about their safety – we simply need to give them a voice and ask their opinions. Increased awareness and providing children and teens with the tools they need to protect themselves from cyber-predators who may seek out their personal information or cyber-stalk them is essential. It is equally important to help them protect themselves against anonymous class-mates who cyber-bully.

Moreover, MNet (2005) discovered that parental monitoring of their children's Internet use and restrictions on the information children are permitted to disclose over the Internet increased from 54 per cent (2001) to 75 per cent in 2005. The majority of children felt that instead of having restrictions placed on their use of the technology, they would prefer guidance and tools that showed them how to differentiate between good and bad websites, between predators and genuinely helpful websites. The study reports a desire in children and adolescents to make informed choices towards their own protection. Many were apprehensive that if they had tracking software that recorded their online movements, they would be unable to prove their innocence to teachers or parents when unsolicited pornographic pop-up screens showed up, which they feared would cause them to lose computer privileges (MNet, 2005, p. 11).

These findings suggest that, clearly, schools need to balance free expression with education about what constitutes socially responsible discourse. Educators can emphasize that teasing someone online hurts as much, if not more, than face-to-face bullying. Furthermore, instead of Internet firewalls and blanket or zero-tolerance restrictions, schools need to work with parents and Internet experts to provide educational resources and tools for navigating cyberspace. These responses are arguably more compatible with the protection and participation rights of the Convention.

Cyber-Bullying and the Canadian Legal Landscape

In examining the legal rights of children in Canada, it is also crucial to consider other legal instruments such as the *Canadian Charter of Rights and Freedoms* (1982) and provincial human rights codes. Under section 8 of the Charter all citizens, including children and youth, have the right to be free from unreasonable search and seizure. However these privacy rights are only guaranteed within reasonable limits in a free and democratic society. Furthermore, section 7 of the Charter states that 'everyone one has the right to life, liberty and security of the person.' In the cyber-bullying context, both sections are relevant. The boundaries with respect to the obligations on schools to override search-and-seizure rights in order to check, for example, school computers and personal websites, must be balanced with the right to life, liberty, and security of the person. Furthermore, victims might argue that their rights to life, liberty, and security of the person are infringed under section 7 when schools fail to intervene and protect them from cyber-bullying.

Based on section 1 considerations, the courts generally give priority to the safety of the greater number of stakeholders as justification for overriding privacy rights. In *R. v. M.R.M.* (1998), for example, the Supreme Court of Canada ruled that as long as a school principal is not acting as an agent of the police, he or she can search student lockers if there is a suspicion of hidden weapons or drugs. The high court held that school lockers are the property of schools. Certainly, it could be argued that school computers are also school property; therefore any emails or correspondence between students, as well as websites created using those computers, could be censored. Moreover, Mackay and Burt-Gerrans (2005) explain that the rationale used by the Supreme Court in *R. v. M.R.M.* was that students should already have a lowered expectation of privacy because they know that their school principals or administrators may need to conduct searches in schools, and that safety ought to be the overriding concern in protecting students. The high court explained its interpretation of a safe and ordered school environment:

Teachers and principals are placed in a position of trust that carries with it onerous responsibilities. When children attend school or school functions, it is they who must care for the children's safety and well-being. It is they who must carry out the fundamentally important task of teaching children so that they can function in our society and fulfill their potential. In order to teach, school officials must provide an atmosphere that encourages learning. During the school day, they must protect and teach our children. (p. 398)

While this case suggests that educators may have a legal basis for supervising student speech that originates from school computers, the monitoring of cyber-bullying becomes more complex when it originates after regular school hours. Schools often maintain that cyber-bullying falls beyond their realm of responsibility because it typically occurs off campus. However, other Charter cases seem to refute this point. For example, in *Ross v. New Brunswick School District No. 15* (1996) it was shown that schools must provide conditions that are conducive to leaning. Although the *Ross* case involved the free speech of a teacher who distributed anti-Semitic publications outside of school, the following statement from the ruling has been quoted in almost every Charter argument for a positive school environment: '[S]chools are an arena for the exchange of ideas and must, therefore, be premised upon principles of tolerance and impartiality so that all persons within the school environment feel equally free to participate. As the board of inquiry stated, a school board has a duty to maintain a positive school environment for all persons served by it' (para. 42). Even though Ross's anti-Semitic publications were distributed outside the school context, the court noted that he poisoned the school and classroom environment for his Jewish students within the classroom. They knew about his publications and felt threatened, fearful, and uncomfortable. This viewpoint is highly applicable to the cyber-bullying context. If we are to draw upon the rationale used in the preceding case it would seem that the on-campus/off-campus (physical vs virtual space) distinction is moot. It is the *effect* of the harassment, bullying, and threats – despite the fact that they are made outside of the physical school setting – that is important. If they prevent students from learning in the physical school setting, if they create a poisoned environment for any student, then it is the school's responsibility to address it.

Based on this ruling, it is highly plausible that in balancing student rights to free expression with student safety and equality under section 1, the courts are more likely to rule in favour of the equality (s. 15) and safety rights of students under section 7 in situations involving cyber-bullying. Similarly, in *Chamberlain v. Surrey School District No. 36* (2002) the Supreme Court of Canada ruled, *inter alia*, that banning books aimed at reducing homophobia increased the possibility of violence against children of same-sex families, breaching their equality rights under section 15.

Canadian Human Rights Jurisprudence

The notion that schools have a responsibility to address student speech that originates off campus is also supported by human rights jurisprudence regarding sexual harassment. For example, in *Robichaud v. Canada* (1987) the Supreme Court of Canada ruled that institutions are responsible for providing safe environments for their employees, even if the sexual harassment by a co-worker occurs outside the workplace. The fact that the victims must face their tormentors in the workplace imposes an obligation on the employer to address the problem effectively. This case is very relevant to cyber-bullying. As the high court confirmed in Robichaud, if a victim of harassment has to face the perpetrator within the institution, the institution is responsible for correcting the problem no matter where the harassment actually takes place. The judge reiterated that, in order to eradicate antisocial conditions in society, human rights law must be consistent with Charter principles. Therefore, institutions must ensure that individuals have equal opportunities to learn and work without fear of harassment. In this case, equal opportunity to work or learn was at issue. Section 15 (1) of the Charter reads as follows: 'Every individual is equal before and under the law and has the right to the equal protection and equal benefit of the law without discrimination and, in particular, without discrimination based on race, national or ethnic origin, colour, religion, sex, age or mental or physical disability.'

The preceding analysis of *Ross* (1996), *Robichaud* (1987), and *R. v. M.R.M* (1998) suggests that there is an implied educational Charter obligation on schools. This opinion is firmly solidified in another recent Canadian court ruling. In the case of Azmi Jubran (*Jubran v. North Vancouver School District*, 2002) the plaintiff lived through four years of discrimination in a hostile school environment where school officials and teachers tacitly condoned homophobia. Jubran claimed that he was not homosexual and argued that administrators made few proactive attempts to reduce homophobic attitudes or foster a positive school climate. Homosexuality has been established as an analogous ground under section 15 of the Charter, even though it was not written in at the outset (see, for example, *Vriend v. Alberta*, 1998; *Miron v. Trudel*, 1995; *Egan v. Canada*, 1995; and *Chamberlain v. Surrey School District No. 36*, 2002).

The Canadian Human Rights Tribunal and, subsequently, the British Columbia Court of Appeal noted that whether the students knew or perceived Jubran to be homosexual was irrelevant. The school board had an obligation to provide him with an educational environment free from discrimination, and teachers knew, or ought to have known, that the epithets directed at him were homophobic, discriminatory, and designed to hurt him. Their lack of adequate attention to the issue was not consistent with the broader objectives of human rights in Canada, namely, to eradicate antisocial conditions in society. This can easily be applied to the responsibility of schools to eradicate antisocial conditions in cyberspace among schoolmates.

Educational Solutions

As we explain in the introduction, there has been encouraging progress by Internet safety organizations, some of which have conducted important studies on Internet use by children and adolescents (MNet, 2005; NetSafe, 2005) and have made significant strides in developing interactive online programs that help young people deal with hate crimes, issues of discrimination, and online bullying. MNet has also developed a licensed product for teacher education for use in teacher preparation and professional development programs at the undergraduate and graduate levels. Furthermore, organizations such as Quebec's public legal-education organization Educaloi have worked with schools to develop interactive online courses that teach young people and educators about the law. For example, on the Educaloi website, students can navigate through social scenarios that teach them about the legal repercussions of certain behaviours. Such programs are designed with a view to informing young people about their rights and also encouraging socially responsible behaviour. In collaboration with Shariff, this same organization plans to develop online educational activities related to Internet safety. These initiatives are positive steps towards addressing issues, such as cyber-bullying, through informed programs. They are far more practical and thoughtful than the continued emphasis on children's bullying behaviour that has informed minimally successful anti-bullying interventions to date (Shariff, 2003, 2004).

It is thus crucial for schools and school boards to invest in learning about these programs and collaborating with experts by incorporating some of their lessons into the regular curriculum. This collaboration should not be limited to schools, but ought to involve university teacher education and professional development programs, as well as government officials and academics from inter-disciplinary perspectives. Most important, such initiatives must provide young people with a voice and include their perspectives. As we saw in the MNet (2005) study, young people are keen to find tools to help them authenticate harmful information or predators on the Internet.

Along with these collaborative initiatives, we also contend that schools can thwart the rise of cyber-bullying by incorporating children's rights education programs into the classroom. For instance, in a Canadian study conducted by Covell and Howe (2001b) it was shown that education in the appreciation of rights may result in higher levels of respect among students. In addition to these scholars, White (1996) also states that when children learn about their rights and corresponding responsibilities they may develop a conception of themselves as moral persons. This sense of morality and justice arises when young people learn that they possess the right to participate in their environment and also have the responsibility to make choices that demonstrate respect for the rights of others. This point is crucial in relation to cyber-bullying, as we can teach children not only about their right to express themselves in electronic forums, but also about their responsibility to uphold the dignity of other users.

Scholars such as Boyden (as cited in Wyse, 2001) argue that meaningful and responsible participation cannot be achieved if individuals are not aware of their rights. Accordingly, there is a need to educate both students and teachers about this issue. In the Canadian context this is especially true since, as previously mentioned, few teachers are aware of child rights and most provinces have not adopted the teaching of the Convention into their official curriculum (Covell & Howe, 2001a). Certainly, if child rights are to be respected in the classroom environment, teachers need to be aware of these rights so they adopt democratic teaching strategies, provide students with opportunities to influence decisions, and educate young people about their rights.

While it is true that some teachers have already taken it upon themselves to incorporate child-rights education into their classrooms, specialists argue that these education programs often teach awareness but do not provide students with opportunities to put their rights into action. In other words, there appears to be a gap between rhetoric and practice (Frantzi, 2004). This is not to say that teachers who attempt to implement child-rights education into their classrooms are incapable; rather, it shows that educators need greater resources and professional development in the teaching and implementation of child rights in schools (Johnny, 2005). Moreover, if young people are to learn how to exercise their rights and responsibilities they need to be provided with opportunities to cultivate this capacity. Therefore, schools also need to adopt policies that will allow children to practise respectfully expressing themselves and participating in the school.

Conclusion and Implications

Our review of case law and interpretation of the Convention on the Rights of the Child affirms that schools have legal authority to intervene in matters regarding cyber-bullying. However, as previously mentioned, we do not want to suggest that disciplinary measures for this new form of harassment should merely aim to punish students for their actions. On the contrary, we recognize that school discipline policies are least successful when they merely serve as a reactionary means to deal with unwanted behaviour. While we have argued that schools should monitor inflammatory student speech, it is equally important to recognize that educators have a duty to cultivate an educational atmosphere that is consistent with the moral and political principles essential to expanding democratic values. In other words, when cyber-bullying becomes pervasive within a school we cannot simply place the blame on students. Instead we must look at the values and beliefs that our schools and constitutional principles impart and take educational measures to ensure that these values promote tolerance, acceptance, and decency among students.

As noted by scholars such as Giroux (2003), school discipline is best achieved when it incorporates an element that aims to educate students about both moral and political principles. Giroux argues that 'schools should provide forms of critical education in which ethics and values are used to teach students to keep the spirit of justice alive in themselves, embrace the need to be compassionate, respect the rights of others, and be self-conscious about the consequences of their actions' (p. 94). Building upon this argument, we suggest that schools take a proactive approach to dealing with cyber-bullying by fostering values that steer students towards positive interactions with one another. As shown above, research indicates that young people show a higher level of respect towards one another and an increased sense of self-esteem when they learn about their rights. Therefore, we feel that children's rights education is an integral component of any program that aims to combat cyber-bullying.

It is crucial for educators to teach young people about their right to freedom of expression as per article 13 of the Convention. With that said, it is also important that we discuss the limitations of this article. For instance, the Convention states that children have the right to receive and impart ideas of all kinds. However, this right is subject to certain restrictions, including respect for the rights and reputations of others (2a) and the protection of national security or of public health and morals (2b). Examining these limitations may help children to understand that while they have rights they also have responsibilities towards others. Given that children from minority groups are most often the targets of bullying, it is also crucial for young people to learn about rights that promote acceptance and tolerance. For instance, article 2 of the Convention outlines the importance of protecting children against all forms of discrimination. Likewise, article 14 also states that all children have the right to freedom of religion. Exploring these rights might encourage young people to become more accepting of differences and, therefore, help to alleviate some of the underlying discriminatory attitudes that propel cyber-bullying.

We argue that these proactive children's rights approaches coupled with clear school policies will allow students to learn the skills central to living in a pluralistic and democratic society where citizens have a right to free speech but also a responsibility to engage in socially responsible discourse. Still, the Convention has not been integrated in any meaningful way into training programs for professionals dealing with children. In other words, while children's rights education might provide a viable option for teaching children about social and moral responsibility within both the physical and virtual realm, educators are given insufficient training and resources to make such programs a reality.

The fact that schools use technology to deliver curriculum and assign homework makes it essential that attention is paid to how their students use it. Schools need to recognize and establish standards and codes of conduct with respect to Internet and cellphone use and also define acceptable boundaries for their students' social relationships in cyberspace. While in the past the courts have reasoned that digital harassment falls outside the school's realm of responsibility, it is somewhat difficult to understand this claim given the impact it has on the overall learning environment. As shown in our discussion, even though cyber-bullying might originate from home computers, it has a spillover effect that is creating an unsafe atmosphere within the educational setting.

The advent of new technologies is calling upon schools to re-conceptualize their regulations with regards to student learning and discipline. It is clear that the on/off-campus distinction that was easily definable in the past has become somewhat blurred as student interactions and learning situations continue to take place in the virtual domain. This new reality necessitates boundaries of supervision that extend beyond the traditional classroom setting. As a result, school policy needs to consider virtual contexts as a site for civic and academic engagement and take steps to ensure that interactions within this virtual domain reflect community values and the overall educational mission of the school. While we have argued that schools have a legal basis for extending their reach into cyberspace, we have also suggested that proactive, educational measures are an integral means of dealing with cyber-bullying. School officials are faced with difficult policy and programming issues. They must balance legal constraints such as equality and freedom of expression through innovative, educational responses to address cyber-bullying. There is, therefore, a pressing need for improved professional development courses for teachers, educational administrators, and policy makers.

The status quo exists in schools because, while school officials and teachers have an abundance of information about general bullying, this information is often focused on the behavioural aspects of the students (Shariff, 2004; Shariff & Strong-Wilson, 2005). There is often little knowledge about what responsibilities schools have in educating children to become socially responsible citizens in a democratic society. This problem is driven by a lack of clarity about the legal boundaries of teachers' responsibilities to students, hence our initiative to clarify those responsibilities in this and related journal articles and book chapters (Shariff & Johnny, 2007; Shariff & Gouin, 2005; Shariff, 2005). This is fuelled by the focus on criminalizing young people, zero-tolerance, suspension policies, and student arrests by police (Giroux, 2003; DiGuilio, 2001; Shariff, 2004).

As Shariff has noted elsewhere (2004), the reactive stance and wall of defence adopted by many educators in relation to bullying is likely due to a lack of knowledge. While schools are inundated with information on how to address bullying, educators have little knowledge about its complexities, conditions, and forms. Instead of funding conferences that search for a non-existent 'blueprint' on bullying, it would be more prudent to invest in improved education for educators who need sensitizing to its complexities and devastating consequences.

This knowledge gap could be addressed at the university level, by faculties of education and law, through professional development programs at the undergraduate and graduate levels for teachers, school administrators, counsellors, and prospective lawyers. Further, these classes need to be offered as part of the core degree requirements rather than as electives. To date, law-related education has had minimal success because it has not been grounded in educational theories of relevance to educators (Cassidy, 2000). Courses should draw upon social justice, leadership, and ethics of care theories, as well as cultural studies (Burns, 1978; Foster, 1989; Fullan, 2000; Leithwood, 1999; Noddings, 1992), whereby prospective teachers and administrators consider transformational and democratic leadership approaches that emphasize the protection and participation rights of children and meet the requirements of the Convention on the Rights of the Child and the *Canadian Charter of Rights and Freedoms*.

REFERENCES

Adam, A. (2001). Cyberstalking: Gender and computer ethics. In E. Green & A. Adam (Eds.), *Virtual gender: Technology, consumption and identity* (pp. 209–224). New York: Routledge.

Almog, S., & Bendor, A. (2004). The UN Convention on the Rights of the Child meets the American Constitution: Towards a supreme law of the world. *International Journal of Children's Rights, 11*, 273–289.

Artz, S., Riecken, E., MacIntyre, B., Lam, E., & Maczewski, M. (2000). Theorizing gender differences in receptivity to violence prevention programming in schools. *Journal of the B.C. School Counsellors Association, 22*(1), 7–35.

Baker v. Canada, 2 S.C.R. 817 (1999).

Barak, A. (2005). Sexual harassment on the Internet. *Social Science Computer Review, 23*(1), 77–92.

Boulton, M.J. (1993). A comparison of adults' and children's abilities to distinguish between aggressive and playful fighting in middle school pupils. Implications for playground supervision and behaviour management. *Educational Studies, 19*, 193–203.

Burns, J. (1978). *Leadership*. New York: Harper & Row.

Canadian Charter of Rights and Freedoms, Schedule B, Constitution Act, 1982, Canada Act, c. 11 (U.K.).

Cassidy, W. (2000). Law-related education. Promoting awareness, participation and action. In T. Goldstein and D. Selby (Eds.), *Weaving connections: Educating for peace, social and environmental justice* (pp. 297–322). Toronto: Sumach Press.

Chamberlain v. Surrey School District No. 36, 4 S.C.R. 710 (2002).

Chu, J. (2005, August 8). You wanna take this online? Cyberspace is the 21st century bully's playground where girls play rougher than boys. *Time* (Canadian ed.), 42–43.

Cohen, C. (2002). United Nations Convention on the Rights of the Child: Developing international norms to create a new world for children. In K. Alaimo & B. Klug (Eds.), *Children as equals: Exploring the rights of the child* (pp. 49–72). Boston: University Press of America.

Covell, K. (2005). *Violence against children in North America*. United Nations Secretary-General's study on violence against children in North American Regional Consultation.

Covell, K., & Howe, B. (2001a). *The challenge of children's rights for Canada.* Waterloo: Wilfrid Laurier Press.

Covell, K., & Howe, B. (2001b). Moral education through the 3 Rs: Rights, respect, and responsibility. *Journal of Moral Education, 30*, 29–41.

Devine, D. (2002). Children's citizenship and the structuring of adult–child relations in the primary school. *Childhood, 9*(3), 303–320.

Dibbell, J. (1993, December 21). A rape in cyberspace. *Village Voice*, 38.

DiGiulio, R.C. (2001). *Educate, medicate, or litigate? What teachers, parents, and administrators must do about student behavior.* Thousand Oaks, CA: Corwin Press, Inc.

Egan v. Canada, 2 S.C.R. 513 (1995).

Foster, W. P. (1989). Toward a critical practice of leadership. In J. Smyth (Ed.), *Critical perspectives on educational leadership* (pp. 39–62). London and New York: Falmer Press.

Frantzi, K. (2004). Human rights education: The United Nations endeavour and the importance of childhood and intelligent sympathy. *International Education Journal, 5*, 1–8.

Fullan, M. (Ed.). (2000). *The Jossey-Bass reader on educational leadership.* San Francisco: Jossey-Bass Inc.

Giroux, H. (2003). *The abandoned generation: Democracy beyond the culture of fear.* New York: Palgrave MacMillan.

Glaser, J., & Kahn, K.B. (2004). Prejudice, discrimination, and the Internet. In Y. Amichai-Hamburger (Ed.), *The Social Net: Human Behavior in Cyberspace.* New York: Oxford University Press.

Glover, D., Cartwright, N., & Gleeson, D. (1998). *Towards bully-free schools.* Buckingham and Philadelphia: Open University Press.

Harmon, A. (2004, August 26). Internet gives teenage bullies weapons to wound from afar. *New York Times.* Retrieved August 26, 2004, from http://www.nytimes.com./2004/08/26/education

Herring, S.C. (1999). The rhetorical dynamic of gender harassment on-line. *The Information Society, 15,* 151–167.

Herring, S.C. (2002). Cyber violence: Recognizing and resisting abuse in online environments. *Asian Women, 14,* 187–212.

Howe, R.B. & Covell, K. (2000). Schools and the participation rights of the child. *Education and Law Journal, 10,* 107–123.

Howe, R.B. & Covell, K. (2005). *Empowering children: Children's rights as a pathway to citizenship.* Toronto: University of Toronto Press.

Human Rights Internet (2004a). *Case studies from the Supreme Court of Canada, Baker v. Canada.* Retrieved November 1, 2004, from http://www.hri.ca/ for therecordCanada/vol3/casebaker.htm

Human Rights Internet (2004b). *Case studies from the Supreme Court of Canada, Canadian Foundation for Children, Youth and the Law v. Canada.* Retrieved November 1, 2004, from http://www.hri.ca/fortherecordCanada/vol3/ casefoundationchildren.htm

Johnny, L. (2005). UN Convention on the Rights of the Child: A rationale for implementing participatory rights in schools. *Canadian Journal of Educational Administration and Policy, 40,* 1–20.

Jubran v. North Vancouver School District et al., 10 B.C.H.R.T. (2002).

Katch, J. (2001). *Under deadman's skin: Discovering the meaning of children's violent play.* Boston: Beacon Press.

Leishman, J. (2002, October 10). Cyber-bullying: The Internet is the latest weapon in a bully's arsenal. *CBC News, The National.* Retrieved on January 27, 2003, from http://cbc.ca/news/national/news/cyberbullying/index.html

Leithwood, K. (1999). An organizational perspective on values for leaders of future schools. In P.T. Begley (Ed.), *Values and educational leadership.* Albany: SUNY Press.

Levinson, M. (1999). *The demands of a liberal education.* Oxford: Oxford University Press.

Li, Qing (2005). Cyber-bullying in schools: The nature and extent of adolescents' experience. Paper presented at the American Education Research Association conference in Montreal, Quebec, April.

Lutes v. Board of Education of Prairie View School Division No. 74, [1992], 101 Sask. R. 232 (Q.B.).

MacKay, W., & Burt-Gerrans, J. (2005). Student freedom of expression: Violent content and the safe school balance. *McGill Journal of Education, 40*(3), 423–443.

Miron v. Trudel, 2 S.C.R 418 (1995).

MNet. (2000). *Young Canadians in a wired world: Phase I.* Retrieved on April 2, 2007, from http://www.mediaawareness.ca/english/research/YCWW/phaseI

MNet. (2005). *Young Canadians in a wired world: Phase II.* Retrieved on April 2, 2007, from http://www.mediaawareness.ca/english/research/YCWW/phaseII/key_findings.cfm

Netsafe. (2005). *The text generation: Mobile phones and New Zealand youth – A report of result from the Internet Safety Group's survey of teenage mobile phone use.* Netsafe.

Noddings, N. (1992). The challenge to care in schools: An alternative approach to education. New York: Teachers College Press.

Olweus, D. (2001). Peer harassment: A critical analysis and some important issues. In J. Juvonen & S. Graham (Eds.), *Peer harassment in school: The plight of the vulnerable and victimized* (pp. 3–20). New York: Guildford Press.

Ontario Human Rights Commission. (2007). *The Ontario Safe Schools Act. School discipline and discrimination: Executive Summary.* Retrieved on April 2, 2007, from http://www.ohrc.on.ca/en/resources/discussion_consultation/SafeSchools ConsultRepENG.

Pinheiro, P. (2006). *World report on violence against children.* Geneva: United Nations.

R. v. D.W. and K.P.D., 96 B.C.P.C. (2002).

R. v. M.R.M., 3 S.C.R. 393 (1998).

Razack, S. (1999). *Looking white people in the eye: Gender, race, and culture in courtrooms and classrooms.* Toronto: University of Toronto Press.

Reich, R. (2002). *Bridging liberalism and multiculturalism in American education.* Chicago: University of Chicago Press.

Robichaud v. Canada (Treasury Board), 2 S.C.R. 84 (1987).

Ross v. New Brunswick School District No. 15, 1 S.C.R. 825 (1996).

Salmivalli, C., Lagerspetz, K., Bjorqvist, K., Osterman, K., & Kaukiainen, A. (1996). Bullying as a group process: Participant roles and their relations to social status within the group. *Aggressive Behavior, 25*, 81–89.

Shariff, S. (2001). The email raveger: The legal context of education. Distance education course. Burnaby, BC: Centre for Distance Education, Simon Fraser University.

Shariff, S. (2003). *A system on trial: Identifying legal standards for educational, ethical and legally defensible approaches to bullying in schools.* Doctoral dissertation. Simon Fraser University, Burnaby, BC.

Shariff, S. (2004). Keeping schools out of court: Legally defensible models of leadership to reduce cyber-bullying. *Educational Forum, Delta Kappa Pi, 68(3)*, 222–233.

Shariff, S. (2005). Cyber-dilemmas in the new millennium: Balancing free expression and student safety in cyber-space. Special issue. Schools and Courts: Competing Rights in the New Millennium. *McGill Journal of Education, 40*(3), 467–487.

Shariff, S., (2006). Cyber-dilemmas: Balancing free expression and learning in a virtual school environment. *International Journal of Learning 12*(4), 269–78.

Shariff, S., & Gouin, R. (2005). *Cyber-dilemmas: Gendered hierarchies, free expression and cyber-safety in schools.* Paper presented at Oxford Internet Institute, Oxford University. See www.oii.ox.ac.uk/cybersafety

Shariff, S., & Johnny, L. (2007). Cyber-libel and cyber-bullying: Can schools protect student reputations and free-expression in virtual environments? *Education & Law Journal, 16*(3), 307–42.

Shariff, S, and Johnny, L. (in press). Cyber-dilemmas: The role of the *Charter* in balancing freedom of expression, safety and equality in a virtual school environment. In M. Manley-Casimir (Ed.), *The courts, the Charter and the schools: The impact of judicial decision-making on educational policy and practice.* Toronto: University of Toronto Press.

Shariff, S., and Strong-Wilson, T. (2005). Bullying and new technologies: What can teachers do to foster socially responsible discourse in the physical and virtual school environments? In J. Kincheloe (Ed.), *Classroom teaching: An introduction.* New York: David Lang Publishers.

Spitzberg, B., & Hoobler, G. (2002). Cyberstalking and the technologies of interpersonal terrorism. *New Media & Society, 4,* 71–92.

Steeves, V., & Wing, C. (2005). *Young Canadians in a wired world. Phase II. Trends and recommendations.* Ottawa: Media Awareness Network.

Tavani, H., & Grodzinsky, F. (2002). Cyberstalking, personal privacy, and moral responsibility. *Ethics and Information Technology, 4,* 123–32.

Tinker v. Des Moines Independent Community School District, 393 U.S. 503 (1969).

United Nations. (1989). *Convention on the Rights of the Child.*

Vriend v. Alberta, 1 S.C.R. 493 (1998).

Watkinson, A. (1999). *Education, student rights and the Charter.* Saskatoon: Purich Publishing Ltd.

White, P. (1996). *Civic virtues and public schooling: Educating citizens for a democratic society.* New York: Teachers College Press.

Willard, N. (2005). Educator's guide to cyber-bullying: Addressing the harm caused by online social cruelty. Retrieved July 19, 2005 from http://cyberbully.org

Williams v. Eady, 10 T.L.R. 41 (1893).

Wyse, D. (2001). Felt tip pens and school councils: Children's participation rights in four English schools. *Children and Society, 15,* 209–18.

10 Too Little, Too Late: The Right to Comprehensive Sexual Health Education in Childhood and Adolescence

JOHANNA VAN VLIET AND REBECCA RABY

The provision of sexual health education to children and adolescents is frequently contentious: what should be taught, by whom, and when? Such concerns about sexual health education are shaped by constructions of childhood innocence and adolescent risk-taking; constructions of gender and gender inequality; and conflicting conceptualizations of rights. We will briefly discuss constructions of childhood, adolescence, and gender, as well as general arguments supporting the implementation of effective sexual health education programs. The bulk of this chapter, however, examines two documents relevant to sexual health education in Ontario: the United Nations Convention on the Rights of the Child (CRC) and the Ontario Ministry of Education's Curriculum for Health and Physical Education (Healthy Living strand). In doing so, we weigh the value and applicability of a rights-based argument for sexual health education, ultimately arguing that children's rights to health, information, education, and citizenship training (as outlined in the Convention) support their access to comprehensive sexual health education. However, such a comprehensive education will require some changes to Ontario's Health and Physical Education curriculum.

What Is Sexual Health Education and What Should It Include?

In light of current interest, sexual health programs in public schools are under popular and academic scrutiny (McKay, 2004). McKay describes most Canadian sexual health programs as multifaceted. That is, they strive for positive outcomes (i.e., successful interpersonal relationships and desired parenthood) while attempting to prevent negative ones (i.e., unwanted pregnancy and sexually transmitted infections [STIs]). Such programs reflect concern over young people's engagement in sexual activity, unplanned teen pregnancies, STIs, sexual coercion, and sexual harassment (Levesque, 2000). Levesque claims that it is important for children and youth to understand the biology of the life cycle and to be encouraged to make informed choices regarding their sexuality. Aggleton and Campbell (2000), however, worry that too many sexual health programs conceptualize sex in negative terms, focusing heavily on sex as a precursor to STIs and unplanned pregnancies. Sex is only being discussed in terms of its control and prevention (ibid.) rather than as desire. Reference to rights remains largely absent.

Clearly, there are a number of different approaches to sexual health education. Levesque (2000) identifies two ideological categories of sexual health education, although many programs fall somewhere between these positions. The first follows a restrictive ideology, which strongly advocates abstinence. Generally, within this approach only a narrow set of behaviours are acceptable, with disapproval of contraception, masturbation, diversities in sexual orientation, and premarital sexual relations (ibid.). The second type of sexual health education follows a more permissive ideology. It recognizes sexual behaviour as pleasurable, and accepts diversities in sexual orientation. These advocates believe that abstinence-only education is incomplete and that fear-based teaching will negatively affect the development of healthy relationships in adulthood. These more permissive programs can begin as early as kindergarten and move up through discussions of biology, the psychology of relationships, and the complexities of families. Some programs, although more controversial, cover masturbation and other forms of self-pleasure (ibid.). Following this position, Aggleton and Campbell (2000) agree that sexual health should be taught as an affirmative concept. That is, sexual health should be celebrated for the benefits it brings to one's life, and not simply advocated for successful protection from negative outcomes. Finally, Aggleton and Campbell espouse a life-skills approach to sexual health education, arguing that it is crucial that young people who are already sexually active learn how to handle their sexual health in real-life situations. This latter position is somewhat reflected by Health Canada (2003):

Sexual health education should provide opportunities for individuals to explore the attitudes, feelings, values and customs that influence their choices about sexual health ... Effective sexual health education supports informed decision making by providing individuals with the opportunity to develop knowledge, personal insight, motivation, and behavioural skills that are consistent with each individual's personal values and choices. (pp. 22–23)

A broad, more permissive approach to sexual health education is consistent with our perspective on the type of program that should be made available to children and youth.

The effectiveness of sexual health education is also controversial, depending on both how success is measured and the programs under study. For example, according to McKay (2004), there is an overall acceptance that sexual health programs successfully reduce young people's risks of STIs or unplanned pregnancies. He suggests that the distribution of condoms, for instance, does not promote sexual activity earlier, but rather increases their usage by the young people who are already sexually active. Somers and Surmann (2005) similarly find that school-based sex education decreases sexual risk-taking. However, Levesque (2000) questions the effectiveness that programs have on decreasing STIs and unplanned pregnancies, as belief in the value of condoms does not translate into actual usage. Levesque argues that the ineffectiveness of programs is due to their narrow focus. Most programs and textbooks have not been adapted to meet the current needs of young people, making some material inapplicable to them. Furthermore, most programs are too short in length to effectively modify behaviour. The average school assigns only 6.5 hours each year to all sexual health topics and most schools introduce topics too late (ibid.). Some students have already been sexually active for some time before they are provided information about safe sex methods.

McKay (2004) reports evidence which states that including abstinence along with discussions of safe sex and birth control can help some youth to delay their first time of intercourse. However, as most young people have sex for the first time by the time they are twenty, McKay sees it as their imperative (and right) to access other forms of information. In fact, in the long run, abstinence-only education decreases young people's use of contraceptives. For example, virginity pledges in the United States have led to a small delay in sexual intercourse among younger teens when pledgers are in the minority among their peers, but it has also been found that these young people are less likely to use contraceptives when they do have sex (Bearman & Brückner, 2001).

Why Such Controversy?

There are a number of reasons as to why sexual health education is a particularly charged topic in relation to young people. Whether implicitly or explicitly taught, such education 'conveys images of gender roles, ethics of care, notions of normality, and conceptions of the good society' (Levesque, 2000, p. 953) and plays a role in 'the very construction and definition of adolescent sexuality' (Bay-Cheng, 2003). This type of controversy has kept the topic of sexual health education, and the appropriateness of the subject matter, under heated debate.

Rights-based arguments for sexual health education for young people face the most adamant opposition from some religious groups that favour abstinence-only programs. Currently, American federal funding favours abstinence-only programs (Planned Parenthood Federation of America, 2005). Such programs are also present in Canada. Many from this perspective contend that young people should be told what to do (or not) rather than explore moral questions, since the correct moral decision is already clear. This type of curriculum also tends to be highly gendered (Dimick & Apple, 2005) and assumes eventual heterosexual marriage (Bay-Cheng, 2003). Health-based arguments, or 'health pragmatism' (that young people will have sex nonetheless and therefore should be protected for the social good), have been used to counter such moral authoritarianism (Thomson, 1993). In this chapter, while we touch on health pragmatism, our focus is on the rights to broad sexual health education. As has occurred within same-sex marriage debates in Canada and the United States, some religious groups have argued that religious rights vie with other human rights. Some elements of the Convention on the Rights of the Child recognize the role of religion and will be examined below, although a full engagement with the question of religious rights will not be the focus of this chapter. Suffice it to say, it is difficult to discuss the issue of sexual health education for young people without recognizing that the topic is, as Levesque (2000) reminds us, morally charged.

Such a debate hinges on differing conceptualizations of childhood and adolescence. A belief in childhood innocence is particularly relevant here. Since the nineteenth century, dominant understandings of childhood have framed it as a time of play, asexuality, and ignorance (Robinson, 2005; Kitzinger, 1988). Children are assumed to be asexual until puberty and therefore unable to understand '"adult" concepts

such as sexuality and desire' (Robinson, 2005, p. 68). This time of innocence is, in turn, idealized by adults as pleasurable and free from
concern. Thus, children are understood to be vulnerable and in need of
protection from the adult world for as long as possible; teaching sexual
health education too soon is therefore undesirable. This emphasis on
innocence resonates with the 'care-taker' model (Archard, 2004),
which suggests that children are distinct from adults, cannot make
rational decisions, and lack self-determination. Consequently, parents
must make decisions on behalf of children.

Kitzinger (1988) is concerned about the negative consequences of
such representations of children. The construction of childhood innocence, she argues, stigmatizes the 'knowing' child. For example,
Robinson (2005) observes a Madonna/whore binary that has been
applied to women, and has dichotomized young girls into either
angels or seductive Lolitas: 'Thus, when childhood innocence is
tainted, children are often held responsible' (p. 69). Kitzinger (1988)
suggests that the emphasis on childhood innocence also prevents children from having knowledge that they need to keep themselves safe.
She points to a cultural industry that has eroticized innocence, thus
augmenting the danger to children about that which they are then pre-
vented from learning. Kitzinger challenges assumptions that children
are inherently innocent and helpless, believing this emphasis on biological vulnerability to be an ideology that reproduces children's suppressed social status and constant surveillance.

These conceptualizations of childhood are deeply relevant to
debates around children's rights and access to sexual health education
(Archard, 2004). For example, Pilcher (1997), whose discussion of
several key British court cases is addressed below, argues:

> In contemporary Britain, children are denied rights to knowledge and
> advice about sex on the basis of a conception of childhood 'separateness.'
> The 'rights' that children properly have in this 'orderly' and 'traditional'
> model of childhood are welfare and protection rights, exercised on their
> behalf by parents, rather than self-determining autonomy rights. (p. 315)

In contrast, she cites the Netherlands as a country that introduces sex
education much earlier and has a low rate of teen pregnancies. There,
they have found that education does not promote promiscuity, but the
opposite. Such studies strongly suggest that children can learn about
sexuality without losing their 'childhood' and that, in many respects,

sexual knowledge can empower children, thereby protecting and extending their 'childhood' (ibid., p. 315). Recent literature within the sociology of childhood recognizes children as social agents, partici- pants in the creation of reality, and thinking beings. This is reflected, Aggleton and Campbell (2000) argue, in the CRC, which stresses the right of young people to state their views and have them heard. As illustrated above, this position that frames children as social agents conflicts with dominant conceptions of childhood.

Adolescents are in an uncertain position in relation to childhood. At times, teenagers are characterized as children, and at other times as adults. In the case of sex, it can be argued that they are frequently more likely to be framed as children, and sex to be framed as dangerous (Packer, 1997). This is particularly the case when specifically referring to girls (Raby, 2007). Yet there are constructions of young people that are unique to adolescents, that is, they are in a liminal position of tran- sition, at-risk and hypersexual (Bay-Cheng, 2003; Raby, 2002; Lesko, 1996). These constructions contribute to independent concerns about adolescents' rights to sexual health information. They are thought to be coming into their own as sexual beings, yet to still lack the skills and reflection that many feel are necessary for sexual activity. When ado- lescents are represented by the internal chaos of searching and becom- ing, biological determination, peer influence, and risk-taking, then the dangers of sexual activity are apparent. Consequent adolescent 'irra- tionality' thus threatens teenagers' access to rights (Aggleton & Campbell, 2000). Attempts are thus made to contain young people's desires in the present, through abstinence education, for instance, as these desires are seen to place them at risk (for their selves in the present and in the future) (Bay-Cheng, 2003).

These discourses can also be reframed to support sexual health edu- cation and young people's right to such education, however. If adoles- cents are becoming sexual, they are shaping the meaning of sexuality in their lives and have a right to both present and future sexual health and sexual pleasure as components of this process. If they are beset by hormonal influences and likely to take risks, it is particularly negligent to deprive them of avenues towards safer sexual practices. They have a right to both education and fertility control, 'enabling them to attain adulthood in good health, complete their desired schooling and develop their person' (Packer, 1997, p. 56). To Levesque (2000), the development of citizenship and social participation in both the present and the future require that young people have access to sexual health education, including the opportunity to discuss and examine relevant moral questions.

Constructions of childhood and adolescence affect concrete decision-making around rights. Pilcher (1997) examines how conceptions of childhood and adolescence have played out in the British *Gillick* case, for instance, regarding access to contraceptives without parental consent. The case was temporarily won on the position that parents have rights, young people are inherently immature, parents' rights trump doctors' rights, and children are not persons – all views that uphold generational inequalities. Ultimately, however, *Gillick* was lost on the argument that children have rights when they are competent to fully understand, when a lack of contraception will lead to consequences for the young person's health, and when contraception is in the best interests of the child (a concept to be further examined shortly).

Support for, and Arguments in Favour of, Sex Education

Clearly, there are a number of key arguments in favour of sexual health education (not all of which concentrate on rights), including the potential success of such programs (which we have discussed), countering misinformation, and the demand for such education. Frequently, children and youth are experiencing and exploring their sexualities before they are taught anything in the classroom. As health pragmatists remind us, whether formally educated or not, children and youth will learn about sexuality through questionable sources. Many young people turn towards the Internet, the media, and their peer groups for information about sex (Somers and Surmann, 2005; Bickmore, 1999), which can, unfortunately, be sources of misinformation. For this reason, Bickmore (1999) contends that detailed sexual health education should be taught in the classroom. Somers and Surmann (2005) have found that providing sex education through school is particularly effective for decreasing young people's sexual activity. Moreover, it is effective for schools to advocate for students to engage in responsible Internet communication through the implementation of Internet safety organizations (Shariff & Johnny, this volume).

Many children and parents agree that while such information should be taught by parents, it should also be provided through the education system. Surveys have shown that Canadian parents are generally in favour of schools providing a broadly based sexual health program. That is, they approve of a wide range of topics including puberty and reproduction, relationships, STIs, birth control, sexual abuse, sexual orientation, and abstinence (McKay, 2004). Ninety-two per cent of Canadian young people questioned in one survey conducted by Byers et al. (2003) also agreed to the inclusion of sexual health education in schools. There is a clear demand from children and parents for schools to provide extensive sexual health programs.

Finally, we need to examine constructions of sexuality, gender, and patterns of gender inequality in terms of sexual health education. Levesque (2000) criticizes many sexual health programs for not addressing issues of diversity, gender roles, and sexual orientation. The failure to mention these issues, educating for abstinence until marriage, and focusing primarily on the risks of intercourse reinforces hegemonic ideals of gender and sexuality. Meanwhile, most classrooms will have at least one student who is not heterosexual (McKay, 2004), and others will have children with same-sex parents. Furthermore, by the time children reach middle school, they are aware that gender identity is largely defined by heterosexual behaviour (i.e., girls must seek boyfriends) and marked by inequalities (i.e., the acute stigma of 'slut' disproportionately affecting girls) (Renold, 2005; Tolman, 2002; Tannenbaum, 1999). Bickmore (1999) insists that these stereotypes be addressed as early as possible.

Gender differences are also perpetuated in the portrayals and illustrations of topics in sexual health programs (Levesque, 2000). For example, Hartley and Drew (2001) have found that sexual health education films for young people, made between 1990 and 2000, delegitimize female sexual agency and yet recognize that of males. Elliot (2003) finds that the representation of women in a commonly used New Zealand textbook highlights their passivity in relation to men, their responsibility for reproduction, and their experiences of sex as functional rather than pleasurable. At the same time, Chambers, Tincknell, and Van Loon (2004), Levesque (2000), and Aggleton and Campbell (2000) find that boys receive limited information in some areas of sexual health education in comparison to girls, which denies their rights to such education and implies that girls have a greater responsibility for sexual health and reproduction. Aggleton and Campbell (2000) insist that sexual health education must also attend to boys' self-esteem and life skills by helping them to understand that dominant ideals of masculinity (i.e., suppression of emotions and needing to 'score') jeopardize their sexual health and that of their partners.

A Rights-Based Approach

The above arguments in favour of broad sexual health education are linked to the overall question of rights. In Canada all people have the right to the information needed to prevent negative outcomes of sexual health (i.e., unplanned pregnancies, STIs) and to ensure positive outcomes of sexual health (i.e., healthy reproduction, pleasure, positive self-image) (McKay, 2004). In addition to the knowledge necessary for healthy sexuality, young people must learn the practical life skills to negotiate safe sexual encounters (Aggleton & Campbell, 2000). The Convention on the Rights of the Child states that adults and organizations must ensure that the well-being of young people is taken into account when making policy decisions about them. It also states that children have a right to privacy, a right to access information, a right to confidentiality, and a right to have their views taken into consideration during decision-making processes (ibid.). Under these guidelines, not only do children have the right to sexual health information, but they also have the right to a voice in the development of their education. Unfortunately, few countries have developed their sexual health programs under this rights framework (ibid.). As we examine below, the Ontario curriculum also falls short.

Rights cover a number of different areas and can be grouped into three categories: protective rights (e.g., to safety), welfare or provision rights (e.g., to education or health care), and participation rights (e.g., to have a say) (Lansdown, 1994). The question of rights to sexual health education (and to birth control) would seem to fall into the first two categories. As Packer (1997) argues, it is paramount to young people's health (and consequently, safety) that they have access to information about family planning methods, and to those methods; she documents the high physical and social costs of pregnancy to young women, the high costs of viruses such as HIV and the community costs in terms of consequent lost schooling and employment. Participation rights are also relevant, however: a right to have a say in what happens to your own body, a right to sexual expression (Aggleton & Campbell, 2000), and a right to democratic social participation. Emphasizing citizenship rights, rights advocate Levesque links young people's right to sexual health education to 'the democratic notion that society must prepare youths for their future and for immediate social participation' (2000, p. 953), including participation in decision-making and respect for the rights of others. Canada is a pluralistic society comprising of various coexisting cultural, philosophical, and religious values. Children have the right to the tools and information necessary to become secure, respected, respecting, and contributing members of this democratic society. Thus, sexual health education should address sexual diversity. In sum, the rights argument is strong because it bolsters health pragmatism, attributes status and agency to the child, and opens possibilities for expanded rights (e.g., to democratic citizenship) and links to the rights of others (e.g., through education for diversity).

Despite the potentially broad scope and potential of children's rights, however, this is a topic defined by key sites of tension: When should a child receive sexual health education and how is this decision linked to his or her competence, maturity, and understanding? What must be included in sexual health education, and at what ages? What are the best interests of the child in terms of sexual health education, and who determines these? How do determinations of children's versus parents' (and State's) rights either reproduce or challenge the traditional hierarchy between parents and young people? How or when do children's rights become complicated by cultural or religious traditions?

These questions are all relevant to deeper analysis of the Convention on the Rights of the Child, which Canada has signed. Certain features of the Convention bolster support for sexual health education (Aggleton & Campbell, 2000; Pilcher, 1997). For instance, article 13 states that children have 'freedom to seek, receive and impart information and ideas of all kinds' (United Nations, 1989). This position has been supported by the Committee on the Rights of the Child, which has monitored access to family planning information (Packer, 1997, p. 57). Article 28 stipulates a child's right to education, and article 24 supports a child's right to health care services.

However, many articles, including 13 and 24, are ambiguous in terms of children's versus parents' or even broader community rights. Article 13 includes provisions for restrictions that protect the 'public order ..., or ... public health or morals' (United Nations, 1989). In fact, this provision has been used in the United Kingdom to restrict access to a sex education book for children (Packer, 1997). As Packer points out, sub-paragraph (f) of article 24 makes it unclear 'as to whether it is children or their parents to whom family planning education and services should be made available' (p. 60).[1] Article 17 ensures the child access 'to information and material ... especially those aimed at the promotion of his or her social, spiritual and moral well-being and physical and mental health' (United Nations, 1989) and yet includes a codicil that guidelines must be in place to protect the child 'from information and material injurious to his or her well-being, bearing in mind the provisions of Articles 13 [freedom of expression] and 18 [parental responsibilities]' (ibid.). Well-being, in this context, could be cited in order to deny sexual health education. Article 34 addresses protective rights, indicating that state parties must prevent 'the inducement or coercion of a child to engage in any unlawful sexual activity' (ibid.). Clearly, this is important for addressing child prostitution and abuse, and yet it also has elements that can undermine a child's access to protection. In Britain's *Gillick* case, for example, it was argued that a person supplying contraceptives to a girl under sixteen years of age could be considered an accessory to a crime, for in Britain sexual intercourse is illegal under the age of 16.

Other components of the Convention can also be used to argue against sexual health education. For example, the preamble of the Convention supports the importance of traditions and cultural values 'for the protection and harmonious development of children' (United Nations, 1989). Further, article 5 emphasizes the 'rights and duties of parents ..., to provide, in a manner consistent with the evolving capacities of the child, appropriate direction and guidance in the exercise by the child of the rights recognized in the present convention' (ibid.). Article 18 further supports this position, as 'Parents ... have the primary responsibility for the upbringing and development of the child. The best interests of the child will be their basic concern' (ibid.). Parents might well argue that the best interests of their child are protected through abstinence-only sexual health education, or through no sexual health education at all.

While there are ambiguities in the use of the CRC as a tool to defend children's rights to sexual health education, there are advantages to using the Convention. Packer (1997) argues that ultimately it is a valuable document in this regard, as it argues that children have rights and interests that must be protected, and it supports the agency and empowerment of children. Furthermore, Packer argues that young

---

1 Packer also notes that 'parents' remains undefined. Parents do not necessarily have to be adults. In this case, the adolescent can also be considered a parent if they have already had a child. Yet in terms of preventative health care it only makes sense that the care be there before parenthood.

people's right of access to sexual health education is bolstered through other conventions such as the 1979 Convention on the Elimination of All Forms of Discrimination against Women (or Women's Convention), the International Covenant on Civil and Political Rights, and the International Covenant on Economic, Social and Cultural Rights. Also, the Joint United Nations Programme on HIV/AIDS (UNAIDS) states that young people have a right to information and resources to protect themselves and others against infection through access to education on sex, drugs, and relationships, access to condoms, clean needles et cetera, and access to youth-friendly services with trained personnel (Aggleton & Campbell, 2000). In Canada, the 2003 Canadian Guidelines for Sexual Health Education argues for the availability to all people of accessible, age-appropriate, culturally sensitive materials that respect 'an individual's right to make informed choices about sexual and reproductive health' (McKay, 2004, p. 129). The guidelines define sexual health as 'a state of physical, emotional, mental and societal well-being related to sexuality. It is not merely the absence of disease, dysfunction or infirmity' (Health Canada, 2003, p. 5). The guidelines demand education that is accessible and comprehensive, ideally through the schools.

Two specific areas of argument greatly influence children's rights discourse: the evolving capacities of the child and the best interests of the child. The CRC defines a child as anyone under the age of eighteen and yet this is a fairly arbitrary number complicated by state and cultural diversity (Packer, 1997; James, 2004) and by our shifting conceptions of young people's age of majority over time and between contexts. The CRC to some extent acknowledges this complexity (Archard, 2004). For example, article 12.1 argues that children may express their views on matters affecting them, with 'the views of the child being given due weight in accordance with the age and maturity of the child' (United Nations, 1989). Such a focus on 'the evolving capacities of the child' disrupts the arbitrariness of the age of eighteen and provides flexibility to states and to rights advocates. Nonetheless, it leaves it up to adults to determine the weight that children's views should be given. A more powerful position is one espoused within current literature in the sociology of childhood in which children have 'been re-conceptualized as citizens, equal in value to adults, with a voice to be listened to, and specific viewpoints on their own well-being and the institutions and the social groups with which they interact' (Taylor, Smith, & Nairn, 2001, p. 138).

The best interests of the child are the responsibility of the parent or guardian until these evolving capacities of the child are met. When parents' and children's positions on the child's best interests differ, state policy or decision makers may decide, but Packer (1997) argues that this position undermines young people's competency because they are consistently framed as having less experience and understanding than adults. This leads to an ironic situation: a young person may be sexually active but deemed to lack the competence to seek and obtain contraceptive information even when he or she has made the mature choice of trying to acquire it. Further, the *risks* resulting from a lack of sexual education and safer sex practices are *not* in the best interests of the child. Therefore, a child's protection from harm should mean that she or he has access to sex education and to contraception. Levesque (2000) similarly argues that parental rights 'lose their power when they place children's lives at risk for injury and violence' (p. 974). Ultimately, Packer (1997) finds that, coupled with other Conventions, sufficient enforcement and some clarification, the Convention on the Rights of the Child is useful for supporting young people's rights to sexual health education.

In Ontario, the issue then becomes whether or not these rights are reflected in the province's Health and Physical Education curriculum. Through the following critical examination into the content of the Ontario Ministry of Education's Curriculum for Health and Physical Education (Healthy Living strand), we will demonstrate that this is not the case.

Case Study: Ontario's Health and Physical Education Curriculum (Healthy Living Strand)

The Ontario Health and Physical Education curriculum governs the content of students' learning from grades 1 to 12. It was written by teachers and curriculum staff while drawing upon their experiences in the classroom (S. Durst, personal communication, 8 July 2005). Initiated in February 2003, an on-going curriculum review process is in place to re-examine the document to ensure it is meeting the changing needs of young people. Parents, teachers, students, universities, and other stakeholders all take part in this review process. The next review of the Health and Physical Education curriculum was due to occur in September 2007 (ibid.). While this document provides guidelines for sexual health education, what is actually taught will, of

Table 10.1 Ontario curriculum expectations for 'Growth and Development / Healthy Growth and Sexuality' (grades 1–12)

Grade	Expectations
1	• describe simple life cycles of plants and animals, including humans; • recognize that rest, food, and exercise affect growth; • identify the major parts of the body by their proper names;
2	• distinguish the similarities and differences between themselves and others; • describe how germs are transmitted and how this relates to personal hygiene; • identify the five senses and describe how each functions;
3	• outline the basic human and animal reproductive processes; • describe basic changes in growth and development from birth to childhood;
4	• describe the four stages of human development (infancy, childhood, adolescence, and adulthood) and identify the physical, interpersonal, and emotional changes appropriate to their current stage; • identify the characteristics of healthy relationships; • identify the challenges and responsibilities in their relationships with family and friends;
5	• identify strategies to deal positively with stress and pressures that result from relationships with family and friends; • identify factors that enhance healthy relationships with friends, family, and peers; • describe the secondary physical changes at puberty; • describe the processes of menstruation and spermatogenesis; • describe the increasing importance of personal hygiene following puberty;
6	• relate the changes at puberty to the reproductive organs and their functions; • apply a problem-solving/decision-making process to address issues related to friends, peers, and family relationships;
7	• explain the male and female reproductive systems as they relate to fertilization; • distinguish between the facts and myths associated with menstruation, spermatogenesis, and fertilization; • identify the methods of transmission and the symptoms of sexually transmitted diseases, and ways to prevent them; • use effective communication skills to deal with various relationships and situations; • explain the term abstinence as it applies to healthy sexuality; • identify sources of support with regard to issues related to healthy sexuality;
8	• explain the importance of abstinence as a positive choice for adolescents; • identify symptoms, methods of transmission, prevention, and high-risk behaviours related to common STDs, HIV, and AIDS; • identify methods used to prevent pregnancy;

Table 10.1 (*continued*)

Grade	Expectations
	• apply living skills in making informed decisions, and analyse the consequences of engaging in sexual activities and using drugs; • identify sources of support related to healthy sexuality issues;
9	• identify the developmental stages of sexuality throughout life; • describe the factors that lead to responsible sexual relationships; • describe the relative effectiveness of methods of preventing pregnancies and sexually transmitted diseases; • demonstrate understanding of how to use decision-making and assertiveness skills effectively to promote healthy sexuality; • demonstrate understanding of the pressures on teens to be sexually active; • identify community support services related to sexual health concerns;
10	• describe environmental influences on sexuality; • explain the effects of choices related to sexual intimacy; • identify available information and support services related to sexual health concerns; • demonstrate understanding of how to use decision-making skills effectively to support choices related to responsible sexuality;
11	• describe factors affecting reproductive health in males and females; • demonstrate an understanding of causes and issues related to infertility; • demonstrate the skills needed to sustain honest, respectful, and responsible relationships; • describe sources of information on and services related to sexual and reproductive health; • assess reproductive and sexual health care information and services;
12	• analyze the factors that affect gender roles and sexuality; • demonstrate an understanding of the factors that affect the prevention of behaviour related to STDs, AIDS, and pregnancy; • describe the factors that contribute to healthy pregnancy and birth; • describe the characteristics of healthy, respectful, and long-lasting relationships; • assess the skills needed to maintain healthy, respectful, and long-lasting relationships; • describe the communication skills needed to discuss sexual intimacy and sexuality in a relationship.

course, depend on specific schools and teachers. A final note here: it has been commonplace for individuals with intellectual disabilities to be denied sexual health education (Griffiths, 2003) and control over their own sexuality and reproduction (Owen et al., this volume). Although this issue is far too extensive to be discussed in this chapter,

Table 10.2 Ontario curriculum expectations for 'Personal Safety and Injury Prevention' (grades 1–12)

Grade	Expectations
1	• outline the potential safety risks in the home, school, and community; • describe exploitative behaviours (e.g., abusive behaviours, inappropriate touching) and the feelings associated with them; • identify people who can provide personal safety assistance and explain how to access them;
2	• identify safety rules to be followed in the home, school, and community (e.g., bus safety); • describe types of verbal and physical violence (e.g., name calling, kicking, hitting); • explain the importance of being able to say no to exploitative behaviours (e.g., improper touching), and describe how to seek help;
3	• explain relevant safety procedures (e.g., fire drills); • use a problem-solving process to identify ways of obtaining support for personal safety in the home, school, and community; • identify examples of real and fictional violence (e.g., schoolyard fights, cartoons, movies);
4	• apply decision-making and problem-solving skills in addressing threats to personal safety (e.g., from abuse or physical fighting) and injury prevention; • identify people and community agencies that can assist with injury prevention and violence prevention;
5	• explain how peoples actions (e.g., bullying) can affect the feelings and reactions of others; • apply strategies (e.g., anger management, assertiveness) to deal with personal-safety and injury-prevention situations (e.g., swarming, threatening, harassment);
6	• identify and describe appropriate methods for preventing and treating ailments; • identify the responsibilities associated with caring for themselves and others (e.g., while babysitting); • describe and respond appropriately to potentially violent situations relevant to themselves (e.g., harassment, violence in the media);
7	• describe harassment and identify ways of dealing with it (e.g., by communicating feelings and reporting) • identify people and resources that can support someone experiencing harassment
8	• analyse situations (e.g., violence in relationships) that are potentially dangerous to personal safety; • identify support services that assist victims of violence, and explain how to access them;
9	• describe specific types of physical and non-physical abuse (e.g., manipulation, sexual harassment);

Table 10.2 (*continued*)

Grade	Expectations
	• assess the impact of non-physical abuse on victims;
	• identify the causes of abuse and violence;
	• describe solutions and strategies to address violence in the lives of young people;
	• explain how the school and community agencies are involved in developing strategies to prevent or end the violence in young peoples lives;
	• demonstrate effective personal strategies to minimize injury in adolescence.
10	• There are no expectations listed for this topic in grade 10.
11	• describe different types of violence (e.g., relationship violence; physical, verbal, sexual, emotional);
	• demonstrate an understanding of the causes of relationship violence;
	• identify and analyse the indicators of violence in interpersonal relationships, as well as appropriate intervention strategies;
	• assess solutions and strategies for preventing and eliminating relationship violence;
	• analyse the leading causes of injury and injury-associated deaths among adolescents
	• demonstrate an ability to minimize the risks of injury for adolescents;
	• assess strategies for reducing injuries and injury-associated deaths among adolescents;
12	• analyse the causes of certain types of interpersonal violence (e.g., stalking, date rape, family violence);
	• describe the possible effects of violence on individuals who are exposed to it in their personal lives
	• identify sources of support for individuals exposed to violence;
	• demonstrate an ability to deal with threats to personal safety and the safety of others;
	• explain why adolescents and young adults are overrepresented in traffic fatalities;
	• assess strategies for reducing risks to their own safety and that of others in various situations (e.g., while driving).

Sources: Ontario Government, 1998; 1999; & 2000

our support for school-based sexual health education extends to all young people.

Within the Health and Physical Education document is a strand entitled 'Healthy Living' (Ontario Government, 1998, 1999, & 2000). Various sections are covered within this strand, including two that are paramount to our discussion of sexual health education: 'Growth and

Development / Healthy Growth and Sexuality' (grades 1–8 and 9–12 respectively) and 'Personal Safety and Injury Prevention' (grades 1–12). A complete list of the expectations covered in each section (from grades 1–12) can be found in tables 10.1 and 10.2.

The Healthy Living strand recognizes that children are influenced by media, peers, family, religious leaders, and relatives, and that school-based programs 'add another important dimension to a child's ongoing learning about sexuality' (Ontario Government, 1998, p. 10). Recalling Bickmore's (1999) discussion of the dangers of getting mis-information outside the classroom, the curriculum could further emphasize that school-based programs are available to also clarify misinformation that young people may acquire elsewhere. Acknowl-edgment of young people's right to accurate information would also bring this document in line with the CRC. The curriculum claims to be 'age-appropriate and addressed with sensitivity and respect for indi-vidual differences' (Ontario Government, 1998, p. 10). As will become evident, this does not always hold true when we examine the content of the curriculum more closely. The curriculum attends to the evolving capacities of the child; yet much of the curriculum comes too late. The comprehensiveness and appropriateness of the curriculum will now be examined.

First, bear in mind that few countries have developed their sexual health education programs under a rights framework (Aggleton & Campbell, 2000). Most fundamentally, direct reference to rights would strengthen the document. Within Canada, and elsewhere, general rights education is also lacking (Stasiulis, 2002). We would like to see such broader rights education integrated in the general Ontario cur-riculum. As discussed in Raby (this volume), such an education pro-vides students with experience in decision-making and democratic participation. It fosters a sense of one's own rights as well as others'. Linked to sexual health education, an emphasis on rights supports the right to say no (and yes), rights to education, rights to safety and secu-rity, and the consequent development of self-esteem.

If one examines the content of the curriculum more closely, it will be seen that most of the material covered is addressed too late to fulfil children's rights to education that will promote safety. Most troubling, there is very little in the primary curriculum that addresses personal boundaries and dealing with sexual advances from adults. Such edu-cation would seem necessary to help prevent 'the inducement or coer-cion of a child to engage in any unlawful sexual activity' (United

Nations, 1989). Students in grades 1 and 2 discuss inappropriate touching under the 'Personal Safety and Injury Prevention' section; however, no further reference to sexual harassment is made again until grade 9, which prevents children from having regular discussion of either inappropriate touching or sexual harassment.

In a number of other areas, information also seems to come too late. As part of the concept of human development in grade 3, children learn about the basic changes that occur developmentally from birth to childhood, such as changes in teeth and height. If, however, the study is broadened to examine birth to *adolescence*, children would be introduced to puberty, and would be prepared for the years to come. As it is, the concept of puberty is not introduced until grade 5, through discussions of the primary and secondary characteristics associated with this phase of life. By grade 5, however, some physical changes are already taking place for some children. The effects of environmental influences (i.e., media, culture) on sexuality, available support systems, and decision-making skills around responsible sexuality are not addressed until grade 10. Furthermore, the final expectation in grade 12 is that students will explore the communication skills necessary to converse about sexual intimacy and sexuality within a relationship. Arguably, this last expectation is the most important aspect of sexual health taught within the Ontario curriculum, one that links up with protection, provision, and participation rights. Ensuring that young people are able to discuss sexuality is the primary step in building a healthy sexuality. Only when communication lines are open are young people able to discuss safe sex methods, their moral views of sexuality, and the kinds of relationships they wish to have. Discussing this in grade 12 is important, but only *introducing* it at this grade level is far too late. Somers and Surmann (2005) have found that an earlier introduction to sexual health education decreases risk-taking behaviours.

Reproduction is well covered throughout the curriculum. In the first grade, children describe the life cycle of plants and animals, including those of humans.[2] In grade 3, students study the basic reproductive processes of humans and animals, such as the union of the egg and the sperm. Yet grade 7 is the first year in which sex is discussed, at which

---

2 A rewording to emphasize the life cycle of humans, with reference to plants and animals as alternative examples of the life cycle concept would put human development in the foreground.

point students learn how STIs are transmitted, their symptoms, and ways to prevent them. These expectations imply sexual intercourse, but only indirectly. Grade 8 students identify methods to prevent pregnancy. Grade 11 students study the nutritional, hormonal, and environmental factors that influence reproductive systems. Students in grade 12 review factors that prevent pregnancy, prevent STIs, and provide for healthy pregnancies. However, despite the attention paid to all these topics related to sexual intercourse, nowhere in the curriculum, from grades 1 to 12, does it explicitly state that children will learn about the act of sexual intercourse, and other forms of sexual activity, which would seem necessary to discuss as part of a comprehensive sexual health education. Oral sex, for example, is now reported to be an earlier form of sexual activity than intercourse, and yet does not seem to receive much attention at all.

In fact, and typical of much sexual health education (Bay-Cheng, 2003), the overall tone of the curriculum in regard to young people's experiences and expressions of sex and sexuality is quite negative, emphasizing mainly prevention, control, and a fear of outcomes. This can be seen through the subject matter and the language of the document. For example, students apply decision-making skills to make informed decisions after determining the consequences of participating in sexual activities, yet such terminology as 'consequences' sheds a negative light upon the subject area of sexual health. When growing up, children learn that poor behaviour has 'consequences.' Using such terminology in this context implies that engaging in sexual activities is wrong. The material for grade 9 and 10 contributes to these discussions of protection and safe sex with further discussions of methods to avoid STIs (i.e., abstinence, condoms, oral contraceptives) and the effects that STIs have on intimacy. In general, the tone is negative. Finally, children also learn the importance of hygiene both during and following puberty. This has the potential to be negative if the reason given for the importance of hygiene is because puberty and its concomitant changes are dirty, unpleasant, or something to be ashamed of. A focus on negative consequences fulfils children's right to health in terms of safety. However, healthy sexuality involves much more: a positive body image, self-exploration, and the recognition of desire (Bay-Cheng, 2003). As Tolman (2002) argues, for example, a lack of discourse of desire for girls leaves them vulnerable to sexual risk.

Notably, gender diversity, gender inequality, and sexual diversity are topics rarely covered by the curriculum, yet they are necessary for democratic citizenship (participation rights) and children's safety from bullying (protection rights). Bickmore (1999) argues that there is room for such topics in the curriculum, but that these are avoided because teachers are not mandated to discuss homosexuality. One of the most common ways to incorporate references to sexual diversity, however, is within the topic of bullying. See Bickmore (1999) for a more in-depth exploration of subject areas of the curriculum where sex, gender, and homosexual identity can be incorporated, namely, language arts and social studies.

Within the Health and Physical Education curriculum, however, children in grade 2 learn to distinguish between themselves and others, making use of similarities and differences. The document provides the examples of body size and gender. Although discussing such difference is beneficial to children's development of identities independent of their peers, it is possible that this expectation may foster gender-role stereotyping, such as 'I'm a girl because I play with dolls. He is a boy because he plays with trucks,' and size-related bullying. Rather, this topic can include education in thinking critically about gender-based generalizations. The topics of gender, diversity, and inequality are not addressed again until grade 12, when students discuss the factors that influence gender roles and sexuality. While discussing this in grade 12 is important to students, recall that by the time students reach middle school, we see evidence of sexual harassment (Renold, 2002) and homophobic bullying (Chambers et al., 2004; Bickmore, 1999). As peer aggression is often a precursor to violence (Lacharite & Marini, this volume), beginning such discussions much earlier will help alleviate the development of gender stereotypes, and encourage children to be more open-minded about others' and their own sexuality. Such education needs to include discussion of sexual orientation (McKay, 2004; Bickmore, 1999) and to expand definitions of sex from emphasis only on intercourse (Bay-Cheng, 2003). Importantly, sexual health education also requires discussion of gender inequalities: the objectification of women in pornography and relationship violence, for example (Lenskyi, 1990).

Finally, the curriculum seems to leave out the opportunity for students to engage with moral questions. As Levesque (2000) suggests, engagement with moral questions is important within sexual health education – an imperative distinct from moralized lecturing. For example, students discuss the term abstinence in grade 8 as a positive choice towards healthy sexuality. It is at this time that other methods to prevent pregnancy are also introduced. Abstinence is highlighted as a positive choice to make, without exploration of various social and personal questions around this issue: What constitutes abstinence? What does abstinence mean to me? Is abstinence my only choice? What if I never get married?

If one examines the Health and Physical Education curriculum as a whole, it appears at first to supply young people with education to which they are entitled. At the same time, however, much of the focus is on preventing the negative outcomes of sex (i.e., pregnancy and STIs) and promoting abstinence. Aggleton and Campbell (2000) highlight the importance of sexual health being an affirmative concept. Rather than representing sexuality as a potentially dangerous, frightening, and complicated aspect of life, perhaps educators should reassure young people that it is potentially satisfactory, pleasurable, and rewarding, and provide them with the resources to ensure this is so. Like many other programs, the Healthy Living strand is limited in its scope (Levesque, 2000): too many issues that deserve more attention (i.e., communication, sexual orientation, diversity, rights, pleasure) are left out, or touched upon only briefly.

Levesque (2000) recognizes that many schools introduce topics later than needed. We recognized this trend in the Ontario curriculum as well. Much of the information needs to be moved up at least one or two school years to prepare young people for the experiences they will come across in their lives, rather than providing them with the resources too late (Somers and Surmann, 2005). Providing earlier sexual health education would therefore recognize that young people are exposed to sexual health material from other sources. It would recognize that young people are engaging in relationships early, sexual or otherwise, and it would more adequately recognize young people's rights to health, safety, and education.

The Ontario curriculum addresses both sexual health education and personal safety education. However, they are generally treated as mutually exclusive. Upon closer examination, many topics under the 'Personal Safety and Injury Prevention' section, such as bullying, violence, and abuse can, and arguably should, be taught with reference to sexual health. Recall that the average school devotes 6.5 hours each year to sexual health (Levesque, 2000). If this is true for any school in Ontario, the guidelines for sexual health education cannot possibly be covered thoroughly. Therefore, incorporating more reference to sexual health into the 'Personal Safety and Injury Prevention' section would effectively bolster young people's sexual health education, recognize their rights to personal safety information, and ensure more time for addressing positive features of sexual health education within that curriculum. Similarly, sexual health education can expand from being taught as singular units by being integrated into various other curricula throughout the year.

Also of concern, once young people enter high school, Health and Physical Education is no longer a mandatory course each year. Students in Ontario are only required to complete one year of Health and Physical Education at the secondary school level, and many students may therefore stop taking the course that offers sexual health information. This is a particular problem for the 'Personal Safety and Injury Prevention' section, as the most pertinent information about sexual harassment does not appear until grade 9. Therefore, students who opt out of Health and Physical Education after grade 9 will only be exposed to one year of instruction regarding their rights to personal boundaries. The response to young people's rights to sexual heath education is therefore limited in a number of ways: in terms of what is taught, when it is taught, and how much is taught.

Conclusion

There are a number of key arguments in favour of young people's early access to sexual health education. These arguments are based on health pragmatism, the desires of young people and their parents for such education and, most importantly for this chapter, young people's rights to education, safety, and social participation. Sexual health education for young people is fraught as it is complicated by conceptualizations of childhood innocence and adolescent risk. Nonetheless, young people are sexual beings who must be provided with the information and skills necessary to negotiate the pleasures they may experience and the dangers they may face. Further, their right to such information is grounded in various international documents, the most important of which is the United Nations Convention on the Rights of the Child. However, some of the CRC's features may in fact undermine these rights, and therefore it needs to be strengthened in this respect (Packer, 1997). To work with these issues, we can look at documents closer to home, such as the Ontario Ministry of Education's Curriculum for Health and Physical Education (Healthy Living strand). Based on arguments in the CRC and other international rights-based documents cited above, this curriculum is found wanting. As the 'age-appropriateness' of this document appears to be out-of-date, the curriculum needs to be revised to take into consideration a changing sexual culture with a need for an earlier sexual health education for children and youth. This includes more of a focus on sexual intercourse, as well as on sexual and gender diversity. Finally, to alleviate the negative stigma placed on sexuality (especially for girls), the curriculum should address positive aspects of sexual health rather than primarily focusing on the prevention and control of problematic situations.

The right to a comprehensive sexual health education in childhood and adolescence is paramount to young people's physical, sexual, social, and civic well-being. Unfortunately, it has become evident that this right is commonly overlooked in the design of sexual health programs. Through the thoughtful amalgamation of rights principles (i.e., the CRC) and program planning (i.e., the Ontario curriculum), young people can receive the comprehensive sexual health education to which they are entitled.

REFERENCES

Aggleton, P., & Campbell, C. (2000). Working with young people: Towards an agenda for sexual health. *Sexual and Relationship Therapy, 15*(3), 283–296.

Archard, D. (2004). *Children: Rights and childhood* (2nd ed.). London: Routledge.

Bay-Cheng, L.Y. (2003). The trouble with teen sex: The construction of adolescent sexuality through school-based sexuality education. *Sex Education, 3*(1), 61–74.

Bearman, P.S., & Brückner, H. (2001). Promising the future: Virginity pledges and first intercourse. *American Journal of Sociology, 106*(4), 859–912.

Bickmore, K. (1999). Why discuss sexuality in elementary school? In W.J. Letts IV & J.T. Sears (Eds.), *Queering elementary education: Advancing the dialogue about sexualities and schooling.* Lanham, MD: Rowman & Littlefield Publishers.

Byers, E.S., Sears, H.A., Voyer, S.D., Thurlow, J.L., Cohen, J.N., & Weaver, A.D. (2003). An adolescent perspective on sexual health education at school and at home: I. High school students. *Canadian Journal of Human Sexuality, 12*(1), 1–17.

Chambers, D., Tincknell, E., & Van Loon, J. (2004). Peer regulation of teenage sexual identities. *Gender and Education, 16*(3), 397–415.

Dimick, A.S., & Apple, M.W. (2005). Texas and the politics of abstinence-only textbooks. *TCRecord: The voice of scholarship education.* Retrieved on June, 28, 2005, from http://www.tcredord.org/PrintContent.asp?ContentID-11855

Elliot, K. (2003). The hostile vagina: Reading vaginal discourse in a school health text. *Sex Education, 3*(2), 133–144.

Griffiths, D. (2003). Sexuality and people who have developmental disabilities: From myth to emerging practices. In I. Brown & M. Percy (Eds.), *Developmental disabilities in Ontario* (2nd ed.). Toronto: Ontario Association on Developmental Disabilities.

Hartley, H., & Drew, T. (2001). Gendered messages in sex ed films: Trends and implications for female sexual problems. *Women and Therapy, 24*(1–2), 133–146.

Health Canada. (2003). *Canadian guidelines for sexual health education.* Ottawa: Population and Public Health Branch, Health Canada.

James, A. (2004). Understanding childhood from an interdisciplinary perspective: Problems and potentials. In P.B. Pufall & R.P. Unsworth (Eds.), *Rethinking childhood.* New Brunswick, NJ: Rutgers University Press.

Kitzinger, J. (1988). Defending innocence: Ideologies of childhood. *Feminist Review, 28,* 77–87.

Lansdown, G. (1994). Children's rights. In B. Mayall (Ed.), *Children's childhoods: Observed and experienced.* London: The Falmer Press.

Lenskyj, H. (1990). Beyond plumbing and prevention: Feminist approaches to sex education. *Gender & Education, 2*(2), 217–230.

Lesko, N. (1996). Denaturalizing adolescence: The politics of contemporary representations. *Youth and Society, 28*(2), 139–161.

Levesque, R.J.R. (2000). Sexuality education: What adolescents' educational rights require. *Psychology, Public Policy and Law, 6*(4), 953–988.

McKay, A. (2004). Sexual health education in the schools: Questions and answers. *Canadian Journal of Human Sexuality, 13*(3–4), 129–141.

Ontario Government. (1998). The Ontario curriculum grades 1–8: Health and physical education.

Ontario Government (1999). The Ontario curriculum grades 9 and 10: Health and physical education.

Ontario Government (2000). The Ontario curriculum grades 11 and 12: Health and physical education.

Packer, C.A.A. (1997). Preventing adolescent pregnancy: The protection offered by international human rights law. *International Journal of Children's Rights, 5,* 47–76.

Pilcher, J. (1997). Contrary to Gillick: British children and sexual rights since 1985. *International Journal of Children's Rights, 5,* 299–317.

Planned Parenthood Federation of America. (2005). *Abstinence-only 'sex' edu-*

cation. Retrieved on August 23, 2005, from http://www.plannedparent
hood.org/pp2/portal/files/portal/medicalinfo/teensexualhealth/facts-
abstinence-education.xml

Raby, R. (2002). Tangle of discourses: Girls negotiating adolescence. *Journal of Youth Studies, 5*(4), 425–450.

Raby, R. (2007). Children in sex, adults in crime: Constructing and confining teenagers. *Resources for Feminist Research / Documentation sur la recherche féministe, 31*(3–4), 9–28.

Renold, E. (2002). Presumed innocence: (Hetero)sexual, heterosexist and homophobic harassment among primary school girls and boys. *Childhood, 9*(4), 415–434.

Renold, E. (2005). *Girls, boys and junior sexualities: Exploring children's gender and sexual relations in the primary school*. London: Routledge Falmer.

Robinson, K. (2005). Childhood and sexuality: Adult constructions and silenced children. In J. Mason & T. Fattore (Eds.), *Children taken seriously in theory, policy and practice*. London: Jessice Kingsley Publishers.

Somers, C., & Surmann, A. (2005). Sources and timing of sex education: Relations with American adolescent sexual attitudes and behavior. *Educational Review, 57*(1), 37–54.

Stasiulis, D. (2002). The active child citizen: Lessons from Canadian policy and the children's movement. *Citizenship Studies, 6*(4), 507–538.

Tannenbaum, L. (1999). *Slut! Growing up female with a bad reputation*. New York: Seven Stories Press.

Taylor, N., Smith, A.B., & Nairn, K. (2001). Rights important to young people: Secondary student and staff perspectives. *International Journal of Children's Rights, 9*, 137–156.

Thomson, R. (1993). Unholy alliances: The recent politics of sex education. In J. Bristow & A.R. Wilson (Eds.), *Activating theory: Lesbian, gay, bisexual politics*. London: Lawrence and Wishart.

Tolman, D. (2002). *Dilemmas of desire*. London: Harvard University Press.

United Nations (1989). *Convention on the Rights of the Child*.

11 Special Education Rights: Services for Children with Special Needs in Ontario Schools

SHEILA BENNETT, DON DWORET, AND MANTA ZAHOS

'Welcome to the war zone that is special education in Ontario' reads a front-page article in the *Toronto Star* from 5 December 2005. This article, entitled 'Parents, schools fight $1.8B special needs war,' had as its focus the disconnect between parents of students with special needs and the educators who work with them. 'War zone' is an overly dramatic and media-catchy turn of phrase perhaps, but, it does represent to some extent the deeply rooted complex issues that define the delivery of service to approximately 290,800 children in the province of Ontario. Spread over seventy-two school boards and delivered with loose consistency across those boards, special-education service delivery in the province of Ontario remains rife with differing philosophical orientations towards working with students with special needs, perceived financial and bureaucratic stumbling blocks to progress, and, within schools and classrooms, idiosyncratic variations on the theme of what defines successful and effective practice. This complexity of service and orientation occurs within an atmosphere of sophisticated parent involvement, litigious intervention in program initiatives, and demonstrably more reliance on outcome measures that are meant to prove student success.

There is no dispute that within the legislative framework, both nationally and provincially, there exists a clear mandate to provide services, access, and opportunity to individuals with disabilities. Under the *Canadian Charter of Rights and Freedoms*, enacted in 1982, all are equal before the law, including those with mental or physical disabilities. In the context of Ontario, the Human Rights Code of Ontario (1990) further recognizes the right to dignity and worth of every person without discrimination, including those with disabilities. From an educational perspective, children and youth with disabilities were further protected by the introduction of the *Education Amendment Act* by the Ontario legislature, commonly known as Bill 82, passed in Ontario in 1980, which had at its core universality of access to education for all students.

Four years after the passage of Bill 82 in Ontario, the United Nations Convention on the Rights of the Child (1989) established the international rights of all children to education, regardless of ability. The Convention espouses education for all children with disabilities as a method of achieving full social integration and personal development. Effective access to education is emphasized, alongside training, health care services, rehabilitation services, preparation for employment, and recreation opportunities. Within this framework, children's personalities, talents, and mental and physical abilities are to be developed to their fullest potential.

In Ontario, Bill 82 ensures full access to education programs and services for children with disabilities. Philosophically, the mandate of Bill 82 upholds the United Nations Convention on the Rights of the Child mandate by attempting to establish an equal playing field for children with special needs, and to ensure equality of outcomes wherever possible. Unfortunately, the Convention's ideal of achieving full social integration and personal development for all disabled children is still to be realized in Ontario. Although the legislated establishment of special education (Bill 82) in Ontario is over twenty years old, the province still faces many challenges in meeting the ideal of what constitutes adequate provision of services. Access and opportunity for persons with special needs to the full spectrum of educational opportunities remains open to interpretation by school officials, parents, and students alike.

This chapter begins with a historical account of Bill 82, surveying the treatment of children with disabilities before the bill's enactment and then explaining how this piece of legislation encapsulated key elements that set the stage for special education in Ontario in its current form. The discussion then focuses on current and controversial issues in special education in Ontario, including identification, programming, measurement of achievement, funding, and teacher education.

A Brief History

Before Bill 82, the *Education Act* of Ontario permitted boards of education to offer programs and services for students with special needs.

Unfortunately for students with special needs, universality of access was more of a myth than a reality. School boards, while being able and permitted to provide programs, often made the choice to either not offer these students programs or deemed them 'unable to profit from instruction.' Historically, education for those with disabilities within Canada only came into existence within the last one hundred and fifty years with the development of schools in larger urban centres such as Toronto and Montreal. For the most part, these schools were set up to deal with students with visible disabilities such as blindness or hearing impairment (Winzer, 2005). These types of schools required children as young as five to leave home and sometimes travel to a different province to receive services. As education for persons with disabilities became more readily available, provinces approached the funding and implementation of programs for such students in various ways.

Within Ontario, funds were made available from the Ontario Ministry of Education for programs and services for persons with disabilities, but only if the boards chose to access them. Inequality of service throughout the province was quite prevalent. Some boards, mostly in urban areas, were able to establish programs for children with particular types of disabilities, but not all. For example, the Board of Education of the City of Toronto had programs for slow learners and students with mild intellectual handicaps, while the (then) Metropolitan Toronto School Board ran segregated schools for students identified, at that time, as Trainable Retarded (now referred to in Ontario as Developmentally Disabled). Toronto also had programs for students who were classified as deaf or hard of hearing, autistic, learning disabled, gifted, and behaviourally exceptional. In spite of these many programs available in this larger urban area, in many other parts of the province programs of this nature did not exist. These areas relied on section 34 of the *Education Act*, which permitted boards to exclude students who, according to a board committee, were 'unable to profit from instruction.' These included students who were profoundly developmentally handicapped, who then became the responsibility of the Ministry of Community and Social Services. Such students received daily service in facilities known as 'treatment centres,' which were prevalent throughout the province and staffed, not by teachers, but by childcare workers. In many situations, if parents wanted their child with special needs to receive an educational program, they would move to an area where the education program or service was available.

The Introduction of the Education Amendment Act *(Bill 82)*

Public frustration with the disparity of educational service delivery, fuelled by a growing North American movement towards the recognition of rights for the disabled, became the catalyst for the creation of Bill 82, which had at its core the recognition of the rights of all students to an appropriate and meaningful education. Choice in delivering an educational program was no longer in the hands of individual school boards; they were now required by law to provide appropriate educational opportunities to all children in the province regardless of ability. The intent of Bill 82 was very clear: no longer would the education of students with special needs be optional. As outlined by Weber and Bennett (2004), the requirement of Bill 82 included a mandate that every school board in the province provide special education programs and services for its exceptional pupils. In cases where services could not be provided, the legislation required that boards of education either pay another board to provide those services or find the service in the private sector. Boards of education were also mandated to establish Identification, Placement and Review Committees (IPRCs), their chief function being to identify whether a pupil is exceptional, and then to decide upon a placement for that pupil. As well, school boards were required to implement procedures for early and on-going identification of pupils' learning abilities and needs. The legislation also mandated that parents, and students sixteen years and older, be included in the IPRC process and that an appeal process be available if they are dissatisfied with identification or placement decisions.

   School boards were further required to establish a Special Education Advisory Committee, whose membership consisted of representatives of parent and advocacy groups, to advise on matters of special education programs and services. A comprehensive special education plan would be developed and maintained by each school board in which programs and services are outlined for public and ministry examination. The 'Plan' is updated and amended as necessary to meet the current needs of exceptional pupils (Weber & Bennett, 2004). It was within these parameters that school boards redefined their existing practices, created new practices, and for the first time had a direct mandate under the law to provide services for all students with special needs.

   Subsequent to the implementation of Bill 82, additional regulations were passed to further assist boards in understanding the intent of the legislation and to try to ensure that there was consistency throughout the province in how the bill would be implemented. These changes also reflected the evolving shift, in terms of decision making with respect to the education of students with special needs, from an almost totally school-centred power base to a more equitable distribution of power characterized by shared (parents and educators) decision making with equal representation. Characteristic of this shift was the change in the IPRC regulation now renumbered Regulation 181/98. This new regulation more explicitly defined the composition of the Identification, Placement and Review Committee and the process that school boards follow in making IPRC decisions. Within this regulation the Special Education Appeal Board, available if a parent or guardian disagrees with an IPRC decision, now permitted a parent to bring a representative with them to the IPRC meeting. Within the Appeal Board regulations, both parents and the school board were permitted to choose their own representative for the board, with the third being agreed on by both parties. Changes also ensured that the board make available to parents a parent guide that would provide a comprehensive description of the programs, policies, and services the board had in place for pupils with exceptionalities. It is important to note that Regulation 181/98 required that IPRCs should view regular-class placement as the first choice for placement. Also within the regulation was the requirement that all exceptional students have an Individual Education Plan (IEP) in place that included learning expectations, an outline of special education programs and services the student would receive, how pupil progress would be evaluated, and, for students fourteen years of age and older, a transition plan to post-secondary education, work, or community living.

Bill 82 created a legislative framework that reflected a number of the principles set forth in the United Nations Convention on the Rights of the Child. The legislation provided children with special needs with full rights to an education. It supported due process for children with disabilities and allowed them access to programming and services. It also provided safeguards that protected children with special needs from discrimination on the basis of their disability. The legislation also took into account the rights and duties of parents in decision making and supported the preparation of children with special needs for responsible living. By mandating educational rights for children with special needs Bill 82 created a pathway for upholding children's rights. While some might argue that Bill 82 has succeeded in opening up full access to educational opportunities, others would argue that that door is only slightly ajar. Despite great strides towards the goal of full social integration and personal development espoused by the Convention, there remains within the province a wide discrepancy among special education orientations and service delivery. Factors that influence this variation in service delivery include the issues of identification, programming, measurement of achievement, funding, and teacher education.

Current Issues

Within the province of Ontario the last decade has seen unprecedented changes, which include the introduction of the College of Teachers, the implementation of a provincial curriculum, mandated board amalgamation, as well as changes in reporting and funding procedures. Within the field of special education the issues of the efficacy of identifying students as having special needs, the placement of students in special education settings, and the provision of appropriate programming are among a larger number of concerns being discussed for which solutions are being sought. As mentioned earlier, these issues are being examined amid an atmosphere of increasing public pressure to demonstrate academic success. They will be the basis for the discussion for the remainder of this chapter.

As Ontario actively moves towards the functional inclusion of students with special needs into the regular classroom, there is an ongoing necessity for research-based practices to inform the teaching of these children and youth. The Expert Panel on Literacy and Numeracy Instruction for Students with Special Education Needs was recently established by the Ministry of Education to advise on this issue. The panel's work resulted in a publication entitled *Education for All* (Ontario Ministry of Education, 2005), which was released to school boards throughout Ontario in the spring of 2005. Before its release the Ministry of Education announced the allocation of $25 million to school boards to research the implementation of programs and strategies that support learners with special education needs in terms of literacy, numeracy, assessment, profile development, program planning, evaluation, and assistive technology, and determine best practice. In tandem with these initiatives, the Ministry of Education set up a Working Table on Special Education Reform, whose mandate was to provide recommendations to the minister on a number of issues, including funding, service delivery, teacher training, and student achievement. The work of the Expert Panel, the creation of the Working Table, and the allocation of funds to support students with special needs should most definitely be seen as a positive step in the move towards ensuring appropriate services for students with special needs.

Identification of Students with Exceptionalities

Within the field of special education, the ongoing debate over the use of categories to define and access services for students with exceptionalities remains unresolved. Kauffman and Hallahan, in their book *Special Education: What Is It and Why We Need It* (2005), argue that stigmatization is always present in society and that the dilemma for educators becomes one of managing this reality with empathy, support and accommodation. McPhail and Freeman (2005), by contrast, argue that the classification of certain students through defining them as disabled creates a scenario where the dominant, normal culture strives to bring those who are considered outside the normal range into what is defined as the appropriate culture. They further argue that this elitist defining of what is normal leads to a devaluing of the diversity of learners and the perpetuation of a system designed to promote only failure rather than growth and development.

Within the province of Ontario the process for the identification of students as exceptional is outlined in Regulation 181/98. For many boards, the process begins with a teacher requesting that the in-school team discuss the student's situation and suggest remedial strategies. If the student's educational and/or behavioural difficulties are such that these strategies are not effective, the in-school team can recommend to the principal that an Identification, Placement and Review Committee be held. (The IPRC process can also be instigated at the request of a parent.) This committee, composed of at least three persons including a principal or supervisory officer, will review the student's file and decide on the identification and placement of students they deem as exceptional. In making this decision the committee must

(a) state whether the committee has identified the pupil as an exceptional pupil;
(b) where the committee has identified the pupil as an exceptional pupil, include,

(i) the committee's description of the pupil's strengths and
needs;
(ii) the categories and definitions of any exceptionalities identified by the committee;
(iii) the committee's placement decision;
(iv) the committee's recommendation under subsection 16(2)
regarding special education programs and services if any; and
(c) where the committee has decided that the pupil should be
placed in a special education class, state the reasons for that decision. (Milne & MacKinnon, 2005, p. 613)

When a student is deemed exceptional by an IPRC, it is required that
the student be identified in one of five categories of exceptionality.
Note that in several categories there are subcategories: behavioural;
intellectual (giftedness, mild intellectual disability, developmental disability); communication (autism, deaf and hard of hearing, language
impairment, speech impairment, learning disability); physical (physical disability, blind and low vision): multiple.

Across the province, questions with regard to the adequacy and suit-
ability of these categories exist. Parents and even educators of students
with such conditions as attention deficit disorder and acquired brain
injury, two disabilities not included in the category list, argue that
accessing service for these students can be difficult and confusing.
Often, students with these types of conditions have to be identified
within one of the existing categories in order to access specific types of
services. It can be argued that all boards have the flexibility, within the
ministry regulations and guidelines, to write an IEP without going
through the IPRC process and thus provide services for those students
in need. The counter argument that exists is twofold. First, the inability to utilize the IPRC process in such cases and rely solely on the IEP
eliminates those legislative vehicles that exist for appeal and due
process. Second, if the choice is made to utilize the IPRC process with
the existing categories and the students, for all intents and purposes,
are mislabelled, then their programming and placement will be based
on incorrect and perhaps misleading information. For example,
placing a child with an acquired brain injury, who has severe behavioural difficulties, in a program designed on the basis of behaviour
modification would be at best ineffective and at worst damaging.

If we accept, along with Kauffman and Hallahan (2005), that categories are a necessary element of service delivery, then the question of

the adequacy of these categories to access and service all students with special needs becomes paramount. If, however, we move towards a more egalitarian model, which defines all learners as part of a diverse range, then the question of the adequacy of categories becomes less important and the issue of ensuring due process for students becomes the central issue.

On a broader level, the release of the document *Special Education Transformation: The Report of the Co-chairs with the Recommendations of the Working Table on Special Education* (Bennett & Wynne, 2006) has resulted in a number of recommendations that will likely affect student access to IPRCs across the province. As a result of the report, the ministry has recommended a streamlined identification and review process that would decrease the need for IPRCs for those students who were in special education classes for less than half a day. The argument in support of this recommendation centres around the streamlining of the administrative process that would allow for more teacher time spent with students. Those who oppose such a recommendation express deep concern over the issue of reducing any legislative process that ensures an appeals procedure and protection under the law to one based solely on goodwill. This concern is countered by the argument that parents maintain the right to call an IPRC if they deem it necessary. The response to this is that there is a serious, if not catastrophic, knowledge gap on the part of parents in terms of their 'right' to initiate such a process. How do we in the province ensure that, when goodwill breaks down, parents are knowledgeable enough as educational consumers to begin the necessary legislative process?

Placement of Students in Special Education

Once a student is identified as being in need of special education services, the issue of the environment in which that student receives this programming must be considered. Traditionally, within special education, a cascade of services have been provided that range from self-contained special education settings to full inclusion (Smith, Lukasson, & Crealok, 1995). Most recently, there has been an increased provincial and political emphasis on the inclusion of students with special needs in the regular classroom, as evidenced by the release of the aforementioned report of the Expert Panel, which has as its focus differentiated instruction delivered by regular classroom teachers and an emphasis on the placement of students with special needs in the

regular classroom. The emphasis of this document was, in part, motivated by parent advocacy groups successfully arguing that their children, regardless of their learning needs, had the right to be educated
in their neighbourhood schools.

Following an assessment, the IPRC chooses what is considered to be
an appropriate placement. This decision is communicated to parents
or guardians, and they have fifteen days to provide written notice if
they wish to appeal the committee's decision. As mentioned earlier,
the Special Education Appeal Board is composed of one member
selected by the school board, one member selected by the parent, and
a chair jointly selected by both parties (or, if they can't agree, by the
Ministry of Education's district manager).

The legislation states that the Appeal Board shall meet within thirty
days of the chair being chosen 'in an informal manner' (Milne &
MacKinnon, 2005, p. 684) and shall review all pertinent information
regarding the decision made by the IPRC. The Appeal Board may
invite anyone to their meeting who can contribute information with
respect to the appeal. Once all information has been considered, the
board shall either agree with the IPRC and recommend that its decisions be implemented or disagree, with recommendation to the board
of education about the pupil's identification, placement, or both. The
decisions of the Appeal Board or the decision of the board of education
concerning this issue must be provided to the parents in writing. At
this point the decision is implemented unless a parental appeal is filed
under section 57 of the *Education Act*, which provides for a Special
Education Tribunal to review the decisions of an Appeal Board.

Section 57 of the *Education Act* provides for the establishment of a
Special Education Tribunal as a final level of appeal for parents or
guardians who are not satisfied with the decisions of the IPRC and
Special Education Appeal Board. Section 57(3) states:

Where a parent or guardian of a pupil has exhausted all rights of appeal
under the regulations of the identification or placement of the pupil as an
exceptional pupil and is dissatisfied with the decision in respect of the
identification or placement, the parent or guardian may appeal to a
Special Education Tribunal for a hearing in respect of the identification or
placement. (Milne & MacKinnon, 2005 p. 53)

Members of this tribunal are selected by the Government of Ontario
and have the right to dismiss the appeal or grant it and make such

order as it considers necessary with respect to the identification or placement (Milne & Mackinnon, 2005). It is important to note that tribunals are held in the local school-board jurisdiction and hold their hearings under the auspices of the *Statutory Powers and Procedures Act*. Unlike the IPRC and Special Education Appeal Board, this process is highly formal. Often lawyers for both sides are involved and costs are high. Valeo (2003) writes that all legislation covering the Special Education Tribunal, as well as the IPRC and the Special Education Appeal Board, prohibits discussion of programming. Parents, however, have often appealed to the tribunal because they felt they were not adequately involved in programming decisions for their child at the school-board level. Since 1992 tribunal decisions have included programming recommendations, since it is very difficult to discuss programming separately from placement (Valeo, 2003).

In very few cases in Ontario have the courts intervened once a Special Education Tribunal has reached a decision. In almost all cases the decision of the Special Education Tribunal is final. One case, an exception to the rule, was that of the *Brant County Board of Education v. Eaton* (1997).

Emily Eaton, a twelve-year-old student with cerebral palsy, was unable to communicate through speech, sign language, or other communication systems. In addition, she had a visual impairment and her mobility was accomplished with the aid of a wheelchair. Emily was identified as an exceptional student by an IPRC and placed in a regular class with a full-time assistant. This placement lasted for three years, at which point the IPRC decided to place her in a special education class. Her parents appealed this decision to the Special Education Appeal Board, who upheld the IPRC decision, then to a Special Education Tribunal, who also upheld the decision of the IPRC. The parents sought remedy through the courts, and eventually, after having lost their case in the divisional court, won their case in the Ontario Court of Appeal.

The case was then brought to the Supreme Court of Canada, which overruled the Ontario Court of Appeal and decided in favour of the Brant County Board of Education. This ruling was based on the fact that the Supreme Court found that disability, as a prohibited ground of discrimination, differs from other grounds such as race, because of the vastly different circumstances of each individual (*Eaton v. Brant County Board of Education*). The court ruled that there is no inherent benefit in either integration or segregation, but that placement should be determined by whether or not the pupil can benefit from the advantages that integration provides. The court also reiterated the tribunal's recommendations that special class placement did not relieve the school board and the parents from the obligation to collaborate to meet Emily's needs through cooperation and compromise.

The Supreme Court decision was perceived by boards of education as a 'victory,' allowing IPRCs to place students in segregated settings and thus, according to parents, severely restricting placement options. This decision, still discussed today, highlights the complex conflict between the perception of what constitutes good and appropriate service within education and the reality of what that delivery of service might be when operationalized in the classroom. The delivery of service is predominantly concerned with meeting the needs of individual children. This can result in a conflict between one's philosophical orientation and the type of educational service these children actually receive. The mandate of the United Nations Convention on the Rights of the Child would presuppose that a more 'normal' environment would be optimal. Normalization, while once a common term in special education, has been replaced by the language of inclusion. Along with this linguistic switch has come a shift in focus away from making a child fit within the normal environment towards shifting the environment to be more inclusive of diverse needs. While inclusion as a philosophical orientation would seem to be the appropriate choice for children, the Emily Eaton case demonstrates to us that when issues revolve around the specific needs of an individual child, philosophical orientation alone may not suffice.

The Coalition for Inclusive Education believes that the Supreme Court decision, in the Eaton case, maintains the view that integration is the norm and that segregation can only be used if the board can demonstrate that there are advantages to that type of placement. Their website states, 'The Supreme Court decision supports inclusion for children with disabilities and limits the ability of school boards to segregate them.' The site also states that placement in a segregated class can only occur when all of the following tests can be met:

(i)   It can be demonstrated that specific aspects of the integrated setting which cannot be changed interfere with meeting the child's special needs in that setting;

(ii) It can be demonstrated that there are advantages in the segregated setting which outweigh the loss of the great psychological benefits that come with the integration;

(iii) It can be demonstrated that the child's equality rights and the desired fulfillment of his/her intellectual, social and emotional needs through regular and natural interaction will be met better in the segregated setting than in the integrated setting;

(iv) Empirical, objective evidence demonstrates that the child's needs are not being met in the regular class;

(v) It can be demonstrated that reasonable accommodations within regular classrooms have been seriously and consistently made. Reasonable accommodations include:
   – teacher in-service;
   – ongoing resource consultation;
   – adapting curriculum and instruction;
   – using a variety of teaching and organizational strategies;
   – providing supports such as special equipment, an adult, a volunteer, teacher assistant and peer support;

(vi) If the child can communicate for him/herself and she/he expresses preference for the segregated class. (Community Living Ontario, 2007)

Of major concern to both parents and school boards is that the Supreme Court supports the notion that the decision of placement is determined by what is in the child's 'best interest.' The definition of the Court's wording of 'best interest' is hotly debated between boards of education and parents, and is an issue not yet settled. Within the Ontario school context, a vast majority of the disagreements between parents/guardians and schools are resolved through mutual collaboration between both parties. Both the IPRC and the IEP procedures emphasize the fundamental importance of communication and co-planning to allow for the successful realization of goals. In the case of the IPRC, when these collaborative efforts are at an impasse, the appeals and tribunal procedures come into play as a vehicle for once again finding common ground.

While the collaboration that happens in a school setting as well as the judicial route are available for all parents, it is important to note that the appeal and tribunal route are only available when an IPRC makes a decision regarding the exceptionality or placement of a particular pupil. In many boards in Ontario, pupils receive special education programs and services without the IPRC process being conducted. Recent figures provided by the Ontario Ministry of Education indicate that 191,902 students were identified as exceptional by school boards in the 2005/6 school year. In addition to this number, approximately

100,000 students were not formally identified but still received special education programs and services. This latter group would not be eligible for the appeal process described above. It might be argued that the legislation does allow for parents to call an IPRC at any time and thus put in place the mechanism necessary to pursue both the appeals and tribunal processes, should that become necessary. This argument, though, while true in a factual way, is moot for those thousands of parents who are unaware of the existence of this option.

Programming for Students with Special Education Needs: The IEP

With identification and placement having been agreed to, the focus of the intervention within the special education context now becomes that of programming. Within the legislation itself, the question of programming has historically rested with education professionals, with many disputes or questions being dealt with at the school level between individual teachers and parents. There exists, currently, within the legislation, no means by which parents or guardians can challenge what is designed and implemented within a classroom context with regard to a student's programming. It certainly could be strongly argued that programming matters are best left to those professionals who are trained to make decisions with regard to those types of strategies and practices that would best benefit the learner in a classroom, but as with many educational issues, when special education becomes part of the discussion, passions, opinions, and debate are more common.

According to Regulation 181/98, students identified as exceptional must have an individual education plan (IEP) developed within thirty days of their placement in a special education program. However, in many boards of education throughout the province of Ontario, students can be placed on IEPs without going through the IPRC process. Regardless of whether or not an IPRC has been conducted, an individual education plan, according to the regulation, must contain

(1) specific education expectations for the pupil;
(2) an outline of the special education program and services received by the pupil; and
(3) a statement of the methods by which the pupil's progress will be reviewed.

In addition, the regulation also states that in the development of the plan, the principal shall consult with the parent or the pupil if she/he is sixteen years of age or older and that the plan shall take into consideration any recommendations made by the IPRC or Special Education Tribunal, as the case may be. It is also required that there be a plan for transition to appropriate post–secondary school activities, such as work, further education, and community living. In the development of this transition plan, the principal shall consult with community agencies and post-secondary institutions as she/he considers appropriate (Ontario Ministry of Education, 2004). This plan is supposed to be developed according to a process described in the Ministry of Education guideline *The Individual Education Plan (IEP): A Resource Guide.* This guide is quite comprehensive and attempts to respond to parental concerns that they are not involved enough in the consultation process to determine the educational programming for their child.

The IEP, according to this guide, is a 'working document that identifies learning expectations that are modified from the expectations for the age-appropriate grade level in a particular subject or courses, as outlined in the Ministry of Education's curriculum policy documents' (p. 6). It is also a 'record of the particular accommodations needed to help students achieve his or her learning expectations, given the student's identified learning strengths and need' (p. 6). The IEP can also indicate alternative expectations in program areas not represented in the Ontario curriculum.

The IEP, according to the ministry guideline, is 'an accountability tool for the student, the student's parents and everyone who has responsibilities under the plan for helping the student meet the stated goals and learning expectations as the student progresses through the Ontario curriculum, (p. 6). Though the IEP is the responsibility of the school principal, it is most often prepared by either the pupil's teacher or the resource teacher assigned to the pupil's school. The guide recommends that whoever has responsibility for the IEP should follow a 'team approach' (p. 9), that the process should be curriculum-oriented and follow five phases:

(1) Gather information
(2) Set the direction
(3) Develop the IEP as it relates to the student's special education program and services

(4) Implement the IEP

(5) Review and update the IEP

The guide clearly includes parents in steps 1 and 4, and under the recommendations for step 1 states that 'consultation with the student's parents and the student, school staff, support personnel, and representatives of outside agencies or services is a valuable source of information, and should be a continuous process throughout the development and implementation of a student's IEP' (Ontario Ministry of Education, 2004, p. 13). Once the IEP is completed, parents are asked to sign and indicate if they have been consulted in its development. The IEP is reviewed regularly, and it is expected that parents will be kept up-to-date on their child's progress over each reporting period.

As indicated above, it is important to note that though IEPs are reviewed regularly, parents have no 'rights of appeal' to what is written in an IEP. Only an appeal of the identification and category placement made by an IPRC can be made to an Appeal Board or a Special Education Tribunal.

An IEP must also indicate what modifications or accommodation adjustments are being made for this particular student. In many jurisdictions the terms modification and accommodation are synonymous, but in Ontario they have very specific meanings. Modifications reflect an adjustment of the grade-level expectations the student is expected to achieve and be evaluated on, while accommodations reflect adjustment to the instructional, environmental, or assessment approaches to achieve learning or evaluate student achievement. A pupil's IEP could reflect either accommodation or modifications or both. It is expected that parents should be informed of the differences between accommodation and modification and be aware of what is being considered for their child as the IEP is being developed. Recently, the Ontario Ministry of Education prepared an IEP template that asks teachers completing the IEP to indicate the three different types of accommodations mentioned above: instructional, environmental, or assessment. If a modification is indicated on the IEP, the teacher must then evaluate the student on the grade-level expectation indicated on the IEP. As indicated above, parents are expected to be part of the consultation related to the IEP's development, and before signing off on this document must ensure that they fully understand what they can expect will be the instructional delivery approach for their child and how their child's learning will be evaluated. They also need to understand that evaluation of learning, based on the IEP, though ongoing, will be clearly stated at each regular reporting interval.

The autonomy of educators to create the IEP and thus program effectively for students with exceptionalities has been called into question somewhat by an ongoing dispute in the area of programming for students with autism. Within the area of autism, the Province of Ontario (both the Ministry of Education and the Ministry of Child and Youth Services) was taken to court by twenty-eight families over the provision of treatment for students with autism spectrum disorder. The initial ruling in favour of the parents was overturned by an appeal heard in December 2005 by the Ontario Superior Court of Justice. This appeal challenged the use of a particular treatment: in this case IBI (Intensive Behaviour Intervention). This treatment, currently available to some school-age children, relies on intensive, one-on-one intervention and training for children with autism. Parents and advocates argued that this treatment should be continued past the age of five until such time as the student would be able to perform independently or could no longer benefit from the treatment. A major issue before the courts related to the effectiveness of this particular treatment in comparison to others. If, as argued by parents, this treatment is essential to the success of their children within a school setting, then should school boards be required to provide such treatment? School boards maintain there is a lack of reliable evidence that this treatment, more than others, will result in any type of substantial benefits. They also maintain that there are comparable programs, and that the IBI program is not necessarily appropriate for all students with autism. There is also concern that the adoption of such a program would, for all intents and purposes, mandate its sole use above others that may be considered just as, or more, beneficial to the students. While the initial ruling favoured the parents, the Ontario Court of Appeal overturned the decision. The Supreme Court of Canada decided that an appeal brought by the parents would not be heard, and the decision stands.

A much larger issue is the questioning of the autonomy of school boards, schools, and individual teachers to make what they consider to be the most appropriate programming decisions for students. These types of litigious endeavours, while threatening to call into question the credibility and judgment of educators to decide on what is appropriate programming, can also serve to provide an opportunity for a re-examination of existing services with a focus on improvement.

Defining Achievement for All

Education for All: A Report of the Expert Panel on Literacy and Numeracy Instruction for Students with Special Needs, Kindergarten to Grade 6, developed by the Ontario Ministry of Education in 2005, lists as one of its core beliefs: 'Each students has his or her own unique pattern of learning.' It also states, 'All students can succeed.' This document, which has at its core a focus on universal design and teaching to a diverse range of learners in the regular class, indicates a shift in philosophical orientation within special education in Ontario, away from a category-driven model of service delivery towards a more inclusive focus. While there would seem to be an implicit understanding that success and achievement can be broadly defined, in particular for those students with special needs, there is increased pressure to document and measure that success. As a result, one of the underlying issues in the province's move forward is the goal of realizing higher standards in literacy and numeracy for all, as measured through province-wide testing. The goal is to ensure that 'by 2008, 75 percent of students reach the provincial standard.'

The idea of using provincial testing as a tool for measuring growth in literacy and numeracy skills in students with disabilities is fraught with measurement and conceptual problems. Many students with special needs will be hard-pressed to show growth through a measurement tool, which is one-dimensional in terms of output. For students with special needs, restricting responses to only one modality creates barriers, as do the extremely limited accommodation options available to them through the provincial testing procedures. Given the multiplicity of learning profiles among students with special needs, it seems myopic to assume that only a handful of accommodations can account for the different ways these students show understanding. Furthermore, the instructional methodology used in provincial testing does not necessarily align itself with the learning styles of many students with special needs. If the purpose of assessment is to make decisions about educational programming for students, particularly students with special needs, then provincial testing, in its current form, is not the desired tool for such an endeavour.

Funding Special Education

In July 2004 the Minister of Education announced that new funding and accountability measures would be developed for special education within the province of Ontario. At that time the Minister also announced that the existing funding model would be replaced by one that focused on local outcomes, local decision making, and reduced administrative requirements and created a system of funding that was predictable and sustainable and supported academic improvement and better overall outcomes for students with special needs. The previous funding model, introduced in the late 1990s, focused on the distribution of funds through a combination of total enrolment and specialized funding amounts, called ISA amounts, that were granted on a case-by-case basis. This previous model of funding was criticized for being difficult to administer and overly focused on a deficit-oriented, pathology-based criterion used to qualify an applicant for funds. Criticisms were also levelled at what was perceived to be the necessary disabling of students in order to access funding. Students who were not defined by the severity of their needs risked a discontinuation of their funding. The school system became very careful about reporting too much success for fear of financial ramifications. School boards, parents, and advocates became 'experts' at what was informally termed 'diagnosing for dollars.' As well, school boards became increasingly concerned about what they perceived to be a lack of flexibility in allowing local decision making with regard to funding (Jordan, 2001). Those boards that advocated for inclusive education found the funding model extremely difficult to reconcile with their philosophical orientation and argued vehemently that the funding system, as designed, discriminated against a model based on service to students in the regular classroom.

Currently special education funding across the province has had a version of 'gap funding' that has allowed school boards to continue with their current levels of funding and apply for new dollars on the basis of need. While the Special Education Transformation Document (Bennett & Wynne 2006) recommends the development of an improved funding model that balances the bureaucratic need for accountability while supporting learning, the process for this development is long term. School boards will participate in a collaborative auditing process that will help set the parameters for funding. The model must be transparent, responsive, and flexible. No small challenge. The new, long-term funding model, which has yet to be released, will seek to address some of the perceived shortfalls of the previous system.

Whether a funding structure can be used as a mechanism for creating change in a system of service delivery is one of the central issues within the funding debate. Certainly, given the parameters of the previous funding model, many would argue vehemently that the way the funding model was operationalized created a set of working procedures that pigeon-holed practitioners into certain types of practices. The model created a reallocation of resources, both materials and personnel, that shifted the teaching balances in specific settings. In the case of personnel, in particular, their allocation to filling out forms was perceived by many school boards to be a ludicrous and, in many cases, harmful, redistribution of trained professionals towards bureaucratic tasks and away from students in the classroom.

Those involved in designing the new funding model must grapple with the impact that each decision will have on how students are treated within a school setting. Questions such as 'Does one type of model promote a more or less inclusive type of service delivery?' and 'Should boards have more or less autonomy in making decisions on how money is spent become central?' If the Ontario Ministry of Education espoused a particular philosophical orientation, such as that of inclusion, then the creation of a funding model that pushes practice towards that orientation could be a possibility. The province may choose instead to allow school boards the freedom and autonomy, within loosely structured funding parameters, to allocate monies to support their own philosophical orientation. The ministry may choose to find a balance between the two by providing some structure and allowing some freedom. The outcome remains to be seen.

Preparing and Supporting Educators

There is little doubt that, in general, teachers feel unprepared for their first teaching experience, and to meet the challenges within a school setting. There is also little doubt that the diversity of student populations within what would be considered the regular classroom has also increased. With an emphasis on the inclusion of students with special needs into the regular classroom, many teachers are faced with a wider continuum of learning and behavioural needs than in the past (Lombardi & Hunka, 2001). Teacher candidates preparing to face the challenges of working with students with diverse needs report concerns about their lack of knowledge, their inability to access resources, their lack of knowledge and experience with assessment techniques, and their unfamiliarity with completing Individual Education Plans (Woloshyn, Bennett, & Berrill, 2003).

Certainly across the province there have been consistent calls for increased teacher education, with an emphasis on working with students with diverse needs. The Ontario College of Teachers recently recommended to the minister of education that all faculties of education include, in their pre-service year, a mandatory component dealing with special education. Within teacher induction programs, which are now required for certification within the province, special education is seen as a vital component. These improvements in teacher pre-service training, induction programs as well as continuing education for teachers, and even additional training for administrators across the province have been discussed and, in part, implemented across various school boards and post-secondary institutions.

There is a related need to re-examine the qualifications of teacher/educational assistants, for whom there are currently no provincial provisions for qualification. Many school boards implement their own requirements, but these can be adjusted depending on availability and need. The Special Education Transformation Document recommends that standards be established that define the roles and responsibilities for teachers' assistants and that training requirements be established. The lack of standardized training for teacher/educational assistants and the real concerns about teachers' readiness to work with students with diverse learning needs call into question the provincial commitment to meeting the needs of all students. Given that students with special education needs are, for the most part, our most vulnerable and are in need of our best professional knowledge, there is cause for concern that there is an inequity in service. Faculties of education, within the time parameters they are given, prepare teachers to teach students who are predominantly in the average cognitive range and are ready and able to learn. The additional skills required to work with those students who fall outside of that range are addressed where possible, but many faculties have to rely on mentors in the field or professional development after initial certification to fill in the gaps.

In Ontario, there are a number of positive signs. The Ministry of Education has provided mandates, supported by ministry funding, for a strong, locally developed teacher induction program. Monies and support have also been provided to allow school boards to examine and develop best practices in special education, and many of them have focused on the training of educators. Within the next few years, with the movement towards differentiated instruction for all students within a classroom, the need for highly qualified educational professionals across all levels of service becomes paramount.

Engaging Parents

The involvement of parents within the special education process has been explicitly outlined within the IPRC regulation, as well as in materials provided across the province with regard to the development and implementation of an IEP. While much progress has been made, there continue to be lingering concerns about the level of parental engagement. None would argue that, like any large system or bureaucracy, schools and school boards have a common culture, vernacular, and set of working parameters that, while very familiar from the inside, can often be confusing and intimidating to those who do not work in those settings. While some parents are perhaps more sophisticated than others in this regard, there exists within the area of special education in particular a proportionately larger number of parents who may feel disconnected from the nuances of schooling. That having been said, it often does not take parents long to acquire expertise when it relates to the education of their child. Despite the quick study that some parents engage in, there remains a population of parents whose voice is quelled by the momentum of the special education process. Across the province the Ministry of Education has approved funds for improved parental engagement at the school and school board level. Within the area of special education, the Special Education Transformation Document had as one of its eight foci the need for improved relationships and communication between educators and parents. It was recommended that efforts be made to reduce conflict, provide training in dispute resolution, and include targeted support for parents who might require it. There has resulted a recommendation for the development of an informal dispute and pilot mediation process. Adding a stronger parental voice to the educational process is an effective means of improving education and ensuring parental rights, but it is essential that that voice be informed, collaborative, and listened to.

From the Past into the Future in Special Education

Since the inception of the *Education Amendment Act* some 28 years ago, the speed at which school boards transitioned into comprehensive services for students with special needs has been impressive. The transformation of service had implications not only for those classrooms but also for the system that was now required to support those needs. While many challenges have been met with enthusiasm and creative planning, others remain. The goal of equal access and opportunity has been adopted as a fundamental principle of special education, yet the paths taken to reach that goal can vary.

The method of identifying and categorizing students remains problematic. Some argue that the use of labels limits opportunities and colours perceptions, while others maintain that they are an administrative and treatment necessity. Debate exists over whether the current system of categorization limits the identification of, and therefore the provision of service to, populations such as children with acquired brain injury and attention deficit disorder, which are currently not recognized by the province as distinct categories of exceptionality.

The question of placement, whether it be in an inclusive setting, a self-contained special-education environment, or some variation thereof, remains a hot topic of debate and discussion. Proponents of a self-contained setting argue that the skills needed to promote independence can only be taught with the resources, training, and low student-teacher ratio found in a special education setting, while proponents of inclusion argue that those types of skills necessary to function as an independent adult can best be learned through support within a regular classroom of school-age peers.

Whether the placement is within a segregated or inclusive setting, the need for appropriate programming through the implementation of an Individual Education Plan is paramount. While parents and guardians are encouraged to participate in the creation of this plan, at the current time the specific decisions around the content of a student's programming rest with educators. Currently there is no vehicle for an appeal of programming decisions.

Linked to the creation of quality programming for students are questions surrounding those measures used to assess the effectiveness of this programming. Quantifying the success of educational programs has become an issue across the province, not just within special education. Province-wide testing has become the norm and one of the standards by which, rightly or wrongly, students and programs are measured. Within special education these types of standardized tests have proved to be a poor vehicle for the demonstration of learning. Questions remain with regard to standards setting and the measurement of students with special needs.

Regardless of what decisions school boards make around identification, placement, or programming, the implementation of those decisions often comes down to money. Funding models, which can influence service delivery, program implementation, and placement availability among other things, are often a central theme in special education discussions. Currently, with the province awaiting a decision with regard to how monies will be allocated, there remain many unanswered questions and concerns in this area.

The training of professionals to work with students with special needs is an area of service delivery that requires a closer examination. Whether funding dollars will be allocated in this direction remains a question. Whether the monies provided for induction will require that part of that induction be focused on special education also remains a question. What is not in question is that educators, especially those at the beginning of their careers, for the most part feel ill equipped to deal with the diverse demands of today's classrooms.

The involvement of parents in the decision-making process for working with students with special needs continues to expand. The dollars released by the Ministry of Education this year for parental engagement promote the involvement of all parents, not just those who have children with special needs. There is a clear message within the province's education system that the success of students is inextricably linked to the relationship that schools and the system have with the parental community. Within the area of special education, the development of dispute resolution and mediation is seen as a priority.

Many would argue that the classroom of the twenty-first century in Ontario is a very different place than the one that existed before the rights of the child with special needs was enshrined in Bill 82. This new era requires a more sophisticated type of educator, one who believes that all students have the right to an educational program regardless of the cognitive, physical, social, and emotional needs that they bring with them as they walk through the classroom door.

REFERENCES

Axelrod, P. (1999). *The promise of schooling: Education in Canada, 1800–1914*. Toronto: University of Toronto Press.

Bennett, S., Dworet, D., & Daigle, R. (2001). Educational provisions for exceptional students in the province of Ontario. *Exceptionality Education Canada, 11*(2–3), 99–123.

Bennett, S., Good, D., Zinga, D., & Kumpf, J. (2004). Acquired brain injury: A silent voice in the Ontario education system. *Exceptionality Education Canada, 14*(1), 115–130.

Bennett, S., & Wynne K. (2006) *Special education transformation: The report of the co-chairs with the recommendations of the Working Table on Special Education / Ministry of Education*. http://www.edu.gov.on.ca/eng/document/reports/speced/transformation/trans-formation.pdf

Community Living Ontario (2007). *How the Emily Eaton case affects you and your Child*. www.communitylivingontario.ca/emilyeaton.html

Dworet, D., & Bennett, S. (2002). A view from the north, special education in Canada. *Teaching Exceptional Children, 34*(5), 22–28.

Eaton v. Brant County, SCC 24668, 7 Feb. 1997.

Government of Canada (1982). *Canadian Charter of Rights and Freedoms*.

Jordan, A. (2001). Special education in Ontario, Canada: A case study of market-based reforms. *Cambridge Journal of Education, 31*(3), 349–371.

Kauffman, J.M., & Hallahan, D.P. (2005). *Special education: What is it and why we need it*. Boston: Pearson.

Lombardi, T., & Hunka, N.L. (2001). Preparing general education teachers for inclusive classrooms: Assessing the process. *Teacher Education and Special Education 24*(3), 183–197.

McPhail, J.C., & Freeman, J.G. (2005). Beyond prejudice: Thinking toward genuine inclusion. *Learning Disabilities Research and Practice, 20*(4), 254–267.

Milne, C., & MacKinnon, M. (2005). *Education statutes and regulations of Ontario*. Markham, ON: Lexis Nexis Canada Inc.

Ontario Ministry of Education (2004). *The individual education plan (IEP): A resource guide*. Toronto: Ontario Ministry of Education.

Ontario Ministry of Education (2005). *Education for all: The report of the expert panel on literacy and numeracy instruction for students with special education needs, kindergarten to grade 6*. Toronto: Ontario Ministry of Education.

Province of Ontario (1980). *Ontario Education Amendment Act*, Revised Statutes of Ontario, 1980, c. 129: RSO 1990, c. E2.

Province of Ontario (1990). *Human Rights Code of Ontario*.

Province of Ontario (2000). *Safe Schools Act, 2000*.

Smith, D.D., Lukasson, R., & Crealok, C. (1995). *Introduction to special education in Canada*. Scarborough, ON: Allyn & Bacon Canada.

United Nations (1989). *Convention on the Rights of the Child.*

Valeo, A. (2003). Special education tribunals in Ontario. *International Journal of Special Education, 18*(2), 18–30.

Weber, K., & Bennett, S. (2004). *Special education in Ontario schools* (5th ed.). Palgrave: Highland Press.

Winzer, M. (2005). *Children with exceptionalities in Canadian classrooms* (7th ed.). Toronto: Pearson.

Woloshyn, V., Bennett, S., & Berrill, D. (2003). Working with students who have learning disabilities: Teacher candidates speak out. Issues and concerns in pre-service education and professional development. *Exceptionality Education Canada, 13*(1), 7–29.

12 Bullying Prevention and the Rights of Children: Psychological and Democratic Aspects

MONIQUE LACHARITE AND ZOPITO A. MARINI

Given the systemic and pervasive nature of the behaviours involved, school bullying has come to be regarded as a complex and dynamic phenomenon, encompassing a variety of interrelated issues, ranging from psychosocial maladjustments (Marini, Dane, Bosacki, & YLC-CURA, 2006[a]) to moral concerns (Bosacki, Marini, & Dane, 2006; Arsenio, Gold, & Adams, 2006; Nucci, 2006). In keeping with the contextualizing of bullying as a multifaceted issue, there has been an increasing concern with the 'health' and 'democratic' deficits associated with the experience of bullying and victimization. Thus, in a recent paper, we have argued that owing to its serious and potentially negative long-term consequences, bullying can be regarded as a health issue (Marini, Bombay, Hobin, Winn, & Dumyn, 2000). We further argued that the broadly based Public Health Prevention Model could be adapted as a guide in the development of bullying intervention programs.

The purpose of this chapter is to build on our earlier research and to outline this general model of prevention by highlighting anti-bullying interventions that are based on the 'rights of children.' In this respect, we agree with Olweus (2001) in emphasizing a connection between issues of the democratic right of students and the serious violation of those rights implied in school bullying:

> It is a fundamental democratic human right for a child to feel safe at school and to be spared the oppression and repeated, intentional humiliation implied in peer victimization or bullying. No student should be afraid to go to school for fear of being harassed or degraded and no parent should need to worry about such things happening to his or her child. (Olweus, 2001, pp. 11–12)

School Bullying and Its Consequences

Bullying is a repeated and systematic type of peer aggression that is both physical and psychosocial in nature and found extensively, but not exclusively, in schools (Boyle, 1996; Marini et al., 2006a). In students, bullying can manifest itself in a variety of ways ranging from 'direct' overt acts such as pushing and teasing to more subtle, 'indirect' forms such as social exclusion and emotional isolation (Crick, 1995; Crick & Grotpeter, 1996; Crick & Bigbee, 1998; Marini et al., 2006a; Vaillancourt, Brendgen, Boivin, & Tremblay, 2003) (see chapter 9 for a description of cyber-bullying). Similar diversity has been observed in the participants, including bullies, victims, bully-victims, and bystanders (Farrington, 1998; Olweus, 2001; Pepler & Craig, 1995). For instance, students who bully seem to have greater physical and psychological strength than their victims (Olweus, 1993; Marini, Koruna, & Dane, 2006[b]). In addition, they appear to have little empathy for their peers and a positive attitude towards antisocial behaviours. In fact, a number of reports have suggested that students' attitudes about aggression predict their likelihood to bully others (Jessor, Van Den Bos, Vanderryn, & Costa, 1995; Marini et al., 2006a; Vernberg, Jacobs, & Hershberger, 1999). Overall, bullies tend to exert their 'power' in a large number of domains, picking on those who do not have the physical, cognitive, social, and emotional resources necessary to oppose them (Marini, Fairbain, & Zuber, 2001; Verdugo & Bermejo, 1997).

Students who are victimized tend to find themselves in powerless situations where their voices are not heard and their points of view are not valued. The powerlessness can be seen in concrete terms in the victims' lack of physical and psychological strength, social isolation, insecurity, and loneliness (Boulton & Underwood, 1992; Olweus, 2001).

The third group of participants are the bystanders who make up the largest group of students. These are individuals who tend to 'stand around' when incidents of bullying take place, because of fear or lack of skill. In some cases, bystanders inadvertently contribute to the bullying incidence by their mere presence. On a more positive note, this group has a high potential to be mobilized in intervention programs (Cowie, 2000; Marini et al., 2000; Marini, McWhinnie, & Lacharite, 2004; Salmivalli, 2001).

An emerging group of participants are the bully-victims. These are students who are involved in the dual role of both victim and bully.

There is comparatively little research focused on this group (Craig, 1998; Olweus, 2001). However, there is a growing concern for bully victims, for they appear to be at greater risk of psychosocial maladjustment. In fact, in a recent study we found that about 33 per cent of the students who reported high involvement in bullying or victimization did so as dual participants, that is, they where involved in both (Marini et al., 2006a).

Peer aggression generates a great deal of concern because of its potential to escalate into violence as well as the long-lasting negative psychological consequences for both aggressor and victim (Marini et al., 2000; Olweus, 1993). While few highly publicized incident such as the tragedies of Colombine in Littleton, Colorado, and of Taber, Alberta, can distort the perception of the amount of violence taking place in our schools, there is no denying the fact that bullying is increasingly a major concern for both students and teachers. For instance, about 15 to 25 per cent of the school population is involved in bullying, as a bully, victim, or bully-victims (Marini et al., 2006a). While these figures may fluctuate, depending on the method of reporting used (see Smith & Sharp, 1994), on average 10 to 15 per cent of the students are victimized regularly and 5 to 10 per cent are the victimizers.

The consequences from bullying involvement can be quite severe and the impact can be long-lasting (Craig, Pepler, & Atlas, 2000; Juvonen & Graham, 2001; Olweus 2001). For instance, externalizing types of behaviours have been reported by students who bully, including hyperactivity, delinquency, substance abuse and antisocial disorder (Kaltiala-Heino, Rimpela, Rantanen, & Rimpela, 2000; Rigby, 2001; Kumpulainen, Raesaenen, & Henttonen, 1999). In addition, Wolke, Woods, Bloomfield, and Karstadt (2000) found that bullies and bully-victims scored significantly high in conduct problems and in hyperactivity, and significantly lower on the prosocial behaviour. The frequent occurrence and co-occurrence of mental health problems associated with children involved in bullying emphasizes the importance of understanding the role of bullying as a real risk for psychiatric disorders (Kaltiala-Heino et al., 2000; Ribgy, 2001, 2002).

In regard to victim status, although it is generally assumed that there are multiple determinants of depression and social anxiety, the association between peer relationships and internalizing problems is well established in the general aggression literature and may be especially salient for students involved in bullying. For example, social anxiety and depression are related to victimization (Craig, 1998; Crick

& Bigbee, 1998; Crick & Grotpeter, 1995; Marini et al., 2006a), social isolation (Nangle, Erdley, Newman, Mason, & Carpenter, 2003; Boivin,
Hymel, & Bukowski, 1995), and other serious behavioural and psychological outcomes, including loneliness, disordered eating, substance abuse, and suicide (Birmaher, Ryan, & Williamson, 1996;
Swearer, Grills, Haye, & Cary, 2004). Social anxiety, which is particularly common among youth, is associated with school avoidance or
refusal, suicidal ideation, substance abuse, and conduct problems
(Harrington, Rutter, & Fombonne, 1996; Levy & Deykin, 1989). Given
the stability of antisocial behaviours as well as victimization status, the
significant link between bullying experiences and maladjustment
highlights the importance of developing effective intervention.

Bullying and Its Prevention

Prevention can take many different forms depending on when it
occurs in the progression of a particular behaviour. In regard to bullying, the challenge is to determine when, where, and how to intervene
in the long chain of potential points of opportunity so as to stop the
possible progression (Kazdin, 1993). The difficulty with any form of
intervention is deciding which component of the target behaviour
should receive intervention and what form that intervention should
take (Kazdin & Kendall, 1998). Given the multitude and complexity of
the possible factors involved in bullying as well as the heterogeneity of
the population affected, it appears that a broad-based system-wide
approach has more potential to be effective than a narrowly focused
approach (see Smith, Pepler, & Rigby, 2004):

Effective intervention requires recognition of the pervasive and systematic nature of bullying behaviour. Therefore, since bullying
impacts the school system at so many levels, it is reasonable to propose
a proven multilayered framework that can assist in this endeavour. We
are proposing that the Public Health Model can be an effective framework and a potentially useful guide for the development of bullying
prevention strategies (see Marini et al., 2000).

The Public Health Prevention Model:
Primary, Secondary, and Tertiary Levels of Prevention

While the Public Health Model has been used extensively in medical
contexts, we have been advocating its use in relation to psychological

health in general and school bullying in particular (see Marini et al., 2000). According to Felner and colleagues (Felner, Jason, Moritsugu, & Farber, 1983), the basic goals of prevention include optimal development, reduction of environmental risks, avoidance of maladaptive behaviour, and enhancement of coping skills and abilities. Thus, we believe that the three levels of intervention outlined below appear promising for the reduction of peer victimization and the prevention of psychosocial maladjustment.

Primary Prevention

Primary prevention can be defined as any intervention that promotes or improves well-being and the positive adjustment of entire groups. Part of the reason for this approach is to avoid labelling or stigmatization (Bloom, 1979). A general example of a primary prevention is a social-skill program geared to promoting adaptive interpersonal behavioural and positive peer relations. This is relevant to bullying since, as mentioned earlier, a number of studies indicate that children's early patterns of peer interaction and acceptance remain stable over time (Crick & Grotpeter, 1996; Loeber & Hay, 1997), as children characterized by poor peer relations are more vulnerable to later interpersonal disorders (Caplan, Bennetto, & Weissberg, 1991; Coie, Christopoulos, Terry, Dodge, & Lochman, 1989; Farrington, 1998; Feindler & Kalfus, 1990; Loeber & Hay, 1997; Weissberg & Allen, 1986).

Secondary Prevention

While primary prevention attempts to target all the members of a 'given population,' thus creating a 'blanket effect,' secondary prevention is targeted more at a specific population of individuals who are showing the initial signs of a particular disorder or are at risks to do so. The main objective of this level of intervention is the prevention of the secondary effects of a disorder by focusing on early detection and identification and by generally increasing awareness of the warning signs of a target disorder. Identifying the children in need of these programs will go a long way towards preventing future maladjustment problems (Durlak & Jason, 1984). Recently, we have developed a Bullying Identification Model aimed at facilitating identification of a range of bullying behaviours where we have focused on the form, function, and type of involvement (see Marini et al., 2004; Marini et al., 2006b).

Tertiary Prevention

In general, tertiary prevention refers to rehabilitation efforts aimed at reducing the effects of a disorder that is usually chronic in nature. Hence, this level of prevention attempts to limit the damage or deterioration caused by an established maladaptive behaviour (Felner et al., 1983; Goldston, 1984; Leventhal, Prohaska, & Hirschman, 1985).

Program interventions directed toward children who have been identified as having a social deficit are a typical example of tertiary prevention (Caplan, Bennetto, & Weissberg, 1991). For example, tertiary prevention may include education and training of special-needs individuals or ESL students involved as victims of bullying (Marini et al., 2001; Marini et al., 2006b).

Children's Right to a Healthy and Secure School:
A Framework for the Development of a Rights-Based
Anti-Bullying Prevention Program

Having argued that bullying can be seen as a psychological problem that can be addressed as a health issue, we are also prepared to argue that other aspects of bullying can be seen as a democratic issue. In this section, we will highlight how children's understanding of rights along with interventions at the primary level can form a solid foundation for an anti-bullying program. We will also argue that for a bullying prevention program to be successful it must be embedded in the curriculum, which will increase its comprehensiveness and the likelihood of it having a positive impact on the life of students and the entire school community. Effective primary prevention is very much like the workings of a two-sided balance beam: the emphasis is on reducing antisocial behaviour, on the one hand, and increasing prosocial behaviour, on the other.

The focus at this level of intervention should be on the development of a board-wide safe school policy (now ministry-mandated in most provinces) with detailed anti-violence prevention plans. It is worth pointing out that while it may be the law to have a safe school policy in place, the specificity of such a policy is very much left to the discretion of school boards. Hence, one is quite likely to encounter a disparity in the implementation of similar policies.

In addition to policies directed specifically at reducing risks, there should be parallel policies designed to encourage and promote social development on a board-wide level. As mentioned, while reducing risks is important, so is the creation of possible opportunities for social cognitive development, which are driven by a positive desire to increase general well-being (Larson, 2000; Massimini & Delle Fave, 2000; Seligman & Csikszentmihalyi, 2000).

The focus should be on the development and implementation of an appropriate curriculum that prevents violence by raising awareness about its destructive consequences. This can be achieved by integrating issues of bullying into the instructional material through activities such as drama, books, and films. The overall goal of these activities should be to create a school climate that promotes values such as equality, respect, and caring (Johnston & Johnston, 1998; Purkey & Novak, 1996).

Since a central feature of bullying is the powerful against the powerless, any intervention strategies should be aimed at rectifying this imbalance of power through some well-placed social engineering. Thus, socio-cognitive training directed at improving students' understanding of social interaction is a desirable primary prevention strategy, because a large number of children suffer from poor peer relationships, and the quality of children's social interactions affects the development of maladjustment (Coie et al., 1989; Kaplan, 1999; Weissberg & Allen, 1986).

While it is unrealistic to expect students to be able to work out 'bullying problems' on their own, it is important that they play an active role in attempts to reduce such behaviours. Bullying is not just a problem of individuals, it is a relationship problem (see Pefer & Craig 1995). Given the influence of peer groups and reputational factors in maintaining the behaviour of bullies and victims, it is largely unrealistic to expect students to alter the dynamics of bullying without adult support. Thus, there is a critical need for multi-level intervention. A promising approach against peer victimization is a type of intervention that requires students to take a central and proactive role. Such is the case with the implementation of a program based on children rights.

The Parallel between Children's Rights and Maslow's Hierarchy of Needs

As already mentioned elsewhere in this book, on 20 November 1989 the United Nations Convention on the Rights of the Child (CRC) was adopted by the 159 member states of the U.N. General Assembly. This event is generally regarded as a turning point for children as well as for organizations that provide services to them such as educators, medical professionals ,and protection agencies. From a psychological perspective, the Convention outlined a developmental model of the child wherein each right included was essential for healthy growth and development, both physical and psychological (Wilcox & Naimark, 1991). Wilcox and Naimark indicate that the rights presented by the CRC influence the ways in which psychologists and other professionals interact with children in therapeutic, research, and educational settings. An example of this is the work of Covell and her colleagues (see Covell, 2001; Covell & Howe, 1999; Howe & Covell, 2005, 2007), building on the CRC, which identifies that children's rights fall into three categories. The first are the rights of provision, which recognize the right of all children to basic social and economic needs such as health care and education. The second are the rights of protection, describing the right children have to protection from harmful practices such as abuse, neglect, and exploitation. The third and final category are the rights of participation, by which children have rights to be heard on all matters that affect them (Covell, 2001).

Children's rights as outlined in the introduction of this book, and as represented by Covell (2001) can be compared to the framework established by Maslow's hierarchy of needs (Maslow, 1954; Maslow & Lowery (1998). Maslow identified a pyramid of needs, whereby some of the more basic needs (i.e., food and safety) acquire higher importance and must be met in order for the subsequent level of needs to be considered a priority. The needs pyramid was established to outline how human needs are layered, and thus convey a sense that a strong foundation must be in place in order for an individual to attain the higher-level needs. For instance, Maslow believed that one must have his or her physiological needs, such as shelter and food, met in order to be able to be concerned about higher-level needs such as belonging and self-actualization. Thus, it can be argued that an individual may not be as concerned for their safety if he or she is urgently preoccupied with looking for food to survive. As individuals climb the pyramid, the nature of needs change from external to internal. Maslow's (1954) main assertion was that unless the physical/external needs are met, individuals are not likely to be concerned about internal/psychological needs such as self-actualization and transcendence.

Maslow's model can been compared to child rights in that an

infringement of one's rights can be considered a roadblock on the hierarchy of needs. For example, if a child's basic needs for food and shelter are not being met, this is a direct infringement of his or her right to the provisions outlined by the CRC. If a comparison is made between Maslow's hierarchy of needs and Covell's (2001) three categories of child rights, one can make connections between the needs as suggested by Maslow (1954) and the categories of rights suggested by Covell (2001).

Thus it can be argued that when children's needs are not met it can lead to psychological difficulties that are intertwined with the democratic difficulties faced when their rights are infringed. For example, if a child is being victimized at school, his or her need for safety and belonging is not being met. According to Covell's (2001) model of rights, this child is being denied his/her right to protection. This potential parallel relationship suggests a similar framework underlying children's needs and children's rights, which will be revisited later in the chapter. Our focus now turns to the concept of bullying as an infringement of child rights as defined by the CRC.

Bullying as an Infringement of Children's Rights

As already mentioned, research has indicated that school bullying is a systematic abuse of power repeated over time (Olweus, 2001; Lopez, 2002; Smith, 2000). The CRC establishes that it is a child's right and a society's duty to ensure that a child lives violence-free and safe from physical and emotional harm. Unfortunately, as indicated by numerous reports, bullying continues to be a pervasive problem in schools.

The first right discussed at the beginning of the chapter was the right to safety from abuse. According to Kumpulainen et al. (1999), bullying among children can be regarded as a form of abuse, as it is intentional, unprovoked, and aimed at causing pain and distress. Furthermore, this type of widespread peer abuse can impact safety concerns. For instance, Kochenderfer and Ladd (2001) reported that over 75 per cent of children had been bullied at some point in their school career, and many children fear verbal threats (Zirkel, 2003; Howard, 2002), with at least 30 per cent of students in a study reported not feeling safe at school (Nairn & Smith, 2002). Children have the right to an education that meets their needs. As can be expected, children identified bullying as one of their top dislikes at school (Alderson, 1999).

Safe Learning Environment

> We are keeping our commitment to help restore respect and responsibil-
> ity in Ontario's publicly-funded school system. Parents, teachers and stu-
> dents have told us that students learn better and teachers teach better
> when they are in a safer environment.
>
> Janet Ecker, Ontario Minister of Education (2001)

With the growing awareness of children's rights, and the adoption of
the guidelines in the CRC, education systems have been put under the
microscope in regard to their ability to promote the CRC's goals. What
does this mean for education systems? It means that all children have
a right to an education that enables them to reach their fullest potential in relation to healthy physical, intellectual, emotional, and social
development. In addition, all children have a right to be protected
from physical, psychological, and sexual abuse, including protection
from racism and discrimination. These are only a few of the rights
listed in the Charter, but are the ones most relevant to education
systems and ensuring their enforcement is considered to be the
responsibility of schools. With the CRC challenge to education
systems, policies have been developed throughout the world to ensure
these rights are being met. Provinces across Canada have developed
policies and handbooks to promote children's rights. Governments
have funded policy development such as Ontario's *Safe Schools Act*,
School Codes of Conduct, and Violence Free Schools Policy (Ministry
of Education and Training, 1994). In 2000, the *Safe Schools Act* was
amended to include a zero tolerance policy (Lawson, 2003).

Attempts to Manage Bullying in School: The Limitations
and Unintended Consequences of Zero Tolerance Policies

The zero tolerance policy outlined as part of Ontario's *Safe Schools Act*
has been implemented widely across Canada (and the United States,
under separate acts), and was initially implemented to help ensure the
safety of all students. It was developed in order to establish set guidelines and expectations on how schools are to deal with violent, aggressive, and non-compliant behaviour in schools and to promote respect,
dignity, and safety (Lawson, 2003). The policy outlines specific punishments for inappropriate behaviours by using suspension and
expulsion more often as well as police involvement in disciplinary
measures (ibid.).

The policy seemed like an answer to all the problems schools were having with violent acts. It did not, however, include room for exception or unusual circumstance, and as it was employed more and more, expulsion and suspension rates rapidly increased, leading to another problem altogether. The students who were suspended or expelled were missing out on valuable educational experiences. One of the consequences of misbehaving in school, being expelled, led to an increase in drop-our rates (Lopez, 2002).

One of the most alarming results from the zero tolerance policy is the rate at which it affects minorities and children with disabilities. Lopez (2002) studied schools in the New York City school board populated predominantly by youth from minority groups and found that boys were treated differently than girls with regards to punishment. According to the research, boys from a racially stigmatized group were automatically viewed as threatening and potential problems (ibid.). The smallest altercation would lead to the physical involvement of security guards and automatic police involvement. The Harvard Education Group (2000) supports this notion of differential treatment by pointing out that in Chicago, 73 per cent of students who were expelled were African American, yet this group makes up only 53 per cent of the school population. As the Harvard study explains, the children with problems are being expelled or suspended and the problems are not being dealt with. Morrison and D'Incau (1997) note that as expulsion rates increase, the students who are most at risk are left with no appropriate education. Schools are referring at-risk students more frequently for expulsion as a way to get rid of problems. These students are those with learning difficulties, emotional and family problems and those identified for special education (ibid.).

The Harvard Education Group (2000) identifies school safety as a critically important issue, especially because school remains one of the safest places for children and youth. They view the zero tolerance policy as wrong and as an infringement on the rights of the children as it excludes them from educational opportunities and places them in criminal institutions. It is noted throughout the literature that the original policy has been expanded to include infractions that pose little or no safety concern (Skiba & Paterson, 1999). There are examples that indicate that the victim of bullying was punished for defending himself or a bystander was punished for trying to mediate and prevent bullying from occurring (Harvard Education Group, 2000). According to the researchers, this policy ultimately denies some children's right to an education by not providing alternative placements (Lopez, 2002; Harvard Education Group, 2000).

Skiba and Paterson (1999) attest that we lack solid evidence to supports the use of harsh policies to improve school safety such as the adoption of the zero tolerance policy. While the original aim of the zero tolerance policy was to protect children and promote individuals' right to be safe at school, the policy neglected the rights of those students whom it punished: their right to an education and their right to the mental-health or educational services they require to deal with their personal issues. In theory, the policy makes sense. In practice, many students are punished for acts that may be a result of another influence, for example, from home, community, bullying, or school failure. Zero tolerance teaches students that we must suspend individual rights and liberties in order to preserve safety in school. A zero tolerance policy should indicate that while certain behaviours will not be ignored and will be responded to in a consistent manner, that does not make certain penalties automatic (Lagana, Bareham, Clark, & Chandler, 1994).

Ontario's Safe Schools Policies

The Ministry of Education and Training in the Province of Ontario has developed two policies called the 'Student Code of Conduct' and 'Violence Free Schools' that are being implemented by school boards across the province. Bill 206, the Student's Code of Conduct 2000, requires that every school board develop a written policy on student conduct in consultation with students, parents, teachers, and principals (Svidal, 2000). The policy must address physical violence, sexual assault, vandalism, and the use or possession of firearms or other weapons, narcotics, alcohol, and tobacco (Svidal, 2000; Ministry of Education and Training, 2000). This notion of establishing a code of conduct promotes positive behaviour in students and makes it clear that negative behaviour such as bullying, harassment, and peer pressure are not acceptable. It serves as a preventative action in order to combat violence in schools. When school boards introduce zero tolerance policies they must take care not to violate the policy's requirement that discipline in schools is to be administered fairly (Lagana et al., 1994).

Similarly, the Ontario Code of Conduct requires school boards to ensure that violators have access to counselling and penalty options that allow them to continue their education (Svidal, 2000). Svidal indicates that the Safe and Caring Schools policy (adopted from the Ontario Code of Conduct) resulted in positive outcomes such as an increase in achievement level, fewer disciplinary problems, and more team participation. Students understood the expectations, felt good about themselves, and were motivated to be successful participants in the school community.

According to Ministry of Education documents (1994, 2001), schools must help all students to learn how to handle conflict and anger in non-violent ways and prepare them for responsible citizenship. Violence has the effect of hurting the health and welfare of an individual. As outlined in the ministry documents (1994, 2001), violence can be physical, verbal (oral or written), emotional, sexual, or racial and can be directed against one individual or a group of individuals. Violence can also be expressed in acts of vandalism and property damage. The Ontario Ministry of Education suggests a number of predominantly behavioural strategies in their Violence-Free Schools Policy documents (1994). Unfortunately, these strategies tend to be rather general and not particularly focused on rights-based intervention.

Nairn and Smith (2002) have identified school bullying as being an infringement of children's right to be protected from mental and physical violence at school (article 19). The CRC also indicates that it is the responsibility of the state to take all appropriate legislative, administrative, social, and educational measures to protect a child from all forms of physical or mental violence (Nairn & Smith, 2002). When Nairn & Smith asked children to give their suggestions for dealing with bullying in schools, the students' suggestions closely mirrored the guidelines of the zero tolerance policy. Forty-six per cent felt that the bullies should be punished with detention, and not being allowed in school because they put others at risk. The students believed that the bully should receive a punishment that fits the crime in the form of suspension and expulsion (Nairn & Smith, 2002). They also believed that teachers should intervene and help the bullies and victims to talk things through.

The findings of Nairn and Smith (2002) point out two important issues. First, students are identifying components of the safe schools and zero tolerance policies that they feel should be in place, but they also indirectly suggest the need for more consistent implementation and the addition of a prosocial component. Second, the responses of the children identify their lack of understanding of human rights, namely, their own child rights. They do not indicate that their rights or the rights of the bully are not being met by the school system. This concept is further discussed in the next section, where an evaluation of children's own perceptions of rights is presented.

The Development of Children's Understanding of Rights

> Rights are a broad concept, which will be interpreted and promoted or resisted differently, depending on the meaning they hold for particular people – for children and young people and the people who have the most contact with them and power over them.
>
> (Taylor, Smith, & Nairn, 2001, p. 138)

Research has indicated that the study of children's perceptions of their own rights is critical in the overall understanding and implementation of children's rights education (Limber, Kask, Heidmets, Hevener Kaufman, & Melton, 2000). In other words, in order for researchers to advocate, promote, or even discuss children's rights, there needs to be an understanding of how children themselves perceive their rights. Taylor et al. (2001) suggest that adult experts on children's rights will not know what children are most concerned with in relation to their rights, unless adults make themselves aware of children's views.

Sparks, Girling, and Smith (2000) talked with children to gain insight into what conceptions of rules and penalties are meaningful to them. They wanted to establish how children relate to the world of adult authority, for instance, the making and breaking of rules in respect to criminal justice, school discipline, and family discipline. Sparks et al. (2000) hoped to gather information that would help them to draw conclusions as to how children perceive justice and individual rights. When the children identified rule breakers as a problem in society and were given the opportunity to delegate fair punishment, the children had difficulty establishing how they could punish without being bad themselves (Sparks et al., 2000). The children felt that the criminals needed to be taught a lesson and provided with an opportunity for a change of heart or an opportunity to understand the other's hurt. They also identified the importance of saying 'sorry' and discussed the concept of picturing the offender as another human being who deserved another chance. The children also portrayed a sense of vulnerability and talked about the fair distribution of scarce resources (Sparks et al., 2000).

Sparks et al. (2000) noted that these ideas of children give insight into how children interpret the adult world, how they understand the need for punitive systems and were adept at identifying the signs of disorder in society. This study also suggests the moral issues faced when examining child rights and how children are aware and identify these moral issues such as fairness over resources and punishing bad people. Children at young ages identify these moral issues around not only child rights but the rights for all people. If we examine a model of how children's reasoning about rights progresses, we can establish a developmental framework for the moral implications involved in teaching child rights.

Melton (1980) developed a stage model of the progression of children's assertion of and reasoning about their rights. He proposed three levels of developmental progression of children's understanding of their rights. At the first level, children perceive rights as 'what one can have or can do.' Children define their rights based on being able to do certain things or being able to have certain things. They believe that adults have more rights than children because of their physical and authoritarian qualities. At level 2, children understand rights as privileges or 'what one should be able to do or to have.' Children view rights as being dependent on fairness or competence, not on the basis of the permission of an adult. Finally, children at level 3 develop an understanding of rights as 'what one must be able to have or to do as a matter of principle.' Melton suggests that it is at this level that children are able to justify through individual reasoning and the notion of morality that there are abstract principles that define rights, for example, freedom of speech or a right to privacy.

In order to test his model, Melton used the Children's Rights Inventory to identify that there are socio-economic differences whereby children from lower socio-economic families exhibit less mature reasoning about rights. He also found that younger children where more likely to report Level 1 responses where their rights were limited by authority. As children got older they identified fairness or competence as rationale for extending rights, which indicates level 2 reasoning. By the time children reached mid–late adolescence they were more likely to recognize autonomy, freedom of choice, and freedom of expression, all associated with level 3 (see table 12.1).

These results suggest that children develop an understanding of rights along a developmental continuum and that they are not fully aware of their rights until they are almost adults. Morrow (1999) exam-

Table 12.1 Melton's developmental model of children's understanding of rights (1980)

	Level 1	Level 2	Level 3
	Age 5 to 9	Age 10–15	Age 16 and up
Perception by the child	What one can have or do	What one should be able to do or to have	What one must be able to have as a matter of principle (natural rights)
Belief	Adults have more rights than children because they are bigger and more important.	Rights are based on fairness and competence rather than on permission.	Rights are justified by individual reasoning of abstract principles and moral development.
Example	I have to go to bed at 8:00 because mom says so.	I can stay up until 9:00 because I am able to.	It is my right to choose when I go to bed.

ined young children's views about rights and found that although children at younger ages were able to articulate their ideas about rights, they felt that their voices were seldom heard and, if heard, often discounted. The children identified their appreciation for the dignity and respect they are given but they felt that they should have a say in matters which concern them. The children also felt that they lacked autonomy and inclusion in decision making, even in regard to small, everyday issues, and they wanted to have a say and be able to participate in decisions that affect them (Marrow, 1999). Taylor et al. (2001) also found that young people want to be able to express themselves and have their views heard and acted upon. The children in their sample reported themselves to be social actors who are actively involved in the construction of their childhood and their rights.

One of the commonalities that has surfaced as a problem throughout the research is the reporting by the children that they are not aware of the CRC and of the rights that they have (Taylor et al., 2001; Morrow, 1999; Alderson, 1999). Alderson (1999) found that only 5 per cent of his sample had heard of the CRC, 19 per cent said they have heard of it 'a bit,' and the rest said 'not at all.' This is problematic when one is examining children's perception of rights. If children are not aware of their rights, then they will have different views about rights than they would if they were aware of their rights. When children indicate their desire to have their voices heard in decision making, are they aware that this is a right outlined in the CRC or is it because they feel that it is fair for them to be heard? Alderson establishes that in order for children to have rights they need to know what rights are, who sanctions them, and how they can ensure their rights are respected.

The CRC states that all children are to be taught the principles outlined in the Convention. Covell (2001) found that when children learn about their rights as described in the Convention, they show increases in self-esteem, increases in perceived peer and teacher support, and increases in the use of rights by respecting attitudes and behaviour. When children understand that they have rights that are written down in a formal document, they develop autonomy and an understanding of the many ways children's rights are not being respected in their everyday lives.

Implications for Interventions

The issues presented thus far in the chapter challenge and question education systems and policies for protecting children from the detrimental effects of school bullying and victimization. There are legal implications of violence in schools, ethical issues to be considered, and psychological considerations for situations involving peer victimization in school settings.

There have been several situations where school boards have been in legal predicaments because of serious outcomes of school violence and bullying (see Zirkel, 2003). One such example involving a student and a school board is the case known as *Jubran v. North Vancouver School District #44*. This case involved a boy who filed a complaint against the school board regarding harassment and bullying that he experienced during his high school career. He claimed that the school did not protect and uphold his rights. The adjudicating tribunal ultimately held the school board responsible, indicating that it was the school's responsibility to uphold the guidelines in the code of conduct and the school board's obligation to maintain a non-discriminatory environment (Howard, 2002). Howard challenges this decision in part because nowhere in the report does the tribunal indicate that the other students involved in the bullying should bear responsibility for their behaviour or that they were independent moral actors.

In the past, bullying was viewed as a school disciplinary matter rather than a criminal issue. Until recently, with the occurrence of cases such as those previously discussed, Canadian courts have predominantly been making decisions involving very serious cases involving murder or suicide that have stemmed from school bullying (Chisholm, 2004). However, the courts and schools are showing a new intolerance for bullying and establishing the need to classify bullying as a crime. Verbal threats are now being recognized by the courts as a criminal offence (as an infringement of basic human rights) and students are being charged under the *Youth Criminal Justice Act, 2003* (Chisholm, 2004).

Controversy and Ethical Considerations

Article 42 of the CRC calls for children's rights education wherein children are to be taught the principles outlined in the CRC (Covell, 2001). As a fundamental right, children should be taught about their rights. Covell notes that when children learn about their rights as described by the CRC they report on increases in self-esteem, and in perceived peer and teacher support. They also have an understanding of their rights and those of others, as is demonstrated by their respecting the attitudes and behaviours of each other (Covell, 2001). A study of rights education in Nova Scotia reported improved classroom environments and student behaviour (ibid.). When students were describing what they learned, they suggested that rights education was an effective agent of moral education.

In addition, David (1999) identifies several reasons why children's rights remain a constant challenge to implement. These include the fact that the CRC code identifies a child as a human being with a full array of rights and public authorities must now be accountable for safe-guarding these rights. Child welfare is no longer based on a child's needs, which can be subjective, but on a child's rights, which are more objective. Adults, namely those in power, need to change their beliefs about the role of the child and implement appropriate legislation and policies to ensure these rights are being met. David (1999) also indicates that the articles regarding civil rights are extremely difficult to implement because they require adults to allow children to actively participate in decisions that affect them, which is not what has traditionally been done in the past. Educational issues encompass more than just access to education, but also protection against discrimination and violence. This suggests a more moral approach, as opposed to the traditional welfare approach, which is not readily accepted by education policy makers (David, 1999). It is obvious that the larger problem lies with the policy makers as they are the ones with the power to influence society at large. Unless these fundamental changes are made, schools, teachers, and health professionals can only do as much as the government allocates funds for. Rights education will become a tool for reducing violence in schools in Ontario when the minister of education recognizes the importance of teaching children about their rights as a way to promote the rights of all children.

Rights Education

The final section of this chapter will focus on how rights education can be an effective agent of socio-moral education. MacDougall (1994) suggests that the ability that children have in understanding power makes them better able to deal with conflict and power struggles, such as those involved in bullying. When children are able to name or put words to an emotion or to a behaviour, they are then able to act consciously and responsibly. However, children need to be taught how to promote their own rights, particularly when dealing with bullying. According to Howe and Covell (2005, 2007), important connections can be made between rights, needs, and wants. As well, explicit links must be made between bullying and rights by asking questions such as: 'What rights are being violated for the bully, the victim, the bully-victim and the bystander?' Thus, a rights education program that is based on a developmentally appropriate content outlining moral responsibility and the rights and needs of all children has a great deal of potential as an anti-bullying intervention.

In fact, Decoene and De Cock (1996) reported a link between the exposure of children (3–12 years) to a rights education program and an increase in support for the general values of rights, tolerance, and multiculturalism. During the program, children asked questions about the rights of others, raised issues concerning the value of diversity and tolerance, and showed considerable sensitivity to the themes of peace and justice. It has also been suggested that children's beliefs about their own rights may affect their attitudes about the rights of others (Ruck, Keating, Abramovitch, & Koegel, 1998). Similarly, research by Covell and Howe (1999) indicates that there is a link between children's knowledge of their rights and more positive attitudes on their part towards those with differences. They suggest this can be explained in two ways: first, as mediated by improved psychological well-being or, second, as mediated by empathy (Covell & Howe, 1999, 2001). Either way, rights education serves the purpose of improving the way children treat each other. The question that remains is how and when will such rights education be implemented?

There is significant evidence that suggests that the education of children's rights can be integrated into the existing school curriculum and can yield significant positive outcomes (Covell & Howe, 1999, 2001; Decoene & De Cock, 1996; Howe, Covell, & O'Leary, 2002). Covell and Howe (1999) have developed a curriculum that integrates the fifty-two articles of the CRC and the pre-existing curriculum in areas such as health for grade 5 and 6 students. This curriculum has also been adapted for grade 8 students with direct links to the health and social studies curriculum (Howe et al., 2002). Both studies assess the use of the rights curriculum in many schools in Nova Scotia using a control group. The results indicate that the students who were exposed to the rights curriculum had a broader and more accurate knowledge of children's rights compared to children who did not receive the curriculum (Covell & Howe, 1999; Howe et al., 2002). The contagion effect was also supported by the results, meaning that students who received the curriculum perceived their classmates to be more accepting of ethnic minority children, and perceived greater levels of peer and teacher support (Covell & Howe, 1999). The children exposed to the rights curriculum developed an understanding that needs were to be given dominance over wants (Covell & Howe, 1999). As mentioned earlier, the comments made by the children exemplify the connection between rights and needs as identified by Maslow (1954). Children understand and value their rights as well as equality, education, health care, and protection from abuse. The children who were not exposed to the curriculum stated that they did not understand what it means to have rights or they only understood rights in terms of freedoms and wants (Covell & Howe, 1999). This implies an understanding of the developmental nature of rights education, whereby children begin to understand and distinguish their rights from their wants.

According to Covell and Howe (2001), there are many reasons to support children's rights education. For instance, it may be necessary for children to feel respected and special for them to treat others with respect and to demonstrate responsible social behaviours. In addition, children who learn about rights express a more accurate and abstract understanding of what rights are and an understanding of the importance of rights for all. It is important for educators to understand that it is not possible for children to learn about their rights without also learning about how rights can be violated in serious ways such as through poverty, abuse, and exploitation. The empathy elicited by such knowledge is expected to impact the emerging social concepts of late childhood and early adolescence. Also, children will learn that rights may sometimes be in conflict; for example, one's right of expression may conflict with another's right of respect. The incidence of bullying could decrease if and when children understand bullying in terms of its being a serious infringement of their rights.

Finally, it is suggested that this increase in perceived peer support would decrease the incidence of bullying as a result of the other factors that are associated with increased perceived peer support. Children feel connected, feel safer, and as a result are less likely to be bullied. Similarly, it can also be suggested that when children feel accepted and feel as though they are well liked, they will be less likely to bully others.

Conclusion

There has to be a recognition that part of the population involved in bullying may suffer from educational and psychological difficulties of varying degrees of severity, which may require the intervention of school systems as well as outside agencies (see Cunningham & Cunningham, 1998; Offord, 1989; Offord, Boyle, & Racine, 1991). The challenge here is deciding what should be implemented, since current practices, as they stand, are not serving the needs of all students. The focus should be on creating a school environment that promotes respect, dignity, and non-violence for all. When children are treated with respect and dignity, they will in turn treat others in this manner if this is the expectation established within a school. Lawson (2003) suggests that a way to create safety for everyone inside and outside of school is to take up inclusiveness practices, and to tap into the unique cultural knowledge and differences that all students bring to school with them. The school must reach out to the community to build partnerships and address issues of power, especially in areas highly populated with minority groups (Lawson, 2003). Schools also need to implement rights training and educate students about their rights in order to help them establish what should be acceptable or not acceptable in respect to conduct and discipline. A combination of many agencies and systems will need to come together to promote the rights of children and at the same time diminish the occurrence of bullying in schools.

'Providing young people with an opportunity to grow and develop in a safe and respectful society is a *shared responsibility* in which schools play an important role' (Letter from deputy minister, dated 9 March 2006, commenting on Ontario's Bill 212, Safe Schools Strategy).[1] With the policies in place and a growing awareness of children's rights and of the social components that infringe these rights, such as school bullying, policy makers, school boards, community organizations, and educators need to establish programs and guidelines specific to rights education as a means of bullying intervention. The research strongly indicates that bullying is an infringement of children's rights in more than one aspect. Now it remains the responsibility of school systems and other organizations working with children to use this information for intervention and ultimately prevention. These methods will need to include multidisciplinary efforts to work with children on all the aspects discussed in this chapter: rights education, violence prevention, and psychological intervention for bullies and victims. It is with these programs in place and all parties working for the same goal that an intervention program will be effective in alleviating the many problems associated with bullying in schools.

REFERENCES

Alderson, P. (1999). Human rights and democracy in schools: Do they mean more than 'picking up litter and not killing whales'? *International Journal of Children's Rights, 7*, 185–205

Arsenio, W.F., Gold, J., & Adams, E. (2006). Children's conceptions and displays of moral emotions. In M. Killen and J.G. Smetana (Eds.), *Handbook of moral development*. Mahwah, NJ: Lawrence Erlbaum Associates Publishers.

Bernstein, J.Y. & Watson, M.W. (1997). Children who are targets of bullying. *Journal of Interpersonal Violence, 12*(4), 483–494.

Birmaher, B., Ryan, N.D., & Williamson, D.E. (1996). Depression in children

1 Bill 212 annuls sections 306 to 311 of the *Education Act* and replaces them with new standards that address the suspension and expulsion of students. The most relevant aspect of the new changes in relation to the present chapter involves the list of criteria for suspension, which include specific references to bullying, and the fact that bullying is now considered as serious as bringing a weapon to school.

and adolescents: Clinical features and pathogenesis. In K.I. Shulman, T. Mauricio, and S.P. Kutcher (Eds.), *Mood disorders across the life span.* New York: Wiley-Liss.

Bloom, B.L. (1979). Prevention of mental disorders: Recent advances in theory and practice. *Community Mental Health Journal, 15*(3), 179–191.

Boivin, M., Hymel, S., & Bukowski, W.M. (1995). The roles of social withdrawal, peer rejection, and victimization by peers in predicting loneliness and depressed mood in childhood. *Development and Psychopathology. Special Issue: Developmental processes in peer relations and psychopathology, 7*(4), 765–785.

Bosacki, S.L., Marini, Z.A., & Dane, A. (2006). Voices from the classroom: Pictorial and narrative representations of middle school bullying experiences. *Journal of Moral Education, 35*(2), 231–245.

Boulton, M.J., & Underwood, K. (1992). Bully/victim problems among middle schoolchildren. *British Journal of Educational Psychology, 62*, 73–87.

Boyle, J. (1996). Bullying as a social problem in schools. In B. Gillham & J. A. Thomson (Eds.), *Child safety: Problem and prevention from preschool to adolescence* (pp. 141–159). London: Routledge.

Caplan, M., Bennetto, L., & Weissberg, R.P. (1991). The role of interpersonal context in the assessment of social problem-solving skills. *Journal of Applied Developmental Psychology, 12*(1), 103–114.

Chisholm, A. (2004). Bullying, schools and the law. *Teaching & Learning, 1*(3), 22–30.

Coie, J.D., Christopoulos, C., Terry, R., Dodge, K.A., & Lochman, J.E. (1989). Types of aggressive relationships, peer rejection, and developmental consequences. In B.H. Schneider, G. Attili, J. Nadel, and R.P. Weissberg (Eds.), *Social competence in developmental perspective.* NATO Advanced Science Institutes series. Series D: Behavioural and social sciences, vol. 51. New York: Kluwer Academic / Plenum Publishers.

Covell, K. (2001). Children's rights education: A new reality for teachers. *Education Canada, 41*(2), 16–19.

Covell, K., & Howe, R.B. (1999). The impact of children's rights education: A Canadian study. *International Journal of Children's Rights, 7*, 171–183.

Covell, K., & Howe, B.R. (2001). Moral education through the 3 Rs: Rights, respect and responsibility. *Journal of Moral Education, 30*(1), 29–41.

Cowie, H. (2000). Bystanding or standing by: Gender issues in coping with bullying. *Aggressive Behaviour, 26*(1), 85–97.

Craig, W. (1998). The relationship among bullying, victimization, depression, anxiety and aggression in elementary school children. *Personality and Individual Difference, 24*(1), 123–130.

Craig, W.M., Pepler, D., & Atlas, R. (2000). Observations of bullying in the playground and in the classroom. *School Psychology International, 21*, 22–36.

Crick, N.R. (1995). Relational aggression: The role of intent attributions, feelings of distress and provocation type. *Development and Psychopathology, 7(2)*, 313–322.

Crick, N.R. (1996). The role of overt aggression, relational aggression and prosocial behaviour in the prediction of children's future social adjustment. *Child Development, 67*, 2317–2327.

Crick, N.R. & Bigbee, M.A. (1998). Relational and overt forms of peer victimization: A multiinformant approach. *Journal of Consulting and Clinical Psychology, 66(2)*, 337–347.

Crick, N.R., & Grotpeter, J.K. (1996). Children's treatment by peers: Victims of relational and overt aggression. *Development and Psychopathology, 8(2)*, 367–380.

Crick, N.R., & Grotpeter, J.K. (1995). Relational aggression, gender, and social-psychological adjustment. *Child Development, 66*, 710–722.

Cunningham, C.E., & Cunningham, L.J. (1998). Student-mediated conflict resolution programs. In R.A. Barkley (Ed.), *Attention-deficit hyperactivity disorder: A handbook for diagnosis and treatment* (2nd ed.). New York: Guilford Press.

David, P. (1999). Implementing the rights of the child: Six reasons why the human rights of children remain a constant challenge. *Prospects, 29(2)*, 258–263.

Decoene, J. & De Cock, R. (1996). The children's rights project in the primary school 'De vrijdagmarkt' in Bruges. In E. Verhellen (Ed.), *Monitoring children's rights* (pp. 627–636). The Hague: Martinus Nijhoff.

Durlak, J.A., & Jason, L.A. (1984). Preventive programs for school-aged children and adolescents. In M.C. Roberts & L. Peterson (Eds.), *Prevention of problems in childhood*. Toronto: John Wiley & Sons.

Farrington, D.P. (1998) Youth crime and antisocial behavior. In A. Campbell and S. Muncer, (Eds.), *The social child*. Hove, Eng.: Psychology Press / Erlbaum (UK) Taylor & Francis.

Feindler, E.L. & Kalfus, G.R. (Eds.) (1990). *Adolescent behavior therapy handbook*. Springer series on behavior therapy and behavioral medicine, 22. New York: Springer Publishing Co.

Felner, R.D., Jason, L.A., Moritsugu, J.N., & Farber S.S. (Eds.) (1983). *Prevention psychology: Theory, research, and practice*. Toronto: Pergamon Press.

Goldston, S. E. (1984). Defining primary prevention. In J.M. Joffe, G.W. Albee, & L.D. Kelly (Eds.), *Readings in primary prevention of psychopathology* (pp. 31–35). London: Vermont Conference on the Primary Prevention of Psychopathology.

Harrington, R., Rutter, M., & Fombonne, E. (1996). Developmental pathways in depression: Multiple meanings, antecedents, and endpoints. *Development and Psychopathology, 8*(4), 601–616.

Harvard Education Group (2000). Opportunities suspended: The devastating consequences of zero tolerance and school discipline policies. *Education Week,* June 21.

Howard, P. (2002). Following-up on Jubran: Boards, bullying, and accountability (*Jubran v. North Vancouver School District #44*). *Education Canada, 42*(3), 1–3.

Howe, B.R., & Covell, K. (2005). *Empowering children: Children's rights education as a pathway to citizenship.* Toronto: University of Toronto Press.

Howe, B.R., & Covell, K. (Eds.) (2007). *A question of commitment: Children's rights in Canada.* Waterloo, ON: Wilfrid Laurier University Press.

Howe, B.R., Covell, K., & O'Leary, J. (2002). Introducing a new grade 8 curriculum in children's rights. *Alberta Journal of Educational Research, 48*(4), 302–313.

Jessor, R., Van Den Bos, J., Vanderryn, J., Costa, F.M. (1995). Protective factors in adolescent problem behavior: Moderator effects and developmental change. *Developmental Psychology, 31*(6), 923–933.

Johnston, D.W., & Johnston, R.T. (1998). Teaching students to manage conflicts in diverse classrooms. In J. W. Putnam (Ed.), *Cooperative learning and strategies for inclusion: Celebrating diversity in the classroom* (2nd ed.). Baltimore, MD: Paul H. Brookes Publishing Co.

Juvonen, J., & Graham, S. (Eds.) (2001). *Peer harassment in school: The plight of the vulnerable and victimized.* New York: Guilford Press.

Kaltiala-Heino, R., Rimpela, M., Rantanen, P., & Rimpela, A. (2000). Bullying at school – an indicator of adolescents at risk for mental disorders. *Journal of Adolescence, 23,* 661–674.

Kaplan, H.B. (1999). Toward an understanding of resilience: A critical review of definitions and models. In M.D. Glantz & J.L. Johnson (Eds.), *Resilience and development: Positive life adaptations.* New York: Kluwer Academic / Plenum Publishers.

Kazdin, A.E. (1993). Adolescent mental health: Prevention and treatment programs. *American Psychologist, 48*(2), 127–141.

Kazdin, A.E., & Kendall, P.C. (1998). Current progress and future plans for developing effective treatments: Comments and perspectives. *Journal of Clinical Child Psychology, 27,* 217–226.

Kochenderfer, B., & Ladd, G. (2001). Variations in peer victimization: Relations to children's maladjustment. In J. Juvonen & S. Graham (Eds.) (2001), *Peer harassment in school: The plight of the vulnerable and victimized.* New York: Guilford Press.

Kumpulainen, K., Raesaenen, E., & Henttonen, I. (1999) Children involved in bullying: Psychological disturbance and the persistence of the involvement. *Child Abuse & Neglect, 23*(12), 1253–1262.

Lagana, N., Bareham, S., Clark, J., & Chandler, M. (1994). *Safe school communities: An information and policy guide for the prevention of violence.* Vancouver, BC: British Columbia School Trustees Association.

Larson, R.W. (2000). Toward a psychology of positive youth development. *American Psychologist, 55,* 170–183.

Lawson, E. (2003). Re-assessing safety and discipline in our schools: Opportunities for growth, opportunities for change. *Orbit, 33*(3), 1–5.

Leventhal, H., Prohaska, T.R., & Hirschman, R.S. (1985). Preventive health behaviour across the life span. In J.C. Rosen & L.J. Solomon (Eds.), *Prevention in health psychology* (pp. 192–235). London: Vermont Conference on the Primary Prevention of Psychopathology.

Levy, J.C., & Deykin, E.Y. (1989). Suicidality, depression, and substance abuse in adolescence. *American Journal of Psychiatry, 146*(11), 1462–1467.

Limber, S., Kask, V., Heidmets, M., Hevener Kaufman, N., & Melton, G. (2000). Estonian children's perceptions of rights: implications for societies in transition. *International Journal of Children's Rights, 7,* 365–383.

Loeber, R., & Hay, D. (1997). Key issues in the development of aggression and violence from childhood to early adulthood. *Annual Review of Psychology, 48,* 371–410.

Lopez, N. (2002). Rewriting race and gender high school lessons: Second-generation Dominicans in New York City. *Teacher's College Record, 104*(6), 1187–1203

MacDougall, J. (1994). *Violence in the schools: Programs and policies for prevention.* Toronto: Canadian Education Association.

Marini, Z.A., Bombay, K., Hobin, C., Winn, D., & Dumyn, P. (2000). From peer victimization to peer mediation: A public health approach to the prevention and management of school bullying. *Brock Education, 10,* 1–29.

Marini, Z.A, Dane, A., Bosacki, S., & YLC-CURA. (2006a). Direct and indirect bully-victims: Differential psychosocial risk factors associated with adolescents involved in bullying and victimization. *Aggressive Behaviour, 32,* 551–569.

Marini, Z.A., Fairbain, L., & Zuber, R. (2001). Peer harassment in individuals with developmental disabilities: Towards the development of a multidimensional bullying identification model. *Developmental Disabilities Bulletin, 29,* 170–195.

Marini, Z.A., Koruna, B., & Dane, A. (2006b). Individualizing interventions for students involved in bullying and victimization: Helping students who are bully-victims. *Contact, 2,* 1–10.

Marini, Z.A., McWhinnie, M., & Lacharite, M. (2004). Preventing school bullying: Identification and intervention involving bystanders. *Teaching and Learning, 1*, 17–21.

Marini, Z.A., Spear, S., & Bonbay, K. (1999). Peer victimization in middle childhood: Characteristics, causes and consequences of school bullying. *Brock Education, 9*, 32–47.

Maslow, A. (1954). *Motivation and personality*. New York: Harper.

Maslow, A., & Lowery, R. (Eds.). (1998). *Toward a psychology of being* (3rd ed.). New York: Wiley & Sons.

Massimini, F., & Delle Fave, A. (2000). Individual development in a bio-cultural perspective. *American Psychologist, 55(1)*, 24–33.

Melton, G.B. (1980). Children's concept of their rights. *Journal of Clinical Child Psychology, 9*, 186–190.

Morrison, G., & D'Incau, B. (1997). The web of zero-tolerance: Characteristics of students who are recommended for expulsion from school. *Education and Treatment of Children, 20* (3), 316–336.

Morrow, V. (1999). We are people too: Children and young people's perspectives on children's rights and decision making in England. *International Journal of Children's Rights, 7*, 49–170.

Nairn, K., & Smith, A. (2002). Bullying at school: secondary students' experiences of bullying at school and their suggestions for dealing with it. *Youth Studies Australia, 21*(3), 37–44.

Nangle, D.W., Erdley, C.A., Newman, J., Mason, C., & Carpenter, E. (2003). Popularity, friendship quantity, and friendship quality: Interactive influences on children's loneliness and depression. *Journal of Clinical Child and Adolescent Psychology, 32*(4), 546–555.

Nucci, L. (2006). Education for moral development. In M. Killen & J. Smetana (Eds.), *Handbook of moral development* (pp. 657–681). Mahwah, NJ: Lawrence Erlbaum.

Offord, D.R. (1989). Conduct disorder: Risk factors and prevention. In D. Shaffer, I. Philips, and N. B. Enzer (Eds.), *Prevention of mental disorders, alcohol and other drug use*. Rockville, MD: U.S. Department of Health and Human Services.

Offord, D., Boyle, M., & Racine, Y. (1991). Children at risk: Schools reaching out. *Education Today*, March/April, 16–18.

Olweus, D. (1993). *Bullying at school: What we know and what we can do*. Oxford, UK: Blackwell.

Olweus, D. (2001). Peer harassment: A critical analysis and some important issues. In J. Juvonen & S. Graham (Eds.), *Peer harassment in school: The plight of the vulnerable and victimized* (pp. 3–20). New York: Guilford Press.

Ontario. Ministry of Education and Training (1994). *Violence-free schools policy.* Government of Ontario.

Ontario. Ministry of Education and Training (2000). *Ontario schools' code of conduct.* Government of Ontario.

Ontario Ministry of Education and Training. (2001). *News release: Province moves forward with safe schools strategy.* Government of Ontario.

Pepler, D., & Craig, W. (1995). A peak behind the fence: Naturalistic observations of aggressive children with remote audiovisual recording. *Developmental Psychology, 31,* 548–553.

Purkey, W.W., & Novak, J.M. (1996). *Inviting school: A self-concept approach to teaching, learning, and democratic practice* (3rd ed.). Belmont, CA: Wadsworth Publishing Co.

United Nations. (1989). *Convention on the Rights of the Child.*

Rigby, K. (2001) Health consequences of bullying and its prevention in schools. In J. Juvonen & S. Graham (eds.), *Peer harassment in school: The plight of the vulnerable and victimized.* New York: Guilford Press.

Rigby, K. (2002). Bullying in childhood. In P.K. Smith & C.H. Hart (Eds.), *Blackwell handbook of childhood social development.* Oxford, UK: Blackwell Publishers.

Ruck, M., Keating, D., Abramovitch, R., & Koegel, C. (1998). Adolescents' and children's knowledge about rights: Some evidence for how young people view rights in their own lives. *Journal of Adolescence, 21,* 275–289.

Salmivalli, C. (2001). Group view on victimization: Empirical findings and their implications. In J. Juvonen & S. Graham (Eds.). *Peer harassment in school: The plight of the vulnerable and victimized.* New York: Guilford Press.

Seligman, M.E.P., & Csikszentmihalyi, M. (2000). Positive psychology: An introduction. *American Psychologist, 55,* 5–14.

Skiba, R., & Paterson, R. (1999). The dark side of zero tolerance. *Phi Delta Kappan, 80*(5), 372–379.

Smith, A. (2002). Interpreting and supporting participation rights: contributions from sociocultural theory. *International Journal of Children's Rights, 10,* 73–88.

Smith, P. (2000) Bullying and harassment in schools and the rights of children. *Children & Society, 14,* 294–303.

Smith, P.K., Pepler, D., & Rigby, K. (Eds.) (2004). *Bullying in schools: How successful can interventions be?* New York: Cambridge University Press.

Smith, P.K., & Sharp, S. (Eds.) (1994). *School bullying: Insights and perspectives.* London: Routledge.

Sparks, R., Girling, E., & Smith, M. (2000). Children talking about justice and punishment. *International Journal of Children's Rights, 8,* 191–209.

Svidal, S. (2000). Preventing school violence aim of a private member's bill (School Amendment Act). *ATA News, 34*(17), 4–5.

Swearer, S., Grills, A., Hayes, K., & Cary, P.T. (2004) Internalizing problems in students involved in bullying and victimization: Implications for intervention. In D. Espelage and S.M. Swearer (Eds.), *Bullying in American schools: A social-ecological perspective on prevention and intervention* (pp. 63–83). Mahwah, NJ: Lawrence Erlbaum Associates.

Taylor, N., Smith, A., & Nairn, K. (2001). Rights important to young people: Secondary student and staff perspectives. *International Journal of Children's Rights, 9*, 137–156.

Vaillancourt, T., Brendgen, M., Boivin, M., & Tremblay, R. (2003). A longitudinal confirmatory factor analysis of indirect and physical aggression: Evidence of two factors over time? *Child Development, 74*, 1628–1638.

Verdugo, M.A., & Bermejo, B.G. (1997). The mentally retarded person as a victim of maltreatment. *Aggression and Violent Behaviour, 2*, 143–165.

Vernberg, E., Jacobs, A., & Hershberger, S. (1999). Peer victimization and attitudes about violence during early adolescence. *Journal of Clinical Child Psychology, 28(3)*, 386–395.

Weissberg, R.P., & Allen, J.P. (1986). Promoting children's social skills and adaptive interpersonal behaviour. In B.A. Edelstein & L. Michelson (Eds.), *Handbook of Prevention*. New York: Plenum Press.

Wilcox, B., & Naimark, H. (1991) The rights of the child: Progress toward human dignity. *American Psychologist, 46*(1), 49

Wolke, D., Woods, S., Bloomfield, L., & Karstadt, L. (2000). The association between direct and relational bullying and behaviour problems among primary school children. *Journal of Child Psychology and Psychiatry, 41*(8), 989–1002.

Zirkel, P. (2003). Bullying: A matter of law? *Phi Delta Kappan*, September, 90–91.

d Responsibility:

ry School Conduct Codes and

duction of Passive Citizenship

REBECCA RABY

Young people spend an inordinate amount of time in schools, and it is these institutions, it is presumed, that teach them not only academic but social and citizenship skills. The latter are addressed, in part, through school codes of conduct. Such codes invariably and necessarily focus on governance in the present, but also often address the preparation of young people for future citizenship and employment. This paper examines secondary school codes of conduct in terms of their stated goals and styles of presentation. It will be argued that while there are tensions within these codes in terms of the kind of citizenship being created, it is overwhelmingly a passive, individualized citizenship, based on welfare and protective rights, and cultivated through obedience.

This paper examines codes of conduct from individual public, secondary schools in the Niagara and Toronto regions. These codes address grades 9 through 12 (ages 14–17), the last phase of public schooling in Ontario. Codes of conduct often include a preamble outlining the intent of the code, specific school rules, and the consequences of their infraction. Occasionally the logic behind school rules is also spelled out. These codes of conduct are created under the aegis of Ontario's *Safe Schools Act* and codes of conduct devised by the Toronto and Niagara school boards. An analysis of the specific rules listed in school codes of conduct may be found elsewhere (Raby, 2005). This paper concentrates instead on sections of these conduct codes that directly address the stated intent of the code in terms of such concepts as citizenship, rights, responsibilities, and respect. Readers are asked to bear in mind that the presentation of such codes of conduct is quite distinct from how they are executed and experienced within the school setting.

Children as Participatory Citizens

Rights and Citizenship

Citizenship is a broad concept that theorist T.H. Marshall understood to include civil elements, such as the rule of law, political elements, such as the right to vote, and social elements (Roche, 1999). Citizenship is also about formal equality and rights, rights that can be loosely divided into passive and active forms. Citizenship can include protective and provision rights, for example (Alvineri & de-Shalit, 1992; Lansdown, 1994), rights that can be considered passive, although they require advocacy (Taylor, Smith, & Navin, 2001). Protective rights address safety from discrimination, abuse, and injustice; for children, this includes protections that adults do not share, from neglect and abuse for instance (Archard, 2004). Provision rights include access to health care, education, recreation, and so forth. 'Active' conceptualizations of citizenship are evident in what Taylor et al. refer to as participation rights, premised on rights to speech, representation, information, and participation in decision making (Beauvais, McKay, & Seddon, 2002; Hart, 1992; John, 1995). Active citizenship also includes the ability to realize these rights through political, democratic engagement. Within this more active model, individual rights are coupled with democratic engagement and, arguably, investment in community.

Young people's lack of independence, unequal social position, and liminality complicate their relationships to citizenship and have led to their exclusion from full citizenship (Beauvais et al., 2002). An understanding of children as citizens and as rights-bearers has been broadly advocated only quite recently. Devine (2002) argues that essentialist notions of childhood incompetence undermine young people's potential for *active* citizenship in particular, as 'Children's rights [are] defined negatively in terms of protection from abuse and inadequate care ... rather than in terms of empowerment' (p. 316). The controversial nature of children's participation rights is evident in the tension between the caretaker and liberation approaches (Archard, 2004). Rights in liberal societies have been linked to autonomy, rationality, and the ability to make wise decisions (Alderson, 1999). The caretaker approach argues that children do not have the ability to make choices of their own and must therefore have their rights exercised by an adult on their behalf, thus problematizing participation rights, which must be exercised by those who possess them (Archard, 2004). In fact, to such protectionists, it is the *prevention* of choice for children that ensures they will be able later to make reasoned choices as educated adults. Liberationists counter that 'presumed incapable of making choices for themselves, children are denied the opportunity to show that they can' (ibid., p. 74). Rather, children do have the ability to make choices and should have the right to exercise this ability. These divergent positions together illustrate a tension in current views of children, a tension that is also reflected in school codes of conduct. Many expect children to be obedient in a society that also prizes liberal values of independence and freedom (Alderson, 1999); so how do obedient children in turn become such independent, decision-making adults?

Archard himself opts for a middle position, one similar to the 'partial citizenship' espoused by Jeremy Roche (1999). He observes that while children may have far more cognitive competence than they are often given credit for, that knowledge increases with age and depends upon varying levels of maturity. Consequently, Archard argues that 'older children, that is teenagers, can exercise rights of self-determination' (2004, p. 93). Yet he also lays bare the injustice in denying rights to children on the basis of their lack of skills when we fail to teach these skills – an issue relevant to *all* children. In concurrence with Archard's reasoning, we can examine secondary schools as ideal sites for young people to exercise such self-determination and, concomitantly, to hone their skills in democratic citizenship. Indeed, Covell and Howe contend that schools *must* educate children 'to exercise their rights to participate' (2001, p. 109). Yet a detailed examination of school rules suggests that while many profess to cultivate self-discipline and responsibility, overall codes of conduct are widely based on a model of inequality between students and teachers, a cultivation of obedience, and passivity in the face of top-down punishment. Codes of conduct therefore follow the caretaker model in which children are prepared for future self-governance and decision making through an absence of active, participatory rights in the present.

Citizenship can also be examined through governmentality studies. Building on and extending from the work of Michel Foucault (1978), governmentality studies characterize modern governance as diffuse and successful through honing self-discipline. Nicholas Rose (1999) defines governmentality as 'all endeavors to shape, guide, [and] direct the conduct of others' (p. 3). Rather than maintaining authority through top-down applications of power (Kelly, 2003), governance is conducted through 'shaping and utilizing [people's] freedom' (Rose, 1999, p. 54). The emphasis, therefore, is on self-governance and self-discipline, in which people regulate themselves. Such processes are particularly resonant with neo-liberalism. Examination of codes of conduct suggests that they attempt to create subjectivities (e.g., the 'respecting' student and the 'responsible' citizen) who have internalized their own governance (Raby, 2005). Yet, this governance does not replace a sovereign, top-down punishment of teenagers.

Children's Participatory Rights and Education

An interest in children's participatory rights has become quite strong over the last decade, particularly within the sociology of childhood, which has emphasized children as citizens, social agents, and social participants (James & Prout, 1990). While children may have different skills from adults, they remain competent in a way that is frequently underestimated (Smith, 2002). Children's entitlements to participation rights have thus been advocated by various activists and researchers, some directly focusing on young people's participation rights in schools (Alderson, 1999). Children's rights have also been enshrined in the United Nations Convention on the Rights of the Child (CRC), with children having the right to free expression and to be consulted on decisions that directly affect them. Within this document, there is some tension regarding participation rights, however (Archard, 2004), some of which have already been outlined within this volume (e.g. Shariff & Johnny, chapter 9; van Vliet & Raby, chapter 10). While children are to have a say in matters that directly affect them, their participation rights are limited by what adults, including teachers and principals, consider to be in the best interests of the child.

In Canada, the *Charter of Rights and Freedoms* has been examined in relation to children's rights and education, with some concerned that the Charter undermines the operation of schools (Dennis, 1996; Harte & McDonald, 1996). Yet courts have found that 'to maintain control of schools and ensure they operate smoothly, educators need to be allowed to infringe on some of the *Charter* rights of students' (Dennis 1996, p. 16). Such infringement has been supported in cases of search and seizure when there are reasonable grounds for suspicion of a school violation and in a case of detention, for example (ibid.). Harte and McDonald (1996) argue, however, that owing to the Charter, school officials need to demonstrate that a school rule is reasonable, necessary, and legitimate. Rules must be clear and linked to an educational and/or disciplinary rationale, and students need an opportunity to provide their side of the story (ibid.). Others argue that it is necessary for young people to be participants in developing school codes of conduct (Schimmel, 2003).

Despite children's rights, agency, responsibilities, and abilities to participate (Devine, 2002; France, 1998; Roche, 1999; Such & Walker, 2005), young people are also conventionally understood to be incomplete, at risk, and in need of guidance (Griffin, 1993; Lesko, 1996), beliefs that legitimize school rules and their enforcement. In fact, as Alderson (1999) observes, schools are highly disciplined environments: 'Discipline is rigorously imposed through the body: prescribed clothing and hair length, proscribed ornaments, injunctions about when and where to sit or stand, to keep still, not to run and, most frequently of all, not to talk' (p. 188). Teachers can reprimand and punish without accountability or justification, while students rarely have any recourse or independent advocate for appealing detentions or suspensions; furthermore, attendance is compulsory (Alderson, 1999). Children's views remain absent from decisions regarding such matters as school choice, testing, or how schools are run (Lansdown, 1994). In the case of school rules, this chapter demonstrates that few address due process or students' participation. Similar findings are evident in David Schimmel's examination of thirty student handbooks from Florida, Ohio, Massachusetts, and New York (2003) and Ramon Lewis's Australian study (1999) of three hundred schools' codes of conduct from secondary and primary schools.

Collection of Codes of Conduct

The codes of conduct examined here were collected in 2003 and 2004. Some schools make their codes available on their websites, but many do not. Niagara and Toronto school boards were contacted to determine the best way to collect these codes. The District School Board of Niagara collected all public, English secondary-school codes on my behalf. The Toronto District School Board instructed that I collect the codes from each individual school. Letters to schools and follow-up phone calls yielded 51 (52%) of the Toronto schools' codes. In Niagara, I received 21 (95%) of the relevant school codes. Of this total of 72 codes, 17 Niagara codes and 40 Toronto codes were examined for this study, as only these codes included some kind of commentary to frame the codes in terms of their goals or expectations beyond a simple

Table 13.1 Stated goals of codes of conduct

Stated goals of codes	Niagara (*n*=17)	Toronto (*n*=40)	Total (*n*=57)
Opening statement of goals	11 (65%)	24 (60%)	35 (61%)
Focus on development of the individual student	9 (53%)	15 (37.5%)	24 (42%)
Focus on promotion of self-discipline specifically	8 (47%)	2 (5%)	10 (17.5%)
Development of students as part of wider community specifically	0 (0%)	5 (12.5%)	5 (9%)
Overt expectation of maturity or responsibility in the present	1 (6%)	3 (7.5%)	4 (7%)

listing of the rules. These 57 codes differ in length and detail. They cover a diversity of schools in terms of size, region, and program specialty, although I received very few from alternative schools. French, private, and Catholic school codes are not examined here. All school names listed here are pseudonyms.

Analysis of Codes of Conduct

These school codes of conduct have been read through a number of times. For this paper, I organized code goals and expectations into categories of presentation, specifically in terms of provision rights, welfare and participation rights, respect, responsibility, and citizenship. As I worked with these categories, four themes were developed: being and becoming; self-discipline and obedience; responsibility and respect; and passive and individualized citizenship.

BEING AND BECOMING

Is a student expected to be a responsible and self-disciplining person in the present, or do schools identify themselves as having a role in developing students as citizens? How do they engage with students as both beings in the present and as people discursively constructed as incomplete 'becomings' (Lesko, 1996)?

Of the 57 codes under study, only 11 (65%) of the Niagara codes and 24 (60%) of the Toronto codes included a clear, opening statement of goals. Of these 35 codes, 24 identified the school's role in the overall *development* of the individual student, with ten specifically focusing on self-discipline and five emphasizing the development of students' membership in the school and wider community (see table 13.1).

> ... to promote a school environment conductive to effective learning and the development to self-discipline in all students, trust and mutual respect (Niagara District code; Smithson Secondary, Niagara)
>
> Our purpose is to assist young people to become self-disciplined, self-directed individuals who take responsibility for themselves and their education (Huntington Collegiate, Toronto)

Those emphasizing self-discipline were concentrated in Niagara, while those emphasizing the wider community were in Toronto. In contrast, only four schools overtly expected such maturity or responsibility in the present. Most schools simply stated the rules that students were expected to follow, and framed them in terms of respect or responsibility.

Overall, then, 42 per cent of school codes understand students as developing and see the role of the school in shaping that development. This approach focuses on young people as becoming – though not in the immanent, minoritarian, and transformative way that Skott-Myhre and Tarulli discuss in this volume (chapter 3); rather, youths are being shaped and are to shape themselves for future adulthood (Lesko, 1996). At the same time, most schools also require that students face immediate consequences for what they do. This recognizes the student in the present and can be seen to be the teaching of consequences. However, there is little recognition of students' agency in the present, nor of how they are being shaped or developed as self-disciplining subjects, except through punishment. These patterns will be developed in the presentation of the remaining themes below.

SELF-DISCIPLINE AND OBEDIENCE

Linked to the above question of being or becoming is this tension, evident in many Niagara codes of conduct, between self-discipline and obedience. A professed goal of a number of codes is the development of self-discipline. Yet, the emphasis is, at the same time, on obedience. As stated above, 10 (17.5%) of the schools identified the goal of developing student self-discipline. Emphasis on self-discipline was especially high in Niagara at 47 per cent, consistent with Lewis's Australian findings, wherein students' self-discipline was the number one ration-

Table 13.2 Rules and expectations

Rules	Niagara (*n*=17)	Toronto (*n*=40)	Total (*n*=57)
Students are expected to obey or to follow rules	9 (53%)	13 (32.5%)	22 (38.5%)
Students are to accept punishment	5 (29%)	0 (0%)	5 (9%)
Rules ensure an educational environment	0 (0%)	8 (20%)	8 (14%)

ale provided for school codes (1999). Other explanations Lewis found included protecting student rights (rarely a stated goal in the codes of conduct under study here), meeting the needs of each student, promoting intellectual development, promoting citizenship, providing an orderly and happy environment. Beyond an overt emphasis on self-discipline, many codes within this study focus on responsibility and respect, concepts that also link up with a cultivation of self-discipline.

Emphases on citizenship and becoming resonate with governmentality studies and developmentalism, as they foster a self-regulating subject and recognize that this is a gradual process. Yet many schools, especially in Niagara, emphasized obedience. Nine (53%) Niagara schools and 13 (32.5%) Toronto schools were very clear: students are expected to follow the rules and to be obedient (see table 13.2). Five Niagara schools also state that students are to accept punishment when it is given; for instance, 'When disciplined, a student will be expected to be courteous and obedient' (Trent Secondary, Niagara). Almost all schools follow the stated goals of their codes of conduct with a list of rules and the consequences for their infraction. Overwhelmingly, rules are presented as non-negotiable, often unexplained and negative, which suggests that students are not capable of self-discipline or self-regulation. These findings concur with Schimmel's American findings, in which most rules he studied focused on prohibitions (2003).

While an emphasis on obedience is valuable for establishing order, and it is favoured by teachers and parents, this approach 'has been criticized as emphasizing irrational obedience to authority' (Lewis, 1999, p. 54). Schimmel argues that 'codes of conduct that rely on control and punishment to teach responsibility and self-control are usually ineffec-

Table 13.3 Responsibility

Required responsibility	Niagara (n=17)	Toronto (n=40)	Total (n=57)
Some mention of responsibility	12 (71%)	25 (62.5%)	37 (65%)
Rights linked to responsibilities	5 (29%)	11 (27.5%)	16 (28%)
For learning	4 (23%)	7 (17.5%)	11 (19%)
For learning of others	2 (12%)	3 (7.5%)	5 (9%)
For following rules	2 (12%)	2 (5%)	4 (7%)
For safety	,0 (0%)	2 (5%)	2 (3.5%)
For schools reputation and property	0 (0%)	4 (10%)	4 (7%)
To respect rights of others	1 (6%)	1 (2.5%)	2 (3.5%)
To resolve conflicts	0 (0%)	2 (5%)	2 (3.5%)
To respect authority	1 (6%)	0 (0%)	1 (2%)
To respect property	1 (6%)	0 (0%)	1 (2%)

tive and counterproductive' (2003, p. 23), teaching instead that break-ing rules is about not getting caught. Emphasis on punishment, the lack of positive reinforcements, limited explanation for the rules, and the top-down nature of the presentation of rules to students suggests that internalized self-discipline is less likely to be fostered than situ-ated obedience, or 'conformity to what are someone else's rules' (Lewis, 1999, p. 55). A similar disjuncture is evident when we examine the rules' emphases on responsibilities and respect.

RESPONSIBILITIES AND RESPECT

Responsibility and respect were common concepts presented in the codes of conduct. Thirty-seven (65%) schools include some mention of responsibility (see table 13.3). Students are expected to take responsi-bility for themselves, their actions, their environment, and their learn-ing. Most common forms of respect mentioned within the codes were for authority, property, the self, and others (see table 13.4). In Toronto, 8 (20%) schools also discuss respect for diversity. Both responsibility and respect are concepts that can be linked to self-discipline, although codes of conduct ultimately ground both in obedience.

Recent conceptualizations of citizenship have shifted from an emphasis on citizens' rights, particularly welfare rights, to linking

Table 13.4 Forms of respect

Respect	Niagara (*n*=17)	Toronto (*n*=40)	Total (*n*=57)
Mentioned in codes	16 (94%)	36 (90%)	52 (91%)
Linked to responsibility	2 (12%)	2 (5%)	4 (7%)
For authority/staff	5 (29%)	11 (28%)	16 (28%)
For property (school, others', neighbours')	11 (65%)	17 (42.5%)	28 (49%)
For self	6 (35%)	13 (32.5%)	19 (33%)
Mutual respect	1 (6%)	10 (25%)	11 (19%)
For others	6 (35%)	23 (57.5%)	29 (51%)
For environment	0 (0%)	3 (7.5%)	3 (5%)
For diversity	0 (0%)	8 (20%)	8 (14%)
For law and country	0 (0%)	4 (10%)	4 (7%)
For learning process	0 (0%)	4 (10%)	4 (7%)
For school community	1 (6%)	1 (2.5%)	2 (3.5%)
For rules	1 (6%)	0 (0%)	1 (2%)

rights with associated responsibilities, suggesting a mutual relationship between citizen and state (Wong & Wong, 2004), active social participation (France, 1998), and individualization (France, 1998). Reflecting such an emphasis, sixteen (28%) of the schools under study specifically linked rights and responsibilities.

> Mature behaviour is characterized by an awareness that every right carries with it a corresponding responsibility (Track Collegiate, Toronto) Education is a right which carries certain responsibilities (including following the rules) (Augusta Collegiate, Toronto)

Lewis (1999) found that 40 per cent of the schools he studied made a similar linkage.

Some behaviour codes frame students' protective rights as inherent, and associated responsibilities as learned, with one purpose of the school being to develop personal responsibility (a form of self-discipline), frequently indicated in the codes through obedience to the rules. In contrast, many schools present students' protective rights as *contingent* on fulfilling certain responsibilities:

> Individual rights imply responsibilities (Brookes Collegiate, Niagara)
> Education is a right, which carries certain responsibilities. One of these responsibilities is to abide by certain rules of behaviour (Beecham Collegiate, Toronto)

In these instances, rights and citizenship are earned. France (1998) is concerned with such a linkage between rights and responsibilities, however. In his research with working-class youth in Britain, France found that the young people often felt no sense of community obligation or responsibility owing to their surveillance and exclusion. They were assumed to be social problems and therefore had little stake in the community. These young people needed to experience themselves as having rights in order to feel a sense of responsibility.

Further, the suggested responsibility is individualized, passive, and meant to foster self-regulation. One consequence of such self-regulation is that 'disadvantage and exclusion are re-framed as matters of choice and not of structural processes' (Kemshall, 2002, p. 43), with the person who does not adequately respond to such self-regulation being blamed and subjected to mechanisms of control and repression. Those who fail to self-regulate in turn experience the sovereign power of the school, such as through detention, suspension, expulsion, or other consequences outlined in the schools' conduct codes and the province's zero tolerance policy. Yet for all students, responsibility is another facet of self-discipline, framed through following set-out, top-down guidelines.

This pattern of linking self-discipline to obedience is especially evident in references to respect. Loosely following David Middleton's typology (2004), 'rights respect,' or human respect, is a kind of respect that everyone is entitled to simply by the very fact of being a person. Earned, or merit, respect is linked to having done something that others, in turn, respect. It suggests worthiness. Differential, or status, respect is respect based on social custom and can be linked to an ascribed or achieved status; in the latter case, status respect overlaps with earned respect.

Power is clearly relevant to these definitions. Helen Jones (2002) supports a rights-respect approach when she argues that with regard to positions of unequal power, respect for those with less is particularly important. In her British study of young people's interpretations of respect, Jones found that they value respect that is shown through listening to their opinions and taking them seriously, valuing their contributions, recognizing their self-identifications in the present, and accepting that they will change. They value respect that is mutual and developing over time, rather than inherently owed to someone in a particular position. Based on these findings, Jones suggests that one-way respect for authority is obsolescent and therefore bound to fail, for 'it epitomizes a form of social relationship that does not reflect the current lives and culture of young people and many adults' (p. 352). In a study of youth values in Britain, Thomson and Holland (2002) also found that while values have generally remained the same across generations, young people are more likely to question the legitimacy of authority. Rather than respect being inherent in a position, young people often believe that respect must be earned and reciprocal. Middleton (2004) also argues that both merit and status respect first require equal, reciprocal 'human respect.'

Rights, earned, and differential respect are all evident in the school rules. Some schools specifically state that everyone is deserving of respect, including the student (rights respect). Many schools, particularly Toronto schools (generally much more so than those in Niagara) also emphasize respect for others (rights respect). This is where anti-harassment, anti-bullying, and non-violence policies are discussed. For many Toronto schools there is a strong emphasis on respect for diverse cultures and races, and some also address sexual orientation under respect for others. Through this emphasis on respect, schools link the conduct of the self to a relation to others (White and Hunt, 2000), suggesting a more communitarian than individualist ethic. In contrast, the frequent emphasis on respect for authority draws on status respect and is framed in terms of social hierarchy, with respect manifested through obedience. As Brookes Collegiate (Niagara) states, 'Respect for authority is required on the job and at large.' Some Niagara schools also state that students must be respectful while they are being disciplined.

One code notes that 'you cannot respect others until you respect yourself' (Massey School, Niagara). Overall, 19 schools (33%) mention some form of self-respect. Robin Dillon (1992), drawing on Stephen Darwell's distinction between recognition and appraisal respect (1977), argues that recognition self-respect, like rights respect, means 'responding to oneself with the kind of respect all persons are owed simply because they are persons.' Such respect is gained through receiving respect from others, paying attention to ourselves, avoiding self-neglect, and reclaiming oneself from oppression. Middleton (2004) concurs, adding that we must recognize our own worth in order to be committed to social justice. Arguably, such self-respect is fostered through participation rights.

Within the codes of conduct, it is frequent for certain rule infractions to be listed alongside an appeal to self-respect, however. This is the case for prohibitions on provocative clothing, swearing, drugs, and alcohol, for example. To be treated with respect requires certain behaviour, which suggests merit, or appraisal, self-respect determined through 'positive appraisal of oneself' in relation to outside standards of excellence or worth (Dillon, 1992, p. 54). But rather than evaluating oneself in relation to outside standards of excellence, it is implied that students are evaluated as deserving *unless they behave otherwise*. Self-respect exists through compliance with external criteria rather than through exceeding them. Thus, obedience and self-control are markers of self-respect, rather than students' intrinsic worth as people with moral rights.

Several other concerns can be raised in reaction to these criteria. First, 'provocative' clothing, particularly female clothing, is presented as incompatible with self-respect, which reinforces a marginalization and problematization of female sexuality. Second, by emphasizing that self-respect requires certain kinds of dress or avoidance of certain activities, a justification is provided for undermining 'respect for others' if the individuals involved do not seem to respect themselves. For example, if students who wear provocative dress are considered to lack self-respect, then responsibility for their marginalization is thus shifted onto themselves rather than the social control of female sexuality and 'slut-bashing' from others (Tanenbaum, 1999). Third, it is interesting that use of drugs and alcohol is presented as incompatible with self-respect. Arguably, both sex and alcohol are presented to Western young people as markers of adulthood. To respect oneself, a student must do so *as an adolescent* and according to rules specific to adolescents, a category distinct in definitions of self-respect from what they are supposedly in the process of becoming (Raby, 2005).

Emphasis on respect can be seen as another attempt at governmentality and regulation of the self that is legislated in a top-down manner. Respect is presented as an important, internalized characteristic that is alternatively inherent, something that can be lost, and something that some (such as those in authority) require more than others. Respect, as presented here, reinforces individual responsibility. Of all the forms of respect presented, self-respect is the most directly related to self-discipline. It entails learning to value a certain understanding of the self, through obedience and saying 'no' to a variety of activities, rather than through pro-activity, participation, or self-knowledge.

Passive and Individualized Citizenship

Ontario's Code of Conduct states that 'responsible citizenship involves appropriate participation in the civic life of the school community. Active and engaged citizens are aware of their rights, but more importantly, they accept responsibility for protecting their rights and the rights of others' (2001, p. 2). Despite this call for active citizenship, almost all codes under study instead emphasize passive citizenship through a concentration on protective and welfare rights rather than participation rights (see table 13.5). There are three key areas in which participatory rights can be addressed in school rules: (1) Through stating students' participatory rights; (2) through students' involvement in the creation and review of school rules; and (3) through a stated right of appeal. All are rare within the codes under study, findings that concur with those Lewis identified in Australia (1999) and those found by Schimmel in the United States (2003).

Importantly, welfare and protective rights were common within the codes under study, although participation rights were not. Here, welfare rights focus almost exclusively on rights to education. This is mentioned in 11 (65%) of the Niagara codes and 14 (35%) of the Toronto codes. Protective rights, raised in 11 (65%) Niagara codes and 11 (27.5%) Toronto codes, centre on rights to safety, particularly in terms of safety from bullying or harassment. Participation rights are infrequently mentioned, and therefore I have been generous in my interpretation of participation. In this light, 5 (29%) Niagara and 5 (12.5%) Toronto codes mentioned some kind of participation right. In Niagara, such participation included acceptance of students as valuable individuals, respect of opinion, and willingness of staff to act as a mediator. In Toronto, such participation included the right to make friends, to get involved in the school, to discuss matters with staff, to appeal, and to be accepted as a valuable individual. For the most part, participation rights were not stated, however.

Devine (2000), Roche (1999), and others have advocated that active

Table 13.5 Forms of rights

Forms of rights	Niagara (n=17)	Toronto (n=40)	Total (n=57)
Welfare rights (education)	11 (65%)	14 (35%)	25 (44%)
Protective rights (safety)	11 (65%)	11 (27.5%)	22 (38%)
Participation rights	5 (29%)	5 (12.5%)	10 (17.5%)
Teacher's rights and responsibilities	3 (18%)	1 (2.5%)	4 (7%)

citizenship requires young people to be participants in the process of making decisions about things such as their time use and the rules in schools. The Ontario Code of Conduct, both Toronto and Niagara school board policies, and some Toronto school codes state that students are involved in the construction of these rules; laudably, most schools involve students in such construction, although few formally cite this in their codes of conduct (see table 13.6). While this is an important movement in the direction of student involvement, there is little room for all young people's *frequent* or *consistent* participation in the making of these rules, particularly as school rules are increasingly homogenized across the province or across school districts. Roche argues that 'the older the child is the more objectionable it is to fail to consult or take into account their wishes and feelings' (Roche 1999, p. 483). Yet Lewis found that Australian primary schools were far more likely than secondary schools to outline the need for student participation in creating their rules than secondary schools. At the time when young people are closest to the age of majority, and presumably more experienced in decision making, they are *less* likely to be involved as *bona fide* participants in the organization of their schools. DeRoma, Lassiter, and Davis have found that teenagers 'feel better about the situation, themselves, and their relationship with the parent when parents involve them in the disciplinary decision-making process' (DeRoma et al., 2004, p. 430). Students, similarly, seek and value such participation in schools (Denton, 2003; Thorson, 1996). Ultimately, Devine concludes that 'children's capacities as active agents are underutilized, with consequent negative implication for children's construction of an identity as citizens within the school' (2002, p. 316). This is certainly the case here.

We can also examine democratic citizenship through access to an appeal process. Part of democratic citizenship, social participation, and the legitimacy of law is the right to give your side of the story, the

Table 13.6 Involvement and recourse

Stated in codes	Niagara (*n*=17)	Toronto (*n*=40)	Total (*n*=57)
Code of conduct created by staff, parents and students	2 (12%)	6 (15%)	8 (14%)
Code of conduct endorsed by staff, parents, and students	0 (0%)	2 (5%)	2 (3.5%)
Code updated regularly	0 (0%)	3 (7.5%)	3 (5%)
Codes grounded in law, school board ...	2 (12%)	11 (27.5%)	12 (21%)
Explanation of rules given	1 (6%)	5 (12.5%)	6 (10%)
Formal right of appeal	1 (6%)	1 (2.5%)	2 (3.5%)
Informal appeal	1 (6%)	4 (10%)	5 (9%)
Conflict resolution	1 (6%)	4 (10%)	5 (9%)

right to a fair hearing, and the right to appeal (Covell & Howe, 2001; John, 1995; Pritchard, 1990). Lansdown concurs that schools must have 'genuine avenues of complaint, backed up by access to independent advocacy for situations where children feels [*sic*] they have been mistreated or ignored or abused in any way' (1994, p. 39). Notably, only two schools, one in Niagara and one in Toronto, referred to any formal appeals process, the most comprehensive of which was Ingram Collegiate in Toronto: 'Students can discuss matters with teachers, staff, Board of Education, Minister of Education, trustee ... on any matter ... If you feel rights infringed upon, there is an Appeal Procedure and can file a complaint with Ontario Human Rights Commission.' Several other schools informally mention that issues may be discussed with administration or teachers.

Participation rights are infrequent within codes of conduct. Rights (and responsibilities) are also individualized. Only two (12%) Niagara schools refer to some kind of community-linked citizenship, including either the school community, the wider community, or both. Six (35%) refer to respect for others. In Toronto, 16 (40%) refer to community-linked citizenship, 23 (57.5%) to respect for others, and 8 (20%) to respect for diversity. Otherwise, the emphasis is on a more individualized responsibility, individual rights, and respect rather than on investments in the wider community. Thomson and Holland's position is that young people's focus on individualized responsibility and shift from acceptance of ascribed authority is linked to the much wider patterns of detraditionalization and individualization described by German theorists Ulrich Beck and Elizabeth Beck-Gernsheim (2002). This examination of school codes of conduct suggests that such individualization is also perpetuated in the governance of students.

A Different Kind of Code

Evidence of active citizenship was found where schools discussed participatory rights, where rights to speech and student representation were evident, and where an appeals process was described. While most schools have student representation through student councils, and school boards require student representation in the making of the rules, statements of student involvement and participatory rights are rare in these codes. The few schools that do provide greater possibilities for student involvement, or more egalitarian presentations of school rules, include mediation for resolving disputes and explain a grievance process that students may initiate.

Short of these forms of enhanced participatory rights, there are other tactics that educators can employ when developing rules which gesture towards rules that better foster democratic citizenship. Rules can address parents' and teachers' rights and responsibilities as well as students' (Lewis, 1999) in order to educate students about the mutuality of rights and to include all school actors within the codes of conduct (see table 13.5). Codes can include pre-emptive, positive strategies that encourage cooperation, tolerance, self-esteem, and pride rather than only including punishments within codes of conduct (Lewis, 1999), approaches Lewis found to be more likely in Australian primary than secondary schools. In this study, only four schools in Niagara and four in Toronto mention that an intent of the code of conduct is to foster school pride or positive memories. Rewards for appropriate behaviour are not mentioned. Codes can explain the rationale behind the rules, yet only 6 (10%) of the codes under study include such a rationale. In his American study, Schimmel (2003) also found that rationales for rules were rarely clear, particularly around dress-code details and prohibitions against electronic devices. Finally, codes can explain students' rights, including the right to participation, right to free expression, and right to appeal (Schimmel, 2003).

More broadly, exciting collaborative rule-making initiatives have been introduced in several American schools, cultivating skills in democratic participation, developing investments in school, decreasing discipline problems (Effrat & Schimmel, 2003), and creating student ownership of the rules (Schimmel, 2003). For example, Denton (2003) describes the Jefferson Committee, established in 1987 in Kingston High School in New York State. This committee included representatives from various stakeholders in the school, with the largest representative group being students. The Jefferson Committee drafted a code of conduct, then continued to review the code, with student representation from all classes, and to make decisions about its application. Included in the code was the provision for a process for students to provide their side of the story and for a public meeting to which students at large can bring their concerns. One of the goals of the committee is student empowerment by providing them with not just the skills for democratic decision making but with real influence in how their school was run. A special issue of *American Secondary Education* (Denton, 2003) provides this and several other examples of such projects.

Conclusion

This study is limited owing to its concentration on codes rather than practice and owing to the variation between codes in terms of comprehensiveness. Further, codes of conduct are simply one area in which rights and citizenship are evident within a school. This paper has not investigated citizenship education within school curricula, for example, although others argue that such education is currently absent in much Canadian school curricula (Stasiulis, 2002). Nonetheless, codes of conduct are planned documents that frequently outline goals and philosophies of student discipline. They are the official documents used to educate students about their schools' expectations.

Overall, the codes of conduct studied here follow the caretaker model of children's rights, with young people understood to be in the liminal position of becoming. In the present students are framed as either non-citizens, citizens who must illustrate their citizenship through obedience, or citizens-in-process who must also be obedient. Ironically, whatever the stated goals of the schools, in most instances students are being groomed to be citizens through techniques that deny them participation rights and the necessary skills for democratic decision making, community building, or participatory politics (Burfoot, 2003). As Pilcher argues, there is a conception of childhood 'separateness' that limits the kinds of rights young people may access to welfare and protection rights. Yet students should and do have rights to participate in the present. They also have the right to the skills for such participation in their futures. Of course, as Stasiulis argues, 'even if Canadian institutions were to affirm children's right to be heard and taken seriously, the realization of such rights would surely be undermined by the decline of opportunities for democratic decision-making in most major Canadian institutions' (2002, p. 527). She points to a general Canadian disaffection, as many feel they have little influence on the federal government and other levels of decision-making. If we are going to prepare young people for democratic citizenship, we need to genuinely desire an active, participatory, rights – knowledgeable citizenship for adults as well.

REFERENCES

Alderson, P. (1999). Human rights and democracy in schools: Do they mean more than 'picking up litter and not killing whales'? *International Journal of Children's Rights, 7*, 185–205.

Alvineri, S., & de-Shalit, A. (1992). *Communitarianism and individualism.* Oxford: Oxford University Press.

Archard, D. (2004). *Children: Rights and childhood* (2nd ed.). London: Routledge.

Beauvais, C., McKay, L., & Seddon, A. (2002). A literature review on youth and citizenship: Executive summary. CPRN discussion paper, from http://www.cprn.com/cprn.html.

Beck, U., & Beck-Gernsheim, E. (2002). *Individualization: Institutionalized individualism and its social and political consequences.* London: Sage Publications.

Burfoot, D. (2003). Children and young people's participation: Arguing for a better future. *Youth Studies Australia, 22*(3), 44–51.

Covell, K., & Howe, B.R. (2001). *The challenge of children's rights for Canada.* Waterloo: Wilfrid Laurier University Press.

Darwall, S.L. (1977). Two kinds of respect. *Ethics, 88*(1), 36–49.

Dennis, A. (1996). Student discipline and the charter. *The Canadian School Executive, 15*(8), 13–17.

Denton, P. (2003). Shared rule-making in practice: The Jefferson Committee at Kingston high school. *American Secondary Education, 31*(3), 66–96.

DeRoma, V.M., Lassiter, K.S., & Davis, V.A. (2004). Adolescent involvement in discipline decision-making. *Behavior Modification, 28*(3), 420–437.

Devine, D. (2002). Children's citizenship and the structuring of adult-child relations in the primary school. *Childhood, 9*(3), 303–320.

Dillon, R.S. (1992). Toward a feminist conception of self-respect. *Hypatia, 7*(1), 52–69.

Effrat, A., & Schimmel, D. (2003). Walking the democratic talk: Introduction to a special issue on collaborative rule-making as preparation for democratic citizenship. *American Secondary Education, 31*(3), 3–15.

Foucault, M. (1978). 'Governmentality.' In G. Burchell, C. Gordon & P. Miller (Eds.), *The Foucault effect: Studies in governmentality*. Chicago: University of Chicago Press.

France, A. (1998). Why should we care? Young people, citizenship and questions of social responsibility. *Journal of Youth Studies, 1*(1), 97–111.

Griffin, C. (1993). *Representations of youth: The study of youth and adolescence in Britain and America*. Cambridge: Polity Press.

Hart, R. (1992). *Children's participation: From tokenism to citizenship*. Florence, Italy: UNICEF International Child Development Centre.

Harte, A.J., & McDonald, K. (1996). Implication of the charter for school discipline. *Canadian School Executive, 15*(7), 3–6.

James, A., & Prout, A. (1990). *Constructing and reconstructing childhood: Contemporary issues in the sociological study of childhood*. Basingstoke, Bristol: Falmer Press.

John, M. (1995). Children's rights in a free-market culture. In S. Stephens (Ed.), *Children and the politics of culture*. Princeton, NJ: Princeton University Press.

Jones, H.M.F. (2002). Respecting respect: Exploring a great deal. *Educational Studies, 28*(4), 341–352.

Kelly, P. (2003). Growing up as risky business? Risks, surveillance and the institutionalized mistrust of youth. *Journal of Youth Studies, 6*(2), 165–180.

Kemshall, H. (2002). Effective practice in probation: An example of 'advanced liberal' responsibilisation? *The Howard Journal, 41*(1), 41–58.

Lansdown, G. (1994). Children's rights. In B. Mayall (ed.), *Children's childhoods: Observed and experienced*. London: Falmer Press.

Lesko, N. (1996). Denaturalizing adolescence: The politics of contemporary representations. *Youth and Society, 28*(2), 139–161.

Lewis, R. (1999). Preparing students for democratic citizenship: Codes of conduct in Victoria's 'schools of the future.' *Educational Research and Evaluation, 5*(1), 41–61.

Middleton, D. (2004). Why we should care about respect. *Contemporary Politics, 10*(3–4), 227–241.

Ontario Government. 2001. Ontario Schools Code of Conduct. Toronto: Queens Park.

Pritchard, B. (1990). Fundamental justice in student discipline. *The Canadian School Executive, 9*(9), 3–5.

Raby, R. (2005). Polite, well-dressed and on time: Secondary school conduct codes and the production of docile citizens. *Canadian Review of Sociology and Anthropology, 42*(1), 71–92.

Roche, J. (1999). Children: Rights, participation and citizenship. *Childhood, 6*(4), 475–493.

Rose, N. (1999). *Power of freedom: Reframing political thought.* Cambridge: Cambridge University Press.

Schimmel, D. (2003). Collaborative rule-making and citizenship education: An antidote to the undemocratic hidden curriculum. *American Secondary Education, 31*(3), 16–35.

Smith, A.B. (2002). Interpreting and supporting participation rights: Contributions from sociocultural theory. *International Journal of Children's Rights, 10,* 73–88.

Stasiulis, D. (2002). The active child citizen: Lessons from Canadian policy and the children's movement. *Citizenship Studies, 6*(4), 507–538.

Such, E., & Walker, R. (2005). Young citizens or policy objects? Children in the 'rights and responsibilities' debate. *Journal of Social Policy, 34*(1), 39–57.

Tanenbaum, Leora. (1999). Slut! Growing up female with a bad reputation. New York: Seven Stories Press.

Taylor, N., Smith, A.B., & Nairn, K. (2001). Rights important to young people: Secondary student and staff perspectives. *International Journal of Children's Rights, 9,* 137–156.

Thomson, R., & Holland, J. (2002). Young people, social change and the negotiation of moral authority. *Children and Society, 16,* 103–115.

Thorson, S. (1996). The missing link: Students discuss school discipline. *Focus on Exceptional Children, 29*(3), 1–12.

United Nations (1989). *Convention on the Rights of the Child.*

White, Melanie, and Alan Hunt. 2000. Citizenship: Care of the Self, Character and Personality. *Citizenship Studies, 4*(2), 93–116.

Wong, C.K., & Wong, K.Y. (2004). Universal ideals and particular constraints of social citizenship: The Chinese experience of unifying rights and responsibilities. *International Journal of Social Welfare, 13,* 103–111.

Contributors

Karyn Audet, Simon Fraser University, Faculty of Education

Marjorie Aunos, University of Quebec in Montreal, Department of Professional Services (DSP), West Montreal Readaptation Center

Sheila Bennett, Brock University, Faculty of Education

Don Dworet, Brock University, Faculty of Education

Angela Evans, University of Toronto, Human Development and Applied Psychology

Maurice Feldman, Brock University, Department of Child and Youth Studies

Judy Finlay, Ryerson University, School of Child and Youth Care

Leanne Gosse, Brock University, Department of Psychology

Dorothy Griffiths, Brock University, Department of Child and Youth Studies

Candace Johnson, University of Guelph, Department of Political Science

Leanne Johnny, McGill University, Department of Integrated Studies in Education

Karen Kurytnik, Simon Fraser University, Faculty of Education

Monique Lacharite, Brock University, Department of Child and Youth Studies

Lucy Le Mare, Simon Fraser University, Faculty of Education

Zopito Marini, Brock University, Department of Child and Youth Studies

Glenys McQueen-Fuentes, Brock University, Department of Dramatic Arts

Tom O'Neill, Brock University, Department of Child and Youth Studies

Frances Owen, Brock University, Department of Child and Youth Studies

Landon Pearson, Carleton University, Landon Pearson Centre for the Study of Childhood and Children's Rights

Rebecca Raby, Brock University, Department of Child and Youth Studies

Kim P. Roberts, Wilfrid Laurier University, Department of Psychology

Carol Sales, Brock University, Department of Organizational Behaviour, Human Resources, Entrepreneurship and Ethics

Shaheen Shariff, McGill University, Department of Integrated Studies in Education

Hans Skott-Myhre, Brock University, Department of Child and Youth Studies

Karen Stoner, Brock University, Department of Child and Youth Studies

Christine Tardif-Williams, Brock University, Department of Child and Youth Studies

Donato Tarulli, Brock University, Department of Child and Youth Studies

Johanna van Vliet, Brock University, Department of Child and Youth Studies

Sherri Young, Indian and Northern Affairs Canada, Nunavut Regional Office

Manta Zahos, Brock University, Faculty of Education

Dawn Zinga, Brock University, Department of Child and Youth Studies